Western Frontiersman Series
XIX

SITE OF THE GRAVE OF SERGEANT CHARLES FLOYD
An 1832 oil painting by George Catlin. A view from the west
looking toward the Missouri River.
Courtesy of the National Collection of Fine Arts, Smithsonian Institution.

Only One Man Died

The Medical Aspects of the Lewis and Clark Expedition

by

Eldon G. Chuinard, M.D.

THE ARTHUR H. CLARK COMPANY
Glendale, California
1979

To My Wife Fritzi

To My Daughter Beverly

To My Son Robert

Who, through the years,
have shared with me the story and the trail
of Lewis and Clark

Contents

Illustrations

Not only were they to be the executive officers, the leaders, in an exploration that would thus alone tax their time and abilities, but they must needs be, also, astronomers, ethnologists, geologists, engineers, physicians and surgeons, mineralogists, diplomatists and statesmen, naturalists, botanists, geographers, topographers, and meteorologists. In a word, all that was to be done that would have a lasting value was, virtually, laid upon the backs of two men. Of soldiers, hunters, rowers or watermen, interpreters, there were enough, but not one man of the medical profession to bind up wounds, mend broken limbs, or cure fevers, was there sent along, nor was there a solitary man of scientific attainments provided to relieve the leaders of a portion of such work.

Olin D. Wheeler, *The Trail of Lewis and Clark*, pp. 45-46

One of the things most difficult to understand . . . is that an expedition as equipped as this one was for the exploration of the continent, should have gone out upon a journey of 8000 miles, to be absent from civilization for two and a half years, without a physician as a member of the party.

Frank H. Garver, "The Story of Sergeant Charles Floyd," *Mississippi Valley Hist. Assoc. Proc.*, 1908-9, pp. 82-83

. . . certainly the most serious defect in the organization of the expedition was the lack of some trained scientist, who should also have been a medical man, and thus united the professional functions of a physician, surgeon and naturalist.

Elliott Coues, *History of the Lewis and Clark Expedition*, I, Introduction, p. xx

CORPS OF DISCOVERY

THOSE LEAVING FT. MANDAN,

USUALLY REFERRED TO AS THE PERMANENT PARTY.

It may seem strange at first view, that I should call upon command-ing officers to take care of the health of the men under their command, or that I should expect that they would pay any regard to the sickness incident to an army. I hope, however, (in the sequel) to shew that upon them especially depend the health and comfort of the soldiers; and that the medical staff are only to be regarded as adjutants, in the recovery of the sick.

James Tilton, *Economical Observations of Military Hospitals,* (1813) p. 46

1. Captain Meriwether Lewis
2. Captain William Clark
3. Sergeant John Ordway
4. Sergeant Nathaniel Pryor
5. Sergeant Patrick Gass
6. Private William Bratton
7. Private John Colter
8. Private John Collins
9. Private Peter Cruzatte
10. Private Robert Frazier
11. Private Joseph Field
12. Private Reuben Field
13. Private George Gibson
14. Private Silas Goodrich
15. Private Hugh Hall
16. Private Thomas Proctor Howard
17. Private Francois Labiche
18. Private Jean Baptiste La Page
19. Private Hugh McNeal
20. Private John Potts
21. Private George Shannon
22. Private John Shields
23. Private John B. Thompson
24. Private William Werner
25. Private Alexander H. Willard
26. Private Richard Windsor
27. Private Joseph Whitehouse
28. Private Peter Weiser
29. Interpreter George Drouillard
30. Interpreter Toussaint Charbonneau
31. York, Clark's servant
32. Sacagawea[1]

33. Baptiste Charbonneau — "Pomp"

Of the original corps leaving Wood River, Sergeant Charles Floyd had died, Private Moses Reed had deserted, and John Newman was discharged. The list does not include those who went up the Missouri to winter at Fort Mandan and return in the spring with Corporal Warfington. And, of course, Lewis' dog Scannon made the journey.

---

[1] The spelling of Sacagawea is used except when spelled otherwise within quotes, rather than Sacajawea or Sakakawea. For reasons, *see* Irving Anderson, "Sacajawea? — Sakakawea? — Sacagawea?" *We Proceed On,* Vol. i, No. 3, 1975, p. 10.

CHRONOLOGY

July 5, 1803	Lewis leaves Washington
August 30, 1803	Lewis leaves Pittsburgh (in his letter of June 19, 1803, to Clark, Lewis calls Pittsburgh "the intended point of embarkation.")
October 26, 1803	Lewis and Clark leave Louisville
December 12, 1803	Lewis and Clark arrive at Wood River
December 20, 1803	U.S. takes possession of Lower Louisiana
March 10, 1804	U.S. takes possession of Upper Louisiana at St. Louis; Lewis present at ceremonies
May 14, 1804	Lewis and Clark leave Camp DuBois
November 2, 1804	Lewis and Clark arrive at the Mandans
April 7, 1805	Lewis and Clark leave the Mandans
July 16, 1805	Lewis and Clark arrive at the Great Falls
July 25, 1805	Lewis and Clark arrive at Three Forks
December 7, 1805	Lewis and Clark arrive at Fort Clatsop
March 23, 1806	Lewis and Clark leave Fort Clatsop
September 23, 1806	Lewis and Clark arrive at St. Louis

IMPORTANT MEDICAL EVENTS
RELATING TO LEWIS AND CLARK

1721   Zabdiel Boylston (1679-1766) successfully performed smallpox inoculation for the first time in America

1751   The Pennsylvania Hospital, the first in America, was established

1751   Leopold Auenbrugger (1722-1809) described auscultation

1757   Thomas Walker (1715-1794) of Virginia, first trephined a bone for osteomelyetis

1765   First American medical school organized: the University of Pennsylvania

1798   Edward Jenner (1749-1823) published work on vaccination

1800   Benjamin Waterhouse (1754-1846) introduced vaccination into the U.S.

1803-1806   THE LEWIS AND CLARK EXPEDITION

1812   James Parkinson (1755-1824) reported the first case of ruptured appendix as the recognized cause of death

1819   Rene Laennec (1781-1826) invented the stethoscope

1842   Crawford Long, M.D. (1815-1878) introduced ether anesthesia

1844   Horace Wells (1815-1848), a dentist, introduced nitrous oxide anesthesia

1852   Anthonius Mathijsen (1805-1878) a Dutch physician, introduced Plaster of Paris (calcium sulfate, gypsum) bandages

1855   Pierre Bretonneau (1778-1862) suggested germ theory of disease

1861   Louis Pasteur (1822-1895) introduced bacteriology, established practice of pasteurization

1867   Joseph Lister (1827-1912) published his principles of anti-sepsis

1868   Carl Wunderlich (1815-1877) introduced clinical thermometry in the study of disease

1871 Edwin Klabs studied the bacteriology of gunshot wounds

1879 Albert Neisser (1855-1906) discovered the gonococcus

1880 Charles Laverau (1845-1922) discovered the parasite of malaria

1881 Carlos Finlay (1883-1915) first proposed that the mosquito Aedes aegypti was responsible for yellow fever

1892 Octave Terrillon (1844-1895) published his technique of asepsis

1905 Fritz Schaudinn (1871-1906) discovered the Treponema pallidium, the cause of syphilis

In Appreciation

The study of history is a wellspring of inspiration and dignity to the professional man.   H. Martin Deranian, D.D.S.[1]

I have been asked many times, "How did you, a doctor, become interested in the Lewis and Clark Expedition?" It is interesting to look back over the years and recall how this developed.

I attended a one-room country schoolhouse near Kelso, Washington. I remember hearing students in a class ahead of me recite something of the story of Lewis and Clark, and thinking how long ago it was that they had made their journey. I was then about ten years old, in 1914. It really had been a long time ago that Lewis and Clark came to the Northwest — eleven times my age ago, then! Today Lewis and Clark do not seem so remote — not quite three times my age ago!

I also remember reading that Patrick Gass lived to be ninety-nine years old, and was the last man of the Lewis and Clark Expedition to die. He died in 1870, ten years before my father was born — which provided added emphasis that Lewis and Clark belonged to ancient times!

History has been a constant interest to me. In my early years of medical practice it came to my attention that there had not been a physician accompanying Lewis and Clark to take care of the men, and yet only one man lost his life. This

---

[1] H. Martin Deranian, Aesculapius, Vol. i, No. 1, p. 6.

impressed me greatly, and as time permitted, I studied the Lewis and Clark journals in detail and read extensively about all the aspects of the Expedition. I traveled the full extent of the Lewis and Clark Trail, some of it many times, and — gratefully — before so many dams covered much of it. Libraries and historical societies were visited, and revisited, and correspondence with many people helped widen the vista of the Lewis and Clark story. Perhaps the most thrilling experience in all these travels was that of walking in the deeply rutted portions of the Expedition's Trail in the high mountains of Idaho, clearly seen today as it was when Lewis and Clark walked along it almost two centuries ago.

Pleasure and propriety call forth a long list of those who have been helpful in providing information, assistance and encouragement in the writing of this book. My heart directs my first thanks to those to whom I have dedicated this book: my wife, daughter and son. Many of our vacation days have been diverted to travel and research along the Lewis and Clark Trail. My wife has spent many hours proofreading this book and making valuable suggestions. My daughter, Mrs. Beverly Forrest, with her master's degree in English, has been most helpful in the composition. My son, also an orthopedic surgeon, has contributed many medical suggestions.

A special note of thanks for assistance and friendship goes to Becky and Sam Johnson of Redmond, Oregon. Despite the accumulation of much material from many years of sporadic research, this book might not have been written without the generous assistance of The S. S. Johnson Foundation. A continuation of gentle nudgings from many friends who knew of my intention to "someday" write a full-length book was finally brought to fruition when Becky and Sam Johnson made funds available from their Foundation to Lewis and Clark College to provide secretarial help. When their keen interest was manifested to the point of making a grant available, I could evade the challenge no longer. Second only to the efforts of the author, their generosity has made this book possible.

And early and continuous encouragement to pursue my interest in writing this book was provided by Governor (now U.S. Senator) Mark O. Hatfield, of Oregon. For his frequent inquiries — and nudgings — about its progress, my thanks!

Sincere thanks also go with high priority to Lewis and Clark College, especially to President John Howard and Librarian James Pirie. The latter has arranged for the detailed manuscript work, and has hovered over the project with genuine interest and valuable suggestions.

A book on Lewis and Clark could not be written without access to the material of the Missouri Historical Society, The American Philosophical Society, The Alderman Library of the University of Virginia, The National Library of Medicine, The Montana Historical Society, The Virginia Historical Society, and the generous help of their staffs.

I owe particular thanks to the following members of the Missouri Historical Society: Mr. George R. Brooks, Director; Mr. Charles Van Ravenswaay, Former Director; Mrs. Fred C. Harrington, Librarian; Miss Barbara Kell (now Mrs. F. David Strudell), Reference Librarian; Miss Dorothy A. Brockhoff, Reference Librarian; Mr. Ernest A. Stedler, Archivist; and Mr. John B. Dotesman, Assistant Archivist.

Special thanks also go to Dr. William E. Lingelbach, Librarian (deceased); Mr. Murphy D. Smith, Associate Librarian; Mrs. Gertrude D. Hess and Mrs. Carolyn B. Milligan, of the American Philosophical Society.

The service and help from the National Library of Medicine has been invaluable. I wish to particularly express my thanks to Mr. Charles Roos, Head, Documents Section; to Dr. John B. Blake, Chief, History of Medicines Division; and to Miss Mary E. Grinell, Head, Reference Section. The National Library of Medicine is a prime source of early Army medical history.

The Alderman Library of the University of Virginia at Charlottesville is a storehouse of invaluable material dealing with Lewis and Clark and Jefferson. Donald Jackson, who edited the *Letters of the Lewis and Clark Expedition with Related Documents,* is now at the Alderman Library editing the George Washington Papers. His book is "an absolute must" for anyone doing research on Lewis and Clark, as the many references to his work in this volume give testimony. I also wish to thank Mr. Edwin Berkeley, Manuscripts Librarian of the Alderman Library, and his staff.

The Portland Public Library has provided constant and courteous help with evident interest in this project, especially by arranging inter-library loan service. I would like to especially thank Miss Louise Pritchard (retired) and Mrs. James Pirie.

I asked Norman David, M.D., friend and professor emeritus of Pharmacology at the University of Oregon Medical School, to review the list of drugs purchased by Meriwether Lewis to be taken on the Expedition, and to make suggestions about their probable usage by Lewis and Clark and their status in current pharmacology. Dr. David provided me with some sixty pages of detailed review of the drugs with scientific data and much interesting commentary — far more material than I could use in the book. He has helped immeasurably to evaluate the medicines used by Lewis and Clark. I have urged Dr. David to submit his detailed paper to a pharmacology journal; it should come to public record because nothing has been published which contains detailed and scholarly work of the calibre of Dr. David's regarding the drugs used on the Lewis and Clark Expedition. For his help, and abiding friendship of many years, I express my sincere gratitude.

This also affords an opportunity to express my appreciation for the friendships which have developed with other Lewis and Clark authors through the years. These friends have seemed to have a vicarious pleasure in this project, and their continued interest has added to the stimulus to complete it, and their counseling and specific help has been most valuable. Among the scholar-friends who have provided such help and inspiration it is a pleasure to list Paul R. Cutright, Donald Jackson, Ingvard Eide, Ernest T. Osgood, John Logan Allen, and John Bakeless. Sincere respect accompanies my thanks.

To Ralph Space of Orofino, Idaho, my thanks for piloting Mr. and Mrs. Ray Forrest of Walla Walla, Washington, Mrs. Chuinard and myself over the high Lolo Trail in the Rocky Mountains; and to Mr. and Mrs. Wilbur Werner of Cutbank, Montana, for piloting Mr. and Mrs. Robert Lange, Mrs. Chuinard and myself to Camp Disappointment and the Two Medicine River fight site of Lewis with the Indians; and for their enthusiastic instruction in bringing the Lewis and Clark story vividly alive for us in these areas.

Mr. Robert Lange and Mr. Irving Anderson of the Oregon Lewis and Clark Trail Committee have helped immeasurably in providing information, reading copy, making valuable suggestions, and providing the continued flow of the Lewis and Clark aura which I hope has seeped into this book.

I wish to thank Colonel (now deceased) and Mrs. Clark J. Lawrence, present owners of Castle Hill, Virginia, the former home of Dr. Thomas Walker, guardian of Thomas Jefferson, for the kindly receptions given to Mrs. Chuinard and myself on our several visits to Dr. Walker's old home.

Sincere thanks are due and given with appreciation to those who patiently typed this manuscript: Marianne DesBouillons and Jackie Youngblood; and to Janice Garber for proofreading and copying; and to Charlotte Glenk and Beverly Eagle for typing many letters of inquiry seeking information from many sources.

I also wish to express grateful appreciation to Arthur H. Clark and Robert A. Clark, of the Arthur H. Clark Company, who have given generously of time and expertise in helping this neophyte author develop an acceptable production.

Encouragement and help in writing this book has come from many people and many institutions. One is always haunted with the thought that in attempting to express appreciation to an all-inclusive list of those to whom a sincere "thank you" is due, some very deserving person will be omitted. No attempt will be made, therefore, to compile such a list, but I do want to express my sincere gratitude to the many, many others throughout the country who aided in the research and preparation of this work.

E. G. CHUINARD, M.D.

Introduction

". . . bring back your party safe. . ." Jefferson's instructions to Lewis, June 20, 1803 [1]

It is almost one and three-quarters centuries since Lewis and Clark led their little army of intrepid explorers through the trans-Mississippi west and brought them safely home. After all these years we can look back on their great feat with wonder and admiration; we may even feel a sense of disbelief as we sit in our easy chairs and read their journals. But a sense of reality comes to those who will drop away from civilization for a time and follow what is left of their trail, and contemplate the conditions under which they made their journey: literally pulling and pushing tons of merchandise up the Missouri River, meeting Indians both hostile and friendly, securing an uncertain day-by-day food supply from an always changing countryside, existing on an uncertain and unbalanced diet varying from fresh, wholesome buffalo meat to dog and infected salmon pemmican, crossing vast mountains of ice and snow, enduring the incessant cold at Fort Mandan and the incessant rain at Fort Clatsop, facing narrow escapes from grizzly bears, floods, boat accidents and precipices, treading in self-made moccasins on snow and ice and rocks and prickly pears, enduring hail storms and boiling sun and mosquitoes on their naked backs, paying for indulgences with the Indian

---

[1] Donald Jackson, *Letters of the Lewis and Clark Expedition with Related Documents, 1783-1854* (Urbana, 1962), pp. 61-66.

maidens with blue beads and venereal disease — all of this, and yet *proceeding on* with good discipline and good humor, dancing to Cruzatte's fiddle after a strenuous day, the captains writing their notes in the evening by candlelight with hands made mobile by devoted hearts.

This small army commanded by Lewis and Clark was composed of the healthiest young men that the rigors of frontier and army life had produced. But the healthiest of physiques can bend and break under extreme conditions of work, cold, hunger and disease. The corps was not very far along on its journey before they were no longer the "robust, healthy young men" which Lewis and Clark recruited for the Expedition. The unbalanced diets of meat off the countryside, supplemented with bacterially infected food brought by Indians, and a mixture of berries and roots, did not set well with their gastrointestinal tracts. The plethora of boils which persisted throughout the journey gives evidence of malnutrition, perhaps including profound scurvy. Clark constantly complained of rheumatism and boils and abscesses. Lewis was ill to the point of hardly being able to sit astride a horse. Recurrent dysentery, malaria, pleurisy, venereal disease and injuries kept debilitating the men. Both of the captains and most of their men survived serious diseases and near-fatal accidents, and yet —

Incredibly, over this journey of eight thousand miles and 28 months, *only one man died!* And he died before the Expedition had gotten very far away from St. Louis — long before they came to the grueling winters at Fort Mandan and Fort Clatsop, and crossed and recrossed the formidable Rocky Mountains.

How was it possible that these men could undertake and return safely from such an expedition so gloriously? Back in the states they had been given up for lost, but on September

23, 1806, the captains and their men floated into St. Louis to an impromptu and joyous reception. Lewis wrote to Jefferson on the very day of his arrival in St. Louis: "Sir: It is with pleasure that I announce to you the safe arrival of myself and party at 12 oClk today at this place with our papers and baggage. . . *The whole of the party who accompanied me from the Mandans have returned in good health,* which is not I assure you, to me one of the least pleasing considerations of the Voyage." [2]

We read in an historical journal in the early 1900s: "One of the things most difficult to understand is that an expedition as equipped as this one was for the exploration of the continent, should have gone out upon a journey of eight thousand miles, to be absent from civilization for two years and a half, without a physician as a member of the party." [3] Coues noted in 1893 the lack of a medical man, calling it "the most serious defect in the organization of the expedition." [4] And Wheeler wrote: "Of soldiers, hunters, rowers or waterman, interpreters, there were enough, but not one man of the medical profession to bind up wounds, mend broken limbs or cure fevers, was there sent along." [5] And yet — *only one man died.*

How, then, did this corps of men succeed in this miraculous feat? Wheeler ascribed a great portion of their success to "rare good luck" [6] and we should not discredit Clark's great and humble declaration that "we ought to assign the general safety of the party to a singular interposition of providence,

---

[2] Jackson, *Letters,* p. 319, 324.

[3] Benjamin F. Shambaugh, *Proceedings of the Mississippi Valley Historical Assoc.,* 1908-09.

[4] Elliott Coues, M.D., *History of the Expedition under the Command of Lewis and Clark* (N.Y., 1893), i, p. xx. Hereafter cited as Coues, *History of Lewis and Clark.*

[5] Olin D. Wheeler, *The Trail of Lewis and Clark, 1804-06* (N.Y., 1904), i, p. 46. Hereafter cited as Wheeler, *Trail.*   [6] *Ibid.*

and not to the wisdom of those who commanded the expedition." [7]

This author believes that there was one aspect which contributed immeasurably to its success, and which, in all the extensive writings about the Lewis and Clark Expedition, has been largely ignored. DeVoto commented: "There are several articles on medicine and medical practice, but this interesting if rather unimportant subject has not been exhausted." [8] To this author this subject is interesting *and* important; and it has been my effort in this book to exhaust the subject — without exhausting the reader — so that we might better assess the significance of the medical aspects of the Expedition as they contributed to its success.

Much has already been written in respect to the attributes of skill and leadership of the two captains. Without the assistance of a medical education, they took care of all illnesses and injuries of their men and themselves, and rendered health care to the Indians. Their miraculous accomplishment in caring for the health of their men through all the vicissitudes of the journey attests to their devotion and skill as physicians.

To comprehend the full import of the accomplishments of Lewis and Clark, it is necessary to study and to contemplate deeply the contemporary world in which they lived, including the medical world, which is revealed by the study of army, colonial, frontier and Indian medicine. The medical practice and health care of the time of Lewis and Clark is also revealed by the study of two doctors who touched the Expedition in some way: Benjamin Rush and Antoine Francois Saugrain. If attention to them seems disproportionate, I plead in answer, with Emerson, that "There is properly no History; only Biography."

[7] Jackson, *Letters*, p. 359.
[8] Bernard DeVoto, *The Course of Empire* (Boston, 1952), p. 622.

Although Lewis and Clark made no specific contribution to medical practice, their efficient common-sense leadership was as evident in the health care of their men as it was in all aspects of the Expedition. Although neither captain had had any training in chemistry or anatomy, the generally non-scientific basis of medical practice at that time permitted these two men of natural ability to care for their men as well as a graduate physician of the day might have done. Thus I have not hesitated to write of Lewis and Clark as "Captain-physicians." Lewis wrote of Clark: "My friend Capt. C. is their (the Indians) favorite physician. . ." — a generous and unselfish tribute; but Clark modestly wrote that the Indians had "an exolted oppinion [sic] of my skill as a phi[si]-cian." [9] Clark was really not a captain, but history has so accepted him. And although neither Lewis nor Clark possessed medical degrees, they were true physicians in the most "exolted" concept of the word.

This book is not meant to be another general and complete review of the story of the Expedition. Terrain, climate, geography, biology, botany and the commercial aspects are muted, being mentioned to orient the reader in time and place, and mainly for the purpose of indicating their effects on the health of the men. The heat and sand and buffalo of the plains, and the snow, cold and lack of game in the Rocky Mountains, are important in this book only as they affected the health of the men — and as the health of the men affected the success of the Expedition. Only enough of the geography, climate, edibles and Indian customs are excerpted from the journals to indicate the health problems that the Expedition faced in certain locations and conditions. The physical demands, dangers and food supply, the health of the Indians whom they

---

[9] Reuben Gold Thwaites, ed., *Original Journals of the Lewis and Clark Expedition* (N.Y., 1904-05), IV, p. 358-60. Hereafter cited as Thwaites, *Journals*.

contacted — all had a bearing on the health of the men, and therefore the scope of medical reference is considerably more extensive than the recounting of specific diseases and their treatments.

This Expedition lost only one man on the journey of eight thousand miles and twenty-eight months. The two captains, without a doctor, took care of all the diseases and injuries which afflicted the men of the Expedition. In comparison, ten years later, the overland portion of the Astor Expedition under Wilson Price Hunt, became undisciplined and fragmented, with loss of life, and accomplished few of its objectives. It is my hope that this book will reflect that the discipline and health care of the men by the captains contributed to their *esprit de corps* as well as to their health, and that their health service to the Indians was one of the important adjuncts to their natural diplomatic skills in dealing with the red men.

The medical aspects of the journey itself are told in the original interesting phraseology and phonetic spelling of the journals kept by the captains and other members of the Expedition. Verbatim quotations from the journals and from other authors are used extensively in order to present their thinking accurately and with their original flavor rather than by paraphrase. At the risk of redundancy and tiresomeness, the day-by-day quotations relative to health are presented in detail. And if the reader wearies from this seeming repetition — like daily sick call in the army — it may serve to emphasize what it was like for the men of the Expedition. So it happened, and so it is recorded.

It is most probable that Lewis and Clark could not and did not note every medical incident. This is very apparent by the fact that only three men are listed as having had syphilis. Occasionally one of the other journalists mentions an illness not recorded by the captains, as pointed out in the notes.

Whitehouse particularly had notes about his own afflictions which were not recorded by the captains.

Six men are not listed in the captains' journals as having been ill or injured: John Colter, John Collins, Hugh Hall, Francois Labiche, Patrick Gass and John Thompson. However, it is most unlikely that these six men really escaped having some illness, injury or nutritional problem. The journal notes often refer to one, two, several, or "all of us" as being ill. All members of the corps were involved in the near-starvation that plagued the Expedition at times. Often the journals designate "the party" as being troubled by some affliction.

The captains themselves were plagued as frequently with illness and injury as anyone, although they may have entered notes in the journals more consistently about their own troubles because of having been more acutely aware of them.

The sickest members of the Expedition were Charles Floyd, who died; and Sacagawea and her papoose, both of whom were so ill that the captains despaired of saving their lives. Lewis might have been mortally wounded by the gunshot wound inflicted by Cruzatte, but it was fortunately superficial. Two of the three "Salt Makers" (Bratton and Gibson) also had severe, protracted illnesses.

I hope this book will be for those who read it, what writing it has been for me: a revelation of how our forefathers survived with almost no health care, and how, at the time of Lewis and Clark, there was coming the dawn of scientific medicine. Lewis and Clark accomplished their great feat while health care was still an unscientific morass; theirs was one of the best organized demonstrations of the status of health care at the beginning of the nineteenth century. And it was a most perfect demonstration of Tilton's statement that ". . . upon them (the officers) especially depend the health and comfort of the soldiers." [10]

Jefferson's eagerness to explore the trans-Mississippi country was tempered by his concern for the health and life of the
explorers. In his instructions to Lewis he stated:

> As it is impossible for us to foresee in what manner you will be
> received by those people, whether with hospitality or hostility, so
> it is impossible to prescribe the exact degree of perseverance with
> which you are to pursue your journey. We value too much the lives
> of citizens to offer them to probable destruction. Your numbers
> will be sufficient to secure you against the unauthorised opposition
> of individuals or of small parties: but if a superior force, author-
> ised, or not authorised, should be arrayed against your further
> passage, and inflexibility determined to arrest it, you must decline
> its further pursuit, and return. In the loss of yourselves, we should
> also lose the information you will have acquired. By returning
> safely with that, you may enable us to renew the essay with better
> calculated means. To your own discretion therefore must be left
> the degree of danger you may risk and the point at which you
> should decline, only saying we wish you to err on the side of your
> safety, and to bring back your party safe even if it be with less
> information.

And near the end of his instructions to Lewis, Jefferson wrote:
"To which I have only to add my sincere prayer for your safe
return." [11] Although Jefferson's stated purpose for the Expedition was commerce, he held the health and lives of the men
of the Expedition above all other considerations.

If the author has conveyed the intent of this book, its pages
should reveal that the safe return of the Expedition was
accomplished to a great extent because of the dedicated
attention of the captains to the health care of their men.
Whitehouse, one of the diarists of the Expedition, bespoke
such sentiments, undoubtedly for all the men, when he wrote

---

[10] James Tilton, *Economical Observations of Military Hospitals* (Wilmington,
1813), p. 27. Hereafter cited as Tilton, *Economical Observations*.

[11] Jackson, *Letters*, pp. 64, 66.

of "my utmost gratitude . . . for the humanity shown at all times by them (the captains)." [12] The men were always cheerful, hard-working and loyal, with many of the diarists starting their notes with such salutations to the day as "a pleasant morning," "a cool, cloudy morning," "a fair morning" — and always, always the note: "we proceeded on." And there were no forty hour weeks and no coffee breaks!

Within the pages of this book is the story of one of the most dedicated and heartwarming — and efficient — records of health care ever rendered by leaders who were not physicians by licensure, but truly great physicians in native ability and devotion. Their great accomplishment gives eternal testimony to Ben Franklin's adage "Want of care does us more damage than want of knowledge." They accomplished all their Commander-in-Chief requested, they secured a part of a continent for their country, and they expressed pride that this was done while *only one man died.*

---

[12] Paul Cutright, "The Journal of Private Joseph Whitehouse," *Bull. of Mo. Hist. Soc.*, Vol. XXVIII, No. 3, p. 160. Hereafter cited as Cutright, "Jour. of Whitehouse."

BOOK ONE

The Medical World
of
Lewis and Clark

Disease has played a dominant role in the destiny of the human race. It has destroyed old races and cleared the terrain for new ones which were hardier, more resourceful and more intelligent. It has defeated armies, paralyzed trade, altered the economic life of nations. It has wiped out old castes and created new ones. It has destroyed explorers and colonizers, scattered their settlements and determined the ownership of continents. It has also profoundly affected the lives of great leaders who have left their impress on history. It has influenced their thoughts, altered their dispositions, dominated their deeds. Its influence on the minds of great thinkers has changed the course of human thought, its influence upon the minds of great statesmen has altered the history of nations. Struck down by it with dramatic suddenness, great leaders, armies and nations, like ships without helmsmen, have crashed on the rocks.

Ralph Major, M.D., *Disease and Destiny*, p. vii

I

Army Medicine

. . . The health, hardihood and efficiency of an army depend very much if not entirely upon the wise and prudent conduct of the commanding officers. James Tilton [1]

"The War of the Revolution was the making of medicine in this country . . . " wrote Fielding Garrison.[2] Lewis and Clark served in the army, spending some of their time under General Anthony Wayne,[3] who was a veteran of the Revolutionary War and a strict disciplinarian. Therefore they were familiar with army routines, including those pertaining to health care. A knowledge of the medical practice of the Revolutionary War serves as a background against which to evaluate the medical aspects of the Lewis and Clark Expedition. Although the medical records of the Revolutionary War are very sketchy, they do give information about the type of medical diseases and the treatment used. These were not records of the kind familiar to us today; they were more in the nature of observations or memoirs.

"A century has elapsed since the American Revolution, and in the interim, much has been written and published concerning it. But there is still something to be supplied. Compar-

---

[1] Tilton, *Economical Observations*, p. 34.

[2] Fielding H. Garrison, M.D., *An Introduction to the History of Medicine* (Phila., 1966), p. 376.

[3] "Mad Anthony" Wayne (1745-1796) was so-called because of his daring. He was one of Washington's generals during the Revolutionary War and remained in the army for a time thereafter.

atively little has ever been accessible to the public concerning the medical department of the Army of Patriots." [4] This statement by John Cockran, Director General of Military Hospitals, is still as applicable today as when it was published in 1884. The hospitals in the Revolutionary War were a disgrace, being used mainly as a depository for soldiers who were so ill they could not keep up with the rest of the army, and who were expected to die. Hospital records were essentially nonexistent so far as patient care was concerned.

Cockran wrote from his headquarters on the east side of the Hudson River on August 29, 1781, to the Board of War to state his problem — which was representative of all the problems of the medical men and their patients: "Our Army, till within a few months, has been remarkably healthy. But Dysentary, Intermittant and remittant fevers, with a few putrid diseases begin to prevail." [5]

This note was about as favorable a one as was ever dispatched by any medical personnel regarding the state of health of the American Revolutionary Army. As would be expected, the soldiers in the field were always in better condition than those in the hospitals, mainly because they were on the move rather than squatting in their own filth, and because they could forage for food. Although the doctors in the Revolutionary Army always needed to plead for medical supplies, food supplies were even shorter, and needed by all men — the sick, the marching and the fighting men. Cockran also wrote: "I am sorry to inform you that I found the Hospital entirely destitute of all kinds of stores, except a little vinegar, which was good for nothing — and frequently without bread or beef for many days — so that the doctor, under those circumstances, was obliged to permit such of the patients as

---

[4] John Cockran, "Medical Department of the Revolutionary Army," in *Mag. of Amer. Hist.*, Vol. xii (1884), pp. 241-259. [5] *Ibid.*, p. 257.

could walk into town to beg for provisions among the inhabitants." [6]

Army medical diseases and problems differed considerably during the days of Lewis and Clark from those of today, but still there are some similarities: the main problems consisted then, as now, in respiratory diseases, infections and trauma. There were only a few cases of malignancy, degenerative arthritis or cardiac failure. Probably the main differences are those related to sanitation and nutrition. As with all medicine of its time, army medicine and health practices were exceedingly poor by today's standards. This was especially true of sanitation, of which there was barely a vestige of modern concept and practice. This is understandable and excusable, considering the lack of knowledge about bacterial infections.

Many of the doctors practicing in their communities were poorly trained, even by the standards of their day. Packard states that: "It has been estimated that at the outset of the war for independence there were upward of thirty-five hundred practitioners of medicine in the colonies, of whom no more than four hundred had received medical degrees." [7] Ashburn quotes Toner as finding that of about twelve hundred physicians serving in the armed forces during the Revolution, only one hundred had medical degrees.[8]

The lack of a formal medical degree must not be construed as synonymous with poor training and ability. Many very able doctors were trained through the apprenticeship system, serving under competent older doctors. It is probable that the less competent doctors, who could not make a living in their community, drifted into the army. However, the army was

---

[6] *Ibid.*, p. 249.

[7] Francis R. Packard, *History of Medicine in the United States* (N.Y., 1931), p. 628.

[8] P. M. Ashburn, *A History of the Medical Department of the United States Army* (N.Y., 1929), p. 5. Hereafter cited as Ashburn, *Medical Dept.*

fortunate to have many outstanding, dedicated physicians who worked hard in caring for the specific ills of the soldiers, and also in developing a medical department of the army.[9] Some effort was made to conduct board examinations for army physicians,[10] but many "doctors," incompetent even by the prevailing low standards, managed to obtain commissions. This was true particularly during the years of the poorly organized and undisciplined Revolutionary Army. Jackson says, "The United States Army was still sending its post surgeons, in 1810, copies of the works of physician Thomas Sydenham, who flourished in the late seventeenth century"[11] — hardly a current treatise in 1810, but medicine had changed little in the preceeding century.

General Washington complained to Congress about the regimental surgeons, "many of whom are very great rascals, countenancing the men in sham complaints to exempt them from duty, continually complain of each other, and bickering to the detriment of the sick."[12] Many army doctors deserted along with the soldiers. Much of their work was deplorable, even by the standards of their time. A vicious cycle existed: the army physician was given little authority and very few supplies, which discouraged him and made his work ineffective, and in many cases this resulted in irresponsibility being added to incompetence. Indeed, when the history of military medicine of the Revolutionary War is reviewed, it adds em-

---

[9] It was not until Sept. 1780 that the medical department of the Continental Army was adequately organized.

[10] James Thacher wrote: "On the day appointed, the medical candidates, sixteen in number, were summoned before the board for examination. This business occupied about four hours; the subjects were anatomy, physiology, surgery, and medicine. . . Six of our number were privately rejected as being found unqualified." James Thacher, *A Military Journal of the Revolutionary War* (Boston, 1827), p. 31.

[11] Donald Jackson, "Some Books Carried by Lewis and Clark," *Mo. Hist. Soc. Bull.*, Vol. xvi, No. 1 (1959), p. 12. Hereafter cited as Jackson, "Books."

[12] Washington's letter to Congress, Sept. 24, 1776.

phasis to the amazement that such an ill and ill-kept army
struggled through to victory in spite of the excellent leadership of Washington and the help of Lafayette and Rocham-
beau.

Packard, in evaluating the medicine practiced by the army
physicians stated that ". . . they were not necessarily
men of education, and when such, they were almost certainly
swayed by the teachings of Benjamin Rush, who believed in
the specific almost magical powers of calomel, tartar emetic
and the lancet. Devoted and earnest as they were, . . .
it is somewhat doubtful if the good they accomplished
counter-balanced the harm they did." [13]

Bacteriology, hygiene and preventive medicine were unknown sciences. Certain health measures had been practiced
on an empirical basis among all peoples. It was recognized
generally that one could "catch" a disease. The stench of
decaying food and bodies and human excreta made it unpleasant enough to have them buried away from stationary
camps, thus also providing some health protection. It was
known empirically that clean water supplies were important,
and that the latrines should be placed downstream from the
camp.

Today the United States Army hospital is considered the
acme of health care for the soldier; but in the years of the
Revolution and for a time thereafter, a prime cause of army
desertions was to get away from the army hospitals. This is
reflected in the opinion of a doctor, James Tilton, who wrote
at the time: "It would be shocking to humanity to relate the
history of our general hospital, in the years 1777 and 1778,
when it swallowed up at least one half of our army, owing to
a fatal tendency in the system to throw all the sick of the army

---

[13] Packard, *History of Medicine*, p. 625.

into the general hospital; whence crowds, infection and consequent mortality too affecting to mention." [14]

The main health affliction of the soldier was "camp fever;" it also was known as putrid fever, or jail fever, and was probably typhoid fever. Tilton wrote:

> The putrid diarrhoea was generally the result of dregs of other camps and hospital disease; and was the most intractable disorder of any we had to deal with. The patient would often be able to move about, with little or no fever, his skin remarkably dry and dusky, and constant drain from bowels. . . Multitudes melted away, as it were, of this miserable complaint, and died. The only expedient I ever found effective for their relief was to billet them in the country, where they could enjoy pure air and a milk diet. . .[15]

Tilton also stated that the soldiers' health was much better in their camps than in the army hospitals because of the better sanitary routine. He observed: ". . . the Americans have outdone all their predecessors in the pomp and extravagance of their hospital arrangements, and have surpassed all other nations, in the destruction and havoc thereby committed on their fellow citizens." [16]

Tilton was writing of the medical conditions prevailing at the time of the Expedition when he outlined the following advice addressed to commanding officers, in Part II of his *Economical Observations on Military Hospitals*. These remarks reflect the implied responsibilities of the commanding officers of an expedition conducted by military men, such as the Lewis and Clark Expedition.

> I shall . . . advert to those ways and means, by which military officers have it much in their power to prevent and alleviate the ordinary sickness and distress of an army.

---

[14] Tilton, *Economical Observations*, p. 13.
[15] *Ibid.*, p. 61.   [16] *Ibid.*, p. 13.

For these purposes, discipline is of the first consequence. Without it, there can be neither health nor comfort in an army.

Cleanliness is essential in all conditions of life, but especially to soldiers. . . Officers, therefore, should be very solicitous to protect their men, as well as themselves, from the dreadful effects of filth and nastiness. . . Bathing should be encouraged in warm weather. . . That the camp may be kept free from excrementitious filth of every kind, a penalty should be annexed to dropping anything of this kind within the bounds of the encampment. If adjacent to a river or running stream, every thing of this sort may be thrown into it and swept away. Even the privies might be built over it to great advantage. Otherwise deep pits should be sunk and all excrementitious matters and filth of every kind thrown into them and covered with a layer of dirt every day. When privies are sunk in the earth, they should always be to the northward and eastward of the camp; for the winds blowing from these quarters, being cool, neither raise the effluvia in the same quantity nor exalt them in the same degree, as do the warmer southern and western breezes.

Keep the Camp clean and you run no risk of infection, otherwise it become more dangerous to the health and lives of officers and men, than the weapons of the enemy.

Diet is another article of immense consequence to a soldier.

Hardihood is another article the American soldiery are not sufficiently attentive to. A delicate soldier is very ridiculous indeed. Hardihood sufficient to resist smaller accidents, is essential to the safety of a warrior, as well as his efficiency in duty. [Lewis and Clark repeatedly expressed this opinion when discussing in their correspondence the type of young men they wanted for their Expedition.]

Not only the body, but the mind of a soldier should also be trained, in subserviency to health. The influence of the mind upon the body is astonishing. A sense of honor and reputation should, therefore, be cultivated, in every soldier, by all possible means.

From what has been said, I trust it will be sufficiently apparent that the health, hardihood and efficiency of an army depend very much, if not entirely upon the wise and prudent conduct of the commanding officers.

Tilton also had specific recommendations for the physicians of the army, in Part III, addressed to the Medical Staff. In treatment of patients with jail, or camp fever, he advised:

> After bleeding, . . . a vomit was deemed of excellent use, by opening and squeezing the glands of the body, and thus shaking from the nervous system, the contaminating poison, before its impressions are fixed.
>
> In American hospitals, we were accustomed to give Calomel, in various forms, according to circumstances: sometimes alone, or mixed with opium, tartar emetic, neutral salts, etc. The following prescription will be found of extensive use and should always be kept as an official:
>
> Take of Calomel two drams; Opium one dram; Tartar Emetic fifteen grains, Syrup enough to make sixty pills. Here it may be observed that each pill contains two grains of calomel, one grain of opium and one-fourth of a grain of tartar emetic. Of these one pill may be taken every night, or night and morning, according to exigency of the case.
>
> This form of medicine may be used, not only in all contagious and infectious diseases, but in all fevers whatsoever, where the inflamatory diathesis prevails; and may be regarded as the most powerful of all antiphlogistic remedies. I do not recollect to have seen it tried in inflammations of the stomach and bowels; but in ordinary colics it may be regarded as specific.

In writing of his own bout with jail fever, Tilton said, "My friend Doc Rush paid kind attention to me; . . ."[17]

One of the best records of army life during the Revolutionary War was that of James Thacher.[18] Thacher's journal records the privation and suffering of the soldiers, their many diseases and poor food and clothing, and the constant effort to get medical and personal supplies for themselves.

Epidemics and plagues were always feared, and it had been noted that these occurred where population was congested. Various kinds of fevers were accepted as entities in them-

---

[17] *Ibid.*, pp. 58-59.   [18] Thacher, *A Military Journal.*

selves, rather than the fever being a manifestation of several illnesses; thus there was camp fever, jail fever, remittant fever, intermittant fever — many of which were probably malaria or typhoid fever. Very little was known about a balanced diet, and therefore malnutrition was an almost constant condition of the soldiers. This permitted certain nutritional diseases such as scurvy, and a health status of poor resistance to any disease. In severe cases of scurvy, where the gums became ulcerated and bleeding, it was sometimes possible to pick loose teeth out with the fingers.[19] Packard writes that even in the War of 1812, "The troops suffered severely from malaria, typhoid, dysentary, diarrhea, rheumatism, ophthalmia, peripneumonia and probably influenza. The great scourges were the intestinal and the respiratory infections." [20] It is impressive that venereal diseases were mentioned very little by those who wrote of the health of the Revolutionary Army; men were too sick with other afflictions, and too hungry and poorly clothed, to give much complaint to such accepted "routine" army accompaniments. Venereal diseases were probably accepted like the "cooties" of World War I — a part of army life. Ashburn writes "among soldiers it [syphilis] is so prevalent that no reproach follows it, either from their comrades or from many of their officers." [21]

When one considers the horrible condition of a city during a plague or an epidemic, wherein the illness is quickly spread because of proximity of people, and where there are no specific medical remedies, and where food supplies are short and malnutrition complicates the disease, it is not too difficult to comprehend the even more terrible conditions that must have afflicted the armies of the Revolutionary War when they had to march and fight in addition to being ill and malnourished.

[19] Ashburn, *Medical Dept.*, p. 27.
[20] Packard, *History of Medicine*, p. 628.   [21] Ashburn, *Medical Dept.*, p. 10.

"Hospitals," commented Rush after the Revolutionary War, "are the sinks of human life in an army. . . They robbed the United States of more citizens than the sword." [22] Of course, these were not hospitals in the modern sense. Florence Nightingale [23] was not to add her gentle touch and firm discipline to hospital care until the Crimean War (1854-1856). The beginning of ambulance service was not to come into existence until Larry [24] organized squads to pick up the wounded from the battlefield and transport them on litters to the hospitals, during the Napoleonic wars; these hospitals were little more than first aid stations.

Probably Jones' treatise on gunshot wounds was still being used in the Army when Lewis and Clark were soldiers with General Wayne. Jones states:

> The first intention, with regard to wounds made by a musket or a pistol ball, is, if possible, to extract the ball, or any other extraneous bodies lodged in the wounded part. The next object of attention is the hemorrhage, which must be restrained, if practical, by tying up the vessels with the proper ligatures. . .
>
> In order to extract the ball, or foreign body . . . advise as little search with the probe or forceps as possible, as all irritation on these occasions increases the consequent pain and inflamation . . . we ought not to attempt the extraction of anything which lies beyond the reach of the finger, though if the ball can be felt under the skin, in an opposite direction to the wound, it ought immediately to be cut upon and taken out. . .[25]

No member of the Lewis and Clark Expedition was to receive

22 Quoted by Nathan G. Goodman, *Benjamin Rush: Physician and Citizen* (Phila., 1934), p. 88. Hereafter cited as Goodman, *Rush*.

23 Florence Nightengale (1822-1910) founded the modern nursing profession.

24 Dominique Jean Larry (1766-1842) was a prominent military surgeon under Napoleon, who recognized and rewarded his ability.

25 John Jones, M.D., *Plain Concise, Practical Remarks on the Treatment of Wounds and Fractures, to which is added a short appendix on Camp and Military Hospitals* (1775), pp. 69-73.

a gunshot wound except Captain Lewis; fortunately, this was near the end of the trip and was a relatively superficial wound with the ball not remaining lodged in his body.

An example of the "profound and confused" thinking used in an attempt to explain the medically unknown is found in Jones' book:

> From what has been said, it is evident, that the bark is one of the best remedies hitherto discovered, for contracting vessels, and restoring their due action upon the blood, when too great a quantity of that necessary fluid is lost by profuse hemorrhage, provided the larger wounded vessels are secured by proper ligature from future bleeding. It also not only secures the most tender solids and small vessels from being dissolved by the acrimony of any matter absorbed and returned into the whole mass of blood, from large wounds or lateral abcesses, but it likewise preserves the texture of the blood itself, from being too much broken, or rendered too watery from the same cause which would otherwise produce a fatal, colliquative hectic.[26]

Jones also recommended that the army should provide one blanket for each soldier instead of one for each tent! Today's soldiers would be amused at further recommendations for their proper care as outlined by Jones:

> To prevent the ill effects of moisture in camps, trenches should be made around the tents to carry off the water, and it is of great importance to allow the soldiers plenty of straw, and to have it frequently changed. . . If a soldier's bedding could be raised to a small height from the ground, particularly in damp situations, it would certainly contribute much to the preservation of his health, the tent should be well open and aired every day the weather will allow it.
>
> The wearing of wet clothes is a common source of a great many complaints, for which reason . . . they ought to be allowed fires in the rear of the camp, to dry their clothing, an indulgence which has been found to be of great benefit.[27]

[26] *Ibid.*, p. 73.   [27] *Ibid.*

By the above standards Captains Lewis and Clark took good care of their men, although at times a sudden deluge of rain probably made them regret that they had not dug a trench around their tent — when they had a tent!

Jones' book shows that the army doctors were as concerned with effluvia and miasmata as were the civilian doctors; he writes, "to obviate the effects of putrid air from marshes and stagnating waters, the encampment should be frequently changed."

Jones emphasized the importance of adopting a routine for the placement of privies and strict penalties for the soldier who "eases" himself in other locations. Layers of dirt should be placed periodically in the privies. They should be properly placed "according to the usual stationary winds." His latter concern was not because the winds might be ill-smelling, but because anything "noxious" might contain "putrid effluvia" which "can never be compensated by diet or medicine."

Remembering that Jones' book was published in 1775, and was thus available to Benjamin Rush, it may very well have been that the latter obtained considerable encouragement to embark on his new theories and practices of medicine from the following paragraph from Jones:

> An implicit adherance to the opinions of others, without exercising our own reason, has been the source of that blind attachment, which men in all ages, have paid to the authority of names and characters, and the best understandings have been so much fettered by these shackles, as to overlook the most obvious truths, and even then some enlightened and liberal minds, have dared to deviate from the beaten track, and boldly pointed out the absurdity of antiquated errors, it is with no little difficulty, that men who have been long bigotted to forms can be induced to adopt more just and rational notions of practice.[28]

---

[28] *Ibid.*, p. 17.

A communication to the House of Representatives on December 3, 1807, from Secretary of War Henry Dearborn, indicated that a regiment of approximately nine hundred infantrymen would be entitled to one surgeon at $45 a month, and one surgeon's mate at $30 per month. This would mean approximately one surgeon for four hundred and fifty men. At this rate the Lewis and Clark Expedition certainly was not entitled to have a physician in their corps. However, Zebulon Pike, who left St. Louis on his expedition to the West in 1806, had Dr. John Robinson with his party of only twenty-four men.[29] Dr. Robinson was a son-in-law of Dr. Saugrain (see Chapter x).

When the record of the American military hospitals is reviewed, it is evident that the sick soldiers of the Revolutionary Army would have fared better if they had not been hospitalized, but had been permitted to wander off across the countryside to seek food and rest, fresh air and fresh water. However, in fairness to the hospitals and the doctors, it must be recognized that it was the severely wounded and moribund patients who were hospitalized, and thus it would be expected that the death rate would have been higher than among the less afflicted and non-hospitalized.[30]

Toner, in referring to the report of the surgeons in General Gates' army in 1776, states that this report included a "catalog of Medicines most necessary for the Army," and listed calomel, opium, gum guiacum, camphor, myrrh, Peruvian bark, Virginia snakeroot, epsom salts, and those old reliables —

29 Elliott Coues, *The Expeditions of Zebulon Montgomery Pike,* ii (N.Y., 1895), p. 359.

30 Statistics must always be interpreted with judgment. Statements are seen today to the effect that the maternity death rate in some hospitals is higher than with home deliveries; it must be kept in mind that the serious, complicated pregnancy cases rarely remain at home, and thus add disproportionately to the hospital morbidity and mortality.

rhubarb, tartar emetic, ipecac and jalap — without which no eighteenth century medicine chest was complete.[31] This is very much like the list of medicines accumulated by Lewis for the Expedition.

It is doubtful if the previous army service of Lewis and Clark provided them with much specific training, or even a good example, for providing medical care to the men of the Expedition. However, they were surely impressed with the generally prevailing situation in the army at that time: the commanding officer was responsible for the health of his men. The soldiers themselves knew the general basic remedies employed by doctors, both civilian and military, which included the universal methods of purging, vomiting, bleeding — and more of the same.

[31] J. M. Toner, *The Medical Men of the Revolution* (Phila: Collins Printer, 1876), p. 38.

II

Indian Medicine

For a long time our ethnic arrogance foreclosed any serious attention to the medical knowledge which the "savages" might have. [1]

Indians were called "savages" by the white man mainly because of their religious beliefs and practices — they were not Christians. They were also savages in comparison with the more learned Europeans and Orientals who had developed arts and literature far beyond any accomplishment of the most advanced Indian tribes. The white man also was more learned in such sciences as astronomy, mathematics, anatomy and chemistry; insofar as the latter two sciences can be considered parts of medicine, the white man was far in advance of the Indian. In medical practice, however, the American Indian in many regards was the equal of his white conqueror.

What the Indian did not have was immunity and resistance to the new diseases brought by the white man, principally malaria and smallpox. These two diseases decimated whole nations. The white man's advantage with these diseases was in his immunity, not in his drugs (although vaccination for smallpox was on its way).

It has been stated by several authors that the native inhabitants of the North and South American continents were the healthiest in the world until the advent of the white man's diseases. From the Smithsonian report of 1941, Fenton con-

---

[1] Virgil J. Vogel, *American Indian Medicine* (Norman, 1970), p. 4.

cluded that the following diseases were brought from Europe and Africa: venereal diseases, tuberculosis, measles, scarlet fever, diphtheria, chicken pox, smallpox, typhus, typhoid, malaria, yellow fever, and yaws, Malta fever, leprosy, and trichinosis.[2]

It is hardly appropriate to speak of the different medical practices of the white man and the Indian prior to the last century, because medicine as it is known today was not part of the health care of either the white man or the red man. The American Indian had learned to do what the white man had done in Europe: he utilized the various herbs which were available to him in his community on the basis of empiricism.

Mysticism and religion were interwoven with health practices in the white man's life as well as with the red man. It took centuries for the barber and the surgeon to become separated in the white man's society, and even today a residuum of this association is evident in the continuing custom of the British medical graduate reverting from his title of "doctor" to "mister" when he becomes a surgical specialist. And the barber pole still contains red, the symbol of blood.

When the white man came to North America he left behind most of the herbs which had been available to him for medicine, and it was a natural consequence that Indian herbs would become a part of his medical armamentarium in the new world. Several specific Indian drugs which were unavailable to the white man in the Old World have become valuable parts of the American pharmacopoeia, such as insulin, cocaine, quinine, ipecac, and witch hazel.[3] Several plants have

[2] Quoted by David J. Davis, M.D., in "The Medical History of the Columbus Voyages," *What's New*, No. 184 (1954), p. 11.

[3] Major writes: "The Spaniards, on their arrival in Mexico, were amazed at the size of the Aztec materia medica. Francisco Hernandez (1517-1587) found the names of more than 3000 plants used by the Aztecs in the treatment of disease." Ralph H. Major, M.D., *A History of Medicine* (Springfield, 1954), p. 12.

provided flavoring and palatability, such as sassafras tea, while having very little medicinal value. As commerce developed, and as experience proved their efficacy, the important drugs of the Old World and the New World became assimilated into a more universal pharmacopoeia. The rationale of Indian medicine was obscured by the overlay of rituals and incantations,[4] few of which became integrated into the health practices of the white man; neither were they totally disregarded, as evidenced by the itinerant Indian medicine shows which were popular even into this century along the fringe of advancing American civilization. Even today ignorant attraction to the occult has not disappeared entirely from the white man's health practices.

Indian medical practices varied from tribe to tribe, based partly on traditional rituals in the hands of the shaman or medicine man,[5] and probably more on the availability of different plants in the various regions. The Indian's use of plants was based entirely upon empiricism; he, as well as the white man, did not know the ingredients which provided the observed effect, and neither had available to them the techniques of chemical titration which could establish uniform dosages. Some Indian tribes developed crude but extensive pharmaceutical uses of plants, which were recorded by them,

[4] "Most of the general works dealing with American Indian medicine dwell upon the shamanistic aspects. While ritual played an important part in Indian curing procedure, there was also extensive use of what has been called rational therapy." Vogel, *American Indian Medicine*, p. 68. Most travelers-diarists noted the interplay of the superstitious, ritualistic aspects and the seemingly rational procedures in Indian health practices. Carver, as early as 1776-78, commented on this point: "Notwithstanding this superstitious method of proceeding, it is very certain that they have acquired a knowledge of many plants and herbs that are of a medicinal quality, and which they know how to use with great skill." Jonathan Carver, *Travels Through the Interior Parts of North America* (Minneapolis: Ross and Haines, Inc., 1956), p. 305.

[5] George Catlin painted a medicine man of the Mandans, where Lewis and Clark wintered in 1804-05, showing his appurtenances. *See* reproduction in George Catlin, *North American Indians* (London, 1841) Vol. i, plate 15, p. 34.

permitting a present-day retrospective reviewer to admire the rough accuracy of their dosages.

Indian health care was not confined to the use of drugs and superstitious incantations. The Indian universally rendered equally good care in the treatment of fractures as did the white man up to and during the time of Lewis and Clark. He utilized such standard procedures as splinting, traction and immobilization, and he was very knowledgeable about the healing time of various bones. Stone appraises Indian orthopedic practices very highly: "On the whole, their skill in the care of wounds, fractures and dislocations equalled and in some respects exceeded that of their white contemporary."[6] The Indian also had an extensive armamentarium for the treatment of burns, ulcers and infections, using a variety of poultices, heat, washing and dressing of wounds, and incision and drainage of abcesses. Gordon writes that "The American Indians handled their wounds, empyemas, fractures and dislocations as well, if not better, than the 18th century white physicians. Their method of removing a retained placenta preceded Credé by a hundred years. The Indians definitely added 59 drugs to our modern pharmacopeia, including cascara sagrada."[7]

There is evidence that certain tribes of Indians had perfected crude techniques of trephining, thus letting out the "devils" to relieve headaches. Not all Indian patients who might fit the present day diagnosis of neurosis and psychosis were subjected to trephining. They were often revered as possessing supernatural powers, and were usually tolerated and permitted to be loose in the community. This attitude toward the demented individual is in considerable contrast to

[6] Eric Stone, "Medicine Among the American Indians," *Clio Medica* (Paul B. Hoeber, Inc., 1932), p. 83.

[7] Maurice Bear Gordon, M.D., *Aesculapius Comes to the Colonies* (Ventor, N.J., 1949), p. 11.

the practices inflicted by the white man on himself, as shown by Benjamin Rush's account of his findings regarding the treatment of the insane in a Pennsylvania hospital.[8]

The Indians possessed a good degree of knowledge about basic physiological processes, such as sweating, constipation, emesis, menstruation, and parturition. The sweat bath was universally and extensively used for a variety of conditions; the Lewis and Clark Journals relate how they used the Indian sweat bath to effect a miraculous cure on their return journey. Constipation was treated with purging herbs, and horns and animal bladders were used to administer enemas.

The intelligence of the Indians in health practices, both in understanding the natural processes of the body and in treatment, is no better exemplified than in their knowledge that sucking with the mouth on open, infected and poisoned wounds and snake bites (if nothing was swallowed), did not admit the infection and poison into the body.

Stone observed that ". . . they [the Indians] had an advantage over their military opponents of the first part of the nineteenth century and earlier, in that they were treated individually in their own lodges and so were not subject to 'hospital gangrene,' which wreaked so much havoc in the military hospitals of the day."[9]

The white man's type of warfare, with its fixed positions both in battle and when not fighting, contributed greatly to his health problems. On the contrary, the Indian was constantly on the move, and left his filth behind him. He also tended to isolate and even abandon the injured, disabled and diseased; whereas the white man, more humane in his motives, would stay behind to care for his less fortunate fellows.

In a way, the Indians also practiced a considerable amount

8 Goodman, *Rush*, pp. 255-71.

9 Stone, "Medicine Among the American Indians," p. 78.

of preventive medicine. They knew that greasing the body
for warmth, wearing moccasins instead of using multiple
layers of clothing in stiff shoes, and sleeping with their feet
to the fire [10] resulted in minimal amounts of freezing and
frostbite. Rush wrote: "I do not find that the Indians ever
suffer in their limbs from the action of cold upon them. Their
moccasins, by allowing their feet to move freely, and thereby
promoting the circulation of the blood, defend their lower
extremities in the daytime, and their practice of sleeping with
their feet near a fire defends them at night." [11]

Childbirth practices were universally understood, and were
quite uniform among the Indians. Parturition was almost universally treated as an uneventful occurrence, but they did
have practices relating to complicated births, as was shown by
the account in the Journals of Lewis and Clark when Sacagawea's son was born. The use of the powdered rattles of the
rattlesnake, as given to Sacagawea, was not restricted to the
Mandan tribes; Vogel cites the same usage among the Choc-
taw Indians.[12] The mother usually cared for herself during the
delivery, with cleansing and swathing, and then she promptly
resumed her routine activities; a similar incident is related
by Lewis and Clark in their journals among the Shoshone
Indians.[13] Suffocation was often used (hopefully with the
proper dosage!) to produce a degree of unconsciousness, and
thus relaxation, in severe and protracted labor.[14] Suffocation

---

[10] That the white man learned the value of the Indian practice of sleeping with
the feet to the fire is shown by James Tilton's description: "The best hospital I ever
contrived was upon the plan of an Indian hut. The fire was built in the midst of
the ward . . . the patients laid with their heads to the wall round about, and
their feet were all turned to the fire." Ashburn, *Medical Dept.*, p. 31.

[11] Dagobert Runes, *The Selected Writings of Benjamin Rush* (N.Y., 1947), p.
267.

[12] Vogel, *American Indian Medicine*, p. 92. An excellent review of obstetrical
concepts and practices among the Indians is given by Vogel on pp. 231-36.

[13] Thwaites, *Journals*, III, p. 40.

was also used to produce lack of awareness of pain in surgical procedures. Alcoholic drinks and manual restraint of the patient during surgery were used crudely by both the Indians and the white man.

Although parturition was recognized almost universally by the Indians as a normal process, menstruation was treated as an "unclean" occurrence; at this time the Indian woman was often segregated. Lewis and Clark recorded that some tribes had special lodges for the women to use during their menses.

Benjamin Rush was not the only colonial doctor to recognize the values of Indian medicine. Dr. Benjamin S. Barton [15] of the medical faculty of the University of Pennsylvania, stated in an address delivered before the Philadelphia Medical Society that ". . . the Indian materia medica . . . contains but few substances as inert as many of those which have a place in our books on this science and on other parts of medicine." Dr. William Bartram,[16] a Philadelphia botanist with whom Lewis conferred at the direction of President Jefferson, also had noted and written about the efficacy of the Indian medical substances. Many other colonial doctors wrote papers and delivered addresses on the value of Indian drugs, which reflected the good appraisal generally placed on these drugs by the colonial physicians.

One of the best pharmacopoeias of Indian medicine is found in a narrative by John Hunter. He had been taken cap-

---

[14] Benjamin Rush reports such a case. See Runes, *Writings of Benjamin Rush*, p. 269.

[15] Dr. Benjamin S. Barton (1766-1815) was a Philadelphia physician and botanist, extensively educated in Philadelphia and abroad. He taught with Dr. Benjamin Rush at the Univ. of Penn. Med. School, and was known as the "Father of American materia medica." Jefferson and Lewis hoped that Barton would help write the botanical part of the report of the Lewis and Clark Expedition, but he never got to it.

[16] Dr. William Bartram (1739-1823) was a Philadelphia naturalist who helped Dr. Barton with his material.

tive by the Indians when he was an infant in a frontier settlement in Ohio, so young that he remembered no white people except a little golden-haired girl. He lived among the Indians until he was nineteen years of age. He was educated in London and there wrote his book, which includes two chapters on the pharmacopoeia of the Indians. He shows how the Indians developed a usage of herbs which produced opposite effects, like constipation and diarrhea, menorrhagia and amenorrhea. Many of these drugs are still in use today. He cites the use of the nut of the buckeye tree as a remedy for diarrhea, and states that the leaves as well as the nuts have a high narcotic quality. He writes that Dr. McDowell [17] of Danville, Kentucky, made several experiments on himself to determine the analgesic effect of the buckeye, and concluded that "the effects were very similar to what three grains of opium would have produced in the same length of time." [18]

Hunter, as have other historians of Indian medicine, recounts that the Indians universally used the old reliables — blood-letting,[19] purging, sweating, and vomiting — in the gen-

---

[17] Ephraim McDowell (1771-1830) is noted for having removed a 22-pound ovarian tumor from Mrs. Jane Crawford on Christmas Day, 1809. The good doctor had put her behind him on his horse and brought her sixty miles to his home. The operation was done before anesthesia and asepsis were a part of surgery. Despite the threats of ignorant neighbors, he proceeded with the surgery with the patient strapped to his kitchen table. She had an uneventful recovery, and 25 days later, made the return horseback ride to her home. She lived to be 78. Dr. McDowell was honored on a U.S. postage stamp issued in 1959.

[18] John Hunter, *Memoirs of a Captivity Among the Indians of North America* (London: Longman, Hurst, Rees, Orme, Brown, and Green, 1823), Ch. 17, 18 and 19. Scully also has written a modern review of the use of medicinal herbs by the Indians. *See* Virginia Scully, *A Treasury of American Indian Herbs* (N.Y., 1970).

[19] Beltrami records in detail a technique of Indian blood-letting: "They bleed their patients, or, to give a better idea of the process, they lacerate the skin with a knife, or sharpened bone, and sometimes even with a gun-flint; then, applying the large end of a horn to the incision, they suck the blood through the other end, discharging it from their mouth as successive repletions require it till they have drawn the quantity prescribed." J. C. Beltrami, *A Pilgrimage to Europe and America*, II (London: Hunt and Clark, 1828), pp. 255-56.

eral treatment of diseases. They also used such universally recognized health practices as heat, poulticing, rest, and cleanliness. Daily bathing was almost a ritual among some Indian tribes. The Indians recognized that sores created by burns usually cure themselves, and that chronic indolent ulcers, if burned by escharotics, often could be stimulated to heal.

In consideration of the pre-historical land connection between Asia and Alaska, it is interesting that the centuries-old oriental practice of acupuncture never became a part of the health practices of the North American Indians. Vogel and other writers on Indian medicine have given no account of acupuncture,[20] although many Indians used blistering and a few used moxa.[21]

The white man had great respect for the health practices of the Indians, rarely disparaged them, and often admired and adopted them. Lewis and Clark participated in this general attitude of their fellow white men toward Indian medicine, questioning some of their practices and using some, as a reading of their journals will show.

---

[20] I checked this by personal correspondence with Vogel; he wrote: "I have found no mention of this practice by American Indians. Moxa and scarification were used, but application was at the seat of the trouble, and not at some other location, as in acupuncture." Vogel also sent to me a copy of a short, excellent review on acupuncture by Frances Lang, published in *Ramparts* (Oct. 1971), pp. 12-16.

[21] Moxa is the practice of burning a splinter of wood on the skin in the area of the body which is painful, or the supposed seat of the trouble. *See* Vogel, *American Indian Medicine,* pp. 181-83.

III

Colonial and Frontier Medicine

Many of a frontier doctor's methods sound curious today . . .
because he was a prisoner of the medical thought of his time.
Richard Dunlop [1]

As indicated by the preceding review of Indian medicine,
colonial and frontier medicine in America was a combination
of health practices brought from Europe with those of the
Indians. The use of regional drugs based upon empiricism
intermingled with ignorance and superstition provided the
main basis for the "do-it-yourself" health practices of the
countryside. Many of the early American "doctors" assumed
their titles without training of any kind, or after an indefinite
apprenticeship with an established physician.[2] However, the
physician as we know him today was slowly evolving. His
practice of "physic" was separating him from the barber surgeon, and his emphasis on treatment of illness was separating
him from the botanist. The increasing study of the developing
sciences of anatomy, physiology and chemistry was providing
a scientific basis for his profession.

The young colonial doctor who sought the epitome of
training and recognition traveled to Europe for study in the
medical centers, where he was usually granted a degree. The

---

[1] Richard Dunlop, *Doctors of the American Frontier* (N.Y: Doubleday and Co.,
1962), p. 3.

[2] In the century preceding Lewis and Clark, only one in nine "doctors" in Jefferson's native state of Virginia had a degree, according to Toner. *See* J. M. Toner,
Contributions to the Annals of Medical Progress (Washington, D.C: 1874), p. 106.

first medical classes in the colonies were held in 1765 in
the Medical Department of the College of Philadelphia.[3]
". . . It has been estimated that even a decade after the
first native school was founded in 1765, ninety-five percent
of American practitioners held no medical degrees whatever."[4] In 1800 there were only five medical schools in the
United States which gave a medical degree, and many of
these degrees were honorary. "Up to and including 1800 there
had been granted medical degrees in the u.s. to a total of 312
individuals by three successive schools in Philadelphia, three
in New York City, and one each in Cambridge, Massachusetts
and Hanover, New Hampshire. However, deducting honorary degrees to older men leaves about 250 men who graduated under instruction."[5]

It is manifestly unfair to lump all physicians into one group
in attempting to make an appraisal of colonial physicians. At
the beginning of the nineteenth century, only about one in
ten physicians had a medical degree. This degree did not
always assure quality performance on the part of the physician. A two-year medical course in which each year consisted
of only six months of lectures, and a second year which was
a repetition of the first, did not provide much knowledge or
practical training, and did very little to ensure those ingredients which contribute to making a truly good physician:
integrity, dedication and native judgment and ability. Most

---

[3] In 1765 William Shippen and John Morgan founded the Medical Department
of the College of Philadelphia, which soon became the University of Pennsylvania.
King's College followed in 1768, Harvard Medical School in 1783, and Dartmouth
in 1798. Wydham B. Blanton, *Medicine in Virginia in the Eighteenth Century*
(Richmond, Va: 1931), p. 81. The University of Mexico created the first chair of
medicine in America in 1580. *See* Major, *History of Medicine,* ii, p. 714.

[4] Richard Shryock, "European Backgrounds of American Medical Education
(1600-1900)," *JAMA*, Vol. 194, No. 7 (Nov. 15, 1965), p. 119.

[5] Frederick C. Waite, "The Professional Education of Pioneer Ohio Physicians,"
Ohio State Arch. and Hist. Qtly., Vol. 48, No. 3 (1939), p. 190.

of the physicians of the time were trained as apprentices to older physicians; as with formal medical education, the result depended upon the trainer and the trainee. Many men who became designated as physicians through the apprenticeship method were better physicians than those who displayed a medical certificate. On the other hand, it was sometimes difficult to differentiate between the physician who was trained in a short apprenticeship by an inadequate doctor and the plentitude of quacks who cruised the countryside.

The colonial doctor who could keep himself from becoming too involved in the arguments about the theories of "physic," or perhaps who was so insolated that he did not have another doctor with whom to argue, and who could keep his mind open and alert, could learn much from the Indians regarding good health practices. In particular he might gain knowledge of the methods of dress for long journeys on the frontier and what herbs and foods previously unknown to the white man would be beneficial to him. Many of these isolated doctors came to rely mainly on Indian medical practices, particularly for their supply of drugs.

Most babies were delivered by mid-wifery, a practice imported from the old country. To some extent it probably was based on prudery, but it is also probable that the mid-wife was more at home in the "delivery bedroom," and as well or better trained in its routine than the untrained and uninitiated male doctor. Both fetal and infant death rates were high, often approaching fifty percent. Puerperal or childbirth fever was common, but doctors were as unknowledgeable about its cause and impotent in treating it as were the mid-wives.[6]

---

[6] It remained for Ignase Semmelweis (1818-1865) of Vienna and Budapest, and Oliver Wendell Holmes (1809-1894) of Boston to relate uncleanliness to sepsis in the 1840s. At first they were both disparaged by their colleagues when they insisted that it was the doctor's unclean hands that brought the infection to the mothers. Bacteriology as a science was not yet known.

"Plantation medicine" was almost an institution in the South. Medical supplies were purchased and stored in large quantities, much as in a modern hospital pharmacy, and were dispensed by the plantation owner or overseer to family and slaves. Patent medicines were available everywhere for the cure of everything.

At the time of Lewis and Clark there was only one medical periodical in the United States, the *Medical Repository*, which had been established in New York in 1797. It is not probable that this journal reached many of the frontier towns. On the other hand, many doctors kept in touch with their colleagues through their personal correspondence. Benjamin Rush carried on extensive correspondence throughout the colonies. There was considerable writing about health in the newspapers and other publications, even to the printing of advice and prescriptions in newspapers by physicians.

The medical students and practitioners today would have good reason to look upon the medical world of Lewis and Clark's time as being quite sterile. Essentially there was no opportunity for a medical education, no hospitals as we know them today, and no medical journals. And yet there was a definite ferment, a stirring, a dissatisfaction with the status quo, a determined inquiry.

Licensure to practice medicine was very slow in coming. The first such law was passed by South Carolina in 1817; thus Lewis and Clark were free to "practice" on their corpsmen.[7] The farther the distance from the large centers of population, the more licensure was replaced with license. Occasionally some enterprising individual with a copious amount of intes-

---

[7] The first law was passed by South Carolina in 1817, followed by Mississippi in 1819, and Alabama in 1823. The first examining board under a medical practice act was established by Mississippi at the time of its licensure law; it was not until 1876 that the second law requiring medical board examinations was passed, this time in California. See *JAMA*, Vol. 216, No. 11 (June 1971), p. 1791.

tinal fortitude matched by irresponsibility, would assume the title and role of doctor, and become a predator on his fellow men. The poor recipients' ignorance added plausibility to what they could not understand. But perhaps all must be forgiven with the understanding that everyone was muddling along, doing their best under the circumstances, particularly when, from our present-day vantage, we read of the ludicrous scholarly writings of the medical leaders of the day, such as Benjamin Rush. Thomas Jefferson fairly summed up the use of medical practice in his day in a letter to Dr. Caspar Wistar: "Thus, fulness of the stomach we can relieve by emetic; disease of the bowels, by purgative; inflammation cases, by bleeding; intermittance of Peruvian bark; syphilis by mercury; watchfulness, by opium." [8]

The first permanent medical school west of the Alleghenies, the University of Cincinnati College of Medicine, was established in 1821 by Daniel Drake. Well-trained medical men, some of whom possessed degrees were moving west along the Ohio River, following the great waterway used by the westering immigrants, to serve the larger settlements. These frontier doctors encountered more ignorance and superstition among the frontier people than in the eastern states, and they had little scientific basis to combat it.

A reading of the prescriptions published by Peter Smith in 1812 in his *Indian Doctor's Dispensatory* will reflect with great honor on the medical practices of Lewis and Clark. While Lewis and Clark's men were receiving reasonable care from their captain-doctors, Peter Smith advocated through the Ohio and Mississippi Valleys such prescriptions as:

Description No. 62 for Wens: The patient must wash the wen morning and evening in his own urine, and once a day he must

---

[8] Quoted by Blanton, *Medicine in Virginia*, p. 198. *See also* Appen. ɪɪ, herein.

grease it with grease broiled out of a wooden pot lid, such as in old times they used on their dinner pots. Probably the marrow out of an old baconed hog's jaw would do as well . . . should the above fail to break the wen, a hubbed toad may be just knocked in the head and laid upon it; this, it is said, will surely break it.[9]

In consideration of the present-day teachings of mouth-to-mouth resuscitation, Peter Smith's description No. 51 will certainly elicit less contempt and ridicule:

> Let a person of good strong lungs apply his mouth to the sufferer's holding at the same time his nostril and blow his breath (as we say) as hard as he can into the sufferer's lungs; he must then leave him to expire while he gets his own breath, and then repeat the effort as soon and as often as he can, perhaps a hundred times, if self-respiration does not take place sooner.[10]

When Lewis and Clark were having great demands made upon them by the Indians for eyewater, which the captains dispensed freely for diplomatic rapport, they might have appreciated having a few gallons of eye water prepared according to prescription No. 23 in Dr. Smith's *Dispensatory:*

> Take 3 gills — take a spoonful heaped up of white vitriol and the same quantity of common salt, calcine them together on copper, or a piece of earthen, or on coal, stiring it with a stick, until it becomes a gray powder; then put it into a bowl, and add to it three gills of rain water. Strain it through paper, or a fine rag, two or three double — then add two tablespoonfulls of white sugar and a lump of blue stone, as big as a large grain of Indian corn, and bottle it for use . . . This eye water cures the western country sore eyes, which are scarcely, if ever relieved by old eyewaters.[11]

Probably Lewis had never heard of this special eye-water for "western country sore eyes," or he might have included it in his medical supplies!

---

[9] Peter Smith, *The Indian Doctor's Dispensatory* (Cincinnati, 1812), pp. 77-78.
[10] *Ibid.,* p. 69.   [11] *Ibid.,* pp. 42-43.

John Bradbury traveled about the area of St. Louis in 1809-11 and recorded much about the health status and care of this frontier town. He noted the prevalence of malaria (ague [12]) and the same erroneous ideas of its cause (miasmata and effluvia of the low lands), as well as the various methods of treatment. Scurvy also was generally recognized by the soldiers and trappers who were confined to a restricted diet for extended periods of time, and there was general recognition that a diet of "greens" would cure the condition.

In addition to scurvy, malnutrition contributed to the ease with which infections were contracted. Pneumonia was a constant and unrelenting killer, especially among the infants. "Fevers" were forever prevalent, but especially the "autumnal fevers" — the ague, or malaria. Maguire says: ". . . it does appear that the ague was the most common disease in this country during the early colonizing and frontier periods." [13] The Peruvian bark was used for all fevers, and of course its quinine gave specific relief in malaria.

James shows how common-place was the recognition of the omnipresent ague by the following description:

> The cold stage commences with a sensation of langour and depression, attended with almost incessant yawning and a disinclination to motion, soon followed by shivering, and a distressing sensation of cold. These symptoms pass off gradually, and the hot stage succeeds. The degree of fever is usually somewhat proportioned to the violence of the cold fit, and respiration becomes full and frequent, the face flushed, and the skin moist, and the patient falls of a heavy slumber; on waking after some time, extreme

---

12 "Ague" is a corruption of *aigu*, the French word for "sharp," used to describe the sharp elevations of fever. The other name for this disease, malaria, also comes from the French and means "bad air" — a reference to the swamps from whence came the "effluvia" and "exhalations" — and mosquitoes!

13 Edward F. Maguire, "Frequent Diseases and Intended Remedies on the Frontier (1780-1850)," Unpub. MA Thesis (St. Louis Univ., 1953), p. 6.

langour and exhaustion are felt, though few symptoms of fever remain.

Intermitting fevers are of such universal occurrence in every part of the newly settled country to the west, that every person is well acquainted with the symptoms, and has some favorite method of treatment. . . The Peruvian bark is much used, but often so injudiciously as to occasion great mischief.[14]

Maguire points out that it was not during the cold months of winter that people usually died, but during late summer and early autumn (mosquito months!). "It was during this period that typhoid epidemics came and went." Consistent with this observation, Charles Floyd of the Expedition died on August 20.

Lewis and Clark were restrained and sophisticated in their medical practice, compared to the crude prescriptions quoted above. Lewis particularly had had contact with good medical practitioners and their advice. The instructions from Drs. Rush, Wistar and Saugrain served as a buffer to the possible enticements of the patent medicine vendors. The availability of the medical supplies purchased by Lewis in Philadelphia and carried by the Expedition countered any tendency to stray from the established armamentarium of medical treatment. Occasionally Lewis resorted to a "home remedy," as when he made a decoction of the choke cherry. Clark might have indulged himself in spurious cures if not restrained by circumstances to the contents of the medicine chest, as indicated by his use of ridiculous health practices after he returned home. But, all things considered, the captains practiced a high quality of health care on their men, impressively free from questionable home-remedy, frontier practices.

[14] Edwin James, *An Account of an Expedition from Pittsburgh to the Rocky Mountains*, ii, p. 322.

IV

Blood-letting

*Hemmorrhages seldom occur, where bleeding has been sufficiently
copious.*   Benjamin Rush [1]

Blood-letting has been used as a means of health treatment
by almost all peoples of the world. The earliest historical
accounts indicate that the practice was already in existence
before the advent of recorded history. Probably its usage was
exceeded only by vomiting and purging as therapeutic meas-
urse to cure diseases, and the greater use of these procedures
undoubtedly was due to their relatively easier applicability.

Blood-letting necessitated the use of certain equipment,
and certain daring on the part of the blood-letter. Various
instruments were used; basically anything that was sharp,
such as a knife or the edge of a rock. Ordinary knives were
used frequently, but a specific knife, called a lancet, was
developed which provided very little refinement of the procedure. The scarifier, a rough instrument to produce superficial lacerations and perforations of the skin, was also used.

In certain parts of the world leeches were used as a means
of blood-letting. The use of a sucking leech is repellent today,
but it was acceptable to many patients because it adhered
painlessly and let loose when it had engorged itself — all of
which was less gruesomely impressive to the patient than
incising a vein and watching the blood flow into a receptacle.

---

[1] Benjamin Rush, "Defense of Blood-Letting," in *Medical Inquiries and Observations,* iv (3rd ed.; Philadelphia, 1809), p. 295.

Garrison quotes Broussais: "As many as 10 to 50 leeches were applied at once . . . of the scarcity of leeches in Broussais' time, Baas records that in the year 1833 alone 41,500,000 leeches were imported into France. . ." [2]

That the lancet became the symbol of the physician just before and during the time of Lewis and Clark is evidenced by the title of a book on the life of General Hugh Mercer, *With Sword and Lancet*.[3] Although Mercer was a physician, he served as a general in the Revolutionary Army and lost his life at the Battle of Princeton.

Along with the lancet a variety of receptacles to collect blood for purposes of measurement and evaluations of its appearance and consistency became established over the centuries. Abel states that "the first European representation of bleeding occurs on a Greek vase circa 500 B.C." [4] He also quotes Hippocrates as writing in the fifth century B.C. that "venesection holds first place in conducting the treatment," and this great and early teacher of medicine, known respectfully as the "Father of Medicine," listed almost every known medical condition as an indication for blood-letting.

Many households contained a lancet and a bleeding bowl, and such items were part of the equipment of "bleeders." Bleeding was a function of the barber-surgeons, until during the last century of its use it was performed mainly by physicians.

There must have been a first incident of willful bloodletting, as well as a definite reason for it, however unsound it may have been, based on today's knowledge. It is probable

[2] Garrison, History of Medicine, p. 427.

[3] Gen. Hugh Mercer, *With Sword and Lancet* (Richmond, Va: Garrett & Massie, 1941).

[4] A. Lawrence Abel, M.D., "Blood-Letting," *JAMA*, Vol. 214, No. 5 (Nov., 2, 1970), pp. 900-01. The issue of *JAMA* in which the article appears has on its cover four color reproductions of beautiful bleeding bowls from the author's (Abel's) collection of 450 items.

that some apparent improvement in a patient occurred as a result of an accidental hemorrhage; for instance, some patient with headache and dizziness because of hypertension may have been relieved of these symptoms following a copious traumatic hemorrhage. This may have led to experimenting with the use of deliberate blood-letting to observe possible salutary effects in other conditions — and such beneficial effects, imaginary or otherwise, may have been noted. The next step would have been for blood-letting to have become incorporated into the teaching system, by Hippocrates, Galen, Harvey, Sydenham and others.[5]

Almost all of the great medical teachers were staunch advocates of the therapeutic value of blood-letting. Cullen,* the leading medical teacher of Edinburgh, was a proponent of the advantages of bleeding. His reasoning is not quite clear to today's medical men:

> When the violence of reaction, and its constant attendant, a phlogistic diathesis, are sufficiently manifest, when these constitute the principle part of the disease, and may be expected to continue throughout the whole of it . . .   blood-letting is the principle remedy, and may be used as far as symptoms of the disease may seem to require, and the constitution of the patient will bear.[6]

Benjamin Rush was the most noted exponent of profuse blood-letting for all conditions during the time of Lewis and Clark. He wrote about bleeding one of his daughters when she was but six weeks old, and bleeding one of his sons twice before he was two months old. "In both cases, life appeared to be saved by this remedy."[7]

[5] When this author was an intern and resident during 1934-39, "bleeding" was done in certain instances: removing blood from a hypertensive patient and giving it to an anemic patient. This was done regularly before the days of blood banks.

* William Cullen's theories greatly impressed Benjamin Rush.

[6] Quoted by Benjamin Welsh, M.D., *A Practical Treatise on the Efficacy of Blood Letting* (Edinburgh, 1819), pp. 125-26.   [7] Rush, "Defense," p. 300.

Again Rush wrote that he "drew six and thirty ounces of blood, in the year 1806, at three bleedings from Mr. Israel Jacobs in the ninety-first year of his age, in a bilious fever, in the course of a few days. He was cured by this remedy, and at this time, July 29, 1809, enjoys good health." [8]

Modern medical practice would hardly approve the following treatment by Dr. Rush:

> In the month of March, 1795, Dr. Physick requested me to visit, with him, Mrs. Fries, the wife of Mr. John Fries, in a malignant fever. He had bled her four times. After the fourth bleeding, her pulse suddenly fell, so as scarcely to be perceptible. I found her hands and feet cold, and her countenance ghastly, as if she were in the last moments of life. In this alarming situation, I suggested nothing to Dr. Physick but to follow his judgment, for I knew that he was master of that law of the animal economy which resolved all her symptoms into an oppressed state of the system. The doctor decided in a moment in favor of more bleeding. During the flowing of the blood, the pulse rose. At the end of three, ten, and seventeen hours it fell, and rose again by three successful bleedings, in all of which she lost about thirty ounces of sizy blood. So great was the vigor acquired by the pulse, a few days after the paroxysms of depression, which have been described, were relieved, that it required seven more bleedings to subdue it.[9]

Rush also wrote: "Bleeding has been charged with being a weakening remedy. I grant that it is so, and in this, its merit chiefly consists. The excessive morbid action of the blood-vessels must be subdued in part in a fever, before stimulating remedies can be given with safety or advantage." [10]

The speciousness of his reasoning is exemplified by his statement that "the corpulency of a patient should regulate the use of the lancet. A butcher of great observation informed me, that a fat ox did not yield more than from one-half, to one-third of the quantity of blood of a lean one. . . Of

---

[8] *Ibid.*, p. 301.   [9] *Ibid.*, pp. 311-12.   [10] *Ibid.*, p. 315.

course, less blood should be drawn from fat, than from lean people, under equal circumstance of disease." [11]

Rush extends his indications for the use of bleeding to the reduction of fractures and dislocations. He writes:

> In dislocated bones which resist both skill and force, it has been suggested, that bleeding, till fainting is induced, would probably induce such relaxation in the muscles as to favor their reduction. This principle was happily applied, in the winter of 1795, by Dr. Physick, in the Pennsylvania hospital, in a case of dislocated humerus of two months continuance. The doctor bled his patient till he fainted, and then reduced his shoulder in less than a minute, and with very little exertion of force. The practice has since become general in Philadelphia, in fractures of large bones, where they resist the common degrees of strength employed to reduce them.[12]

If the practice of bleeding was established in Philadelphia in 1795 as an adjunct to the reduction of fractures and dislocations, apparently Rush did not impart this information when he gave medical instructions to Lewis. Securing relaxation of the muscles is a prime necessity to permit the manipulator to reduce a dislocation or fracture. The four attempts of the captains which were required to reduce Sergeant Pryor's dislocated shoulder on the way up the Missouri may be an indication that relaxation was not readily obtained. But Lewis and Clark did not bleed Pryor — at least they did not mention it in the journals.

A review of all of Rush's writings and practices seems to indicate that his reasoning for blood-letting was as follows: he considered fevers a result of the morbid condition of the blood-vessels, and thought that blood-letting changed the morbidity of the blood-vessels, as evidenced by the change of pulse. Bleeding assisted sweating, vomiting, and diarrhea as nature's way of depleting the body of its morbid elements.

[11] *Ibid.*, pp. 337-38.   [12] *Ibid.*, pp. 378-79.

The indefinite and illusory phraseology used to explain pathological processes which were not understood, and the irrational treatment of them, are no better exemplified than in Rush's statement that

> . . . the higher grades of fever depend upon morbid and excessive action in the blood-vessels. It is connected, of course, with preternatural sensibility in their muscular fibers. The blood is the most powerful irritant which acts upon them. By abstracting a part of it, we lessen the principal cause of the fever. The effect of blood-letting is as immediate and natural in removing fever, as the abstraction of a particle of sand is to cure any inflammation in the eye, when it arises from that cause.[13]

He felt that nosebleeds were evidence of a need for blood-letting, and emphasized that "By artificial blood-letting, we can choose the time and place of drawing blood, and we may regulate its quantity by the degrees of action in the blood-vessels." [14]

Rush wrote voluminously in "defense of blood-letting." He cited its advantages to include the following:

> it frequently strangles a fever, when used in its forming state, and therby saves much pain, time, and expense to a patient; it imparts strength to the body, by removing the depression which is induced by the remote cause of the fever. It moreover obviates a disposition to faint, which arises from this state of the system; it induces sleep . . . sleep sometimes stole upon the patient while the blood was flowing; it prevents effusions of serum and blood. Hemmorrhages seldom occur, where bleeding has been sufficiently copious.[15]

That Benjamin Rush believed and practiced what he preached cannot be doubted; at the time of his own illness he bled himself, or designated that someone should bleed him. Mrs. Rush wrote of her husband's terminal illness:

---

[13] *Ibid.*, p. 288.   [14] *Ibid.*, p. 289.   [15] *Ibid.*, p. 295.

At nine o'clock in the evening of Wednesday, the fourteenth of April, 1813, Dr. Rush, after having been as well as usual through the day, complained of chilliness and general indisposition, and said he would go to bed. While his room was preparing and a fire making, he became so cold that he called for some brandy and drank it; he then went to his room, bathed his feet in warm water, got into a warm bed, and took some hot drink; the fever soon came on, attended with great pain in his limbs and in his side; he passed a restless night, but after daylight a perspiration came on, and all the pains were relieved except that in his side which became more acute. He sent for a bleeder, and ten ounces of blood taken from his arm with evident relief.[16]

Many critics have felt that perhaps George Washington was bled too extensively, even unto death; this can hardly be proven, inasmuch as he had a septic sore throat and probably pneumonia, both great killers prior to the recent advent of antibiotics. The exact amount of blood removed from George Washington is unknown,[17] although he probably received copious and repeated bleedings, and Dr. Elisha C. Dick objected to the amount of bleeding. George Washington initiated his own blood-letting — "he procured a bleeder in the neighborhood, who took from the arm in the night, twelve or fourteen ounces of blood."[18]

Recently it has been reported by cardiologists that there may be some therapeutic value to restricted blood-letting in the treatment of heart disease. This report suggested that blood-letting reduced the viscosity of the blood, thus permitting freer circulation, and also advanced the idea that anemia promoted the better growth of blood vessels.[19] Blood-letting

[16] Quoted from Gordon, *Aesculapius*, p. 472.

[17] Pepper states that Washington was bled "an estimated gallon and a pint" within 24 hours. O. N. Perry Pepper, M.D., "Benjamin Rush: Theories on Blood Letting after One Hundred and Fifty Years," *Trans. and Stud. of Coll. of Physicians*, Vol. 14 (1946-47), p. 122.

[18] Quoted from Blanton, *Medicine in Virginia*, p. 305.

[19] George E. Burch, M.D., and Nicholas P. DePasquale, M.D., reference made in *JAMA*, Vol. 182, No. 5 (Nov. 3, 1962), p. 56.

is a standard part of the current treatment for polycythemia vera, a condition where the red blood corpuscles are produced too abundantly.

The indications for blood-letting became very voluminous and confused in accumulated medical literature. The condition of the pulse — its strength, rapidity, bounding or soft quality — was the main indication for bleeding. Great attention and emphasis was given to the pulse because it was easily examined. However, other conditions provided indications for bleeding: the presence of any type of fever, or sweating; even a simple complaint of not feeling well might be sufficient cause for this procedure. The "sizy" appearance of drawn blood was an indication for more blood-letting.

One of the best testimonials to blood-letting was given by Welsh:

> Blood letting is, in reality, the surgery of the physician. . . When he makes use of phlebotomy, he boldly and at once, enters the great reservoir from which all our sluices are derived, and at once draws off the quantity necessary to produce the change required. Hence it is, that in all ages, whether disease was conceived to arise from a corrupted humerus, from plethora, or the overaction of blood vessels . . . this remedy has been more or less employed for this purpose. For its action is so manifest and immediate, the relief of urgent symptoms so palpable, that little argument could be required to persuade mankind of its utility.[20]

Blood-letting continued to be popular as a treatment for many medical conditions long after Lewis and Clark's time. In his *Diseases of the Mississippi Valley*,[21] published in 1850 and 1854, Drake advocated the extensive use of bleeding,

---

[20] Welsh, *Blood Letting*, p. 156.

[21] Daniel Drake (1785-1852) was a graduate of the Medical Dept. of the Univ. of Pennsylvania. He is noted for his *Diseases of the Interior of North America* and his contributions to medical education through his efforts in helping establish the Medical Dept. of Cincinnati College (now the Univ. of Cincinnati College of Medicine).

especially in the treatment of ague, the omnipresent disease of the Ohio and Mississippi valleys.

But there was no unanimity of opinion among medical leaders regarding the value of blood-letting. Those who believed in blood-letting felt that the blood was the site of disease, and therefore the indicated treatment was to "deplete" it. Those who opposed blood-letting, including Edward Jenner, the discoverer of vaccination, felt that depleting blood effected the patient's condition as a whole and not just the blood. However, bleeding continued to be a part of the universal armamentarium of medical practice up to the time of the American Civil War.

Venesection could be a lucrative part of the physician's services. Sir Astley Cooper[22] describes a Mr. Lucas who made "£300 per annum by bleeding." Dr. Bernard Farrar's Account Book in 1811-12 lists the cost of venesection as fifty cents.[23]

That blood-letting was not confined to the art and finesse of the physician is evidenced by prescription Number 72 of Peter Smith's *Indian Doctor Dispensatory* which gave direction that enabled any person to bleed a member of their family or a friend in need. Smith gave explicit commentary under the headings: 1. How to bleed; 2. Where to bleed; 3. When to bleed; 4. When not to bleed.[24] His indications and instructions are no more ridiculous than those of the "regular doctors."

The following quotation from Welsh expresses the effect of blood-letting more succinctly and correctly than anything else that has ever been written about it: "The most obvious effect of blood-letting is, to diminish the quantity of circulating

---

[22] Sir Astley Cooper (1768-1841) was a leading English surgeon who was baroneted for removing a wen from the head of George IV.

[23] Dr. Bernard Farrar, "Dr. Bernard Farrar's Account Book of 1811-1812," manuscript at the Missouri Hist. Soc. Dr. Farrar was a leading early St. Louis physician.

[24] Smith, *Indian Dr.'s Dispensatory,* p. 86.

blood." [25] He lists the following advantages of blood-letting: alteration of the pulse in various ways, reduction of fever, relief of delirium and coma, and relief of pain, constipation, diarrhea, and sleeplessness. "It removes depression and morbid congestion, it calms the respirations, it diminishes thirst and improves the appetite, it mitigates all the uneasy sensations." The author summarizes that "the utility of blood-letting in fever depends almost solely on its being copiously drawn. Bleeding should be repeated . . . until four fifths of the blood contained in the body are drawn away." This suggestion to continue bleeding until four-fifths of the patient's blood was drawn away was an ignorant and hazardous one; the average amount of blood in the human body was not known when blood-letting was practiced extensively. Today we know that the average quantity of blood in a human adult is five quarts. Welsh would have removed up to four quarts. The unit of blood removed by a modern blood bank is about one pint, or about one-eighth the amount Welsh thought it was safe and even desirable to remove.

Bryan [26] indicates that blood-letting in America began to decline after 1830, which means that this decline began not too long after the death of Benjamin Rush in 1813. This change, Bryan indicates, was initiated by the impressive questioning and teaching of Hall in England and Louis in France. Neither Hall nor Louis advised abandonment of blood-letting, pleading only for restraint. Textbooks published after the American Civil War made very little reference to blood-letting, and its use in medical practice likewise diminished. Bryan states that "during the Civil War, the Confederate Surgical Manual condemned the time-honored absurdity of

---

25 Welsh, *Blood Letting*, p. 156.

26 Leon S. Bryan, Jr., "Blood-Letting in American Medicine, 1803-1892," *Bull. of the Hist. of Medicine*, Vol. 38, No. 6 (Nov.-Dec., 1964), pp. 516-29.

De Aderlating (The Bleeding)
By the Dutch painter, Jacob Ochtervelt, born in Rotterdam about 1635.
The original is in possession of the Goudstikker Collection, Amsterdam.
Courtesy of Antiphlogistine Laboratories

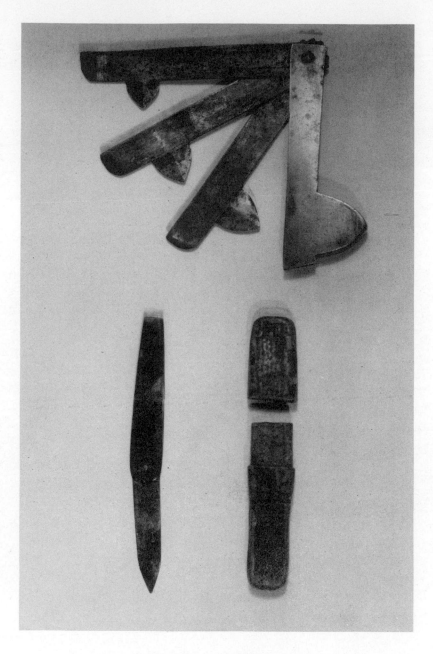

LANCET WITH CASE
That shown was owned by Daniel Boone, and is probably
representative of the ones used by Lewis and Clark.
Courtesy of Missouri Historical Society, St. Louis.

venesection" for most conditions. Just as Benjamin Rush had questioned medical practices of his day, so too his medical practices in turn came under close scrutiny and questioning — and change.

Most medical textbooks no longer mentioned blood-letting as a therapeutic procedure after 1870. However, in his first textbook published in 1892, William Osler listed several indications for blood-letting, most of them related to cardiac and pulmonary congestion.[27]

Although blood-letting has not been a part of routine medical practice for a century, it is important to be aware of its wide-spread usage in order to put the medical practice of Lewis and Clark in perspective. It must be realized that it was the most emphasized single method of health practice by both physician and layman during the time of the Expedition. Lewis and Clark were equipped for their Expedition with many medicines — and with "six best lancets." They did blood-letting for a multitude of conditions, for trauma as well as for many illnesses. They did not hesitate on occasions to bleed their patient repeatedly, or to bleed themselves. However, unless they failed to record each incident, they did not bleed as often as Rush would have had them do. There is no record of the amount of blood removed in any of the bleedings noted in the journals. There is occasional reference to the state of the pulse; otherwise the indications for bleeding are not stated.

As army men, both Lewis and Clark had had previous practice in the art of venesection. It was the responsibility of the commanding officer to be equipped with medicines and supplies to take care of the illness and trauma of the men. William Clark records in his journal while an army officer in 1793 that

27 William Osler, *The Principles and Practice of Medicine* (N.Y: D. Appleton & Co., 1892).

he was equipped with a lancet and bled men on several occasions.[28]

That bleeding was a highly regarded universal therapeutic practice is shown by the following quotations from the two ends of the Lewis and Clark Trail. In writing about the health of citizens of Louisiana, Trudeau stated in 1791 that "work people" had a high mortality "because of the badly founded preconceptions of some against bleeding, and the lack of a good blood-letter for others." [29]

In his journal about Astoria, Franchere wrote of the high mortality among the Indians, "whom a timely bleeding or purgative would have saved . . ." [30] Cox, a fellow clerk of Franchere in the Astor expedition, writing in his journal about the six years he spent on the Columbia, relates that in treating contusions, the Flathead Indians "generally bleed, either in the temples, arms, wrists, or ancles, with pieces of sharp flint, or heads of arrows." [31]

In consideration of the universality of bleeding for everything, of Lewis having been tutored by Rush "the Bloodletter," of the captains' own demonstrated use of this therapy, and of the continuing affliction of the men of the Expedition, it is very fortunate that many were not bled to a state of anemia and lowered resistance that might have been fatal.

---

[28] From the unedited and unpublished brief diary of William Clark, in the possession of the Missouri Hist. Soc.

[29] Quoted from Louis Houck, *History of Missouri*, II (Chicago, 1908), p. 28.

[30] Gabriel Franchere, *Narrative of a Voyage to the Northwest Coast of America* (N.Y., 1854). The idea of the general efficacy of bleeding in the minds of the laity is exemplified by Franchere, a clerk of the Astor expedition, writing in his journal: "There are charlatans everywhere, but they are more numerous among savages than anywhere else. . . As soon as a native of the Columbia is indisposed, no matter what the malady, they send for the medicine man, who treats the patient in the absurd manner usually adopted by these imposters, and with such violence of manipulation, that often a sick man, whom a timely bleeding or purgative would have saved, is carried by a sudden death." p. 256.

[31] Ross Cox, *The Columbia River*, I (London, 1831), p. 248.

BOOK TWO

Preparation
for the Expedition

V

The President and His Captains

This is our national epic of exploration, conceived by Thomas Jefferson, wrought out by Lewis and Clark.   Elliott Coues [1]

Bernard DeVoto stated that the Lewis and Clark Expedition is "unequaled in American history and hardly surpassed in the history of exploration anywhere." [2] This statement was made after the Byrd Antarctic Expedition, and before the astronauts' landing on the moon. However, DeVoto's statement probably will forever be correct from the standpoint of contributions to the development of the United States. This monumental exploration did not develop full-blown overnight, but was the culmination of years of dreaming and planning by Thomas Jefferson, the fortuitous unfolding of political circumstances, and the entrusting of the exploration to two of the most extraordinary captains of history.

THOMAS JEFFERSON

April 13, 1743 — July 4, 1826

Thomas Jefferson probably possessed the most versatile, imaginative and brilliant mind of any of our presidents. He also richly combined the qualities of idealism and pragmatism, with the discerning ability to emphasize one or the other as occasion demanded. All of these qualities were soon evidenced when Napoleon fortuitously made the whole Loui-

---

[1] Coues, *History of Lewis and Clark*, ɪ, vi.

[2] Bernard Devoto, *The Journals of Lewis and Clark* (Boston, 1953), p. xliv. Hereafter cited as Devoto, *Journals.*

siana Territory available for purchase, soon after Jefferson assumed the presidency and had persuaded Congress to authorize the Lewis and Clark Expedition.[3] Though his political philosophy was idealistically attuned to states' rights, and in opposition to federalism, he pragmatically executed the purchase of the Louisiana Territory without the consent of the several states in Congress. A precedence was thus established regarding the importance and continuing role of the federal government in expanding the territory and power of the United States, as well as the power of the executive branch of government.

Jefferson acquired the Louisiana Territory without military action or loss of life. He was equally concerned that the Lewis and Clark Expedition be completed similarly; he repeatedly expressed concern about the health of the men of the Expedition. He wrote of his concern about the "risk of valuable lives,"[4] and called his proposed expedition "perilous."[5]

When colonial charters were granted by England along the Atlantic seaboard, the chartered lands extended interminably to the west. Lands bought from the colonial governments by private individuals also extended westward indefinitely. George Washington, Benjamin Franklin, Thomas Jefferson and many other colonists of means owned such lands. As early as 1756 a scheme was underway to explore these lands, with the enterprise to be led by Dr. Thomas Walker.[6] Thomas

---

[3] Thomas Jefferson had the very able help in Congress of Rep. Samuel L. Mitchell, M.D., who was very interested in the Louisiana Territory. He later became a U.S. Senator from N.Y.

[4] Thwaites, *Journals*, I, p. xlvii.   [5] Jackson, *Letters*, p. 21.

[6] For an account of this plan, *see* Ann Maury, *Memoirs of a Hugenot Family* (New York: Geo. P. Putnam & Co., 1853), pp. 31, 390-91.

Dr. Thomas Walker was born in Queens County, Va., on Jan. 25, 1715. When his time of life was completed 79 years later on Nov. 1, 1794, he had seen the Old Dominion become an important state of the new nation, and had participated in many of the events that had brought this nation into existence.

When Peter Jefferson, Thomas' father, died at the family home at Shadwell, Va.,

Jefferson was about thirteen years old when these plans
were developing. With Walker's home only about two hours

in 1757, Dr. Thomas Walker, old friend and family physician who lived down the
"old road" about eight miles, attended him in his last illness, just as he had cared
for the family on many previous occasions.

Young Thomas was 14-years-old when his father died. He was to come under the
increasing influence of Dr. Walker, because the will of Peter Jefferson, written into
the clerk record book at Albermarle Courthouse — America's first courthouse and
the oldest still in use — named Dr. Thomas Walker as a guardian of the young
Jefferson. Without a doubt the two men closest to Thomas Jefferson were his father
and Dr. Thomas Walker. The close interest of these two men is shown by an ex-
cerpt from Peter Jefferson's will: "Whereas I have a right to and interest in certain
lands on the Branches of the Mississippi River in Partnership with Doctor Thomas
Walker. . ." Peter Jefferson's will is still legibly extant and well protected at the
Albermarle Courthouse in Charlottesville, Va.

It probably was the good doctor-guardian who first lifted the curtain of Thomas
Jefferson's vista of the West, and instilled in him an interest and vision that re-
mained with him all of his life. It had been Thomas Walker with his companion,
Peter Gist, who first explored westward into the Blue Grass country and named the
Cumberland Gap and the Cumberland River. When Thomas Jefferson wrote his
Notes on the State of Virginia many years later, he referred several times to Dr. W.
who had given him information about "the West." (An old confederate Army song
pays tribute to Dr. Walker: "the first white man through the Cumberland Gap was
Dr. Walker, an English chap.") The Boone Wilderness Trail later passed through
this gap and along it went many settlers to the Blue Grass country, and on down
the Ohio — eventually to follow the Lewis and Clark Trail to the Pacific Coast.
Dr. Walker kept a journal of his trip through the Cumberland Gap, which was
published by F. Marion Rust, *Kentucky's First House — A Journal of Dr. Thomas
Walker* (Barbourville, Ky: The Advocate Publishing Co., 1940).

Dr. Walker came into possession of extensive lands in Albermarle County by
marrying the widow of Nicholas Meriwether in 1741; this lady was the second
cousin of George Washington. In 1765 he built a home on his domain of 17,000
acres. Although the house was comparable in size to any in the countryside, it was
not conceivably large enough to provide room for the twelve children who came
along to bless his marriage. This house, Castle Hill, still stands today, restored and
maintained by its present owner, Mrs. Clark J. Laurence, as it was in Dr. Walker's
time.

During the Revolution, Castle Hill was on the route of Tarleton and his raiders
who were heading for Charlottesville to capture Gov. Thomas Jefferson. Tradition
says that when Tarleton appeared and demanded breakfast, the gracious doctor,
aided by his effective mint juleps and a contrived late breakfast, was able to permit
a warned Jefferson to escape by sending a messenger on a fast horse. This was the
famous ride of Jack Jouett — second only to the better known ride of Paul Revere.
It occurred on June 3, 1781. This ride is recounted interestingly in Lee Meriwether,
My Yesteryears (St. Louis: Mound City Press, 1942), pp. 3, 4.

away, it is very likely that this young man, with his naturally inquisitive and visionary mind, was right in the thick of all the discussions and activity, and was very much impressed. Thomas Jefferson was never to lose interest in the western country. Many other men were to stimulate his interest, but he probably owed most to a man of medicine, Dr. Walker.

In 1783 Thomas Jefferson had requested of General George Rogers Clark,[7] who had been the savior of the "Old Northwest" for the United States, that he lead an expedition under the sponsorship and for the benefit of private individuals, to explore the lands beyond the Mississippi. The prospects of the rich fur trade and the nebulous Northwest Passage augmented the tantalizing dreams of these men. The Columbia River had not yet been discovered by Captain Robert Gray (1792). Clark's personal fortunes, and perhaps Jefferson's and his associates' also, were not on high tide — nothing came of this proposal.

But the dream was not to die; its vivid continuance was contributed to by a young adventurer named John Ledyard.[8] Ledyard approached Jefferson in Paris in late 1785, where the latter was on diplomatic duty, with the proposal that he cross the western country from the west to the east. This young man was more of a dreamer than Meriwether Lewis, who was to appear later, but lacked the latter's practical organizational

---

[7] George Rogers Clark (1752-1818) was the oldest brother of William Clark of the Lewis and Clark Expedition. See John Bakeless, Background to Glory (Phila: J. B. Lippincott Co., 1957).

[8] John Ledyard (1751-1789) had an imaginative and roving nature. He left Dartmouth College and accompanied Capt. Cook on his last voyage, in 1776-79, about which he published a journal (James K. Mumford, ed., "John Ledyard's Journal of Captain Cook's Last Voyage" [Corvallis: Oreg. St. Univ. Press, 1963]). Ledyard and Jefferson stimulated each other with their visions of western North America. For other books on John Ledyard see Jared Sparks, The Life of John Ledyard (Cambridge, 1829); Kenneth Mumford, John Ledyard, An American Marco Polo (Portland: Binfords & Mort, 1939); and Helen Augur, Passage to Glory (N.Y: Doubleday & Co., 1946).

ability. In spite of his courage, he was waylaid by the Russian queen when he had almost reached Kamchatka, Siberia, preparatory to crossing North America.

In 1789, Captain John Armstrong,[9] at the instigation of Secretary of War Henry Knox (and quite possibly at the instigation of George Washington, who also possessed lands in the West), started up the Missouri River alone, but was quickly discouraged by the report of the warlike attitude of the Indian tribes.

In 1793, Thomas Jefferson was again trying to find a capable leader to make the exploration of the western lands. The American Philosophical Society of Philadelphia, of which Jefferson was then vice-president, started a subscription to fund the Expedition. Andre Michaux,[10] a French botanist working in the United States, was engaged to lead this effort. Michaux was interested in the project, and probably would have recorded a great deal of scientific knowledge regarding botany. However, he became entangled in complicated political machinations involving Spain, France and the United States, giving evidence that he was incapable of the diplomatic abilities which Lewis and Clark later demonstrated in dealing with the Indians.

Jefferson wrote comparatively brief instructions for Michaux in January of 1793, but expressed concern for the botanist's health: "It is strongly recommended to you to expose yourself in no case to unnecessary dangers, whether such as might effect your health or your personal safety. . . ."[11]

---

[9] Capt. John Armstrong (1755-1816) left his station at Louisville alone in a canoe and traveled only a short ways above St. Louis.

[10] Andre Michaux (1746-1802) was a prominent French botanist and the father of F. A. Michaux, M.D., who also traveled and recorded botanical findings in this country. *See* the latter's *Travels to the Westward of the Allegeny Mountains . . . in the Year 1802* (London, 1805).

[11] Thwaites, *Journals*, VII, p. 204.

It certainly was not just Jefferson's interest in developing his personal lands which was the reason for his continued interest in the West. He was aware that Mackenzie had crossed the territory which is now Canada in 1793, and that English, Spanish and Russian as well as American vessels were carrying on an increasingly brisk trade with the Indians along the Northwest coast. The tenuous balance of power in this area is evidenced by the fact that even with the claims of the United States by right of discovery of the Columbia River by Captain Gray in 1792, and the crossing of the Louisiana and Oregon country by Lewis and Clark in 1804-5, the latter region continued to be under joint sovereignty of Great Britain and the United States until 1846. The persistent dreaming and plotting of Thomas Jefferson in great part helped determine that the Louisiana Territory and the Oregon Country would eventually belong to the United States.

French explorers, voyageurs, trappers and settlers sparsely populated the Mississippi Valley from the Great Lakes to New Orleans in the late eighteenth century. Although Spain nominally ruled this country along with Mexico, very little was done to encourage the settling of Spanish people. But Spanish officials controlled the port of New Orleans. The Americans moving west down the Ohio River and across the bluegrass country in their eager search for virgin agricultural land had only the Mississippi River and the port of New Orleans as avenues to the world markets. They soon found themselves in a commercial and political conflict with the Spanish authorities, who closed the port to them. Fulfilling the prophecy of Dr. Saugrain,[12] they began putting pressure on the local Spanish authorities as well as the American government. Thus, when Thomas Jefferson became president in 1801, he was presented with demands by the western fron-

---

12 *See* page 196, herein.

tiersmen to actualize his long-standing dream of directing the nation's attention westward, particularly to the problem of the Port of New Orleans.

In a not too secret message to Congress on January 18, 1803, Jefferson proposed that the federal government finance an expedition to the West, for which he outlined a combination of objectives: trade with the Indians, "literary pursuits," and exploration for the illusory Northwest Passage. Congress acquiesced to this request, as well as to the estimated expenses of $2500.[13] This amount was not expected to be the total expenditure for the Expedition, inasmuch as funds from the War Department were to be available. By his authority as an army officer Lewis could and did requisition supplies and men along the Ohio River and in and around St. Louis.

Securing approval from Congress for financial support of the Expedition, and coincidentally setting a precedent for the authority and power of the federal government, was a stroke of genius culminating Jefferson's unrelenting plans for western exploration — and expansion. These lands would be secured by the federal government, and the states of the future would be the creation of the federal government — no longer would the federal government be a totally restricted instrument created by the states. States'-rightist Jefferson had become a Federalist!

THE LOUISIANA PURCHASE

We shall delineate with correctness the great arteries of this country: those who come after us will extend the ramifications as they become acquainted with them, and fill up the canvas we begin.
                                                            Thomas Jefferson [14]

---

[13] The full cost of the Lewis and Clark Expedition has been estimated to have been $38,722.25. *See* Grace Lewis, "Financial Records of the Expedition to the Pacific Ocean," *Bull. of the Missouri Hist. Soc.*, Vol. x, No. 4 (July, 1954), pp. 465-89. *See also*, Jackson, *Letters*, pp. 419-31.

[14] Thomas Jefferson wrote these prophetic words to William Dunbar in his letter of May 25, 1805. Jackson, *Letters*, p. 245.

A most fortuitous combination of events in the history of the United States was the purchase of the Louisiana Territory and the Lewis and Clark Expedition. The Louisiana Purchase eliminated potential international complications by making it unnecessary for this expedition to cross territory claimed by other nations when it ascended the Missouri River. It also provided a territorial bridge to the Oregon Country, thus strengthening the claim of the United States to this area. The accomplishments of Captain Gray and Lewis and Clark provided a firm claim for the United States to the Oregon Territory. But it was the immigrations along the Oregon Trail to the Willamette Valley in the 1840s that emphasized the old maxim that possession is nine-tenths of the law. If Louisiana had remained in the possession of France or Spain, and if the English had moved down from Canada in strength, the Oregon country would have been cut off from the United States, and the emigrant wagon trains probably would never have rolled across the plains.

Exploring the Missouri River was a persistent dream of Thomas Jefferson, and the Lewis and Clark Expedition was the fruition of this dream. Instead of referring to "two fortuitous events" — the Louisiana Purchase and the Lewis and Clark Expedition — perhaps it is more proper to recognize Thomas Jefferson's ascendency to the Presidency of the United States as *the* fortuitous event. The Presidency provided Jefferson with the power to stimulate Congress to authorize the Lewis and Clark Expedition. The subtlety of his request to Congress for $2500 to fund the expedition as a literary and commercial venture probably did not fool the Congress.[15] Jefferson had repeatedly shown his awareness of the importance of Louisiana to the United States, not only

[15] Jefferson's confidential message to Congress, Jan. 18, 1803. Jackson, *Letters,* p. 10.

to secure the commercial privileges of the Mississippi and Missouri Rivers and the possible colonization into their valleys, but also to remove foreign powers from the North American continent.

Early in the Jefferson administration the farmers of the Ohio Valley made complaints to their government about the difficulties they were having in depositing their cargo at the Spanish port of New Orleans. Jefferson probably welcomed the complaints of the farmers, as they provided him an argument to place before Congress in support of his plans. To solve this problem, it was first conceived that the United States might buy lower Louisiana if attempts to make commercial arrangements with Spain continued to be fruitless. But it was certainly evident to Jefferson that securing only lower Louisiana would not give the United States assurance for an uncomplicated trans-Mississippi exploration.

Jefferson provided in his will that his tombstone list three of his accomplishments: author of the Declaration of Independence,[16] author of the Bill of Rights of the State of Virginia, and founder of the University of Virginia. Probably genuine modesty (or possibly awareness that no mention of it would provide greater emphasis) prompted Jefferson to omit mention of the Presidency. Posterity will not find fault with the importance of the items he chose, but it was the Presidency that enabled him to implement the Louisiana Purchase and the Lewis and Clark Expedition — thus extending into the lands so acquired the benefits of those things which he chose to list on his tombstone. Wheeler thinks that "it is not improbable that in history Jefferson's reputation will stand higher for the exploration than for the acquisition [of Louisiana]."[17] Certainly Wheeler is correct in recognizing

---

[16] For an account of the Declaration of Independence, *see* Dumas Malone, *The Story of the Declaration of Independence* (N.Y: Oxford Univ. Press, 1954).

[17] Wheeler, *Trail*, i, p. 1.

that the exploration was conceived and implemented by Jefferson alone, whereas a combination of circumstances and people contributed to the Louisiana Purchase.

LaSalle staked a claim to the Mississippi Valley for Louis xiv of France in 1682, thus making France the first European country to take possession of the Mississippi Valley and those lands which it drained. Because of insufficient interest and other demands, France did not succeed in establishing a strong colony in Louisiana, and Louis xv ceded it to Spain in 1762 to prevent it from falling to England. When Napoleon became Emperor of France, his dream of empire began to encompass the New World; accordingly, he forced the recession of Louisiana to France in the Treaty of San Ildefonso in 1800. This was a fortuitous event for the United States, because it enabled France to "legally" sell Louisiana to the United States; but the Spanish continued to administer the government of Louisiana and thus continued their intrigues against the United States.

When the secret treaty of San Ildefonso became known, Jefferson immediately recognized that he should shift his efforts to settle the Louisiana-Mississippi River problem from Spain to France. Therefore he directed the American Minister to France, Robert R. Livingston, to attempt to purchase lower Louisiana. Napoleon was uninterested in the sale of Louisiana at first because of his own ambitions to build a strong new France. In 1802 he assembled an army of 28,000 soldiers — a large army indeed for those days — under his brother-in-law, General LeClerc, to sail to New Orleans. The army stopped at Santo Domingo on the way to put down a rebellion. Toussaint L'Overture, leader of the native revolt, is often eulogized for defeating this large army of France, but it was actually Yellow Fever which decimated the French forces — the same Yellow Fever which Benjamin Rush had fought so heroically in Philadelphia in 1793. The French troops which were destined for New Orleans did not get beyond Santo Domingo, and very few of the soldiers returned to their native France. Thus did disease play a part in helping to fulfill the dreams of Jefferson and the destiny of our young Republic.[18]

Soon after the catastrophe in Santo Domingo, Livingston made his proposal of purchase to Napoleon. In May of 1803 Napoleon again found himself at war with England. He realized that he could not support the war with England and at the same time protect Louisiana from the English navy. Despite the urgent advice of his brothers to the contrary, Napoleon decided to relieve himself of the defense of Louisiana and to obtain money to support his war by offering to sell Louisiana in its entirety to the United States.[19]

Napoleon's sudden offer to sell the whole of Louisiana posed a problem for the negotiators; they had no specific authority from Congress to purchase all of Louisiana and certainly did not have any financial appropriations for such a goal. Communication by slow-moving packet ships did not facilitate the immediate answer Napoleon wanted, now that he had made up his mind. Probably feeling assured of their President's attitude from previous discussions, Livingston and Monroe did not hesitate. On April 30, 1803, the treaty was

---

[18] Illness had much to do with the fortunes of Napoleon Bonaparte. When the British were facing defeat at Waterloo, instead of pushing his advantages on the battlefield, Napoleon seemed to have lost his noted ability to make the right decisions at the right time, and let opportunity slip by while he nursed his painful hemorrhoids and cystitis. See David Howarth, Waterloo: Day of Battle (N.Y: Atheneum, 1968), pp. 52-56.

[19] Napoleon was very aware of his predicament, stating that "I know the full value of Louisiana. . . But if it escapes from me, it shall one day cost dearer to those who oblige me to strip myself of it [the English] . . . I have not a moment to lose in putting it out of their reach . . . and it appears to me that in the hands of this growing power [the United States], it will be more useful to the policy and even to the commerce of France, than if I should attempt to keep it." Wheeler, Trail, I, p. 7.

signed by these two men for the United States and by Barbe
Marbois for France.[20] It was ratified by Congress on October
17, 1803.

Lewis had completed his journey down the Ohio River and
arrived at Camp DuBois outside of St. Louis on December 12,
1803. He was privy to all of Jefferson's information and thus
knew that Louisiana now belonged to the United States.
However, official transfer of "Upper Louisiana" did not occur
until March 10, 1804; Lewis was present at the ceremony that
raised the American flag over the land across which he was to
lead the Corps of Discovery.

There was a fairly clear concept in the minds of everyone —
Americans, French, Spanish, and English — about the land
area of the lower portion of Louisiana, but the northern and
western reaches of the Louisiana Territory were not definite.
Thus the explorations of Lewis and Clark became important
in acquiring information about this new territory of the United
States, as well as laying a claim for the future acquisition of
the Oregon Country.

In securing the Louisiana Territory for the United States,
the little army of Lewis and Clark was fortunate that in spite
of health problems throughout its travels, it was not decimated by Yellow Fever as the French were, or by smallpox
which wiped out entire Indian villages.

JEFFERSON AND MEDICINE

Thomas Jefferson was one of the most versatile of all our
presidents — statesman, architect, educator, author, and to no
little extent, a physician.[21] As with most physicians of his day,

---

20 Napoleon is supposed to have said: "This accession of territory, strengthens
forever the power of the United States. I have just given to England a maritime
rival, that will sooner or later humble her pride." Eva Emory Dye, *The Conquest*
(Chicago, 1902), p. 143.

21 Blanton states of Jefferson: "As a man of science Jefferson was even more
versatile than Franklin. His interest ranged from mechanical invention to agricul-

DOCTOR THOMAS WALKER
Guardian of Thomas Jefferson.
Courtesy of Advocate Publishing Company.

CASTLE HILL, HOME OF THOMAS WALKER
Near Jefferson's birthplace at Shadwell, Virginia.
The author and Mrs. Clark J. Lawrence, present owner, shown on the lawn.

THOMAS JEFFERSON
An 1800 painting by Rembrandt Peale. As he appeared
when beginning preparation for the Expedition.
Courtesy of the Peabody Institute, Baltimore.

THOMAS JEFFERSON'S MEDICINE CHEST
Having lived with Jefferson for two years, Lewis was
probably familiar with this chest and may have
chosen one similar to it for the Expedition.
Courtesy Jefferson Memorial Foundation, Monticello.

he did not have a degree. However, he had a great interest in "physic" and a large medical library, and read and wrote extensively on medical subjects. He participated in what seemed to be a sort of "round-robin" of letters on health of the day. Discussion of one's own and others' health was a favorite topic of everyone who could write, and Jefferson's correspondence shows that he exchanged comments and prescriptions concerning health with many of his medical and non-medical friends.

Jefferson's libraries contained over a hundred volumes of medical books,[22] and his correspondence shows that he was familiar with much of their content. Although he placed great confidence in a portion of the medical profession, particularly his medical friends, he had considerable disdain for the medical profession as a whole.[23] His writings show that he was aware of the unscientific fallacies that formed the basis of much medical practice. He wrote in a famous letter to one of his medical friends, Dr. Caspar Wistar:

Having been so often a witness to the salutary efforts which nature makes to re-establish the distorted functions, he [the physician] should rather trust to their action, than hazard the interruption of that, and a greater derangement of the system, by conjectural experiments on a machine so complicated and so unknown as the human body, and a subject so sacred as human life. Or, if the appearance of doing something be necessary to keep alive the hope and spirits of the patient, it should be of the most innocent character.

ture, botany, geology, paleontology, and medicine." Blanton, *Medicine in Virginia,* p. 187. For a good account of Jefferson and medicine, *see* pp. 187-200.

22 *See* Appen. I, herein.

23 Cutright says: "He had strong personal reasons for this distrust. Before he had attained the age of forty-two, he had lost his father and mother, his closest friend (Dabney Carr), his favorite sister (Jane), three children (two daughters and his only son), and — the bitterest blow of all — his beloved wife, Martha." Paul Cutright, "Meriwether Lewis Prepares for a Trip West," *Bull. of the Missouri Hist. Soc., Vol.* XXII, No. 1 (Oct., 1966), pp. 9-10.

In this same letter, he might have been thinking of his friend Benjamin Rush when he wrote: "From the scanty field of what is known, he launches into the boundless region of what is unknown. He establishes for his guide some fanciful theory . . . of depletion by the lancet and repletion by mercury, or some other ingenious dream. . ." He continues: "I have lived myself to see the disciples of Hoffman, Boerhaave, Stahl, Cullen, Brown, succeed one another like the shifting figures of a magic lantern," and if he had lived long enough, Jefferson could have added his friend Rush to this list; he vigorously disagreed with Rush's prolific use of bleeding and purging. "It is in this part of medicine that I wish to see a reform, an abandonment of hypothesis for sober facts, the first degree of value set on clinical observation, and the lowest on visionary theories." [24]

Jefferson emphasizes repeatedly in his letter to Dr. Wistar the importance of clinical observation.[25] "The anatomical and clinical schools, therefore, are those in which the young physicians should be formed . . . his mind must be strong indeed, if, rising above juvenile credulity, it can maintain a wise infidelity against the authority of his instructors, and the bewitching delusions of their theories." Jefferson expresses his concern and hope that there will be established "sound principles in this branch of science, the most important of all others, being that to which we commit the care of health and life."

These are noble expressions from the third President of the United States, and well qualify him for his accomplishment of including in the University of Virginia when it opened in

[24] *See Appen.* II and Paul Leicester Ford, *Writings of Thomas Jefferson,* IX (N.Y., 1898), pp. 81-85.

[25] Jefferson was anticipating Haggard's comment about the first half of the nineteenth century: ". . . the spirit of investigation and observation was widely extended." H. W. Haggard, *Devils, Drugs and Doctors* (N.Y: Harper and Brothers, 1929), p. 394.

1825 a school of medicine as one of the seven independent divisions of instruction.[26] In spite of Jefferson having placed emphasis upon the clinical aspects of medicine, the medical teaching was conducted entirely without the students having patient contact.

When Jefferson writes, as he does to Dr. Wistar, he seems to deride the "adventurous physician" (as he did Dr. Mesmer[27]) and at other times to support him (as he did Dr. Waterhouse). But a careful reading will show that Jefferson is consistent. He derides charlatanism and assumption, and calls for careful investigation and observation. Therefore, he feels strongly that "I have no doubt that some diseases not yet understood may in time be transferred to the table of those known." He succinctly stated his derision of all pompous ignorance: "Nothing betrays imbecility so much as the being insensible of it." [28]

Jefferson's concern and comprehension regarding all matters of human health are shown in his instructions to Lewis regarding the Expedition, both in relation to the Indians and to the men of the Expedition. Jefferson instructed Lewis to "carry with you some matter of the kinepox, inform those of them [the Indians] with whom you may be of its efficacy . . . ." [29] There was good reason for Jefferson to want Lewis

[26] R. Hall Courtney, "Jefferson on the Medical Theory and Practice of His Day," *Bull. of the Hist. of Medicine,* Vol. xxxi, No. 3 (1957), p. 241.

[27] Franz Mesmer (1733-1815) was an Austrian medical doctor. He passed through phases of astrology and magnetism before arriving at his concept of an occult force to which people were susceptible and which could influence disease. His demonstrations aroused a great public following, but a committee of the French Academy of Sciences (on which Benjamin Franklin served) condemned him as a charlatan. Undoubtedly Mesmer was using hypnotism, familiar to the priests of Egypt and India, and which today has a respected place in the work of medicine and psychology. *See* Rudolph Marx, M.D., *The Health of the Presidents* (N.Y: G. P. Putnam's Sons, 1960), pp. 54-56.

[28] Ford, *Writings of Jefferson,* ix, p. 328, letter to Benjamin Rush.

[29] Jackson, *Letters,* p. 64.

to use vaccination on the Indians. Smallpox had for centuries been a great killer of the white man, who was now bringing it to the Indians; if vaccination could protect these Indians who had developed no natural immunity to smallpox, it would be a great proof of its effectiveness. The story of smallpox and its final mastery is one of the most interesting annals in medical history. Jefferson played an important role in that story in America [30] and Lewis might have played an equally important role in protecting the Indians if Jefferson's plans for Lewis to vaccinate them had been fulfilled.

In his *Notes on Virginia*,[31] Jefferson wrote about medicinal herbs and mineral hot springs and the effect of climate on health. His correspondents included leading medical men and scientists in Europe as well as America. Jefferson kept as detailed a record regarding his vaccinations of his patients and slaves as he did of his farm's activities. He wrote to Dr. Henry Rose, "I received from Dr. Waterhouse of Boston some vaccine matter of his own taking and some from Dr. Jenner of England just then come to hand. Both of them took well, and exhibited the same identical appearances in the persons into whom they were inserted. I inoculated about 70 or 80 of my own family, my two sons in law as many." [32] Jefferson goes on to describe the local and systemic response in each individual. One of the early problems with vaccination was transporting the vaccine material and keeping it active. Jefferson developed an effective means of transportation, which consisted of placing the vaccine matter in a small corked vial inside a larger, water-filled tube. Also, Jefferson's carefully collected data

[30] Robert H. Halsey, M.D., *How the President, Thomas Jefferson, and Dr. Benjamin Waterhouse Established Vaccination as a Public Health Procedure* (N.Y., 1936), p. 55. Hereafter cited as Halsey, *Jefferson and Waterhouse*.

[31] Jefferson, *Notes on Virginia* (1953 ed.).

[32] For the entirety of this letter, dated Oct. 23, 1801, *see* Edwin M. Betts, Thomas Jefferson's Farm Book (Princeton, N.J: Princeton Univ. Press, 1953), p. 18.

helped establish the time and means of collecting the pure virus from patients.

Inoculation [33] had been the only specific protection against smallpox. It was first introduced into this country in Boston in 1721 by a clergyman, Dr. Cotton Mather (1663-1728) and a physician, Dr. Zabdiel Boylston (1679-1766). Most of the physicians opposed the procedure at first. Dr. Boylston inoculated his family, slaves and patients, and only six died of 241 inoculated — an impressive record at that time. Inoculation was practiced extensively in the Revolutionary War armies, and greatly reduced the death rate from smallpox. (Lewis had been inoculated while serving in the army.) It was done by the transmission of an adulterated strain of the true smallpox infection to the host at a time when he was in excellent health.

But smallpox continued to be one of the most devastating diseases of the world — until the work of Edward Jenner (1749-1823).[34] Jenner's work did not receive immediate rec-

---

[33] Major writes: "No one knows who began the practice of inoculation against smallpox. The Chinese are said to have practiced inoculation since the most remote time. Their method consisted of blowing a powder made of dried smallpox crusts into the nostrils of the subject. In India, the same method was practiced by Brahmin priests during a religious rite in honor of the god of smallpox. The practice of inoculation first came to the attention of the medical world, and of the public at large, after its introduction into England." When the Boston epidemic of smallpox in 1721 came to an end, "it was found that the death rate of those not inoculated was one in ten, while in the inoculated only one in sixty-eight died." *See* Major, *History of Medicine,* pp. 115-16; 121-22.

[34] Major states that smallpox seems to have started in Abyssinia. "In Japan it appeared first in the eighth century, while it did not reach Siberia until the seventeenth century. . . The first epidemic of Smallpox in the Western Hemisphere appeared in the West Indies only fifteen years after the voyage of Columbus. It exterminated entire tribes of Indians. In 1570 the Spaniards carried the disease into Mexico and more than three million natives perished. The disease appeared in Boston as early as 1649. . ." *See* Ralph H. Major, M.D., *Disease and Destiny* (N.Y: Appleton-Century Co., 1936), p. 113.

"At the time of Edward Jenner it was estimated that every tenth person in Europe died from smallpox." Quoted from *JAMA*, Vol. 177, No. 6 (Aug. 12, 1961), p. 446. Jenner was a small-town doctor who was astute enough to listen

ognition or approval, but the delay was a short one. The value of smallpox vaccination was soon known in the United States. In 1799 Dr. Benjamin Waterhouse (1754-1846), professor of medicine at Harvard, received a copy of Jenner's work and discussed it in an article in the *Columbian Sentinel,* under the title of "Something Curious in the Medical Line." He vaccinated his four children in July of 1800. Dr. Waterhouse's efforts to gain recognition for vaccination required a lot of travail, and probably would not have been successful without the enthusiastic support of President Jefferson.[35]

---

and observe when one of his young patients told him "I cannot take that disease [smallpox] as I have had cowpox." (One hundred years before, Barbara Villiers [1631-1709], the Duchess of Cleveland, and the mistress of Charles II, was told that her king might become disinterested in her if she became marked with smallpox; she answered that she was not afraid because she had had cowpox, and therefore could never have smallpox.) Jenner commented to his teacher and friend that cowpox and smallpox might be the same disease — to which John Hunter gave his famous reply: "Don't think, try! Be patient, be accurate." The smallpox epidemic in 1796 provided Jenner with the opportunity to do so. Thus, James Phipps entered history as the small boy on whom Jenner first tried vaccination, on May 14, 1796, using pus from a cowpox patient named Sarah Nelmes. Phipps developed a small sore and scab, without any systemic symptoms. Six weeks later he was inoculated with smallpox but did not contract the disease. Jenner repeated his experiments with vaccination using cowpox, which uniformly protected patients against subsequent inoculation with smallpox. He published his article in 1798: "An Inquiry Into the Causes and Effects of the Variolae Vacciniae."

[35] Many of Waterhouse's troubles were of his own making. Blake writes: ". . . it is no longer possible to ignore his efforts to restrict the diffusion of vaccine in the late summer and early fall of 1800 in order to profit from a monopoly, or the bonds [contracts] he secured from other practitioners requiring them to submit one quarter of their profits in return for a supply of the virus. . . No one . . . can carefully read the Waterhouse-Spalding-Bartlett letters without concluding that Waterhouse intended to profit from his original monopoly of the cowpox virus [which] fostered the spirit of commercialism which at first damaged the cause of vaccination. . . Knowing the basic facts, the physicians of Boston were fully justified in regarding Waterhouse with suspicion and hostility." John B. Blake, *Benjamin Waterhouse and the Introduction of Vaccination* (Philadelphia: Univ. of Pa. Press, 1957), pp. 73-74. This is in marked contrast to the long-held opinion that Dr. Waterhouse was opposed by the physicians of Boston because they were against vaccination.

Jefferson aided introduction of vaccination to the United States in several important ways: his sponsorship of Dr. Waterhouse; his personal inoculation of his own family, friends and relatives, and the close observations he made thereof; and the dissemination of vaccine matter to many other interested people. Jefferson might also have properly listed on his tombstone his sponsorship of Dr. Waterhouse in introducing vaccination to the United States, and his related activities in establishing its value.

The first vaccination in Philadelphia was done by Dr. John Redmond Cox on his own son. Rush closely observed Cox, and admired and trusted his friend. On April 8, 1802, Dr. Waterhouse wrote to Dr. Jenner: "Dr. Rush has come out full and strong in praise of the new inoculation [vaccination], and has sent me a copy of an eloquent lecture of his on the blessings of the Jennerian discovery." [36] These notes indicate that both Rush and Jefferson urged Lewis to use vaccination and instructed him in its use.

"If Jefferson and his American contemporaries seemed confused about the condition of medicine at the end of the eighteenth century, it was not surprising, for never, probably, had medical thinking in general been in so chaotic a state." [37] It was an age of great ferment in science, in which medicine participated. All medical theorists advanced their ideas while doubting their colleagues, and were doubted in turn. It is not surprising that Jefferson questioned the efficacy of doctors — they doubted and disputed with each other. The absence of a doctor on the Lewis and Clark Expedition might well have been a deliberate act on the part of Jefferson in order to leave the health care of the men in the hands of his practical army captain-physicians.

[36] Halsey, *Jefferson and Waterhouse.*   [37] *Ibid.,* p. 245.

Meriwether Lewis
August 18, 1774 — October 11, 1809

*Of courage undaunted; possessing a firmness and perseverence of
purpose which nothing but impossibilities could divert from his
direction; careful as a father of those committed to his charge, yet
steady in the maintenance of order and discipline; . . . with
all these qualifications . . . I could have no hesitation in confiding the enterprise to him.* Jefferson's memorial to Lewis [38]

Far more was necessary to make the Expedition successful
than to have the approval and finances of the federal government. Just as Jefferson had never lost sight of his dreams regarding the West, he had been constantly assessing the
qualifications of possible leaders of previously planned explorations. With the assumption of the Presidency, he was now
very certain of the nature and the ability of the man he
wanted to lead the Expedition to the West. In fact, he knew
the man's identity.

When Dr. Thomas Walker died at Castle Hill in 1794, a
young man living at his family home, Locust Hill at Ivy Station, over on the other side of Charlottesville, had reached his
twentieth year. He was the son of William and Lucy Lewis,
and they gave him her maiden name, Meriwether. Meriwether's uncle Nicholas had married Mary, a daughter of Dr.
Thomas Walker, the family doctor of Thomas Jefferson's
father.

When Meriwether was five years old his father died of
pneumonia, after exposure in an accident in which he almost
drowned. Less than six months later, the widow married
Captain John Marks. They moved to Georgia for a time, but
after John Marks' death in 1791, Lucy Marks returned to
Locust Hill, where she resided until her death in 1837.

---

[38] Thwaites, *Journals,* i, p. xxvi.

Meriwether was modestly educated in the fashion of the times, with instruction in the arts of reading and writing and scientific Latin nomenclature. Part of his education was self-determined; he loved the out-of-doors with its associated pastimes of hunting and fishing, and acquired the basic knowledge necessary to a frontier woodsman. His self-confidence was evidenced by his frequent trips alone into the forest, and by his applying to Jefferson to lead a contemplated expedition to the West when he was only eighteen years of age.[39]

Another part of Lewis' education and experience which was to be of great value to him on the Expedition was his service in the Army during the Whiskey Rebellion. He rose through the ranks from private to captain, and served under General Anthony Wayne. He wrote to his mother on November 24, 1794 ". . . I am in perfect health . . . I am delighted with a soldier's life." Again he wrote (October 4, 1794) "We have mountains of Beef and oceans of Whiskey and I feel myself able to share it [with] heartiest fellow in camp." [40] In view of his troubles in keeping monetary accounts straight later in life, it is interesting that he became paymaster for his regiment.

Meriwether Lewis' mother was known among family and neighbors for her sturdy kindliness and devotion to everyone. She grew medicinal herbs in her garden and dispensed them to her neighbors with a kindness that evoked a responsive appreciation from all. She rode horseback with her medicines to serve the countryside day and night as would the country

[39] In his letter to Paul Allen on Aug. 18, 1813 (Jefferson's memoir of Lewis), he writes: "Capt. Lewis being stationed at Charlottesville on recruiting service, warmly solicited me to obtain for him the execution of that object." Jackson, *Letters*, p. 589. At this time the designation of leader went to André Michaux.

[40] In a letter to his mother while in the army, Lewis wrote from Pittsburgh about "my governing passion of rambling" and ascribes it to "having inherited it in right of the Meriwether family." *See* Meriwether Lewis Letters, Mo. Hist. Soc.

doctor with his horse and saddlebags.[41] Meriwether probably learned much about the use of frontier medicinal simples from her, and she exemplified and instilled in him an attitude and dedication that later reflected itself in the care of the men whose health was entrusted to him on the famous expedition he was to lead.

His mother's natural interest in health matters also showed in her other two sons. Both Meriwether's full brother Reuben and his half-brother, John Marks, became doctors.[42] On November 3, 1807, Lewis paid for a course of lectures on Materia Medica for John from Dr. Benjamin Smith Barton of the University of Pennsylvania, and a course of lectures on chemistry by Dr. James Woodhouse.

Lewis was a man of complicated and intricate personality. He was a "loner" and a dreamer who loved solitude and the unencumbered life of the woodsman. But he also understood and adapted well to army discipline. He evoked the trust of those above him, like Jefferson, as well as those who were subordinate to him. He was unrelenting in discipline, but fair.

Meriwether Lewis was twenty years old when he enlisted in the army during the Whiskey Rebellion. He stayed with the army and was quickly elevated in rank, indicating ready

[41] "Whenever anybody was sick, grandmother would get on her horse and go and nurse and feed them." This statement was made to this author by Mrs. Sarah Anderson Gordon of Stafford, Va., in an interview on June 29, 1947. She added that she thought that Lewis' brother Reuben (who was a doctor) got much of his medical experience from treating the Indians. See Bakeless, *Partners in Discovery*, for a good account of the "yarb doctor" activity of Lucy Marks, Lewis' mother.

[42] It has been stated that all three of the sons died without marrying, but this seems to be erroneous. Woods states that "Reuben studied medicine, lived on a part of his father's place. Married his cousin, Mildred Dabney, and died without children in 1844. Reuben is buried beside his mother in the small (and unkept) family cemetery at Locust Hill, Ivy Station." See Rev. Edgar Woods, *History of Albermarle County, Virginia* (1901). (Recently a Locust Hill Foundation has been formed to purchase and care for the property, after years of being unkept. Author.)

recognition of his definite abilities. He was serving with the army as paymaster when he received a letter from Thomas Jefferson, dated February 23, 1801. In this letter Jefferson offered Lewis the position of private secretary because "your knowledge of the Western country, of the army and of all its interests and relations has rendered it desirable for public as well as private purposes that you should be engaged in that office." [43] In order to supplement his meager official salary of $500 per annum, Jefferson offered Lewis the privilege of living in his home without cost to him. "You would of course save also the expence of subsistance & lodging as you would be one of my family." What Jefferson meant by the "private concerns of the household" is indicated by the footnote which Jackson appends to this letter,[44] in which he quotes Jefferson's letter to Burwell wherein he mentions that Lewis' duties are more "than a mere Secretary. The writing is not considerable, because I write my own letters." Jefferson probably recognized that Lewis' lack of education, particularly in spelling, did not qualify him to be the composer of letters of state. But he recognized Lewis' qualifications for the future duty he had in mind for him.

In his memoir of Meriwether Lewis (August 18, 1813), Jefferson wrote:

I had now the opportunities of knowing him intimately. Of courage undaunted, possessing a firmness & perseverance of purpose which nothing but impossibilities could divert from it's direction, careful as a father of those committed to his charge, yet steady in the maintenance of order & discipline, intimate with the Indian character, customs, and principles, habituated to the hunting life, guarded by exact observation of the vegetables & animals of his own country, against losing time in the description of objects already possessed, honest, disinterested, liberal, of sound under-

[43] Jackson, *Letters*, p. 2.   [44] *Ibid.*, p. 3.

standing and a fidelity to truth so scrupulous that whatever he should report would be as certain as if seen by ourselves, with all his qualifications as if selected and implanted by nature in one body, for this express purpose, I can have no hesitation in confiding the enterprise to him.[45]

Jefferson knew of Lewis' interest in outdoor life, and specifically of his interest in heading a proposed expedition to the West. Lewis' residence with Jefferson, and the intimate scrutiny provided thereby, convinced Jefferson that Lewis was the man to lead the Expedition. In this same memoir Jefferson writes that, after receiving the authorization from Congress in 1803 for the Expedition, "Captain Lewis who had then been near two years with me as private secretary, immediately renewed his solicitations to have direction of the party." [46]

In his instructions to Lewis, Jefferson of course placed emphasis on geography and commerce, but he also instructed him to acquire information about

the diseases prevalent among them [the Indians], & the remedies they use; moral & physical circumstances which distinguish them from the tribes we know of . . . carry with you some matter of the kine-pox; inform those of them with whom you may be, of its efficacy as a preservative from the smallpox; & instruct & encourage them in the use of it. This may be especially done wherever you winter. [Jefferson recognized that] it is impossible to prescribe the exact degree of perseverance with which you are to pursue your journey. We value too much the lives of citizens to offer them to probable destruction . . . in the loss of yourselves we should lose also the information you will have acquired. By returning safely with that, you may enable us to renew the essay with better calculated means. To your own discretion therefore must be left to the degree of danger you may risk, and the point at which you should decline, only saying we wish you to err

---

45 *Ibid.*, pp. 589-90.   46 *Ibid.*, p. 589.

on the side of your safety, and to bring back your party safe even if it be with less information.[47]

Jefferson was well aware of the dangers to the health and the life of the members of the Expedition. He instructed Lewis further: "To provide, on the accident of your death, against anarchy, dispersion & the consequent danger to your party, and total failure of the enterprise you are hereby authorized . . . to name the person among them who succeeds to the command on your decease. . ."

Despite his recognition of Lewis' native qualifications, Jefferson prudently recognized that Lewis was deficient in some formal technical training. He therefore arranged to have Lewis spend some time in Philadelphia to obtain basic instruction in the sciences of astronomy, geography, botany, and to receive from Dr. Benjamin Rush basic instructions of health care for the men of the Expedition, and suggestions for medicines and medical equipment to be used on the journey.

Jefferson and Lewis wisely decided that the Expedition should have a co-leader. Jefferson left it to Lewis to choose this man, and gave him permission to invest him with a commission of captain. Lewis decided to invite William Clark, a younger brother of George Rogers Clark. It is interesting that Jefferson had invited the elder Clark brother to lead the proposed expedition in 1783, and that Meriwether Lewis had decided in 1803 to invite the youngest of the several Clark brothers to be his co-leader in the new Expedition. Indeed a tribute to the quality of the Clark men!

Before he left Washington to travel overland to Pittsburgh preparatory to descending the Ohio River, Lewis wrote to Clark as follows, under the date of June 19, 1803, inviting him to join him in the Expedition because of ". . . the

---

[47] *Ibid.*, pp. 61-66.

long and uninterupted friendship and confidence which has subsisted between us." From his home at Clarksville, Clark answered on July 18, 1803, as follows: ". . . My friend I do assure you that no man lives whith whome I would prefur to undertake Such a Trip &c. as your self."[48]

Lewis wrote on August 3, 1803, acknowledging Clark's acceptance with language which today would appear unctuous, but this exchange of letters, each expressing earnest admiration of the other as well as dedication to the Expedition, provides an understanding of the basis of their abiding and enduring friendship and leadership. This relationship surely was constantly noted by their men with a salutary effect on their morale.

With all the detailed planning on the part of Jefferson, the omission of a physician to accompany the Expedition is glaring and probably significant. Jefferson must have deliberately planned it this way, with Lewis expected to assume the main responsibility for the health of the men. It is probable that Jefferson felt that a physician was not necessary, perhaps assuming that one of competence could not be induced to make the journey; his uncomplimentary appraisal of doctors in general may have been a determining factor, but it was most likely due to his highly correct appraisal of Lewis' ability as a physician.

Beard states that "American medicine lost a great leader when Meriwether Lewis responded to the urge of adventure instead of to the wings of Panaciea, the daughter of Aesculapius. His natural gifts, if trained, would have undoubtedly qualified him as a most worthy successor to Benjamin Rush. His rare powers of observation, his wide information and his capacity to recognize and to differentiate the various symptoms of disease would have made him one of the great clini-

---

[48] *Ibid.*, pp. 57; 110-11.

cians of his day."[49] There can be little doubt that Jefferson also held this high evaluation of Lewis in regard to providing health care for the men of the Expedition.

Because of the death of Meriwether Lewis by "suicide or murder," there has been considerable reading into his life certain interpretations of incidents pertaining to his personality. It is sufficient at this time and for the purposes of this book to state that there is no indication during the Expedition of Lewis having any mental health problem. He handled all problems, however stressful, with exceeding skill: the discipline of the men, the diplomacy with the Indians, the determination of geographical routes, his own health problems of physical debilitation, sickness, malnourishment, and near-escapes from death.[50]

WILLIAM CLARK
August 1, 1770 — September 1, 1838

. . . there is no man on earth with whom I should feel equal

[49] J. Howard Beard, "The Medical Observations and Practice of Lewis and Clark," *The Scientific Monthly*, Vol. xx, No. 5 (May, 1925), pp. 519-20. Hereafter cited as Beard, "Medical Observations and Practice."

[50] A short time before Lewis started east and met his death on the Natchez Trace, he wrote a morbid prophecy to his "old flame," Theodosia Burr Alston, daughter of Aaron Burr, in which he said "I am going to die, Theodosia, I cannot tell you how I know it, but I do. . . For me, I know that the trail is nearly ended. . . I want to see you once again first. . . I shall be with you in October. . ." But on Oct. 11, 1809, it was "suicide or murder" for Meriwether Lewis. Filmore Norfleet, *Saint-Memin in Virginia: Portraits and Biographies* (Richmond: The Dietz Press, 1942).

Meriwether's half-brother, John, apparently had some mental instability as indicated by a letter from Dr. Harper to Reuben Lewis, dated May 12, 1819, at Albemarle Co., Va: "Our neighborhood has been severely afflicted for some months past, among which your mother's family have had a large share, owing to the Doctor's (probably his half-brother, Dr. John Marks) situation, which has become to appearances hopeless; his insanity has assumed a dangerous appearance so that it has been found necessary to confine him. . ." See Stella M. Drumm, ed., *Luttig's Journal of a Fur Trading Expedition on the Upper Missouri, 1812-1813* (St. Louis: Mo. Hist. Soc., 1920), pp. 150-51. For a discussion of this matter, *see* Jackson, *Letters*, pp. 172-73.

pleasure in sharing them (the fatigues, dangers, and honors) as with yourself.   Meriwether Lewis to William Clark [51]

In his memoir of Meriwether Lewis, Jefferson wrote: "Deeming it necessary he should have some person with him of known competence to the direction of the enterprise, to whom he might confide it, in the event of accident to himself he proposed William Clarke, brother of Genl. Geo. Rogers Clarke, who was approved, and with that received a commission of captain." Actually, Clark was given only a second lieutenant's commission in the artillery. Clark accepted the commission and fulfilled his committment to Lewis and his government, but he was always rankled by this treatment, and immediately resigned his commission when he returned from the Expedition. It might be wondered why Lewis, who informed Clark that he had permission of the President to offer a captaincy, did not remonstrate with his Commander-in-Chief about the Secretary of War's action, when he was on such intimate terms with the President. There is some indication that he did so, but the matter was never pressed by anyone, including Clark.[52] Jefferson knew Clark personally, through Lewis and William's older brother, George Rogers; it is inexplicable that Jefferson did not make good his own and Lewis' commitment to Clark. Lewis always addressed Clark as Captain, and the men of the corps did not know of Clark's lower rank.

President Jefferson had decided on the man he wanted to lead the Expedition, and Meriwether Lewis knew the man he wanted as co-leader. He and Clark had served together in the army, with Clark as his superior. The Clark name was a pres-

---

[51] Jackson, *Letters*, p. 60.

[52] *See* John Louis Loos, "William Clark's Part in the Preparation of the Lewis and Clark Expedition," *Bull. of the Mo. Hist. Soc.*, Vol. x, No. 4, Pt. 1 (July, 1954), pp. 492-93; 508-09. *See also*, E. G. Chuinard, "Thomas Jefferson and the Corps of Discovery," *American West*, Vol. xxii, No. 6 (1975), pp. 4-13.

tigious one in the Ohio Valley. George Rogers Clark had secured the Old Northwest Territory for the United States, and now his youngest brother was to help extend the boundaries of the United States to the Pacific Ocean.

The Clark family was well-known to Jefferson. William Clark was a fellow Virginian of Thomas Jefferson and Meriwether Lewis; he was born near Charlottesville, within a few miles of the birthplace of Lewis, on August 1, 1770. He learned military discipline by serving under "Mad Anthony Wayne" from 1793-96. He grew up to a hardy, competent, frontier manhood due to the combination of his environment, family stock, and military training. His "book learning" was limited; his journal entries justify Vestal's remark that Clark exercised "not only freedom of speech but freedom of spelling," [53] and his contributions to his country justify Dunbar's evaluation that "the man who helps to make an empire may spell as he chooses." [54]

Undoubtedly because of the attachment of George Rogers Clark to the Northwest Territory, the Clarks moved to Kentucky in 1784, when William was fifteen years old. There they established a new home which they called Mulberry Hill, located near Louisville. Mulberry Hill was not just the home of the Clarks; it was also the center of the mingling of frontier society and important personages.

William Clark grew up on the frontier — on the frontier to which Lewis would move to join him, and from which both would extend the western horizons. He was more intimate with the western Indians, and more knowledgeable about western geography than Lewis. He had had more experience in leadership of other men, having led minor expeditions on the western frontier.

[53] Stanley Vestal, *The Missouri* (N.Y: Farrar and Rinehart, 1945), p. 248.

[54] Seymour Dunbar, *History of Travel in America*, quoted in Vinton, *John Colter*, p. 49.

Clark early gave evidence of being an attentive journalist. He kept a very detailed record of his activities in General Wayne's campaign of 1793-94.[55] In this he gives much attention to the anti-Wayne sentiment pervading the army, but also takes time to make comments regarding health. There is not only the recording of specific illnesses and their treatment; he also relates his experiences with desertion and courts-martial, and the scarcity of food and salt — very much as he was to write later in his journal of the Lewis and Clark Expedition.

On May 13 he wrote: "One man very sick. I blead him and gave him a swet. A fall ague." On the fifteenth he wrote: "All is well. I am obj. [obliged] to punish one man for filth." On the seventeenth he noted: "One man sick the usual fall ague;" again, on the nineteenth: "Fall ague as usual." He did not mention whether this "fall ague" was afflicting him or one of the other soldiers. The above quotations show that Clark was conversant with the symptoms of ague, and that, as an officer, he bled a soldier who was ailing. His frequent notations about ague are in contrast to the complete absence of reference to this affliction at Wood River and during the Expedition.

On August 28, 1794, he recorded: "I hate the recolection of the Sufferings of our Wounded, but I am induced here to Say that no set of men in the like disabled situation ever experienced much more want of Conveniancies &c." Thus Clark certainly had a background in meeting and dealing with the problems of frontier army campaigns, including the health of the personnel.

After Clark returned from the Expedition and married his sweetheart, Julia, he made a trip with her and his son, Meriwether Lewis Clark, from St. Louis to Washington, in 1809. As usual, Clark kept a diary, and he noted in it on November

---

[55] This journal can be seen at the Mo. Hist. Soc.

22, 1809: "Set out after Brackfast. Verry cold. Proceeded on to Mr. William Lewises near Salom [Salem, Virginia] & staid all night, his Children have the Hopping Cough. Tied a String around my Child's nake to prevent him taking it.[56]

Clark's credulity for irrational health practices is exemplified by the above quotation. That he continued to be impressed with such ridiculous treatment is evidenced by excerpts from a notebook he kept in 1820. In this he copied a prescription for a cough: "Pine or light wood splinters put into a Bottle of Brandy or Rum and drank 3 or 4 times a day, in small quantities." More than likely most patients chose to use the brandy without the splinters! Clark also placed in his notebook the following: "Croupe amediate relief Bind a large tobacco leaf to the heart, it pukes the child instantly, before any medicine could have effect."[57]

On August 15, 1811, Clark wrote to Nicholas Biddle, who was editing the expedition journals for publication, a chronological letter about himself: "I resigned [from the army on July 1, 1796] and returned to a Farm in Kentucky on which I lived several years in bad health."[58] It is interesting in consideration of his bad health that he would want to join an expedition for which Lewis and he anticipated strenuous "rigours," and for which they demanded prime health and durability from their men. Coues states that "we find him [Clark] on sick-leave in 1795."[59] It is probable that "bad health" seemed of less consideration compared to the challenges of the Expedition. Of such men was our country made!

Clark had a bout of illness soon after joining Lewis. Loos

[56] Donald Jackson, "A Footnote to the Lewis and Clark Expedition," *Manuscripts,* Vol. xxiv, No. 1 (1972), p. 17.

[57] From William Clark's notebook, seen at the Mo. Hist. Soc., dated 1820. This notebook is a collection of miscellaneous entries, none of which refer to the Lewis and Clark Expedition.   [58] Jackson, *Letters,* p. 572.

[59] Coues, *History of Lewis and Clark,* i, p. lxxii.

writes that while Lewis was visiting the Spanish Commandant at Cape Girardeau (approaching St. Louis), ". . . Clark, who had not been feeling very well for a week, remained aboard the keelboat." [60]

Although it is always Lewis who is designated as the more mercurial and temperamental of the two captains, it was Clark who seemed to be the more introspective about his health; a frequent notation of his was "I am unwell." And he probably was — he suffered from arthritis and boils and probably malaria. He may very well have had gout also, in view of his age, sex and heavy meat diet at times. But so often he began his daily journal entry with "a fair morning," even though it had rained all night.

Just as Lewis had contributed to the Expedition before Clark joined their captain-team (making plans with Jefferson, purchasing supplies in Philadelphia and transporting them down the Ohio), so Clark served the Expedition's purposes for an extended time after Lewis' death by diligently pursuing Jefferson's desire to get the journals published. Clark was not too well acquainted in Philadelphia, so Dr. Rush was again asked to help; Joel Marlow [61] wrote to him on January 7, 1810: "I hope to do you a pleasure as well as myself by commanding to your kind attention & friendship Genl. Clarke the companion & colleague of the late Govr Lewis in the voyage of Discovery across the continent. He visits your city to bring forward the publication of that interesting work which Lewis undertook & has left in an infinished state." [62] It was to be a long and frustrating wait before Clark would see the journals published by Biddle-Allen in 1814. To Clark must go the credit for seeing the enterprise through to completion — the

60 Loos, "William Clark's Part in the Preparation," p. 498.
61 Joel Marlow (1754-1812) was a poet and diplomat.
62 Letter seen in American Philosophical Soc. Coll.

publishing of the journals of the Expedition. Rather pathetically, Clark wrote on September 14, 1814, to Biddle: "I have borrowed a Copy of my Book which has reached this place, But have not had time to read it as yet." [63]

Fortunately, in contrast to Lewis, Clark lived many years to serve his city, state and country as an illustrious citizen. He had married his Judith (Julia) for whom he named a river in Montana, and after her death he married her cousin. After serving as Commissioner of Indian Affairs and Governor of the Missouri Territory, the Lieutenant of artillery who was denied a promised captaincy died a brigadier general in 1838. The Clark name has not been dimmed by his many descendants.

The only tribute written to their captains by any of their men is that of Joseph Whitehouse: "I cannot in justice to myself omit saying, that the manly, and soldier-like behaviour; and enterprizing abilities; of both Captain Lewis, and Captain Clark, claim my utmost gratitude; and the humanity shown at all times by them, to those under their command, on this perilous and important Voyage of discovery; I hope will ever fill the breasts of Men who were under their command with the same, and make their characters be esteem'd by the American people, and mankind in general; and convince the generous Public, that the President of the United States, did not displace his judgement, when he appointed them to the command of this party on discovery, which is of so great a magnitude and utility, to the United States and mankind in general." [64]

[63] Jackson, *Letters*, p. 600.

[64] Cutright, "Whitehouse," p. 160. This rather flowery and verbose statement is not in keeping with the sparse and terse notes made by Whitehouse in his journals. This paragraph appears in the copied survival of the original second part of Whitehouse's journal, recently discovered, and owned by the Newberry Lby. in Chicago. The diction suggests that some retrospective editing was done by the copyist.

Two great captains [65] — perhaps their most perfect epitaph is the phrase they so frequently entered in their journals, no matter how hard the day: "we proceeded on."

[65] The two captains were remembered and honored when a Fleet Ballistic Missile submarine was named after them and was commissioned on Dec. 22, 1965. Mrs. William Clark Adreon, wife of the explorer's great-great-grandson, was a matron of honor and her sister, Mrs. Martin F. Engman, Jr., was a co-sponsor. The other co-sponsor was a great-great-grandniece of Lewis, Mrs. William Goodrich Sales. The motto of the ship is significant: "Theirs to Discover — Ours to Defend."

VI

Benjamin Rush

It would appear that one great lesson to be derived from medical history is that there is no necessary relation between the doctor's opinion of his work and the real facts of the case.

Francis B. Packard [1]

Thomas Jefferson literally thought of everything in preparing Lewis for the Expedition to the Pacific Ocean. He directed letters to old friends of his in Philadelphia, asking them to instruct Lewis in basic information sufficient to meet the varied responsibilities of the journey. It is obvious that Jefferson expected Lewis to assume all the responsibility for the professional aspects of the Expedition. The only recruited "specialist" was an interpreter; otherwise, Lewis was to be the geographer, navigator, geologist, naturalist, mineralogist, diplomat — and the physician.

On February 28, 1803, President Jefferson wrote from Washington to Dr. Benjamin Rush in Philadelphia:

> Dear Sir: I wish to mention to you in confidence that I have obtained authority from Congress to undertake the long desired object of exploring the Missouri & whatever river, heading with that, leads into the western ocean. About ten chosen woodsmen headed by Capt. Lewis my secretary will set out on it immediately and probably accomplish it in two seasons. Capt. Lewis is brave, prudent, habituated to the woods, and familiar with Indian manners and character. He is not regularly educated, but he possesses a great mass of accurate observation on all the subjects of nature

---

[1] Packard, *History of Medicine,* p. 631.

which present themselves here, and will, therefore readily select only those in his new route which shall be new. He has qualified himself for those observations of longitude and latitude necessary to fix the points of the line he will go over. It would be useful to state for him those objects on which it is most desirable he should bring us information. For this purpose I ask the favor of you to prepare some notes of such particulars as may occur in his journey and which you think should draw his attention and enquiry. He will be in Philadelphia about two or three weeks hence and will wait on you.[2]

Rush answered Jefferson on March 12, 1803: "I shall expect to see Mr. Lewis in Philadelphia, and shall not fail of furnishing him with a number of questions calculated to increase our knowledge of subjects connected with medicine."[3]

Rush wrote to Jefferson again on June 11, 1803: "I have endeavored to fulfill your wishes by furnishing Mr. Lewis with some inquiries relative to the natural history of the Indians. The enclosed letter contains a few short directions for the preservation of his health, as well as the persons under his command."[4]

Why did Jefferson select Rush to be Lewis' medical tutor? What about the man and his medicine?

Rush was in more than one sense the leading physician of the United States, and he had been so from colonial times. His energy and unfailing readiness to utter and write opinions on all things medical and political made him the most widely known and controversial physician of his day, if not the most

[2] Jackson, *Letters,* p. 18.

[3] L. H. Butterfield, *Letters of Benjamin Rush* (Philadelphia, 1951), p. 858. This is the only paragraph referring to Lewis in a long letter of medical advice to Jefferson. In view of Jefferson's not too complimentary opinion of the medical profession as a whole (*see* Appen. II), it serves to emphasize the high regard Jefferson had for Rush by seeking his advice.

[4] Quoted by permission of R. Stockton Rush. The entirety of this letter can be found in Butterfield, *Letters of Rush,* p. 868.

highly regarded by some of his professional colleagues. He worked devotedly, read voraciously, deliberated on all things, and spoke and wrote voluminously and without restraint.

Benjamin Rush was interested in and contributed to a wide range of community interests. It was inevitable that his inquiring and aggressive nature would find him in the midst of all the conflicting currents of the American Revolution, and most certainly on the side of the rebels. He was one of the five physicians who signed the Declaration of Independence.[5] It was only natural, then, that it was to Benjamin Rush, the outstanding physician and physician-patriot of the colonies and the new nation, a comrade in arms, that Thomas Jefferson sent Meriwether Lewis for medical instruction in preparation for his exploration to the Pacific.

A study of Benjamin Rush is important for two reasons: it offers an insight into the medical practice of his time and therefore into the time of the Lewis and Clark Expedition, and also gives evidence of his direct contribution to this Expedition.

Benjamin Rush was born December 24, 1745, at Byberry Pennsylvania. He early developed the habit of recording facts, quotations and thoughts in a notebook, and his writing and speaking ability were noted by friends and instructors. After graduating from the College of New Jersey (now Princeton) in 1760, the fifteen-year-old Rush returned to Philadelphia and started his medical training, according to the method of the day, by apprenticing himself to Dr. John Redman.[6] This

---

[5] Goodman is in error when he writes that Benjamin Rush was "the only Doctor of Medicine to sign the Declaration of Independence." Goodman, *Rush*, "Preface," and p. 344. There were four other physicians in addition to Rush: Josiah Bartlett of New Hampshire; Lyman Hall of Georgia; Matthew Thornton of New Hampshire; and James McHenry of Maryland.

[6] John Redman (1722-1808) was a leading Philadelphia physician, active in medical education.

proved to be a mutually highly regarded association between student and teacher, and Rush was a devoted and able apprentice to Redman for over five years.

He read widely on medical subjects, and his inquiring nature lead him to make thoughtful observations and comparisons about medical practices. He enrolled for courses in anatomy conducted by Dr. William Shippen [7] and in materia medica by Dr. John Morgan.[8] This constant seeking for new and more medical information lead him to go abroad for further study. Edinburgh was the medical center to which most of the young colonial doctors went who had financial means equal to their medical ambitions.

And so Rush went to Edinburgh in 1766. Here he studied hard; by his diligence and personality he won the attention and the approbation of the great William Cullen, professor of medicine and recognized medical doctrinarian of his time. Rush was most impressed by Cullen, and became a devotee. Medical teaching was more a matter of philosophical opinion than of scientific fact, and a forceful and personable teacher was apt to prevail in the promotion of conflicting theories.

After two years of study, and having presented an acceptable thesis on the digestion of food, Benjamin Rush received his Doctor of Medicine from the medical faculty of the University of Edinburgh, in June 1768.[9] He was only twenty-two

---

[7] William Shippen (1736-1808) was a well-trained and prominent Philadelphia physician. He joined with John Morgan to found the first medical school in the colonies, at the College of Philadelphia.

[8] John Morgan (1735-1789) was a great innovator in medical teaching and practice in Philadelphia. He stimulated the establishment of the first medical school in the colonies in 1765, where he was appointed professor of the theory and practice of physic, the first medical professorship in North America. He early restricted his practice to internal medicine and employed an apothecary to fill his prescriptions — changes from the usual practice of the day.

[9] Goodman, *Rush*, p. 17. The work done by Rush as the basis of the report in his thesis is an indication of his investigative and questioning attitude, and affords a comparison of the superficial research of that time with the intricate, scientific

years old, so he remained in Europe to study and travel.

Rush's catholic interests were shown by his visiting of American artist Benjamin West and the English artist Sir Joshua Reynolds; by his visiting the authors Samuel Johnson and Oliver Goldsmith; by his journeying to Paris where he critically noted many things about the French people besides their lesser quality of medical practice; and by his study of other languages, arts and customs.

When Rush returned to Philadelphia in 1769, he was a polished citizen and physician by virtue of his long training at home and abroad, his extensive travel, and his avidity for knowledge. These traits, combined with his social graces and ability to write and converse fluently and informatively, made him one of the colonies' leading citizens. He was appointed professor of chemistry at the College of Philadelphia, the first such professorship designated in America; he was now a fellow professor on the faculty with his former teachers and sponsors, William Shippen and John Morgan. Besides formal medical school lectures, he gave many public addresses about health, he published extensively on medical subjects, and he carried on a wide correspondence with other doctors on med-

---

medical research of today. Goodman gives the following account: "In commemorating on the thesis Dr. David Ramsay of South Carolina said: 'The eagerness of its author to acquire professional knowledge, induced him to test a medical opinion in a way against which a less ardent student would have revolted. To ascertain whether fermentation had any agency in digestion he made three unpleasant experiments on his own stomach.' He used an emetic three hours after dinner and examined the ejected contents of the stomach. 'By taking five grains of alkaline salt, he first destroyed any acid that might be accidently in it [the stomach], and immediately afterwards dined on beef, peas, bread, and beer. Three hours after dinner, he took an emetic of two grains of emetic tartar.' The contents of the stomach proved to be acidic. Then he tried veal instead of beef, and water instead of beer, and the result was the same. For the third test he used chicken instead of beef or veal, and cabbage instead of peas, and unleavened bread instead of the bread in common use. The result was unchanged. 'From these facts, thrice repeated, an inference can be drawn, that the aliment in the human stomach, in the course of three hours after deglutition, underwent the acetetous fermentation.'"

ical advice. He immediately gave attention to the health needs of the poor, and his accounts give a vivid picture of the congested filth and squalor in which many people lived in Philadelphia at the time.

Most medical education in the colonies was by apprenticeship. At the time of the American Revolution there were only two medical schools in the colonies. The first medical school was founded in Philadelphia in 1765, and the second in New York in 1768. Philadelphia was the center of medical education in America during the colonial years and the first years of the independent states, and Benjamin Rush became the unquestioned leader of his profession in his native Philadelphia. He has been credited with influencing more young medical men than any other physician of his time, and this influence extended for many years after his death. His son James states that a total of 2872 students attended his classes during the years 1779-1812. It has been estimated that Rush helped train more than three thousand physicians in America. One of Rush's students was the future President, William Henry Harrison. He was a founder and a very active member of the College of Physicians of Philadelphia.

Rush's return to Philadelphia was only a few years before the Spirit of 1776 held full and fateful sway. Those years were filled with increasing resentment of the colonies toward a bungling mother country, and Philadelphia was host to most of the organizers and leaders of the developing rebellion. It would have been contrary to Rush's natural revolutionary bent not to be in the thick of the rebel (patriot!) activities. He became an intimate friend and co-worker of Washington, Adams, Jefferson, Franklin, Henry and many other leaders of the revolting colonies. He was elected a delegate from Pennsylvania to the Second Continental Congress, and thereby was destined to sign the Declaration of Independence. He served on many committees, including one to procure medicines and supplies for the army.

Benjamin Rush was one of the outstanding citizens of Philadelphia in many regards other than medical. He was a member of the American Philosophical Society, and served as its vice-president. He helped found the first anti-slavery society in America, and was its president during the first ten years. He was a devout man, practicing formal worship and supporting church activities with his usual zeal. He was a fervent supporter of universal education, and was one of the trustees who staunchly stood by Dickinson College during its early floundering years. He was always actively aligned with those who worked for beneficial civic enterprises. Rush is credited with having been the main prod to Thomas Paine to write his pamphlet *Common Sense,* suggesting the title for the book, and proofreading much of it. He campaigned for a better understanding of mentally disturbed patients, and advocated a more humane treatment of them; this has earned for him the designation of "Father of American Psychiatry." [10]

Rush was a student of the Old Country in both medicine and politics, attempting to evaluate fairly the good therefrom. But he honestly endeavored to sever decisively all valueless and improper attachments, and to establish new medical and political aims and methods. He helped by work and inspiration to establish good medical teaching and practices (for his time) in this country. Gradually it became less popular and less necessary for young men to seek medical education in Europe, thanks to Rush's energetic promotion of medical teaching in this country.

---

[10] So designated by the American Psychiatric Association, on a bronze plaque placed on his grave. The official seal of the American Psychiatric Association bears Rush's portrait. See Carl Binger, *Revolutionary Doctor, Benjamin Rush* (N.Y., 1966).

Rush and His Medicine

Up to the time of Cullen, the great Dutch physician Hermann Boerhaave (1668-1738) was the advocate of the prevailing accepted theories of disease and treatment. Boerhaave taught that illness was caused by "morbid acrimonies" in the blood, and removal of these harmful acrimonies was the basis of his therapy. Thus sweating, vomiting, purging, diuresis and blood-letting formed the main armamentarium of the Boerhaave school. Whereas Borehaave's theory of disease postulated that all trouble was in the "fluids," Cullen taught that the "solids" were the location of all disorders.

Rush early subscribed to the teachings of Cullen. Without the knowledge of the existence of germs, and without the revelations later made possible through studies of microscopic pathology, clinicians were restricted to the interpretations of the obvious gross aspects of disease to explain its cause. Thus it is understandable that the manifestations of the disease process were often accepted as the cause, such as fever and pulse rate; or even incorporated into the treatment, such as purging and vomiting. It is not surprising then, that an inquisitive physician like Rush would develop his own confused idea of the cause of disease, and propound it with all the energy and assured opinion that he brought to the support of all his ideas.

Rush came to believe that the site of all fevers was in the blood vessels — caused by them or related to them — which in turn were affected by the blood; and the pulse — its rate, strength and volume — was a reflection of the action of the blood vessels on the blood. Whether insanity or jaundice, the cause was in the blood vessels — one in the blood vessels of the brain, the other in the blood vessels of the liver. It is hard to determine what Rush really thought the prime trigger was that set off this chain reaction between blood, and blood vessels, pulse and fever. Rush's own words do little to clarify the point: ". . . I have attempted to prove that the higher grades of fever depend upon morbid and excessive action in the blood-vessels. It is connected, of course, with preternatural sensibility in their muscular fibres. The blood is the most powerful irritant which acts upon them." His circuitous reasoning was typical of the medical rationale of the times. He wrote in his *Directions of Preserving the Health of Army Soldiers* in 1777: "it is a well-known fact, that the perspiration of the body, by attaching itself to linen, and afterwards, by mixing with rain, is disposed to form miasmata, which produce fevers." [11]

It is only natural and logical that the main point of Rush's therapy would be to reduce the effect of the "most powerful irritant" by removing some of it. Thus, even though he differed with Boerhaave and Cullen as to the cause of disease, he found it necessary to continue the standby of their therapy, bleeding, as the cornerstone of his own therapy.[12] But he taught and practiced its use with an unprecedented fervor, so that the words "bleeding" and "Dr. Rush" became practically synonymous.

The external causes or conditions which contributed to disease at the time of Benjamin Rush, and which essentially had not changed by the time of Lewis and Clark's Expedition, were expressed in such nebulous terms as "miasmata," "effluvia" and "exhalations" all related to marshes and decomposing material which were harmful to a person when inhaled. The relationship of disease to stagnant water and fresh air was generally noted, and lead Rush to recommend that the swamps be drained and the soldiers be kept constantly on the move.

---

[11] Quoted by Ashburn, *Medical Dept.*, p. 7.

[12] Chris Holmes, "Benjamin Rush and the Yellow Fever," *Bull. of the History of Med.*, Vol. XL, No. 3, p. 253.

As was true with his predecessors, Rush's ideas of the cause
of disease were based more on speculation than on proof, and
served more to stimulate violent argument between the medical practitioners than to provide any new therapy.[13]

The cure-all of blood-letting speeded the slow pulse, and it
slowed the fast pulse. It depleted the body of morbid influ-
ences on the pulse. It assisted the other depleting modalities:
purging, vomiting, blistering. It opened the bowels and also
checked diarrhea. It decreased fever and stopped chilling. It
relieved coma, and also induced sleep. A person could be bled
until syncope was produced, and then bled some more to
relieve syncope. Rush believed that up to four-fifths of the
body's blood could be removed.[14] Nowhere in his writings
does Rush record concern about too much bleeding; of course,
the use of transfusions to restore blood loss was a thing of the
future, or Rush probably would have condemned it in re-
sounding terms.

Rush records the drawing of up to eighty ounces of blood
daily from patients. At a time when the method of bleeding
was often into open pans or onto the ground, with measurement only by estimation, and with no exact knowledge of the
amount of blood in the human body, it is probable that the
stated amount of withdrawn blood was a reflection of the
enthusiasm of the physician.

Busy physicians like Rush often employed technicians to
bleed their patients. The physician would examine the pa-

---

13 The following is an example of Rush's enthusiastic approach that so irritated
his colleagues: "I have formerly said that there was but one fever in the world. Be
not startled, Gentlemen, follow me and I will say there is but one disease in the
world. The proximate cause of disease is irregular, convulsive or wrong action in
the system affected. This, Gentlemen, is a concise view of my theory of disease
. . . I call upon you, Gentlemen, at this early period either to approve or
disapprove of it now." Binger, *Revolutionary Dr.: Rush,* p. 88.

14 "Bleeding should be repeated while the symptoms which first indicated it continue, should it be until four-fifths of the blood contained in the body are drawn
away." Pepper, "Rush's Theories," p. 122.

DOCTOR BENJAMIN RUSH
He was asked by Jefferson to advise Lewis regarding the
health care of the men of the Expedition.
Painted and engraved by Savage in 1800.
Courtesy of College of Physicians of Philadelphia.

Philadelphia June 11th 1803.

Dear Sir!

I have endeavoured to fulfil your wishes by furnishing Mr Lewis with some inquiries relative to the natural history of the Indians. The enclosed letter contains a few short directions for the preservation of his health, as well as the health of the persons under his command.

His mission is truely interesting. I shall wait with great solicitude for its issue. Mr Lewis appears admirably qualified for it. May its advantages prove no less honourable to your administration, than to the interests of science!

The enclosed letter from Mr Sumpter contains some new views of the present military arrangements of France & Great Britain. You need not return it.

From Dear Sir yours
very respectfully & sincerely
Benj:n Rush

Tho. Jefferson Esq.

LETTER WRITTEN BY BENJAMIN RUSH
Addressed to Jefferson in answer to the request for health
rules which Lewis could apply on the Expedition. See text p.222.
Courtesy of the National Archives, Washington.

tient's pulse, and thereby determine the amount of blood to be lost, and the "bleeder" would open the vein with a lancet. Undoubtedly many of these technicians became as expert as today's laboratory technicians who perform venepunctures with needles to obtain blood for laboratory examinations.

The main purpose of drugs was to stimulate and increase the process of depleting the body of the "morbid" elements which were mainly in the blood. Dr. Rush "the bleeder" became almost equally famous for his combined use of mercury and jalap as a purgative, which he used in combined doses of ten grains each several times a day. The "depleting" effect of these pills was no less dramatic than that of bleeding; in fact, it may be rightfully conjectured that many a recipient of these "Rush's pills" considered them to be well named!

Jalap is used very little in modern therapy; its previous use was usually as a laxative. Mercury was used as a purgative, usually given as "calomel" [15] up to the early part of this century, in adult doses of ten to fifteen grains. This combination of calomel and jalap was the composition of "Dr. Rush's Bilious Pills" used so extensively by the Expedition.

Lewis and Clark relied upon mercury in their treatment of syphilis as well as using it as a purgative. Undoubtedly Rush instructed them in the technical use of mercury in the treat-

---

[15] Calomel was introduced into medicinal use by Theodore Turfet de Mayerne in France in the 16th century. *See* Charles H. LaWall, *Four Thousand Years of Pharmacy* (Philadelphia: J. B. Lippincott Co., 1936), p. 266. Mayerne was a 17th century French physician. He was physician to Henry vi of France, and also to James i of England. I am indebted to Roy J. Popkin, M.D., for this reference. Mercury has been one of the most extensively used drugs in medical history. In Rush's pills it was used in the form of calomel, or mercurous chloride, a compound of mercury and chlorine in the proportions of 200 parts mercury to 35.5 parts chlorine. It is a white powder, and thus lends itself well to mix with other medicinal powders, make pills, or incorporate in salves. Its main use in medicine has been as a purgative, and it was used extensively in the treatment of syphilis until the advent of penicillin. Holmes writes that ".   .   .   mercury was used at least as early as the Renaissance by Paracelsus in his administration to syphilitics." Holmes, "Rush and Yellow Fever," p. 254.

ment of syphilis; and probably their experience as army officers had also provided them with knowledge in this regard. The usual method of the administration of mercury for the treatment of syphilis was by the application of salves to the local lesion to the point of salivation and sore gums, then interruption of treatment for a time, then resumption of treatment until the lesions seemed cured. The stimulation of salivation by mercury was looked upon by the practitioners of the day as another evidence of beneficial "depletion" of harmful substances in the body.

The high regard in which calomel was held at the time of the Revolution is shown by the opinion of Tilton: "This Sampsonian remedy has the power of subduing all manner of contagion or infection that we are yet acquainted with. Thus, besides syphilis, itch, and so forth, without fever, it is regarded as specific in smallpox, measles, scarletina, influenza, yellow fever, etc., and is found to be not less successful in the early stages of jail fever. . . Hence it is that in yellow fever, remitting or any other fever, if we can only touch the patients mouth with mercury, we regard him as safe." [16]

RUSH AND YELLOW FEVER

Perhaps nothing in Benjamin Rush's life depicts more vividly his great devotion, drive and opinionated medical ideas than does his association with yellow fever.

Yellow fever had been one of the great health scourges of all time. Primarily a tropical disease, it struck in sporadic epidemics with devastating effects in temperate northern climates. At the time of Benjamin Rush, diseases were classified mainly as types of fever; therefore, it was natural that this fever with accompanying yellow skin would become known as "yellow fever." Nothing was known of its etiology, but it had been observed that it usually broke out near the

---

[16] Quoted by Ashburn, *Medical Dept.*, p. 402.

waterfront of a large port. It was widely accepted that it was the "effluvia" and "miasmata" of the poorly drained and swampy lands which produced the "morbid" unhealthy state of the land and the people.

When yellow fever appeared occasionally in areas where it was not endemic, and therefore where most of the population had not acquired an immunity to it, the mortality rate was very high, often reaching fifty percent. Whole families became ill and died. Commerce came to a standstill, even to the distribution of needed food and other supplies. All transportation and public mingling stopped, except for those people who hurriedly left their infected environs and spread widely into the surrounding countryside. Some doctors and morticians deserted and fled in panic with the others. Homes and streets became immersed in vinegar washes and choked with smoking fires, and a great variety of other ignorant home remedies were used against the epidemic.

The most horrible of all the yellow fever epidemics in North America occurred in 1793 in Philadelphia.[17] Its occurrence was credited to spoiled coffee unloaded on a dock from a ship from Santo Domingo;[18] no credit was given to the crewmen who were ill. The epidemic spread in waves throughout the late summer and autumn. The medical profession of Philadelphia, with very few exceptions, cared for their patients with unrelenting devotion during these months. Several of them even found time to argue about the theories and practice of medicine in relation to yellow fever, and the fervor of their arguments regarding the cause of the epidemic was exceeded only by their ignorance of it.

Dr. Rush's practice probably exceeded that of any other

---

[17] J. H. Powell, *Bring Out Your Dead* (Phila: Univ. of Pa. Press, 1949), provides an excellent, detailed and vivid account of the 1793 epidemic in Philadelphia.

[18] In 1802, yellow fever again played a key role in Santo Domingo, when it decimated the army Napoleon had sent to establish his power in Louisiana.

physician, and no physician exceeded Dr. Rush's attention to his practice; however, he found time to participate without restraint in all the arguments about the proper personal and public health measures to be used in combatting the yellow fever. In Dr. Rush's time it was considered proper to speak and write publicly about another physician's practice, and to write articles advising about treatment, even to the publishing of prescriptions. The artist Charles Willson Peale helped treat his wife by purging and bleeding her according to the directions published by Dr. Rush in a newspaper.

Rush literally worked night and day, seeing patients in his office, and making a round of house calls. As would be expected, his main armamentarium of treatment consisted of purging and blood-letting. He wrote: "I have bled twice in many, and one acute case, four times, with the happiest efects. I consider intrepidity in the use of the lancet at present to be as necessary, as it is in the use of mercury and jalap, in this insidious and ferocious disease." [19] During the height of

---

[19] Rush had been so closely identified with bleeding that he was so portrayed in *The Red City*. The author of this novel has Dr. Rush say of a patient by the name of Schmidt: " 'I must bleed him at once. Calomel and blood-letting are the only safety, sir. I bled Dr. Griffith seventy-five ounces today. He will get well.' The doctor bled everybody, and over and over." *See* S. Weir Mitchell, M.D., *The Red City* (N.Y: The Century Co., 1908), p. 213.

S. Weir Mitchell (1829-1914) graduated from Jefferson Medical College in 1850. He became an eminent physician, particularly noted for his work in neurology. He wrote many medical treatises. Next to Oliver Wendell Holmes, he is America's most noted physician-poet-novelist. He wrote some 30 novels, including *The Red City*. He was in great demand as a dinner speaker; on one occasion he said of Rush: "With reverent doubt of my powers to do justice to the greatest physician this country has produced, I approach the task of briefly recalling to your memories the vivid and emphatic personality of Benjamin Rush." (*See* his Commemorative Address of Jan. 3, 1887, in the *Trans. of the College of Physicians of Phila.*, IX, 1887). A few lines of a poem written by Mitchell are very apropos of Benjamin Rush, and will be humbly and sympathetically understood by all physicians:

Take, then, the thought — That wisdom fades
That Knowledge dies of newer truth.
That only duty simply done
Walks always with the step of youth.

the epidemic Rush wrote to his wife Julia on September 11, 1793: "I have this day visited and prescribed for upwards of one hundred patients, and have not had a single death among them. Four persons in the British minister's family will swell the triumphs of mercury, jalap and blood-letting." [20]

Rush would often precede a corps of bleeders, examining the patient's pulse and indicating the amount of blood to be lost, and the technician followed with his lancet. Powell states that "Jones, Gray, Allen and their helpers bled about eight hundred persons following Rush's perscription." [21] Today, such treatment seems about as rational and impressive as the myriad of ignorant home treatments which were used by the populace, such as the sprinkling of vinegar through the houses and streets, or the carrying of camphor bags and tarred ropes.

One universal treatment used by the people probably had some efficacy: building fires to create an offensive smudge — this probably served to disperse the mosquitoes. It is interesting to read Rush's observations of his patients' skin: "Those small red spots, which have been compared to moscheto bites, occurred in several of my patients." Despite the universal observation that yellow fever and mosquitoes came together, it was to be more than a hundred years before the relationship of the two was definitely established. [22]

---

[20] Butterfield, *Letters of Rush*, p. 659.

[21] Powell, *Bring Out Your Dead*, p. 98.

[22] Dr. Carlos Finlay (1833-1915), of Havana, in 1881 advanced the belief that the mosquito *Aedes aegypti* caused the spread of yellow fever, but it remained for Dr. Walter Reed (1851-1902) and his associates in 1900 to develop conclusive proof of the role of the mosquito in yellow fever. Reed proved by his experiments that contaminated material from yellow fever patients would not infect people, but that a bite from an *Aedes aegypti* mosquito which had previously bitten a yellow fever patient would infect and produce the disease in a healthy person.

It became evident that elimination of the mosquito would control yellow fever. Major William C. Gorgas (1854-1920) showed by an extensive project in Havana that mosquito propagation could be stopped by spraying all open waters with kerosene, thus preventing the larvae from securing air. Yellow fever was eliminated as a serious disease by the wide application of Gorgas' method. His work as Chief

Rush proved his sincere belief in his recommended therapy when he contracted yellow fever himself. He recognized the unmistakable symptoms of the disease, and immediately administered his routine treatment, including bleeding himself of ten ounces. Despite his illness, he worked strenuously all day, became worse in the evening, and took a mercurial purge and bled himself of another ten ounces. He kept working and purging and bleeding, with the consultation of a fellow physician — of course one who agreed with Rush!

The magnitude of the problem in the yellow fever epidemic of 1793 in Philadelphia is indicated by Rush's claim that six thousand citizens of that city owed their lives to the beneficial effects of purging and bleeding. Today, as patients and physicians, we can be grateful that we do not have to decide what is the most efficacious therapy for yellow fever.

Rush's methods of treatment and theories have continued to spark controversy. The following quotations exemplify the opposing points of view regarding the man's life and work:

> His contribution to the Art of Medicine is measurable in the obvious sacredness in which he held human life and his really heroic efforts to preserve it. Certainly nothing more can be asked of a physician, even a great one.[23]

> By virtue of his social and professional prominence, his position as teacher and his facile pen, Benjamin Rush had more influence upon American medicine and was more potent in the propagation and long perpetuation of medical errors than any man of his day. To him, more than to any other man in America, was due the great vogue of vomits, purgings, especially of bleeding, salivation and blistering, which blackened the record of medicine and afflicted the sick almost to the time of the Civil War.[24]

Health Officer was an important factor in the success of the United States in building the Panama Canal. Yellow fever had been one of the main causes of France's failure to complete the canal a few years earlier.

[23] Holmes, "Rush and Yellow Fever," p. 260.

Rush and Army Medicine

That officer . . . will best perform his duty to his men, who obliges them to take the most care of their health.[25]

In the *Pennsylvania Packett* of September 1777, Benjamin

---

[24] Ashburn, *Medical Dept.*, p. 19, fn. A more philosophical and charitable appraisal of Rush — and of medicine — is given by Binger, *Revolutionary Dr.: Rush*, pp. 263-64: "But one should not belittle his substantive accomplishments. Nor should one dismiss his errors with an air of superiority. A hundred and fifty years from now our present convictions and theories in medicine may be looked upon with equal disregard by our descendants, if, indeed, they do not return to his views. In an historical survey, the errors of a great man do not count. What counts are his moral ideal and the push he gives to man's fate. On this score one can only admire Rush, in spite of the unevenness of his thinking. The fact is, he was so persuasive, so passionate, convinced and articulate, that he swept objections before him. And soon he had a devoted bank of student-followers who continued to practice his mistakes. This is the fate of great men — to put a drag anchor in their generation at the very time they are launching it on hitherto uncharted seas. Rush was not unaware of this danger. In a lecture on Hippocrates delivered six years before his work on diseases of the mind was published, he said:

" 'While we thus felicitate ourselves upon the present highly cultivated and improved state of medicine, let us check a disposition to pride, by looking forward to a time when there will probably be the same differences between our degrees of knowledge and those that are to exist hereafter, that now exists between us and Hippocrates. Should discoveries in our science be multiplied but for a century to come, in the same ratio they have been for the last thirty years, this difference will probably take place. Then will the opinions and modes of practice of modern physicians furnish subjects for animadversion, such as you have heard this day upon those of Hippocrates.

" 'Perhaps from the chair which I now occupy, your successors in this seminary may hear expressions of surprise and contempt at our ignorance of the most simple modes of curing diseases which now elude our skill, or of our tedious, painful, and offensive remedies for such as are under the power of medicine. Should the humble labours of your teacher, who now addresses you, attract his notice, I hope he will do him the justice to admit, before he consigns his name and opinions to oblivion, that he experienced the same pleasure in renouncing an old error that he did in teaching a new truth; and that the health and lives of his patients, and the improvement of his pupils were always dearer to him than interest or fame.' "

For an excellent and balanced review of Rush and his medicine, *see* Richard Harrison Shryock, "The Medical Reputation of Benjamin Rush: Contrasts over Two Centuries," *Bull. of the Hist. of Med.*, Vol. xlv, No. 6 (1972), pp. 507-52.

[25] Quoted by David Freman Hawke, *Benjamin Rush, Revolutionary Gadfly* (N.Y: Bobbs-Merrill Co., 1971), p. 326.

Rush published his "Directions for Preserving the Health of Soldiers, Addressed to the Officers of the Army of the United States." He admonished them that ". . . the munificence of the congress, and the skill of physicians and surgeons, will avail but little in preventing mortality from sickness among our soldiers without the concurrence of the officers of the army. Your authority, gentlemen, is absolutely necessary to enforce the most salutary plan, and the precepts for preserving the health of the soldiers."

Dr. Rush clearly understood and emphasized the importance of a disciplined health procedure for the soldiers. The responsible leadership for such a disciplined health routine was placed squarely upon the line officers. Rush placed the services of the physician almost secondary to the importance of the leadership of the commanding officers of the army.

In his directions Rush made five main points to the officers. First, dress should be of flannel instead of linen, as flannel was less "disposed to form miasmata, which produce fevers." [26] Second, diet should "consist chiefly of vegetables," well cooked. Spoiled meats and flour should be avoided. Rum was a part of army diet, but Rush cautioned against its overuse. "The use of rum, by gradually wearing away the powers of the system, lays the foundation of fevers, fluxes, jaundices, and the most of diseases which occur in military hospitals." He advised that the age-old mixture of vinegar and water be used as a substitute for rum. Third, personal cleanliness was important, including the frequent washing of the body, clothing, eating utensils and bedding. The hair was to be worn short on the neck, and combed frequently. The hands and face were to be washed daily, and the body was to be bathed at least three times a week. Fourth, Rush emphasized that the

---

[26] Even into the twentieth century, the use of flannel for covering the chest, usually accompanied with ointments and liniments, was a universal routine in the treatment of colds, bronchitis, pneumonia.

camps must be kept clean, moved frequently, and located away from the "effluvia" of swampy places. Fifth, Rush recognized the age-old problem of army and civilian personnel: that idleness is the bane of everyone, and that a disciplined attention to duty was necessary.

He enlisted as a physician to help General Washington. At the Battle of Princeton he attended a mortally wounded fellow physician, General Hugh Mercer.[27] In later years he wrote that while visiting Washington in his headquarters he observed Washington doodling on a piece of paper "Victory or Death," the countersign of Washington's victorious troops at Trenton a few days later.

Rush was appointed physician-general of the Middle Department of the Army, and was very energetic in learning the conditions of the soldiers and trying to improve them. He studied at first hand the privation and suffering at Valley Forge, during the winter of 1777-78, while General Howe and his English army lived in relative ease in Rush's native Philadelphia, only twenty miles away.

Rush constantly emphasized the need for food and clothing, cleanliness of person and surroundings, and fresh air and water. He wrote that "Hospitals are the sinks of human life in the army. They robbed the United States of more citizens than the sword." [28] He noted and deplored the apalling higher death-rate in the hospitals than in the marching army; but he recognized that the sickest patients went into the hospitals, while those less ill and less apt to die continued with the marching army.

It was a constant struggle for the army doctor to gain a status of authority and respect. The general concept about

---

[27] For an excellent biography of Dr. Hugh Mercer, *see* Joseph M. Waterman, *With Sword and Lancet* (Garrett & Massie, 1941). His service in the Battle of Princeton was as a General, not as a physician. His home and apothecary shop are maintained today by the American Pharmaceutical Society in Fredericksburg, Va.

[28] Quoted from Goodman, *Rush*, p. 88.

the Army surgeon was that he would take care of illness and injury when it occurred; but Rush asked for a participating authority regarding anything to do with the health of the soldiers — in a preventative way, including the duties demanded of them, their food and clothing and play — the encampments — a very imaginative and bold concept when the surgeons were having great difficulty even obtaining necessary medical supplies and food.[29]

Rush resigned his position as physician-general because of the poor medical care and graft in the army; these charges he placed on the head of Dr. William Shippen, Director-General of the Military Hospitals and Physician-in-Chief of the Continental Army. Rush carried the fight to a personal interview with General Washington, who, in the throes of many problems, referred Rush's charges to Congress. Rush, in his vehemence, took this action to be buck passing on the part of Washington and his resignation followed.

Rush never hesitated to offer criticism, by either word or pen, about anyone and anything when he thought it was just. A letter of his to Patrick Henry, in which he was critical of Washington, became entangled in the Conroy Cabal[30] against Washington; Rush later regretted this and tried to prevent the letter from being published. However unfortunate and regrettable this incident was, Rush was not guilty of disloyalty or treason; rather this humane and earnest man was moved to remonstrance by his loyalty to and concern for the soldiers of his country.

Smallpox was a dread disease in the Continental armies, second only to camp fever, and was credited with a mortality

[29] From Rush's *Notebook.*

[30] Thomas Conroy, an Irish immigrant, was obviously looking for trouble, and making it. He was able to make some temporary headway with plans to remove Gen. Washington from his command after the latter lost the battles of Brandywine and Germantown, and after Gate's impressive victory over Burgoyne.

rate of fifteen percent. As usual, where a problem existed, Benjamin Rush gave his attention to it. He became interested in the use of inoculation as a means of reducing the mortality rate, advocating that inductees be inoculated immediately upon entering the army, while they were in generally good health and were thus better able to resist the disease.[31] By this procedure, the mortality rate was reduced to one percent. That Rush believed in this procedure without reservation is attested to by his having inoculated his own children.

When Waterhouse, with the encouragement and assistance of Thomas Jefferson, introduced the smallpox vaccine to this country in 1800, Rush was one of fifty physicians who publicly recommended vaccination to the citizens of Philadelphia, and he predicted that it would annihilate smallpox within a few years. Thus, Rush had vaccination on his mind when Lewis was conferring with him about medical care for the Expedition; it is a reasonable assumption that he instructed Lewis in the technique of its use. Rush's ready recognition of the advantage of vaccination over inoculation gave contradiction to his critics who said he was a stubborn and opinionated man who would never change his mind.

In view of the fact that disease in the armies of the world has contributed much to their failures and consequently the causes, good or bad, for which they fought; and in view of the deplorable health conditions of the Revolutionary Army (with the death rate due to disease exceeding by far that due to combat), it is nothing short of miraculous that the American Revolution did not fold up because of the unhealthy condition of the soldiers, the political bickerings of Congress and

---

[31] Lewis had been inoculated with smallpox when serving in the army. He wrote to his mother from Pittsburgh on May 22, 1795: "I am at present billeted in the house of a Mrs. Butler in order to make preparations prescribed by the surgeons for taking the smallpox. . ." The preparations usually consisted primarily of the taking of strong purgatives.

the far less than universal support of the revolutionary cause by the colonists.

The many defeats inflicted upon the Revolutionary Army were discouraging to a soldier already despondent with hunger, inadequate clothing, and very poor medical attention. Washington's armies moved all over New England; whatever the military tactics of such maneuvering may have contributed to the ultimate victory, it is probable that the constant moving of the soldiers away from the accumulated filth and disease of entrenched camps — and hospitals — contributed in some degree to improving the health conditions, and thus to victory. ". . . the army was always more healthy when in motion, than in fixed camps."[32] Meriwether Lewis was later to make a similar observation when the Expedition was getting ready to start its homeward journey from Fort Clatsop. The small army of Lewis and Clark was fortunate that it was not attacked by a severe contagious disease, and that most of the time it was on the move.

---

[32] Tilton, *Economical Observations*, p. 33.

VII

Lewis Prepares to Go West

. . . A voyage which had formed a da[r]ling project of mine for the last ten years. Meriwether Lewis [1]

Thomas Jefferson had the utmost confidence in Meriwether Lewis, including his capacity to absorb important information and its significance. Although Lewis had no formal training in certain requisites for his future responsibilities, Jefferson knew that with minimal instruction he would rapidly acquire all of the knowledge and technique not already familiar to him.

To better equip Lewis for the anticipated varied responsibilities as leader of the Expedition, Jefferson requested assistance from certain of his friends who were authorities in the recognized center of erudition in the new United States — Philadelphia. Jefferson had become acquainted with these men during his political sojourns to Philadelphia and by association in the American Philosophical Society. Letters of introduction went to Benjamin Smith Barton, a physician but also a botanist associated with the University of Pennsylvania; to Caspar Wistar, also a physician and professor of anatomy at the University of Pennsylvania, and to Robert Patterson, professor of medicine at the university and destined to become Jefferson's Director of the Mint. These men were to combine their instructions to provide Lewis with the basic information and techniques in taking longitude and latitude and in properly describing and classifying plants and animals.

---

[1] Thwaites, *Journals*, i, p. 285.

Jefferson clearly had no plans for a physician to attend the Expedition,[2] so he also wrote to his close friend and co-signer of the Declaration of Independence, Dr. Benjamin Rush, on February 28, 1803, requesting his help in instructing Lewis about the health care of the men who would comprise the Corps of Discovery. No doubt the loquacious Rush, who had a penchant for being involved in any new project, gave Lewis plenty of medical advice.

Dr. Rush provided Meriwether Lewis with a list of health rules to follow in caring for the men under his command. These rules are variously worded and are usually summarized in ten separate statements. The original letter containing these rules has been lost, but Rush wrote them out in his *Common place Notebook*.[3] These rules which Rush committed to his notebook may not be exactly as stated in the communication sent to Jefferson,[4] but undoubtedly the general content is the

---

[2] Coues writes: ". . . the most serious defect in the organization of the Expedition was the lack of some trained scientist, who should also have been a medical man, and thus united the professional functions of physician, surgeon, and naturalist." Coues, H*istory of Lewis and Clark,* i, p. xx.

Lewis and Clark may have sought to take a botanist with them, to act as a "surgeon-herbalist," according to Susan Delano McKelvey in her *Botanical Exploration of the Trans-Mississippi West* (Arnold Arboretum, 1955), p. 68, fn. 3: "In *A Life of Travels,* Rafinesque recounts that, in 1804, . . . he had several offers of employment . . . 'I had once hesitated however when I was told that I might be admitted as Botanist in the expedition which Lewis & Clark were then preparing to survey the Missouri and cross the Oregon Mountains.'" Rafinesque explained that the danger didn't prevent him, but ". . . this journey did not promise any reward, while I had a more remunerative system in Sicily. . ." Constantine Samuel Rafinesque (1783-1840) was a self-taught botanist.

Lewis was to encounter Dr. Ewing Patterson at Wheeling, who seemed interested in going with the Expedition.

The question of why a naturalist-physician was not included in the Expedition is discussed in more detail in E. G. Chuinard, "Thomas Jefferson and the Corps of Discovery: Could He Have Done More?" *American West,* Vol. xxii, No. 6 (Nov. 1975), pp. 4-13.

[3] Rush's *Common-place Notebook* can be seen at the Library Company of Philadelphia (Ridgway).

[4] Eleven rules are frequently listed; *see* Jackson, *Letters,* p. 54. Rush lists 10 in his common-place notebook.

same. There is no evidence among the papers of Jefferson that he received these health rules from Rush or that he sent them on to Lewis. Rush was a copious notemaker and letter-writer, and it is very probable that he also provided Lewis with a personal copy.[5]

When Jefferson was developing plans to have André Michaux lead an expedition up the Missouri in 1793, he included among his instructions very little about the health care of the men of that expedition or of the Indians; however, his only reference to health does show that he was always concerned in this regard: "It is strongly recommended to you to expose yourself in no case to unnecessary dangers, whether such as might affect your health or your personal safety." [6] The more extensive instructions to Lewis about inquiries into the health status of the Indians and health instructions for the men are certainly reflective of Rush's influence.

The rules which Rush gave to Lewis constitute the ten health commandments of the Lewis and Clark Expedition:

1 Flannel worn next to the skin, especially in winter.
2 Always to take a little raw spirirts after being very wet or much fatigued; and as little as possible at any other time.
3 When you feel the least indisposition, fasting and rest; and diluting drinks for a few hours, take a sweat, and if costive take purge of two pills every four hours until they operate freely.
4 Unusual costiveness is often the sign of an approaching disease. When you feel it, take one or two of the opening pills.
5 Where salt cannot be had with your meat, steep it a day or two in common lye.
6 In difficult and laborious enterprises or marches, eating sparingly will enable you to bear them with less fatigue and more safety to your health.
7 Washing feet with spirit when chilled, and every morning with cold water.

---

5 Donald Jackson thinks so. *Ibid.*, p. 55.
6 *Ibid.*, p. 671.

8 Molasses or sugar with water with vit. [victuals] and for drink with meals.
9 Shoes without heels.[7]
10 Lying down when fatigued.

These rules reflect the general health practice of the time in giving attention to fever, with such things as purging, fasting, eating habits and the use of flannel. It is interesting to note Rush's admonition about protecting themselves against fatigue. And he need not have admonished them to apply cold water to their feet; they could not avoid this during a considerable extent of their journey. It is also interesting that Rush did not mention bleeding in his rules, but it is probable he discussed it with Lewis. The "opening pills" to be used in the third and fourth health commandments undoubtedly means "Dr. Rush's Bilious Pills."

His advice to wear shoes without heels meant that the men should wear moccasins. In previous writings Rush had drawn attention to his observations of Indian practices in regard to footwear and foot care. As has already been mentioned, the Indians wore moccasins in all weather, which permitted freer action of the feet muscles, and therefore better circulation, than did the stiff footwear of the white pioneers and soldiers. The Indians also slept with their feet to the fire. Rarely were Indians afflicted with frost bite, and by following Rush's precepts of foot care no man of the Expedition lost even one toe by freezing.

Dr. Rush also provided Meriwether Lewis with a list of questions to guide him in seeking information regarding

---

[7] The advice to use shoes without heels is rule no. 11 in the list used by Jackson, to which is added: "by affording equal action to all the muscles of the legs, will enable you to march with less fatigue than shoes made in the ordinary way." *Ibid.*, p. 54. Such muscle action promotes circulation and warmth as well as developing strength. Most of Dr. Rush's advice is of little pertinence in modern-day health care — except, as an orthopedist, I find constant cause to repeat Rule No. 7 to women who seek care of their feet!

DOCTOR RUSH'S LIST OF HEALTH RULES FOR LEWIS
The original list has been lost, but this list was
hastily scratched in his Commonplace Notebook.
Courtesy of the American Philosophical Society.

A LIST OF MEDICINES
Purchased by Meriwether Lewis from the drug firm of Gillaspy
and Strong through the Schuykill Arsenal of Philadelphia.
Courtesy of the National Archives, Washington.

health practices of the Indians. As can be seen by the listing of these questions under the related topics of physical history and medicine, morals, and religion, there is reflected the same association which prevails to some extent even to this day: that the beliefs and practices of morals and religion have considerable effect on health.

Questions to Merryweather Lewis before he went up the Missouri

i. Physical history & medicine

What are the acute diseases of the Indians? Is the bilious fever attended with a black vomit.

Is Goiture, apoplexy, palsy, Epilepsy, madness . . . ven. Disease known among them?

What is their state of life as to longevity?

At what age do the women begin and cease to menstruate?

At what age do they marry? How long do they suckle the Children?

What is the provision of their Childrn. after being weaned?

The state of the pulse as to frequency in the morning, at noon & at night — before & after eating? What is its state in childhood. Adult life, & old age? The number of strokes counted by the quarter of a minute by glass, and multiplied by four will give its frequency in a minute.

What are their Remidies?

Are artificial discharges of blood ever used among them?

In what manner do they induce sweating?

Do they ever use voluntary fasting?

At what time do they rise — their Baths?

What is the diet — manner of cooking & times of eating among the Indians? How do they preserve their food?

ii. Morals

1 What are their vices?
2 Is Suicide common among them? — ever from love?
3 Do they employ any substitute for ardent spirits to promote intoxication?
4 Is murder common among them, & do they punish it with death?

iii. Religion

1   What Affinity between their religious Ceremonies & those of
    the Jews?
2   Do they use animal Sacrifices in their worship?
3   What are the principal Objects of their worship?
4   How do they dispose of their dead, and with what Ceremonies
    do they inter them?

    May 17. 1803   B. Rush

Clark prepared a longer and more comprehensive list dated
1804 (*see* Appendix iii), probably including suggestions from
various sources and his own reading. Rush's list, given to
Lewis, as printed above, is really not representative of the
usually garrulous communications of Rush, and not at all
representative of either the extent of his medical knowledge
or his medical interest. This deficiency is particularly glaring
for Rush's omission of any reference to smallpox as well as
little reference to his favorite treatment of bleeding. Dr.
Rush's instructions regarding the observation of the Indians'
pulse reflects his reliance upon the state of the pulse in determining the patient's sickness and the required amount of
bleeding. It may be that Jefferson or Rush, or both, helped
Clark compose this comprehensive list.[8]

Lewis had the benefit of advice from the various experts in
Philadelphia regarding instruments and materials he could
obtain in order to enable him to carry out the responsibilities
for which they had trained him. Likewise, Lewis had the
benefit of advice from Dr. Rush regarding the list of medicines
which he should procure for the purpose of maintaining the
health care of his men. It is also probable that he received
medical advice from Dr. Benjamin Smith Barton, inasmuch as
Lewis purchased a copy of Barton's *Elements of Botany* to
take with him on the Expedition.[9]

---

[8] This list can be seen at the Missouri Hist. Soc. in Clark's handwriting. *See*
Jackson's footnote to this list, *Letters*, p. 161.

Lewis obtained all the medical supplies from the drug firm of Gillaspay and Strong of Philadelphia, through Israel Wheelen, purveyor of the Schuylkill arsenal in Philadelphia, and receipted for them himself. This final list was more extensive than an earlier one prepared by Lewis, [10] and probably reflects advice received from his several medical contacts in Philadelphia.

Bill of Gillaspay & Strong for Medicine [11]

Israel Wheelen Purveyor Bought of Gillaspay & Strong the following articles for the use of M. Lewis Esquire on his tour up the Mississippi River, and supplied by his Order: — Viz.

15 lb. Pulv. Cort. Peru	$30.00		4 oz. Laudanum		.50
½ lb. " Jalap	.67		2 lb. Ung. Basilic Flav.,	.50	1.00
½ lb. " Rhei (Rhubarb)	1.00		1 lb. " e lap Cailmin.	.50	.50
4 oz. " Ipecacuan	1.25		1 lb. " Epispastric		1.00
2 lb. " Crem. Tart.	.67		1 lb. " Mercuriale		1.25
2 oz. Gum Camphor	.40		1. Emplast. Diach. S.		.50
1 lb. " Assafoetic	1.00		1. Set Pocket Insts. small		9.50
½ lb. " Opii Turk. opt	2.50		1. " Teeth " "		2.25
¼ lb. " Tragacanth	.37		1. Clyster Syringe		2.75

[9] Dr. Benjamin Smith Barton (1766-1815) was a physician and botanist. His textbook, *Elements of Botany* (1803), was the first American textbook on botany. Lewis paid $6 for this book — not a small price in those days. Botany was closely related to medicine — many of the "ship's surgeons" of Lewis and Clark's time were really botanists, for instance Archibald Menzies (1754-1842), who served as surgeon-botanist on the *Discovery,* under Capt. George Vancouver in 1790.

Lewis also carried, on loan from Barton, to the Pacific and back *The History of Louisiana,* by Antoine LePage du Pratz — for this story *see* Cutright, "Lewis and Clark and Du Pratz," *Bull. of Mo. Hist. Soc.,* Vol. xxi, No. 1 (Oct. 1964), pp. 31-35.

[10] Jackson, *Letters,* pp. 73-74.

[11] A similar but abbreviated list of medicines was ordered by Dr. John McLoughlin of the Hudson's Bay Company, writing from Ft. Vancouver on Nov. 18, 1830, to Capt. William Ryan: "½ lbs. Gum Camphor, ½ lbs. Sulphar Quinine, 12 lbs. Best Peruvian Bark, 1 lbs. acetate Lead, 1 lbs. Crude Opium, 20 lbs. Epsom salts, 4 lbs. Rhubarb Powder." The large quantity of Peruvian bark indicates the extensive prevalence of ague (malaria) in the Columbia River Valley and its tributaries. Peruvian bark constitutes a large proportion of both the McLoughlin and the Lewis medical lists.

6 lb. Sal Glauber	.10	.60
2 lb. " Nitri	.33½	.67
2 lb. Copperas		.10
6 oz. Sacchar. Saturn. opt.		.37
4 oz. Calomel		.75
1 oz. Tartar Emetic		.10
4 oz. Vitriol Alb.		.12
½ lb. Columbo Rad.		1.00
¼ lb. Elix. Vitriol		.25
¼ lb. Ess. Meth. pip.		.50
¼ lb. Bals. Copaiboe		.37
¼ lb. " Traumat.		.50
2 oz. Magnesia		.20
¼ lb. Indian Ink		1.50
2 oz. Gun Elastic		.37
2 oz. Nutmegs		.75
2 oz. Cloves		.31
4 oz. Cinnamon		.20
		$46.52

4. Penis do.		1.00
3. Best Lancets	.80	2.40
1. Tourniquet		3.50
2 oz. Patent Lint		.25
50 doz. Bilious Pills to Order		
of Dr. Rush	.10	5.00
6 Tin Canisters	.25	1.50
3 8 oz. Gd. Stopd. bottles		1.20
5 4 oz. Tinctures do		1.85
6 4 oz. Salt Mo.		2.22
1 Walnut Chest		4.50
1 Pine do.		1.20
		$90.69

Gillaspay and Strong were located at 103 South Second and 234 High streets. Jackson states that the proprietors were probably George Gillaspay, M.D. and Joseph Strong, M.D.[12] This drug firm long ago went out of existence, and there are no known records remaining from its operation. [13] There is no known prescription extant in the handwriting of Benjamin Rush; this has been checked with several of Rush's descendants, some of whom are medical practitioners today.

The list of medical supplies contains one walnut chest and one pine chest, undoubtedly for the purpose of carrying the medical supplies. This notation is interesting in view of the

[12] Jackson, *Letters,* p. 81.

[13] The extensive library and museum of the Philadelphia College of Pharmacy and Science has no additional information regarding this firm. Miss Gertrude D. Hess, Assistant Librarian of the American Philosophical Society wrote in answer to my inquiry: "We have checked the Philadelphia Directories from 1804 through 1811 and find no further listing for the drug firm of Gillaspay and Strong."

tradition that Dr. Saugrain in St. Louis later provided Lewis and Clark with a medicine chest and certain medicines.

Although he undoubtedly made suggestions about the drugs to be taken on the Expedition and their dosages, there is no evidence that Dr. Rush made out the entire specific list of medicines which Lewis purchased. Many of these medicines would be found in the medicine cabinet of most families of the times. There are still people alive who can remember the unpleasantness of assafoedita, a substance totally devoid of any medicinal value, except that it was so ill-smelling that it kept everyone away from the bearer, including those who might have a contagious disease.[14] Lewis and Clark do not record in the Journals that they used this medicine — which probably was appreciated by the men. It may have been used as a means of locating the medicine chest!

The four ounces of laudanum (tincture of opium) seem a small amount for the relief of the amount of pain to be anticipated in such a hazardous journey of thirty to forty people for some thirty months. Perhaps an additional supply was provided by Dr. Saugrain in St. Louis.

The list of medicines includes one substance that unquestionably was specified by Dr. Rush: "50 doz. Bilious Pills to Order of B. Rush." There are several references throughout the journals where some ailing corpsman was given "Rush's bilious pills" by one of the captain-doctors, and often with the added statement, "they operated very well." The probable content of these "bilious pills" was jalap [15] and calomel, [16] each

---

[14] The 1805 *Edinburgh New Dispensatory* states about assafoedita: "It acts as a Stimulant, anti-spasmodic, expectorant, and emmenagogue and amphelmintic." *See* Duncan, *Edinburgh New Dispensatory* (1805), p. 189.

[15] Pulvis (powder) jalap — this word refers to Jalapa, a city in Mexico, where the roots of the Exogonium jalapa and other similar plants were found useful for their cathartic action, with beneficial effect in constipation and water retention of the body. The powder dosage was usually 15-30 grains. *Ibid.*

[16] *See* footnote on page 133.

in the amount of ten or fifteen grains. Such a purgative combination is not used today, and such a dosage would be considered quite heroic; however, this was not an unusual dosage in the hands of a purger like Dr. Rush.

The list also included staples still used today, such as mercury and laudanum (tincture of opium).[17] Opium, of course, was used mainly by Lewis and Clark as a pain-killer, although it undoubtedly had its effect also as a sedative. The sal nitri or saltpetre was used as a diuretic and diaphoretic, for fevers and probably gonorrhea. The half-pound of gum Opii Turk. would have been used to supplement the laudanum. This is the common poppy, the milk of which, when dried, yields opium.

The total expense for medicines and related equipment was $90.60 — not much more than the cost of a modern-day prescription for an antibiotic! One-third of the total amount, thirty dollars, was spent for fifteen pounds of Peruvian bark,[18]

[17] Laudanum was concocted by Phillippus Paracelsus (1493-1541) about 1510. *Medical Properties and Uses.* "Opium is a stimulant and narcotic. Taken by a healthy person, in moderate doses, it increases the force, fulness, and frequency of the pulse, augments the temperature of the skin, invigorates the muscular system, quickens the senses, animates the spirits, and gives new energy to the intellectual faculties. Its operation, while thus extending to all parts of the system, is directed with peculiar force to the brain, the functions of which it excites sometimes even to intoxication or delirium. In a short time this excitation subsides; a calmness of the corporeal actions, and a delightful placidity of mind succeed; and the individual, insensible to painful impressions, forgetting all sources of care and anxiety, submits himself to a current of undefined and unconnected, but pleasing fancies; and is conscious of no other feeling than that of a quiet and vague enjoyment. At the end of half an hour or an hour from the administration of the narcotic, all consciousness is lost in sleep." Geo. B. Wood, and Franklin Boche, *U.S. Dispensatory I* (Phila., 1834), p. 483.

[18] Pulvis Cort. Peru. This is also known as balsam of Peru and as Cinchona. This drug was named for a Countess of Chinchon. It is of the genus of the rubiaceous trees of South America. The bark of this tree contains many alkaloids, the most important ones of which are quinine and quinidine. The bark was used in the crude stage at the time of Lewis and Clark for making concoctions and powders, its specific alkaloids not being known. The bark was also used generally as a tonic; it also had a febrifugal action (to counteract fever). The *U.S. Dispensatory* (1934

indicating that the captains anticipated that "fevers" would be the main health concern of the Expedition. Powders and concoctions of Peruvian bark were used in the treatment of all sorts of fevers, most of which were ague, or malaria. It was not until 1845 that quinine, the active ingredient, was extracted from Peruvian bark.

There is no record anywhere in the principal journals indicating specifically that one of the members had an attack of malaria; however, Lewis records in his journal made during his trip down the Ohio River that he had one such attack of "fevers and chills." In view of the great prevalence of malaria, and of the preparations made for the treatment of these chills and fevers by taking along such a large quantity of Peruvian bark, it is reasonable to conjecture that the absence of recordings in the journals about any malarial attacks was because they were too commonplace to mention.[19] The Peruvian bark, however, was used extensively for many conditions, as the journals record. It is known now to have a tonic, astringent, and antiseptic effect. David[20] calls it the "aspirin of its day."

Fortunately Lewis took along plenty of ingredients to concoct "eye-wash" which they used for diplomatic purposes on the return trip. These drugs included white vitriol (zinc sul-

ed.) mentions that it was the Jesuit missionaries who went to Peru, and not the Indians, who first used an infusion of the bark as a febrifuge in the treatment of tertial ague. Joseph DiPalma said: "Quinine, despite its imperfections, can truly be said to be the drug which changed the destinies of nations. It alone made possible invasion and exploitation of tropical countries." Joseph R. DiPalma, M.D., ed., *Drill's Pharmacolage and Medicine* (3rd ed., New York: McGraw Hill, 1965), p. 1376.

19 The omnipresence of ague in the Ohio and Mississippi valleys is attested by James: "Intermitting fevers are of such universal occurrence in every part of the newly settled country to the west, that every person is well acquainted with the symptoms, and has his favorite method of treatment." James, *Account of an Expedition*, ii, p. 322.

20 Norman David, M.D., professor emeritus of pharmacology of the Univ. of Oregon Medical School, to whom I am greatly indebted for information, advice, and criticism of this chapter.

phate) and sugar of lead (Sacchr. Saturn., lead acetate). The Indians all along the Expedition's route were affected with eye trouble, the causes of which probably included one or more of the following: gonorrhea (ophthalmia neonatorium in the newborn), syphilis, myopia, trachoma (a contagious disease which forms granular growths that obscure the vision), and purulent infections. The vitriols were also used for eye complaints. As with blue beads, Lewis probably wished he had had a larger supply of eye medicines with him, because of the great demand for them by the Indians.

The captains were well supplied with the means of treating their men with the time-honored methods of bleeding and purging, but the medical supply of emetics was comparatively scant. Ipicacuan, obtained from the roots of a Brazilian plant, was generally a favorite producer of vomiting, but the journals indicate it was used sparingly on the Expedition. The gum camphor was used as a stimulant and diaphoretic. The spices were used in decoctions and salves to improve the flavor and aroma.

Also included in Lewis' list of medical supplies was a set of pocket instruments and "one set of teeth instruments." There is no record of dental problems in the journals, except for one or two cases of toothache, even though it is probable that the treatment of syphilis with mercury produced gingivitis and some loose teeth, and the scurvy may have effected the teeth similarly.

The one "Clyster syringe" — clyster is an old word for enema — would seem an inadequate supply for the number of men and the length of time of the Expedition. But it is probable that when problems of constipation arose, the men disdained the clyster syringe in preference to Rush's "bilious pills." Besides Rush's pills, the medicine chest contained several other drugs with purgative effects: jalap, rhubarb, cream of tartar, Glauber's salts, calomel, magnesia, ipecacuan and assafoedita.

Lewis would supplement his medicine chest of purchased drugs with many plants from the countryside: onions, "cous" (Lomatium cous) and slippery elm (ulums fulva) to make poultices; bear's oil and beeswax to be mixed with gunpowder to make ointments — a favorite frontier practice used because of the availability of the ingredients. Plants of pleasant flavor were used, as wild ginger (asarium caudatum), in contradiction to the generally held belief then that the worst tasting medicines were the most effective. Lewis' personal favorite was a decoction of the choke cherry (prunus virginiana).

The inclusion of "4 Penis do." — penis syringes — indicated that the captain-physicians expected gonorrhea to be one of their medical problems, and that they were prepared to treat it with the standard urethral irrigations of the day. The journals record no specific mention of such treatment, however. Saccharum saturni and the balsam of copaiba were the probable drugs used.

The supply of plasters and ointments was essentially innocuous medicines for topical application for cuts, abrasions and blisters. The Bals. Traumat (compound tincture of Benzoin) was also used for dressing abrasions — still its favorite use today.

"3 Best Lancets" and a tourniquet (the latter costing $3.50!) show that Dr. Rush had influenced Lewis regarding the necessity of bleeding, although Lewis, as a military commander of his day, undoubtedly would have provided himself with the instruments for blood-letting.

Lewis also receipted for thirty Gallons of "strong, Spt. wine," for a value of $77.20 — almost as much as was spent for medicinal supplies. [21] It may be fair to consider the wine

[21] Jackson, Letters, p. 97.

as a part of the medicinal supplies, particularly when Lewis was to take on a supply of whiskey in St. Louis. Also, in the list of supplies from private vendors,[22] Lewis has listed drugs in the amount of $77.20 to D. Jackson as Item #21 — the same amount of money paid to the same provider for the thirty gallons of wine. D. Jackson, who provided the wine, listed himself as a druggist at the address of 26 South Third Street in Philadelphia.[23] It cannot be determined from reading the journals whether the thirty gallons of wine were used for medicinal purposes or not.

The item of "8 Oz. Gd. Stopd. Bottles" is interesting. Why would Lewis hazard carrying any of his valuable drugs in breakable bottles? Were these empty bottles to be used later for the division of the medicinal supplies when caches were left at various places on the way west, or division of the medicines when the Expedition divided on the way home?

An important purchase also made by Israel Wheelen for Lewis was "193 lbs. of Portable Soup." This portable soup was contained in lead canisters[24] and may have been either a dry powder or a thick liquid substance. There is no known record of its exact composition; however, it probably was very similar to the portable soups used by armed forces of the time. Cutbush describes the preparation of a portable soup, or "Tablettes de bouillon (Under Direction to Nurses and Orderly Men for the Preparation of the diet, &c. for the sick.)":

> Take calves' feet, 4; the lean part of a rump of beef 12 pounds; fillet of veal 3 pounds; leg of mutton 10 pounds. These are to be boiled in a sufficient quantity of water and the scum taken off. When the meat becomes very tender, the liquor is to be separated

---

[22] *Ibid.*, p. 78.   [23] *Ibid.*, p. 88.

[24] Lewis specifically mentions the portable soup being contained in "canisters" in his note of Sept. 18, 1805; also in his list of supplies he includes "32 Cannisters of P. Soup," Thwaites, *Journals*, vii, p. 239.

from it by expression; and when cold, the fat must be carefully taken off. The jelly-like substance must then be dissolved over the fire and clarified with five or six whites of eggs. It is then to be salted to the taste and boiled down to the consistency of paste, when it is to be poured out on a marble table and cut into pieces, either round or square, and dried in a stove room. Then perfectly hard, they should be put up in close vessels of tine or glass. Powdered rice, beans, peas, barley, celery, with any grateful aromatice may be added; but for the use of the sick it should be made plain.

It may be simply made either of beef, mutton, or veal.[25]

Lewis wrote from Fredricktown on April 15, 1803, to General William Irvine regarding the preparation of portable soup for the Expedition.[26] The soup was prepared by Francois Baillet, cook at 21 North Ninth Street, Philadelphia, who presented a bill on May 30, 1803, for 193 pounds of Portable Soup in the amount of $289.50.[27] The soup was ready in plenty of time and Lewis receipted for it [28] and took it with him overland to Pittsburgh, where he was to embark on the Ohio River.

DeVoto[29] called portable soup an army experimental iron ration. This is hardly a correct description; it was not particularly an iron ration except to the degree that iron was contained in the meat, and it was considerably past the

---

[25] Cutbush, *Preserving the Health,* pp. 314-15.

[26] Gen. William Irvine (1741-1804) was a physician and supt. of military stores with headquarters in Philadelphia. This letter was advertised for sale by the American Autograph Shop, Merion Station, Pa., in Dec., 1939. The advertisement said in part: "Investigation in connection with the most reliable experts of his time convinced him [Lewis] that PORTABLE SOUP, what we would call CANNED SOUP today, was the most reliable and nourishing article, as necessary for the success of the expedition as life itself." Quantity, price and date of delivery were discussed, but apparently not composition. This letter is currently owned by Mrs. Grace Lewis Miller of St. Louis, and is not available for review. However, Mrs. Miller wrote in answer to my inquiry: "In this letter there are no details or directions pertaining to the composition of this soup."

[27] Jackson, *Letters,* p. 28.   [28] *Ibid.,* p. 82.

[29] DeVoto, *Course of Empire,* p. 505.

experimental stage, having been used, in various forms, by armed services of different countries for many years.

Cutbush also gives directions for using the portable soup:

> To make soup from this article, one or two cakes must be dissolved in a pint of boiling water, to which may be added two or three teaspoonsful of powdered rice, or whole rice boiled soft; then add a little dry celery powder or parsley; sometimes a little salt, pepper, cloves, and wine may be added, but this should never be done, unless by direction of the surgeon. If the portable soup be of the consistency of a jelly, in a canister, one tablespoonful will be sufficient for a pint of water. It should never be boiled; as it renders the whole unpleasant, and gives it the taste of glue.[30]

Sir John Pringle (1707-1782) also described the preparation of portable soup: "Having by long boiling evaporated the most cutrescent parts of the meat, [it] is reduced to the consistency of a glue, which in effect it is, and will like other glues, in a dry place, keep sound for years together." [31]

This portable soup became a life-saving measure to the Expedition at times, particularly on the return trip through the Rockies. It might have been more palatable to the men if they had had the several ingredients to add which Cutbush mentioned. And it may have been something of the consistency of glue, inasmuch as the men had to melt snow to obtain the water to mix with the soup. Lewis had the portable soup put in canisters, also indicating that it was a paste or fluid substance. Lead cannisters were then melted to make bullets.

A review of the Philadelphia newspapers in 1803 provides a background for reflection on the list of medicines which Lewis assembled for the Expedition. These papers include advertisements for Dr. Bardwell's Reanimating Solar Tinc-

---

30 Cutbush, *Preserving the Health*, p. 309.

31 Sir John Pringle, *A Discourse upon some late Improvements of the Means of Preserving the Health of Mariners* (London, 1776). Pringle has been called the Father of Modern Military Medicine.

ture, Dr. Atkinson's Genuine Essence of Mustard, and Hamilton's Grand Restorative. The latter preparation was good for "intemperance, lowness of spirits, impurity of blood, hysterical afflictions, inward weakness, barreness, melancholy, gout in the stomach, impotency, obstinate gleets." Lewis and Clark were to use "eye water" frequently among the Indians, but Lewis did not take along some of Dr. Hahn's Genuine Eye Water as advertised in the *Aurora* of March 5, 1803, nor did he add to the supply of Rush's bilious pills some of Dr. Hahn's anti-bilious pills. These pills may have been better than Dr. Rush's according to the advertisement which stated that "they had been found remarkably efficacious in promoting and curing disorders attendant on long voyages."

The *Aurora* of March 2, 1803, contained an advertisement by Dr. John Redmond Coxe about the advantages of vaccination. Although vaccination had been introduced into this country first in Boston, the Philadelphia physicians were quick to adopt this new treatment. It became widely used because of the united urgings of the outstanding physicians of Philadelphia, including Rush. It would be consistent with his enthusiasm for him to urge Lewis to include vaccination materials in his medical purchases. However, there is no specific evidence in this regard, and no record that he gave any instructions to Lewis in its use, although it can be reasonably assumed that the enthusiastic Rush would not have passed up such an opportunity. Lewis' supply of "kinepox material" was given to him by Thomas Jefferson.

It may have been much simpler for Lewis to have engaged the services of a Chinese doctor to take care of the anticipated multiple ills of the Expedition. The *Aurora* carried an advertisement on March 9, 1803, to the effect that "Dr. John Howard, late from Canton   .   .   .   will engage perfectly to cure the cancer, king's evil, gout, dropsy, rheumatism, consumption, colic, cramps, stone or gravel, piles, old ulcers or sores, lameness, deafness, sore eyes, fits, yellow fever, white swellings, phthisic, etc." The advertisement included a list of testimonials for the cure of all these diseases.

John Harrison's Drug and Chemical House advertised the following medicinal substances: juniper berries, verdigris, pearl barley, Glauber's salt, sulphur, crem tartar, allum, copperous, rumca stone, colombo root, cantharides, liquorice ball, red bark, rhubarb root, oil of vitriol, spirits of wine, sweet spirits of nitre, spirits of hartshorn, opium, tapisa, gum myrrh, sago, to list a few.[32]

Lewis was probably too busy in Philadelphia to read the *Aurora* thoroughly. If he had done so, he would have seen the advertisement on March 1, 1803, for an important new book: *MacKenzie's Voyages.*[33] This book was to be studied by Lewis with increasing respect as he and Clark met their own tribulations on their westward journey — eleven years later.

Lewis took with him several books to help him on the Expedition. One of these was *Owen's Dictionary,* of which Jackson says: "Perhaps the most worthwhile aspect of the dictionary to an exploring party was the material on medicine . . . it dealt at length with the ills of man and remedies then in use." [34] It is very doubtful if this dictionary, however reputable, would provide Lewis and Clark with a medical armamentarium much more useful than the advertising doc-

---

[32] Perhaps Lewis recognized what was later expressed in the *Journal of Health*, Vol. I, p. 93, published by an Assoc. of Physicians in Philadelphia in 1830: "The whole history of quackery shows that no reliance can be placed on the pompous annunciations of the venders of nostrums. . ."

[33] Alexander Mackenzie, *Voyages Through the Continent of North America* (London, 1801). Mackenzie had crossed to the Pacific in what is now Canada. Jefferson purchased a copy of it on June 22, 1803 and it undoubtedly intensified his efforts to get his plans underway for an American expedition. The two captains were conversant with it and referred to considerable information in it. Jackson, *Letters,* p. 56.   [34] Jackson, "Books," p. 12.

tors and druggists of Philadelphia, and certainly it was not as authoritative as Dr. Rush.

During the two years that Lewis lived at Monticello with Jefferson as his private secretary, he undoubtedly studied in Jefferson's medical library.[35] This would be consistent with Jefferson having Lewis seek medical instruction from Dr. Rush, and also with Lewis' own natural interest in medicine and health.

Lewis had all of his medical supplies assembled and receipted for by March 27, 1803. His other supplies were also ready, and he had received all of his instructions. He then returned to Washington preparatory to his departure to the West. In his instructions to Lewis dated June 20, 1803, Jefferson wrote: "Your situation as Secretary of the President of the u.s. has made you acquainted with the objects of my confidential message of Jan. 18, 1803 to the legislature. . ."[36] It would be interesting if today we could listen to a tape recording of the conversations between President Jefferson and Meriwether Lewis during their last days together — here was the mingled relationship of the President and his secretary, of the father and his son, of the author and the executor of the Expedition.

On July 2, 1803, Lewis wrote his mother from Washington: "The day after tomorrow I shall set out for the Western Country; . . . For its fatiegues I feel myself perfectly prepared, nor do I doubt my health and strength of constitution to bear me through it; I go with the most perfect preconviction in my own mind of returning safe and hope therefore that you will not suffer yourself to indulge any anxiety for my safety."[37]

---

[35] Jefferson's library included many medical books; see Appen. i.

[36] Jackson, *Letters*, p. 61.

[37] From the Meriwether Lewis letters, Mo. Hist. Soc.

VIII

Down the Ohio

. . . I was seized with a violent ague. . . Meriwether Lewis

Jefferson had already demonstrated many times his utmost faith in Meriwether Lewis. However, he also thought of any possible risk to the Expedition and insurance against it. Thus he suggested to Lewis that he seek a co-leader, leaving this person entirely to the choice of Lewis, and authorized Lewis to give him a captaincy. On June 19, 1803, before he left Washington, Lewis wrote his old friend William Clark, who was in Louisville, proposing that he accompany him as a leader of the Expedition. His long explanatory letter stated in part: "From the long and uninterupted friendship and confidence which has subsisted between us I feel no hesitation in making to you the following communication under the fulest impression that it will be held by you inviolably secret untill I see you, or you shall hear again from me." Lewis then told Clark about the proposed Expedition, and adds: ". . . when descending the Ohio it shall be my duty by enquiry to find out and engage some good hunters, stout, healthy, unmarried men, accustomed to the woods, and capable of bearing bodily fatigue in a pretty considerable degree. . ."

Lewis described his plans for wintering in the neighborhood of St. Louis while assembling and training his expeditionary force, and added, "I shall engage some French traders at Illinois to attend me to my wintering ground with a sufficient quantity of flour, pork &c. to serve them plentifully during the winter, and thus being able to set out in the Spring with a healthy and vigorous party. . ."

Lewis recounted to Clark the details of the objects of the Expedition, including obtaining general information about the Indians such as "the diseases prevalent among them and remedies they use;" — a concise outline of the objects of the Expedition similar to what Jefferson had given to Lewis.

Lewis then came to the pertinent part of his letter:

> If therefore there is anything under those circumstances, in this enterpries, which would enduce you to participate with me in its fatiegues, its dangers and its honors, believe me there is no man on earth with whom I should feel equal pleasure in sharing this as with yourself; I make this communication with the privity of the President, who expresses an anxious wish that you would consent to join me in this enterprise; he has authorized me to say that in the event of your accepting this proposition he will grant you a captain's commission. . .

Clark answered from Clarksville on July 18, 1803 in which he offered to "cheerfully join" with Lewis and "partake of the dangers, difficulties, and fatigue, and anticipate the honors and rewards of the result of such enterprise, should we be successful in accomplishing it. This is an undertaking fraited with many difeculties, but My friend I do assure you that no man lives whith whome I would perfur to undertake Such a Trip &c. as yourself. . ."

In a subsequent letter written from Louisville on July 24, 1803, Clark stated: "I have temperally engaged some men for the enterprise of a description calculated to work and go thro those labours and fatigues which will be necessary. Several young men (Gentlemens sons) have applyed to accompany us — as they are not accustomed to labour and as that is a verry assential part of the services required of the party, I am causious in giveing them any encouragement." [1]

---

[1] The letters cited above are found in Jackson, *Letters,* p. 57 and 112.

Lewis acknowledged Clark's acceptance in a letter dated August 3, in which he said, ". . . be assured I feel myself much gratifyed with your decision; for I could neither hope, wish, nor expect from a union with any man on earth, more perfect support or further aid in the discharge of the several duties of my mission, than that, which I am confident I shall derive from being associated with yourself."[2] The correspondence between these two commanders reflects the deep respect and confidence and mutual trust which abided between them throughout the journey, and which undoubtedly was reflected upon the men, preventing any of the uneasiness that would certainly accompany a distraught relationship between the captains.

Clark promptly became busy in Kentucky, carefully assembling a group of promising young men. His care is reflected in his letter to Lewis from Louisville on August 21: "The young men that I have engaged or rather promised to take on this expedition are (four, &c.) the best woodsmen & Hunters, of young men in this part of the countrey . . . stout likely fellows . . . A judicious choice of our party is of the greatest importance to the success of this vast enterprise."[3] These men being assembled by Clark were to become known as the "nine young men from Kentucky," and they formed a sturdy and talented heart of the corps of the Expedition.

This exchange of letters between Lewis and Clark in which they repeatedly emphasize the importance of the health and endurance of the potential recruits is most interesting in consideration of Clark having resigned from the Army in 1795 due to ill health. His health must have improved in order for him to be so eager to "partake of the dangers, difficulties, and fatigue" with which the Expedition was "fraited." However,

---

[2] *Ibid.*, p. 115.
[3] *Ibid.*, pp. 117-18.

Clark was "unwell" much of the time during the Expedition, apparently with rheumatism, and probably with ague.

Lewis left Washington, D.C., on July 5, 1803, and proceeded overland with a wagon and supplies to Pittsburgh. His journey was leisurely and uneventful, and he did not keep a diary about this short portion of his journey to the west. Pittsburgh was to be his departure point — Lewis designated it as "The intended point of embarcation   .   .   ." down the Ohio River, the Belle Riviere of the French. The Ohio River was one of the great avenues to the west; hunters, soldiers and families gathered from the north and south and converged to meet on this waterway. Overland travel was developing, particularly along the Great Lakes in the north and through the Cumberland Gap into the bluegrass country. But Lewis' choice of the Ohio waterway was the popular and easier route, even though still somewhat perilous to the larger boats of the white men, and still populated along its banks with red men ready to resist the increasing intrusions of these white men. Lewis left Pittsburgh on August 31, 1803, after considerable delay in getting his keel-boat made and assembling a crew.[4]

Because of the low water, Lewis used a couple of wagons for some of the transportation at the beginning of his journey, rather than overload the boat. It was not long before he was almost called upon to exhibit his medical skill. He brought his boat to shore on Brunot's Island,[5] about three miles below Pittsburgh, and permitted a friend to try his air gun.[6]

---

[4] Lt. Moses Hooke states that Lewis left Pittsburgh on Sept. 1. Jackson, *Letters*, p. 199. Although Lewis' first journal entry gives Aug. 30 as his departure date, from other documents it is evident that the actual date of the departure was Aug. 31. *Ibid., p.* 120. Hooke was Lewis' next choice for a fellow commander if Clark had not accepted the offer. It might have been the Lewis and Hooke Expedition — *see* Don Holm, "The Lewis and Hooke Expedition," *Portland Oregonian* (Dec. 12, 1965).

An interesting aspect of the six-week delay of Lewis at Pittsburgh is related in Chuinard, "A Medical Mystery at Fort Clatsop," *We Proceed On*, Vol. III, No. 2.

The ball passed through the hat of a woman about 40 yards distant cuting her temple about the fourth of a diameter of the ball; shee fell instantly and the blood gus (h)ing from her temple we were all in the greatest consternation suppose(d) she was dead by (but) in a minute she revived to our enexprassible satisfaction, and by examination we found the wound by no means mortal or even dangerous. . .[7]

Lewis and his men coasted along with the current, although he was fretful of the slow progress made necessary by the shallow water. Probably his crewmen were unfamiliar with the relatively uncharted Ohio River. But his keelboat held up well on the uncertain river and with the uncertain crew, and none of his goods were lost or damaged.

He wrote in his journal of September 8:[8]

. . . I here [Wheeling] also met with Dr. Patterson the son of the professor of mathematicks in the University of Philada he expressed a great desire to go with me   I consented providing he could get ready by three the next evening [afternoon] he thought he could and instantly set about it . . .   the Dr was to have taken his medicine with him which was a small assortment of about one hundred L [pounds] value [9] . . .   Dr could not get ready I waited untill thre[e] this evening and then set out. . .

Bakeless simply states that the dilatory doctor was too slow.[10]

---

[5] Brunot's Island was named for its owner, Dr. Felix Brunot. Very little was known of the qualifications of this doctor except that he was described as "skilled in the practice of physic." Whatever his qualifications, he seems to have been absent at the time of this incident. *See* Thwaites, *Early Western Travels*, IV, p. 93.

[6] Although there are several references in the journals to Lewis' air gun, there is no detailed description of it. For a good description of the working of the air gun *see* William R. Barbour, "The Guns of Lewis and Clark," *The Gun Digest*, 18th edition (1964), pp. 38-45. *See also* Roy Chatters, "The Enigmatic Lewis and Clark Airgun," *The Record*, Friends of the Library of Wash. St. Univ., Vol. XXXIV, (1973).

[7] Quaife, "Journals of Lewis and Ordway," p. 31.   [8] *Ibid.*, p. 39.

[9] This seems to be a very high value compared to the $90.69 worth of medicine purchased by Lewis in Philadelphia. It probably represents an exaggeration on the part of Dr. Patterson.   [10] Bakeless, *Partners in Discovery*, p. 102.

This reference to Dr. Patterson raises some observations and questions. Thomas Jefferson knew Robert Patterson, the father of the Dr. Patterson of Wheeling, very well. He was professor of mathematics at the University of Pennsylvania, and was held in such high esteem as a friend by President Jefferson that he later appointed him as director of the United States Mint in Philadelphia. On March 2, 1803, Jefferson had written to Professor Patterson, informing him of the planned Expedition, and asking his assistance in tutoring Lewis in the techniques "for taking observations of longitude & latitude . . ." [11]

Jefferson had written to Lewis on April 27, 1803, informing him that "your destination being known to Mr. Patterson . . ." [12] Jefferson was referring to Dr. Robert Patterson, the father of Ewing. The senior Patterson probably knew that Lewis would be passing through Wheeling where his son was practicing medicine. It is also probable that Jefferson was aware that his old friend's son was a physician in Wheeling. Why would he not direct Lewis to contact him, at least for possible advice about frontier health conditions? And why did not the father, who knew of Lewis' proposed journey and had instructed him regarding it, suggest that Lewis contact his son? Also, why did not Dr. Ewing Patterson keep his appointment with Meriwether Lewis — did he lose his enthusiasm and purposely evade Lewis? Or was he legitimately busy with his professional demands? As a physician with more training than Meriwether Lewis had had from Benjamin Rush, with one hundred pounds worth of medicine in his possession, and with an apparent willingness to go on the Expedition, this situation looked like a "natural."

There is nothing in Lewis' journal entry to indicate that he knew of a strained relationship between the Pattersons, father

---

[11] Jackson, *Letters*, p. 21.   [12] *Ibid.*, p. 44.

and son, but he may well have known that much strife existed and why — and thus he availed himself of the opportunity to not wait; otherwise he surely would have been more gracious to the son of one who had helped instruct him for the Expedition. In his letter to Jefferson on May 29, 1803, from Philadelphia, Lewis had written of Dr. Patterson: ". . . he has been extremely obliging to me since my arrival here. . ." [13]

Lewis probably did not know that Ewing Patterson was a chronic alcoholic, and that he had "gone west" to Wheeling to make an effort at rehabilitation. Such an effort was unsuccessful; he died in 1829 at the age of forty-eight. Published letters reveal the pathetic hopes of the family and the equally pathetic, weak attempts of Ewing to cure his alcoholic habit and to re-establish himself in his profession and in the family's graces.[14]

It may have been that Ewing Patterson was really interested in "getting away" again and going with Lewis; he soon left Wheeling and embarked on another journey, as ship's surgeon at St. Domingo in 1805. Although his conduct toward Lewis was not very responsible, Ewing Patterson really had Lewis' offer in mind, as evidenced by the following paragraph from a letter written by Dr. Caspar Wistar to Jefferson on October 6: "Mr. Patterson has lately been informed by his Son that Major Lewis wished him to join the expedition as assistant Surgeon, & in consequence requested me to inform you what I knew of his qualifications. He . . . appeared to devote himself with great industry to the study of Medicine . . . He also appeared very correct & proper in his habits

---

13 *Ibid.*, p. 52.

14 William Irving DuBois, *The Families of Robert Patterson* (Phila., 1847). Ewing is described as "industrious, yet fond of sport and company, inclined to read, but reluctant to study, wayward and open-hearted. . . Coming of age, and having attended two courses of medical lectures, he commenced practise in Wheeling, in the summer of 1803. His stay at that new settlement was of no sort of benefit."

of Life."[15] Either Dr. Wistar did not know young Ewing very well, or the latter developed his excessive use of liquor at a later date.

It is probably fortunate for the Lewis and Clark Expedition that Ewing did not "catch the boat." [16] His weak character probably would have compromised the discipline of the Expedition. Later, on the Missouri, one of the members of the Expedition was to receive seventy-five lashes for breaking into the liquor supply; it is quite conceivable that Dr. Patterson would have received his lashes repeatedly if he had survived the five-month training program at Wood River; and if he had gotten up the Missouri to the Mandan villages, it is almost certain that Lewis, a great disciplinarian, would have sent him back down the river in the spring with Corporal Warfington.[17]

Lewis reached the French settlement of Marietta on September 14, where he noted that: "The fever and ague and bilious fevers here commence their banefull oppression and continue as you approach its mouth." [18] It was two months later, November 13, that Lewis entered in his journal the only reference made by any member of the Expedition to

---

15 Jackson, *Letters*, p. 133.

16 Quaife does not agree with this opinion. He writes: "In view of what the party was to face during the next three years it may well be questioned whether it would not have been wiser to have given Doctor Patterson a little more time to get ready for his journey." Milo M. Quaife, "Some New Found Records of the Lewis and Clark Expedition," *Miss. Valley Hist. Rev.* (June 2, 1915), pp. 114-15. Quaife also writes of Ewing: "It is interesting to reflect upon the probable influence upon such a character of the severe schooling and stern discipline of the exploring expedition, and the narrowness of the margin by which possible future fame and happiness escaped him." Milo M. Quaife, "The Journals of Capt. Meriwether Lewis and Sgt. John Ordway," *Pubs. of the St. Hist. Soc. of Wisc., Coll.,* xxii (Madison,, 1916), p. 39.

17 Corp. Richard Warfington was in charge of ten crewmen, most of whom had gone upriver for the purpose of wintering with the Expedition at the Mandan villages, and returning to St. Louis with the keelboat in the spring, bringing dispatches and collected articles.   18 Quaife, "Lewis and Ordway," 44.

his own personal affliction with malaria.[19] Lewis wrote:
". . . rain[e]d very hard in the ev[en]ing and I was seized
with a violent ague which continued about four hours and as
usual was succeeded by feever which however fortunately
abated in some measure by sunrise the next morning." The

[19] James and Kathryn Smith state in their article on Patrick Gass that "When
some vampire among the clouds of ravenous mosquitoes inoculated him with the
'shaking ague' (malaria), he noted that he was unable to steer his boat." Smith and
Smith, "Sedulous Sergeant, Patrick Gass," *Montana, The Magazine of Western
History*, Vol. 5, No. 3 (July, 1955), p. 23. This statement by these authors caused
me to review Gass' Journal and Jacob's *Life and Times of Patrick Gass* with the
thought that I had missed some reference of Gass to the ague. Although Gass refers
repeatedly, as do the other diarists, to swarms of troublesome mosquitoes, he
nowhere uses the word ague; nor does he state that the mosquitoes caused trouble
to him while steering a boat. A reading of the Smith article without other reference
might easily lead to the assumption that Gass used the words enclosed in the quotations, and that he had malaria — in such ways do historical inaccuracies and
distortions develop. It is not unlikely that Gass and all the men of the expedition
were infected with chronic malaria, but there is no historical substance to make fact
of the assumption.

Ague was endemic in the Mississippi, Missouri and Ohio valleys. That its identity was recognized by expedition members, is indicated by John Ordway's letter of
Nov. 15, 1807 (written after the Expedition's return) to his brother: ". . . I and
Gracey are well at present but Gracey has been sick about 2 months with the fever
and ague. . ." Maguire writes: ". . . It does appear that the ague was the
most common disease in this country during the early colonizing and frontier
periods. So inescapable was it that many refused to regard it as a disease, but like
hard work, a concomitant of the frontier." Edward F. Maguire, "Frequent Diseases
and Intended Remedies on the Frontier (1780-1850)," Unpublished Master's
Thesis at St. Louis Univ. 1953), p. 6.

For an informative reference indicating the nature and extent of this disease at
the time of Lewis and Clark, *see* Daniel Drake, *Malaria in the Interior Valley of
North America*, ed. by Norman D. Levine (Urbana: Univ. of Illinois Press, 1964).
Another reference is Eminett Field Harnie, M.D., *Daniel Drake* (Phila: Univ. of
Pa. Press, 1961). Daniel Drake was a leading medical practitioner and teacher in
the Ohio and Mississippi valleys, and contributed to the early success of the Univ.
of Cincinnati College of Medicine and the School of Medicine of the Univ. of
Louisville. Drake had part of his early medical training from Dr. William Goforth
of Cincinnati, who Lewis met there on his way down the Ohio. Jackson, *Letters*, p.
126.

Levine records the pseudonyms listed by Drake for Malaria: "autumnul, bilious,
intermittent, remittent, congestive, miasmatic, malarial, marsh, malignant, chill-
fever, ague, fever and ague, and lastly *the* Fever."

following day Lewis entered in his journal: "I took a doze of Rushes pills which operated extremely well and I found myself much to my satisfaction entirely clear of fever by the evening . . . felt myself much better but extreemly week." [20] There is no information about when Lewis contracted malaria; probably he had had it for several years. Michaux recorded that Pittsburgh, where Lewis stayed several weeks, was a healthy community, free of "intermittent fevers." [21]

This reference to Lewis having ague is interesting because in Lewis' time all fevers were ascribed to miasmata and putrid exhalations from marshes, with no attention given to the great number of mosquitoes in these marshes. There are many references to the abundance of mosquitoes throughout the Expedition's journey, but there is no further mention of ague. It is also interesting that in the extensive commentary made over the years regarding Lewis death of "suicide or murder," [22] including the various descriptions of his illness before and after he started on his trip up the Natchez Trace on which he died, the possibility of recurrent malarial attacks as explanation for his apparent dementia is seldom cited. Mental confusion was a rather consistent accompaniment to severe cases of malaria with high fever. The first published suggestion that Lewis' chronic malaria could be the cause of his mental "derangement" was Bakeless,[23] and other authors have quoted him.

---

[20] Quaife, op. cit., 47-48.

[21] Michaux, Travels Westward, p. 30. "The air of Pittsburgh and its neighborhood is very healthful; intermittent fevers, so common in the Southern States, are here unknown. . ." Michaux' journey was in 1802. He was the son of Andre Michaux (1746-1802), a distinguished French botanist who headed an abortive attempt to explore the Missouri in 1793, at Jefferson's request.

[22] Vardis Fisher, Suicide or Murder (Denver: Swallow, 1962).

[23] Bakeless, Partners in Discovery, p. 413. Vardis Fisher also refers to Lewis' malaria as a possible cause of his mental condition.

On November 21, Lewis wrote that he had noted mistletoe about the mouth of the Muskingum River, and he seemed to have in mind that perhaps this plant was related to the fact that this same area "is the point at which I date the commencement of the fever and Ague & bilious fever to commence, or become common among the inhabitants of its borders." [24]

Lewis was not as consistent a journalist as was Clark on their journey from St. Louis to Fort Clatsop and back. This same inattention to faithful entries in his journal occurred on his trip down the Ohio River, with no entries between September 18 and November 11. [25] Quaife notes that this was a distance of 694 miles. [26] That Lewis had considerable physical stress, if not illness, on the journey down the Ohio is seen in Lewis' letter of October 3, written to Jefferson from Cincinnatti, [27] in which he tells about a rest period of several days for recuperation.

It was during this time in which Lewis was not committing himself to his journals that he joined Clark at Louisville; it is too bad that this meeting of the two captains was not recorded in the felicitous words they had used in their previous correspondence to each other. They had not seen each other for several years. The high regard in which they remembered each other must have been firmed up immeasureably by this personal meeting and their discussion of the great adventure upon which they were about to embark.

In his final instructions to Lewis, dated June 20, 1803, Jefferson included the specific instruction to "carry with you some matter of the kine-pox; inform those of them [the Indians] with whom you may be, of its efficacy as a preservative from the smallpox; & instruct & encourage them in the use of

---

[24] Quaife, op. cit., p. 53.
[26] Ibid., p. 47.

[25] Ibid.
[27] Jackson, Letters, p. 126.

it. This may be especially done wherever you winter." [28] That
Lewis did carry with him a supply of vaccine is shown by his
letter to President Jefferson from Cincinnati on October 3,
1803: "I would thank you to forward me some of the vaxcine
matter, as I have reason to believe from several experiments
made with what I have, that it has lost its virtue." [29] The directing of his request to Jefferson indicates that it was Jefferson who provided the first supply. There is no record that
Jefferson acknowledged Lewis' request for more "kine-pox,"
nor is there further reference in the journals or in correspondence that the kinepox was sent or received. The failure of
Jefferson to send Lewis more kinepox probably was due to the
difficulty in transporting the live vaccine, a problem which
Jefferson was to help solve.

It is regrettable that Lewis did not place in his diary the
details of his "several experiments." It is most likely that he
had practiced vaccination on several Indians, following a
technique given him by Jefferson or Rush, probably the
former; most likely these vaccinations were done at Pittsburgh as this was the only place where he stopped long
enough to observe the results. His statement that "it has lost
its virtue" indicates that Lewis was familiar with the inflammatory reaction to be expected at the point of vaccination.
Almost every schoolchild is familiar with the usual smallpox
vaccination reaction: a variation from slight erythema and
itching to vesiculation with scab formation; rarely is there
a systemic reaction. The absence of systemic reaction and the
greater protection afforded, are the main advantages of vaccination over inoculation; the latter was used fairly extensively

---

[28] *Ibid.*, p. 61. Halsey states: "This is probably the earliest instruction bearing
on preventive medicine ever given by a president to the officers of an American
government expedition." Halsey, *Jefferson and Waterhouse*, p. 6.

[29] Jackson, *Letters*, p. 130.

in civilian and army life prior to Jenner's introduction of vaccination.

History is generously sprinkled with "ifs." If Lewis had received some virile vaccine from Jefferson he might have been the one to first introduce smallpox vaccination into the St. Louis area, although Harrell has shown that smallpox vaccine was used successfully in the Mississippi territory in 1802.[30] And if the men of the Lewis and Clark Expedition did not possess immunity to smallpox, and if they had met an epidemic of this disease among the Indians such as the latter experienced before and after the time of the Expedition, this

---

[30] Laura D. S. Harrell, "Preventive Medicine in the Mississippi Territory, 1799-1802," *Bulletin of the History of Medicine*, Vol. xl, No. 4 (1966), pp. 364-73. "Letters and documents in the manuscript of the executive journal of the governor of the Mississippi Territory reveal that two youthful and enlightened physicians and a compassionate and resourceful governor doubtless saved the inhabitants of Old Natchez district from a serious smallpox epidemic in the spring of 1802, by the vaccination of an estimated 2/3 of the population and by the isolation of smallpox patients. This was the first recorded mass vaccination in the area." In the above article is reproduced a letter from Governor William C. C. Claiborne from Washington in the Mississippi Territory, dated April 16, 1802, to William Dunbar, in which he states: "It would be a fortuitous circumstance if the Vaccine Matter could be obtained, & I hope that a disappointment will not ensue; — I should esteem it peculiarly unfortunate, if, at this time, we should not be benefitted by this important discovery; — for my part I should think the citizens would act wisely, were they immediately to assemble, and raise by subscription a fund to employ a confidential character to proceed direct to Kentucky, & procure the Matter. — From the account I received of a Cow-pox, it is safe at all Seasons of the Year & so mild in its operation as seldom to require either nursing or confinement."

The above letter is a part of an exchange of correspondence endeavoring to protect the inhabitants of the Old Natchez District from a serious smallpox epidemic in the spring of 1802. An estimated 2/3 of the population was vaccinated by Doctors David and William Lattimore, thus preventing a smallpox epidemic.

Another letter quoted by Harrell shows that successful vaccination was not accomplished without difficulty in procuring a viable vaccine, — reminiscent of Lewis' letter to President Jefferson of Oct. 3, 1803: "Two attempts have been made to avail ourselves of that valuable discovery in Medical Science, the Vaccine of Cow-pox, but I am sorry to inform you, that the Virus which was procured, not being genuine, or having lost its virtue from age, the first attempt failed of success & it is yet doubtful whether the issue of the second will be more fortunate."

small army contingent might have been wiped out as was
Napoleon's army in Santo Domingo.[31]

The two captains continued their journey uneventfully
down the Ohio River and brought their keelboat into the
bustling frontier town of St. Louis, and began seeking for
a place to establish their camp for the recruitment of men and
gathering of supplies for their journey of exploration to the
West.

---

[31] Smallpox has become so extinct in the United States that the U.S. Public
Health Service's Advisory Committee on Immunization Practices and the Committee on Infectious Diseases of the American Academy of Pediatrics have recommended discontinuation of smallpox vaccination. *See* an editorial in *JAMA*, Vol.
218, No. 6 (Nov. 8, 1971), p. 876. This would seem to substantiate Major's statement: "The presence or absence of smallpox is a more reliable index of the intelligence of a people than statistics on illiteracy, their consumption of rum, or even
than that modern device, the IQ." Major, *History of Medicine,* p. 132.

IX

At Camp DuBois

Discipline is of the first consequence. Without it, there can be neither health nor comfort in an army. James Tilton [1]

When this author began delving into the details of the medical aspects of the Lewis and Clark Expedition, it immediately became apparent that there was a hiatus in the records of the Expedition which might include important medical information. Jefferson had prepared Lewis quite adequately for the health care of the Expedition by arranging instruction for him from Dr. Benjamin Rush. Lewis had brought a good array of medical supplies with him from Philadelphia. The advice and perhaps some medicines, which he obtained from Dr. Saugrain in St. Louis, also helped prepare Lewis as a captain-physician for his men. But there was no information available about the health of the men or about medical preparations while the Expedition was readying itself during the five months at Camp DuBois, from December 12, 1803 until May 14, 1804.

St. Louis had a population of only about three thousand in 1803,[2] but the captains knew that it would be better for the health and discipline of the men if they were isolated from "city life." They chose the site on Wood River for the same

---

[1] Tilton, *Economical Observations* (1813) p. 34.

[2] Houck states that "In 1805, the first year after the country had been ceded to the United States, the population of Upper Louisiana increased from 6,028 to 10,120: of this number then only 3,760 were French, 5,000 Americans and 1,200 Negroes, the latter mostly slaves. . ." The St. Louis district was attributed 2,780. Houck, *History of Missouri*, p. 140.

reasons that would determine the locations of future Fort Mandan and Fort Clatsop: plenty of game for food, wood for cabins and fuel, and fresh water. Also, they could look across the Mississippi and see the mouth of the Missouri River, conveniently waiting for them. The captains wanted to stay on the east bank of the Mississippi River; even though the Louisiana Purchase had been completed in Paris on April 30, 1803, it was not officially transferred to the United States until March 9-10, 1804.[3] They did not want to give any occasion for complaints from the Spanish authorities, and thus cause political complications.

The time spent at Camp DuBois was a time of "whipping into shape" the various candidates for enlistment in the corps. Alexander Willard, one of the members of the Expedition, in later years enjoyed telling how his fine physique enabled him to pass the inspection for enlistment in the Expedition. He said there were more than one hundred who failed to pass the examination.[4] There had to be hunters and fishermen to provide food, carpenters and blacksmiths to make and repair physical equipment, voyageurs to row, cordelle, and pole the keelboat and pirogues. The captains divided their efforts, but presented a united front to the members of the corps. Clark worked more directly with the men, drilling and disciplining them and developing the internal organization of the Expedition. The two captains had learned the value of discipline during their army service under "Mad Anthony Wayne" in 1792. (Lewis was under Clark's command at that time.) Lewis sought community contacts and assistance and information and carried on the "external" business.

---

[3] Capt. Amos Stoddard officiated for the United States in receiving transfer of the Louisiana territory. Meriwether Lewis was present as an observer. Two days were required for the ceremony to permit the French flag to replace the Spanish flag for a day as a good-will gesture to the large French popuplation. The following day the tricolor of France was lowered and the Stars and Stripes were raised.

[4] Wheeler, *Trail*, i, p. 122.

Much of the detailed responsibility for the organization and supervision of the corps was delegated to three sergeants: John Ordway, Nathaniel Pryor, and Charles Floyd. Patrick Gass replaced Floyd when he became the only fatality of the Expedition.

For many years there were no detailed records available to give an account of the day-to-day activities at Camp DuBois. It was with considerable excitement and interest, then, that Captain William Clark's dusty notes covering the Camp DuBois period were discovered in an attic in St. Paul in 1953.[5] It was hoped that these notes would contain considerable information about the health organization and practices of the corps — something more than the usual army arrangements for the water supply to be a considerable distance and up-stream from the latrine area.

Might these notes also show that vaccination was practiced by the two captain-physicians? Might they reveal that Jefferson had sent more kine-pox in answer to Lewis' request, and that it had been used on the men of the Expedition?[6] What

[5] This author journeyed to the Minnesota Hist. Soc. in St. Paul with the hope of reviewing these notes, but I was only permitted to view the wrapped manuscripts through the open door of a vault. Miss Lucille Kane, Curator, explained that the ownership of the manuscripts had come under litigation since the family wished to retrieve them. The litigation finally ended with the decision that the manuscripts belonged to the family. They were later sold to the Yale University and were published in 1964. See Ernest S. Osgood, The Field Notes of Capt. William Clark (New Haven: Yale Univ. Press, 1964). An excellent account of the historical background and significance of Clark's Field Notes, and of the trial and its legal vagaries, is given in Calvin Tomkins' article, "Annals of Law; The Lewis and Clark Case," The New Yorker (Oct. 29, 1966), p. 105.

[6] The Expedition was at Wood River for five months before it left on May 14, 1804. That smallpox and vaccination existed near these men of the expedition in both place and time is shown by Harrison's letter to Secy. of War Dearborn, dated May 27, 1805, at Vincennes: "On arrival at this place I will have them (the Indians) inoculated with the vaccine disease that they may avoid the smallpox which is at this time in Kentucky." Jackson, Letters, p. 246. William Henry Harrison (1773-1841) was at this time territorial Governor of Indiana. As Governor and general, he gained a wide reputation that swept him into the presidency, becoming

were the diseases encountered during this winter of five months of stationary life? Lewis was to observe in the journals many months later, as they were preparing to start their journey from Fort Clatsop, that they were always in better health when on the move.[7] Were there other problems affecting the health of the men? What medicines were used; specifically, were there indications that medicines other than those which Lewis brought from Philadelphia were used? Would these notes contain indications that local physicians, particularly Dr. Saugrain, had rendered health care and provided other medicines for the men? And might they also give information about the illnesses and deaths of the men who were supposed to have died at Camp DuBois?

Armstrong states that "the men comprising the expedition were drilled and prepared for their arduous trip. Some of them died of sickness, and were buried in the old Milton Cemetery."[8] Palmer also gives support to the story of the burial of Lewis and Clark's men in the Milton Cemetery; he states "and in my recollection, I could see the sluggish Wood River, down near Alton, on the banks of which Lewis and Clark spent the winter of 1803-1804, and I could see the little Milton Cemetery where the explorers had left some of their men, victims of bilious fever."[9]

The *Wood River Journal*[10] states regarding the Milton Cemetery: "Word handed down from generation to generation about the Lewis and Clark Expedition which started here

the ninth President. At one time he was a medical student of Benjamin Rush; *see* Freeman Cleaves, *Old Tippecanoe* (N.Y: Charles Scribner's Sons, 1939), p. 7, regarding Harrison's brief attachment to medicine.

[7] Thwaites, *Journals*, IV, p. 194.

[8] W. D. Armstrong, *A Condensed History of Madison County* (Alton, Ill: National Printing Co., c. 1925), pp. 36-37.

[9] George Thomas Palmer, *Historic Landmarks Along the Highways of Illinois*, Illinois State Historical Transactions, Publ. 39, 1932, p. 44.

[10] Sept. 19, 1957, Section II, p. 6.

in 1803-4 informs us that two of that party died here and were buried in Milton Cemetery." The paper of the same date shows the oldest legible marker in the cemetery, with the death date of December 15, 1819.

The Alton *Telegraph* of December 11, 1959, contains an historical account of the Milton Cemetery: "Records give 1807 as the date of the first burials, but it is believed that two members of the Lewis and Clark Expedition who died in the winter of 1803-4 at the campsite at the mouth of Wood River were buried there." If any Lewis and Clark men from Wood River were buried in the Milton Cemetery, it would seem that they must have been the nucleus around which the cemetery was developed, or the date of 1807 used by the *Telegraph* is incorrect. Lewis and Clark left Wood River on May 14, 1804, and had completed their journey and returned to St. Louis by September 23, 1806.[11]

Before Clark's *Field Notes* were available there was nothing to contradict these stories about the death and burial in the Milton Cemetery of Lewis and Clark's men, but the *Field Notes* do not mention any deaths; surely any illness serious enough to cause death would have been recorded by Clark. On the basis of present information there is no substantiation of the story that any Lewis and Clark men died at Camp DuBois and were buried in the Milton Cemetery.

Lewis had written to Jefferson for more kine-pox (*see* page 178) for future use; his plans may have included vaccination of the members of the corps as well as the Indians to whom Jefferson had directed its use. It is unlikely that Jefferson would request Lewis to use his time vaccinating the Indians

---

[11] I am indebted to Miss Katharine Moorhead, Librarian of the Madison Co. Hist. Soc., Inc., of Edwardsville, Ill., and to Mrs. Fred C. Harrington, Jr., Librarian of the Mo. Hist. Soc., for research on the story about the deaths and burials in the Milton Cemetery of Lewis and Clark's men. Mrs. Harrington states: "There is no documentation for this statement."

to protect them against smallpox, and not take the same precautions for the men of the Expedition.

Many members of the corps had been transferred from their regular units in the army; thus it is probable that some of them already had been protected against smallpox by inoculation, which was true of Lewis. The ravages of smallpox, and its perennial presence, must have been a matter of concern to the captains and their men. The months spent at Camp DuBois were certainly the ideal time to inoculate or vaccinate the men, but there are no notes indicating that this was done.

Clark's *Field Notes* cover the five months at Camp DuBois and also the journey up the Missouri to the Mandan villages. The published notes contain some information not previously known, including some minor medical aspects, but basically there is nothing new — and nothing to answer specifically the preceding questions.

At Camp DuBois the men were close to the needed sources for laying in all sorts of supplies for the Expedition, and could build their boats and watch the condition of the rivers. From the Collot map of 1796, reproduced in Osgood,[12] Wood River then lay as it does today, its mouth directly across the Mississippi from the mouth of the Missouri River. That this topography of the river prevailed while Lewis and Clark were at Camp DuBois is evidenced by Clark's journal entry for May 13, 1804: "River a Dubais opposet the mouth of the Missourie River." [13]

Clark was particularly responsible for the "examination"

---

[12] Osgood, *Field Notes of Clark*, p. 102, and fn. 3.

[13] Thwaites, *Journals*, I, p. 16. For an authenticated and detailed review of the changing relations of the rivers over the years and the locations of Camp DuBois, *see* Roy E. Appleman, "The Lost Site of Camp Wood," *Jour. of the West*, Vol. VII, No. 2 (April, 1968), pp. 270-74.

given to the prospective recruits for the Expedition. He does not indicate what kind of examination was given to the men; undoubtedly it was not a physical examination as it is understood today, but probably was designed only to determine a man's stamina and skills. Clark had been used to living with and evaluating the men on the frontier; undoubtedly a part of the examination given to each potential recruit was a scrutinizing evaluation of the man's potential adaptability and service to the Expedition — what psychologists today would call an aptitude test.

Once the recruit was accepted into the corps, it was Clark's responsibility to develop his technical skills and to drill and discipline him into a dependable corpsman. Although some of the men were of the frontier-trained calibre, it was necessary to instill in all of them an awareness of their mutual dependency upon communal assistance: obtaining, preserving and husbanding their food, eating off the countryside by the expertise of their own hunters and by trading with the Indians, and supplementing their day-to-day provendering only as necessary from their salt pork and other staples. Although there were specified hunters who could read the animal trails and were good marksmen, these hunters had in turn to depend upon the skill of the gunsmith. And every man had to care for his own gun, to protect his life from an animal or an Indian, and to provide food and clothing, in order to survive.

Each man had to be willing to forego his main duty and be able to supplement other imperative immediate needs, such as all men becoming "watermen" to row or sail or pull the boat out of hazardous situations. There would be times on the journey when all would have to be rowers, or literally be required to act as pack horses. There would be times when safety and success of the Expedition would depend upon their unquestioned response to team discipline. Just as discipline in a modern army is important to a soldier's health and life, so it was with the men of the Lewis and Clark Expedition — and Clark's months of disciplinary training undoubtedly contributed to the healthiness of the corps while on the journey. The "examination" and the discipline and the anticipated future demands did not appeal to all of the recruits. Clark seemingly molded his corps with a firmness that evidenced his agreement with Tilton that "a delicate soldier is very ridiculous indeed." [14]

Future accounts in the journals reveal that several of the men could not swim, and one or two almost lost their lives by drowning. It is remarkable that any of these young men on the frontier had not learned to swim and more remarkable that Clark did not require them to learn while at Camp DuBois. Much of their journey was to be spent on unknown hazardous waters, where even a good swimmer might lose his life. The fate of the Expedition might have been compromised by the drowning of two or three key men. The "rare good luck" to which Wheeler attributes a goodly portion of the success of the Expedition certainly helped take care of these men. [15]

The personal health problems of the men while at Camp Dubois were not great — not as frequent nor as troublesome as would be encountered throughout the journey. And they were well housed and well fed — certainly better than the soldiers Lewis lived with during his army days, as described in a letter to his mother on December 24, 1794: "The situation of the soldairy is truly deplorable exposed to the inclemency of the winter which is about this time completely set in without any shelter more than what eight men can derive

---

[14] Quoted by Stanhope Bayne-Jones, "The Evaluation of Preventive Medicine in the United States Army, 1607-1939," *Office of Surgeon Genl., Dept. of the Army* (Washington, D.C.), p. 48.   [15] Wheeler, *Trail*, I, p. 46.

from a small tent. Many are sick but fortunately few have died as yet." [16]

Clark related in his notes on January 10 how Joseph Field escaped the hazard of floating, breaking ice and that he (Clark) "found that my feet, which were wet had frozed to my shoes." On the same day Clark wrote: "I am verry unwell all day, owing I believe to the Ducking & excessive Cold which I enderwent yesterday,   . ." He repeated on the 11th: "I am unweell I was unweell last night Slept but a little."

On January 25 he wrote: "I was Sick all night." The next day he wrote: "I am unweell all day   .   .   .   the fessic I took yesterday worked to day." On the twenty-seventh he complained that he was still "verry unweell," but later added, "I am some better." Clark does not give any clue as to the nature of his illness; inasmuch as it was wintertime, it is presumable that he might have had a severe cold.

Clark was not introspective by nature, and it is doubtful that he would have made so many references to being "unweell" unless that were truly his condition. From his notes it seems that Clark was more affected with illness while at Camp DuBois than any of his men. He wrote to his brother-in-law, Major William Croghan, from Camp DuBois on January 15, 1804: ".   .   .   I am in tolerable health. I have not been from Camp to any house since my arrival here." [17]

By February 1 and 2 he recorded that he was again "verry unweell" and "verry sick," to which he adds on the third, "(I) take medicine without pain." He makes a similar recording on February 4, and on the fifth he writes that he "sent out Shields to get walnut Bark for pills," and on the sixth he adds "sick take Walnut pills." This is the only reference throughout the journals to the use of "walnut pills." [18]

16 From letter of Meriwether Lewis, Mo. Hist. Soc.

17 Jackson, *Letters*, p. 164.

Clark was "unweell" a lot of the time at Wood River and on the trip; however, this rarely slowed him physically, and seems never to have changed his fortitude and equanimity. Perhaps he had attained from his parents, John and Ann Clark, something of the philosophy written to them by Dr. James O'Fallon: "Suffer no trouble to rest on your mind. It sapps and undermines the most vigorous constitution. A cheerful heart, Temper, and disposition (if uniformally kept up and good sense can do it) is one of the best Preservatives against your, and indeed, against any disease." [19]

[18] Osgood, *Field Notes of Clark*, p. 27. In note 4, Osgood states: "Walnut bark appears in the old pharmacopeias but not in recent ones. The 1808 edition of the *London Medical Dictionary*, 1843, under 'Juglands,' states that the shells are astringent, an ointment of leaves boiled in lard is a useful application for hemorrhoids and old ulcers, and that the bark and catkins are strongly emetic. Dr. F. B. Queen, deceased, Prof. of Pathology at the Univ. of Ore. Med. School, to whom I am indebted for the above, suggested that in 1804, it was probably used as a mild purgative." It hardly is consistent that any drug would have the contrary effects of acting as an astringent and as a purgative.

Peter Smith thought well of the Walnut bark pills, and his mention of them indicates they were well-known on the frontier. His prescription No. 5 describes the making and use of "the Butternut or White-Walnut bark pills:" "[They] are a valuable purge, very easy and safe, to all persons under disease. These pills may be prepared by boiling a kettle of the bark of the butternut tree in water, until you gain the substance of the bark, then strain the liquor and boil it down; when it becomes a thick syrup, take care not to burn it, but simmer it to a substance like hard wax; then put it by in a cup or gally pot, and make it into pills as they are wanted, for if the pills are made up, they will run together and dissolve in a little time. This purge is preferable to any that I know, in a weak and debilitated state of the bowels. It may be taken in as small quantities as you please, for if they do not purge immediately, they act the better as a stimulus and tonic to the system and will produce a good habit of body by repeating them every night, and this may be done for a month together." Smith, *Indian Dr.'s Dispensatory*, p. 28.

The Edinburgh *New Dispensatory*, 1805, p. 240, lists under Juglans Regia (the walnut tree) the following in regard to the unripe fruit: "They have been supposed to possess tonic and anthelmintic virtues. The green rind has been celebrated as a powerful antivenereal remedy; but it possesses no real antisyphlitic virtues, although it forms a very useful addition to the compound decoction of sarsaparilla, where pains of the limbs and indurations of the membranes remain after the venereal disease has been cured by mercury. . . . A decoction of the green rind has also been recommended as a useful application to old ulcers." Duncan, *Edinburgh New Dispensatory*.   [19] Seen in Clark papers, Mo. Hist. Soc.

It is disappointing that the Camp DuBois notes contain a paucity of reference to health conditions. Surely a lot of the other men were "unweell." Although the winter months would help protect them from fresh malarial infections,[20] it would bring other things to trouble them, such as colds, pleurisy, fevers, frostbite. The journals continuously mention the men being afflicted with venereal disease throughout the trip but there is no mention of venereal disease while at Camp DuBois. Although Lewis had been tutored by Dr. Rush, Clark was at least as active as Lewis in the role of physician during the Expedition's journey; and with Lewis absent from Camp DuBois much of the time, Clark had ample opportunity to "practice" on his men. However, there is no mention of treating "the Venerial," nor of the dispensing of much medication, nor the use of the lancet. There is no mention of injury inflicted by one member of the Expedition upon another, even though some disciplinary attention was necessary because of intrusion into the liquor stores. There is no information regarding any specific preparations for the health care of the corps during the impending journey. It can be assumed that the army routine of the day was rigorously followed regarding sanitation. There is no record of use of vaccination or even inoculation.[21]

A fair summary of the health of the men while at Camp DuBois is given by Amos Stoddard in his letter to Secretary

[20] Nevertheless, the men were pestered with mosquitoes; Lewis writes from St. Louis to Clark on May 2: "I send you . . . sixteen Musquitoe nets. . ." Jackson, *Letters*, p. 177.

[21] Eva Emory Dye, in her novelized story of the Lewis and Clark Expedition, *The Conquest*, has Dr. Saugrain ask Lewis: " 'And have you any kine-pox? You must surely carry kine-pox, for I hear those Omahas have died like cattle in a plague.' " After Lewis explains to the doctor that he had written to Jefferson for more kine-pox, Mrs. Dye continues her narrative: "out of his medicine chest in the corner the little Doctor brought tiny vials. 'Sent from Paris. Carry it, explain it to the Indians, use it whenever you can — it will save the life of hundreds.' " pp. 159-60.

of War Dearborn, from St. Louis, June 3, 1804: "His [Lewis']
men possess great resolution and they [are in the best]
health and spirits." [22] The Expedition left Camp DuBois on
May 14, 1804. Clark reported that their party was "Composed
or robust, healthy hardy young men   .   .   ." Sergeant John
Ordway wrote to his "Honored Parence. I am well thank God,
and in high spirits. I am on an expedition to the Westward,
with Capt. Lewis and Capt. Clark   .   .   .   I am so happy to
be one of them pick'd." [23] Confidence pervaded the crew, as
was reflected in Whitehouse's journal on May 14: ".   .   .   we
fired our swivel on the bow hoisted Sail and Set out in high
Sperits for the western Expedition." [24]

But the men, except for some French voyageurs who had
been up the Missouri previously, did not know, and would not
have comprehended, the endurance and work to be demanded of them as they fought their way upstream. The
banks of the river were always precariously unstable because
of the meandering current and the soft soil; it was always
hazardous to anchor their boats near a bank for fear it would
collapse on them. The nature of the river changed constantly,
from narrow, rough rapids to wide, shallow sandbars. A fresh
rain always loosened more trees from the banks and the current hurled them into the path of the boat, or piled them up

---

[22] Jackson, *Letters,* p. 196. Amos Stoddard was a career army officer. As a Major,
in 1804, Stoddard served as the agent and Commissioner of France when the Upper
Louisiana Territory was transferred from Spain to France and then to the United
States. (Spain had retroceded Louisiana to France by the secret treaty of San
Ildefonso, but Louisiana remained under Spanish administration until purchased
by the u.s.) He also served as governor of the Louisiana Territory from 1804-1812.
Stoddard wrote in 1812 that there was generally favorable health in Upper Louisiana, despite the fact that "the exhalations from the swamps and low grounds must
necessarily poison the air." The men of the Lewis and Clark Expedition remained
healthy in spite of their location, where, according to Stoddard, "the pestilential
vapors   .   .   .   accrue from the rivers, and from the decayed vegetable substances produced in great abundance on the bottoms along the borders of them."

[23] Jackson, *Letters,* p. 176.
[24] Thwaites, *Journals,* p. 30.

in impregnable log jams or embarrasses that required hours of labor to chop and saw away. Submerged sawyers threatened to tear holes in the hulls of their boats, with possible loss of the boat and supplies, and even of lives. To fight this formidable combination of the elements, the men had to pull their boats literally hand over hand, in torrential rains or under blazing sun — and if the latter, mosquitoes raised bloody welts on their backs while they dare not let go of the pole or rope. And with such labor throughout the daylight hours, they must also hunt for food and stop for a meal of corn and venison roast or salt pork, and then rest their weary bodies on unsheltered ground. Only man's inherent urge for adventure and uncertain profit could have driven them to the impossible task of pulling and pushing a boat of several tons' burden up such a mean and dangerous water highway as the Missouri River. Only willful, foolhardy ants of men could and would refuse to be conquered. Some men had preceded Lewis and Clark up the Missouri, and many would follow, but none would conquer it so magnificently. The Rocky Mountains were to give their challenge in due time, but first the Missouri — the long, long Missouri.

Despite its furious challenge, the final score would be: "The river runs terrible and strong, unwilling to be mastered. Part of the Lewis and Clark epic is their victory over the Missouri." [25]

---

[25] Quoted from Jeannette Mirsky, *The Westward Crossings* (N.Y: Knopf, 1946), p. 238.

X

Dr. Antoine Francois Saugrain

Persons in indigent circumstances, paupers and Indians will be
vaccinated and attended gratis.   Dr. Antoine François Saugrain [1]

William Clark left Camp DuBois (Wood River) with the
Expedition on May 14, 1804, and proceeded on a sort of trial
run up the Missouri River to Saint Charles, an early French
settlement located about twenty-one miles from the mouth of
the Missouri River. Here Clark did some rearranging of the
load on the keelboat to accommodate for the current and
debris in the Missouri River, and to await Lewis, who was
completing business arrangements in St. Louis. On May 20,
Clark notes in his journal that "at three oClock Capt. Lewis,
Capt. Stoddard accompanied by the Officers & Several Gentlemen of St. Louis arrived in a heavy Showr of Rain. Messrs.
Lutenants Minford & Worriss. Mr. Choteau, Grattiot, De-
loney, Laberdee, Rankin. Dr. Sodrang."[*]

Although Clark knew Dr. Saugrain as one of the leading
citizens of St. Louis and was aware that their Expedition had
benefited from some advice from the doctor, he could hardly
know that Dr. Saugrain's visit to see the Expedition off to the
West was a fulfillment of a phophecy that he had made many
years before. Dr. Saugrain[2] had immigrated to this country

---

[1] St. Louis *Gazette,* Oct. 26, 1809.

[*] Thwaites, *Journals,* I, p. 22.

[2] Antoine Francois Saugrain was born in Paris on Feb. 17, 1763, into an educated
and fairly well-to-do family, distinguished mainly for its activities as librarians and
editors. One sister married Dr. Joseph Guillotine who gave his name to the decap-
itating machine he invented as a humane, painless method of putting criminals to

with many of his fellow Frenchmen and founded the beautiful community of Gallipolis on the Ohio River. Here a fellow countryman, Brissot de Warville, visited him in 1788. De Warville quotes Dr. Saugrain as saying that "the active genius of the Americans is always pushing them forward,"[3] and he predicted that they would cross the Mississippi River and push the Spaniards from Louisiana.[4]

Dr. Saugrain was a protege of Dr. Benjamin Franklin, who received him in Philadelphia, and sent him on his way to Gallipolis on the Ohio River, where he arrived on October 17, 1790. In time the good doctor had displayed his sign "Cabinet de Docteur et Boulangerie." In 1792 Dr. Saugrain "et des autres docteurs de Gallipolis" were busy with a malaria epidemic which took the lives of "un grand nombre d'inhabitants." Thus we know that malaria was recognized in the Ohio Valley a decade before Lewis and Clark started on their journey, and that Dr. Saugrain had accumulated much expe-

death. Dr. Saugrain's family was not of the nobility, but he assumed the designation of Saugrain de Vigni. He was of a studious nature, and having ample opportunity for education, he became widely read, and evinced a bent toward scientific subjects, including chemistry and minerology. His education was widened by extensive travel in Europe and abroad. His travels included Mexico and the young republic of the United States.

[3] "The active genius of the Americans is always pushing them forward. M. Saugrain has no doubt but sooner or later the Spaniards will be forced to quit the Mississippi & that the Americans will pass it, and establish themselves in Louisiana, which he has seen and considers as one of the finest in the universe." Brissot deWarville, *New Travels in the United States of America* (Paris, 1794), i, p. 219.

[4] Baron Francisco Luis Hector de Carondelet (1748?-1807), the Spanish Governor of Louisiana from 1795-1797, shared Dr. Saugrain's impression of the Americans: "The wandering spirit and the ease with which these people preserve their sustenance and shelter quickly form new settlements. A carbine and a little maize in a sack are enough for an American to wander about in the forests alone for a whole month." Carondelet was responsible in part for much of the political intrigues and uncertainties which concerned Jefferson in planning for the Lewis and Clark Expedition, by his fomenting unrest among American settlers and the Indians. The strained relations between Spain and the U.S. were the principle reason that the captains established Camp DuBois on the east bank of the Mississippi, even though the Louisiana Purchase had been consumated.

rience and advice to give the captains regarding this disease when they met later in St. Louis.

After spending a few years in Gallipolis and Louisville, Dr. Saugrain moved on down the Ohio River to St. Louis, as if to make ready to assure the fulfillment of his prophecy. He arrived in St. Louis in 1800, thirty-six years after the founding of this French settlement by Laclede.[5] It was three years later that Meriwether Lewis and William Clark spent five months in the spring of 1803 at their camp at the mouth of Wood River, only a few miles outside of St. Louis. Tradition and fact recount the assistance given by Dr. Saugrain to the two captains: the providing of medicines and medical advice, and the making of thermometers by blowing and calibrating glass tubes which he filled with mercury melted from his wife's Parisian mirror.[6]

The four foot, six inch physique of this former court physician from France was no true measure of the man. Although it was Benjamin Franklin who helped lure him to America, it was his own vision of the West's expanding horizon that carried him westward from the Atlantic seaboard. His capture by the Indians on the Ohio River, and his escape after privation and injury, gave him first-hand knowledge of what moving to the western frontier would mean. Yet move he did, from Philadelphia to Gallipolis, and on to St. Louis, where his work earned for him the title of the First Scientist of the Mississippi

[5] Pierre Laclede (1724-1778). By his orders Rene Auguste Chouteau began building the nucleus of the new town in 1764. Rene and his brother Jean Pierre were the founders of an extensive fur trade and other businesses, and a family which has continued to have an important part in the development of St. Louis.

[6] Dillon calls the melting of mercury from Madame Saugrain's mirror a "hard-to-kill legend." Richard Dillon, *Meriwether Lewis* (N.Y: Coward-McCann, 1965), p. 41. Lew Larkin provides a variation on the mirror story which I have not seen elsewhere: "When Lewis and Clark came up short of thermometers and barometers because there was no mercury, Saugrain prowled the town, and the homes of the rich, and took mercury from all silvered mirrors." *See* the St. Louis *Post-Dispatch*, Mar. 9, 1969.

Valley,[7] and where he helped establish worthy foundations for medical practice in his chosen community.

Although he did not move on into the Louisiana Territory as he predicted the Americans would do, he lived the rest of his life at the gateway to the West, always in contact with and interested in the pursuits of the explorers, fur traders and merchants whose domain was up the Missouri River and beyond. Therefore, it is not by accident that "Dr. Sodrang" came to bid an interested farewell to the two American captains and their crew who represented the "active genius of the Americans."

Brackenridge, who as a youth and young man spent much time in "the west" (the Ohio, Mississippi and Missouri valleys), writes of revisiting Gallipolis and staying with Dr. Saugrain and having his "fever and ague," a further testimony to the presence of malaria in the Ohio Valley in the years immediately preceeding the Lewis and Clark Expedition. Brackenridge also described the doctor's scientific experiments:[8]

> The Doctor had his small apartment which contained his chemical apparatus, and I used to sit by him as often as I could, watching the curious operations of his blow pipe and crucible. I loved the cheerful little man, and he became very fond of me in turn. . .
> The doctor's little phosphoric matches, igniting spontaneously when the glass tube was broken . . . were thought by some to be somewhat beyond mere human power.[9] His barometers and

---

[7] N. P. Dandridge, M.D., "The First Scientist of the Mississippi Valley," *Ohio Arch. and Hist. Soc. Pubs.*, Vol. xv (1906), pp. 192-206. This paper was Dr. Dandridge's presidential address at a meeting of the Amer. Med. Assn. in St. Louis.

[8] H. M. Brackenridge, *Recollections of Persons and Places in the West* (Phila: Kay & Bros., 1834), pp. 40-44.

[9] Apparently Saugrain, who did earlier experiments with friction matches, used both sulphur and phosphorus. "He also knew the formula for making sulphur matches; so while the rest of the world was using flint and steel, Lewis and Clark were able to strike matches far out on the Columbia River! Keeping supplies on hand for experimentation was difficult, but he was resourceful, even scraping the mercury off the back of Madam Saugrain's pier glass (a fine mirror brought from

thermometers with the scale neatly painted with the pen, and the frames richly carved, were the objects of wonder, and probably some of them are still extant in the west. . .

The fortunes of Gallipolis went from bad to worse, and it failed to develop into the successful community envisaged by its founders.[10] This probably was part of the reason for Dr.

France) in order to finish in time the thermometers and barometers he made for those two great explorers to take when they started on their long and perilous journey. . ." William Clark Kennerly, *Persimmon Hill* (Norman: Univ. of Ok., 1948), p. 141. (William Clark Kennerly was a nephew of William Clark, the explorer). *See also* John Francis McDermott, "Gallipolis as Travelers Saw It, 1793-1811," *Ohio Arch. and Hist. Qtly.*, Vol. xlviii (1939), p. 294. McDermott writes that the Reverend James Smith had written in 1795 about visiting Dr. Saugrain: " 'He showed a chemical composition which had the peculiar property of setting wood on fire.' "

Nowhere in the journals or letters of the Expedition is there a definite description of making a fire. They may have used the old Indian wood-friction method, or a magnifying glass when the sun was shining. It is probable that they used flints and gunpowder; this is indicated by Clark's statement of Sept. 10, 1805, that "Cap Lewis gave them [the Indians] a Steel & a little Powder to make fire. . ." Thwaites, *Journals*, iii, p. 61. In the list of supplies Lewis purchased at the Schuylkill arsenal were "30 Steels for striking or making fire" and "100 flints for ditto." *Ibid.*, vii, p. 234.

Perhaps the idea that "Lewis and Clark were able to strike matches far out on the Columbia River" comes from Clark's statement when on the Multnomah (Willamette) River: "I had a small pece of port fire match in my pocket, off of which I cut a pece one inch in length I put it into the fire . . . the port fire caught and burned vehemently, which changed the colour of the fire . . . at this moment the match being exhausted. . ." *Ibid.*, iv, p. 237. It is apparent that whatever Clark meant by using the word "match" he was not describing a match such as we conceive it. The fire was already burning when he threw his "port fire" substance into it.

The property of the spontaneous ignition of phosphorus when exposed to oxygen had been known since its discovery by Brand in 1670. John Walker, an Englishman, is usually credited with developing the first friction phosphorus match; but his invention was not until 1827. Yellow sulphur was first used in the rapid development of the match trade, but caused necrosis of the jaws in workers. This was remedied by the use of sesquisulphide of phosphorus. Today phosphorus is only one of many chemicals used in the machine manufacture of "safety matches." Regrettably, in the usual historical accounts of the development of matches Dr. Saugrain is rarely mentioned.

10 When Brackenridge returned twelve years later, he noted many changes: "Even the pond, which had carried off a third of the French population by its malaria, had disappeared." Brackenridge, *Recollections*, p. 221.

Saugrain's departure, because he did not find in the community the opportunity and challenges to match his scientific inclinations and his education. He moved on down the Ohio River to Louisville. He was not happy there, either, as reflected in his diary entry: "Louisville is a very unhealthy place. . ."

While visiting Clarksville [11] he found a sweet gum tree in the forest; the value of the tree's resin was not yet known by the local people. ". . . and to honor my sojourn in the fort they have planted one in the garden to which they have given the name Saugrain-tree." [12]

In 1800 Dr. Saugrain moved to St. Louis and promptly became a leading citizen because of his services as a physician, his scientific interest, his education, and his friendly and inspiring personality. He again established a laboratory in which he conducted chemical and electrical experiments. He impressed Indians, who were awed with the electrical stimulation received from putting their hands into a bell jar, and touching electrified doorknobs. But not all of Dr. Saugrain's experiments dealt with trickery. As shown by Brackenridge's previous notes, he developed phosphorous matches while he was still in Gallipolis, and he continued with his match-making in St. Louis. Thus there is ample evidence that Dr. Saugrain's invention of friction matches antedated that of A. D. Phillips, who was granted the first American patent in 1836.

Dr. Saugrain's home occupied an entire block in St. Louis, bounded by Second and Third streets and Gratiot and Lombard streets. This block was surrounded by a seven-foot stone wall to keep Indians from running through the prop-

---

[11] The home of George Rogers Clark (1752-1818), William's oldest brother.

[12] Kennerly, *Persimmon Hill*, p. 126. The sweet gum tree (liquidamber styraciflua) exudes a resin used in medicine as an expectorant, and in perfumes — thus the natives appreciated Dr. Saugrain's find.

erty.[13] It was difficult for Indians to understand the boundaries of personal property which the white men had laid out for themselves.[14] Enclosed within the stone walls surrounding the block Dr. Saugrain built his cottage, then one of the finest homes in St. Louis. Here he housed one of the largest libraries in the city.[15] Because of his importance as a physician and a citizen, people of all walks of life came to Dr. Saugrain's home. Eva Emory Dye related that Captain Meriwether Lewis visited Dr. Saugrain in his home;[16] this is certainly a reasonable probability inasmuch as Lewis was seeking advice and help from all the leading citizens of St. Louis in preparation for the Expedition to the West.

Around the house and within the stone wall surrounding Dr. Saugrain's block of land were planted fruit trees, vegetables and herbs. Undoubtedly Dr. Saugrain relied a great deal upon the medicinal herbs which he raised in his own

[13] *Ibid.*, pp. 136-37. This block is now a commercial area, only three blocks from the Jefferson National Expansion Memorial, and could be connected to it without much difficulty. Several buildings around the block have historical markers on them, but there is no historical marker to note Dr. Saugrain and his home. This might be a challenge to the physicians of St. Louis who today enjoy the high prestige for which Dr. Saugrain helped lay the foundation. ("Dr. Antoine Francois Saugrain may be called the father of the medical profession of St. Louis and the profession may feel honored today." Walter B. Stevens, *History of St. Louis: The Fourth City* [St. Louis: Clarke, 1911], p. 568.) Surely he was a vital part of the Gateway to the West. Perhaps the entire Saugrain block could be restored under the aegis of the Federal Historic Sites Preservation Program, as well as the home and surrounding seven-foot wall, which "was used as a park by the early villagers." Perhaps the "delicious astregon vinegar for their *salade*" might be provided for those who might today wish "to step through the little wicket in the high stone wall of Madame Saugrain's garden.

[14] One of the most difficult things that Narcissa Whitman, wife of Dr. Marcus Whitman, had to endure in their mission at Waiilatpu (near present-day Walla Walla, Wash.) was the assumed freedom of the Indians, who stared through the windows and walked through the doors and into any of the rooms. *See* Clifford M. Drury, *Marcus and Narcissa Whitman and the Opening of Old Oregon*, 2 vols. (Glendale: Arthur Clark Co., 1973).

[15] John Francis McDermott, *Private Libraries in Creole St. Louis* (Baltimore: Institut Francais, 1938).   [16] Dye, *The Conquest*, p. 159.

garden to treat his patients. However, he was billed on September 6, 1810, by Mr. Pierre Dorion, for drugs purchased from July 3, 1808 to September 6, 1810.[17]

Because of Dr. Saugrain's recognition as a leading citizen and physician and scientist of St. Louis, Lewis would have naturally gravitated to him in seeking general and specific medical information in the formulation of plans for the Expedition.[18] It is very unlikely that Dr. Saugrain would have made the twenty-one mile trip to St. Charles and back to see Lewis and Clark off on their journey unless there had been a very personal relationship between them.

Dr. Saugrain left many descendants who married into several leading and responsible families of St. Louis.[19] The handing down of tradition through such reliable sources cannot be discounted, and it is this tradition, rather than absolute proof, which holds that Dr. Saugrain helped Lewis and Clark in several ways.[20] Meany reviewed the plausibility of help that the captains might have received from Dr. Saugrain, interviewing in person and by correspondence several of Dr. Sau-

---

[17] Seen in the Mo. Hist. Soc.

[18] There is concrete evidence that Lewis had contact with Dr. Saugrain in the report of the list of articles sent by Lewis to Jefferson from St. Louis. Included in the list is a buffalo hair ball, "presented by Doctr. Anthony Sograine." Jackson, *Letters*, p. 192.

[19] *See* H. Foure Selter, *L'Odyssee Americaine d'une Famille Francaise: Le Docteur Antoine Saugrain* (Baltimore: Institut Francais, 1936), and Elliott Coues, *Expeditions of Zebulon M. Pike* (N.Y: Francis P. Harper, 1895), pp. 11, 397. Coues writes that one daughter of Saugrain, Sophie-Marie, married an American doctor, John Robinson, who accompanied Pike on his expedition to the Rockies. Pike's expedition left St. Louis on July 15, 1806: "Our party consisted of two lieutenants, one surgeon, one sergeant, two corporals, 16 privates and one interpreter." Note that this expedition had a doctor, in contrast to the Lewis and Clark Expedition.

[20] The following is from a letter from Mrs. Kennerly Taylor to Mrs. Eva Emory Dye: "I don't remember if I ever wrote you that Lewis was in St. Louis a short time before they started for the trip, but I think I told you that Grand Father Saugrain prepared the medicine Chest &c. for them." *See* Dye Mss. in the Oreg. Hist. Soc.

grain's descendants, and came to the following conclusion: "that family traditions, abundant and persistent through three generations, must be largely depended upon in lieu of the scant written or printed contemporaneous records," and "that Dr. Saugrain did supply the Lewis and Clark Expedition with a homemade thermometer, some experimental lucifer matches [21] and packages of medicine." [22]

Robinson states that "At Saint Louis they [the captains] became acquainted with Dr. Antoine Saugrain, a physician, surgeon, and scientist of unusual attainments. Dr. Saugrain gave a 'free-hand' course in medicine and surgery to Captain Clark who served as the doctor of the Expedition." [23] This statement is presumptuous and probably inaccurate because Clark remained at Wood River most of the time while Lewis was the one who spent much time in St. Louis.

Among the supplies which were requested by Meriwether Lewis from the Schuylkill arsenal in Philadelphia,[24] and which he brought with him overland to Pittsburgh and used in making temperature recordings on his trip down the Ohio River to St. Louis, were three thermometers.[25] Undoubtedly

---

[21] Various accounts by journalists as quoted above indicate that Dr. Saugrain was working with phosphorus matches. The "lucifer" matches seem to have been made with chlorate of potash, sugar and gum arabic; this was the composition of the friction matches of John Walker (see *Encyclopaedia Britannica*, xv, 45, 1943, p. 6). Thus it is questionable that any matches supplied by Dr. Saugrain to Lewis and Clark were "lucifer."

[22] Edmund S. Meany, "Dr. Saugrain Helped Lewis and Clark," *Wash. Hist. Qtly.*, Vol. xvi (Oct., 1931), p. 377. The *Dictionary of American Biography* (N.Y., 1935), follows Meany very closely: "While the Lewis and Clark expedition was being fitted out in St. Louis, he supplied gratuitously a medicine chest, thermometers, barometers, and matches."

[23] Doan Robinson, *Medical Adventures of Lewis and Clark* (Dept. of Hist. Coll. of S.D., 1924) xii, pp. 53-66.   [24] Thwaites, *Journals*, vii, p. 231.

[25] Thus Will's statement that "No thermometer was purchased for the expedition's use by the public stores. . ." is inaccurate. Drake Will, "Lewis and Clark: Westering Physicians," *Montana, Magazine of Western History*, Vol. xxi, No. 4 (Autumn, 1971), p. 9.

these were thermometers for taking water temperatures be-
caus it was a part of the Expedition's duties to record climatic
conditions. Clinical thermometers for the recording of human
body temperatures were not in use until after the time of
Lewis and Clark.[26] In view of the well-established fact that
Dr. Saugrain had been making thermometers and barometers
in Gallipolis a decade previously, it is reasonable to expect
that he provided Lewis and Clark with additional thermometers, but there is no definite statement in the journals or
elsewhere to this effect.

Three breakable thermometers would hardly suffice for the
duration of the Expedition. The journals record the use of
thermometers, and their loss and breakage. Whatever the
total number of thermometers taken on the Expedition, Lewis
states definitely that the last one was broken on the way west,
on the Lolo Trail, September 3, 1805 (but also gives September 6, 1805, as the date).[27] Lewis' statement makes it
impossible for anyone today to have a thermometer used by
the Lewis and Clark Expedition.[28]

---

[26] The use of clinical thermometers for the recording of human body temperatures started several years after Lewis and Clark. Thomas Clifford Allbutt (1826-
1925), an English physician, is credited with introducing the modern clinical
thermometer in 1870. Various efforts to relate and record both temperature and
disease started in 1626 with the work of Santorious Sanctorious (1561-1636), an
Italian physician. See J. E. Schmidt, *Medical Discoveries* (Springfield: Charles
Thomas, 1959), p. 488.

[27] Thwaites, *Journals*, III, p .51; VI, p. 197.

[28] In recent correspondence with Mrs. Charles E. Michel, Jr., of St. Louis, a
great-great-granddaughter (and married to a great-great-grandson!) of Dr. Saugrain, she writes: "I have been told that the author, John Bakeless, claims to have
in his possession Dr. Saugrain's thermometer which was taken on the Lewis and
Clark Expedition." I wrote to Dr. Bakeless about this; he answered, "Sorry, but
I do not have the Saugrain thermometer, and never have had it." And so rests
another bit of legend.

In a letter from Mrs. Michel to this author on March 17, 1957, she relates a brief
summary of the traditional help given by Dr. Saugrain to Lewis and Clark: "The
articles which he made for the Lewis and Clark Expedition were thermometers, the
mercury for which he scraped from his wife's treasured French mirrors . . .

Although there is no specific record that Lewis consulted with or received advice from Dr. Saugrain regarding health care of the men at Camp DuBois for their future journey, it is reasonable that these two men with their mutual interests and inquiring minds would have discussed this important subject many times. Inasmuch as the good doctor was known to have an unfavorable opinion of bleeding, believing that it depleted the patient, he may have tempered the captains' use of the lancet.

Tradition also relates that Dr. Saugrain provided a medicine chest and certain medicines for the Expedition. This is certainly possible but at the end of the list of medical supplies which Lewis requisitioned from the Schuylkill arsenal in Philadelphia was "1 Walnut Chest $4.50" and "1 Pine do. $1.20." [29] A thorough search of the journals does not mention the use of any medicines throughout the extent of the journey other than the medicines which are listed as having been bought by Lewis through the Schuylkill arsenal in Philadelphia, except for Scotts pills (*see* pages 349-51). It may be that Dr. Saugrain provided medicines which were used only locally at Camp DuBois. Also, a medicine chest and medicines supplied by Dr. Saugrain may have been among those lost in the various boat accidents. In view of the fact that he maintained an herb garden from which he concocted medicinal compounds, it is possible that he may have provided Lewis and Clark with some herb medicines.

The amount of information which Lewis probably obtained from his home-remedy, herb-doctor mother, his instructions

phosphorus matches and pharmaceutical supplies (which included smallpox vaccine, and a barometer   .   .   .)

"It is said that Captain Lewis was fascinated with the Doctor's laboratory, and was a frequent visitor during the preparation of the articles." It will be noted from other references in this chapter that the possession of smallpox vaccine this early by Dr. Saugrain was not an impossibility, although improbable.

[29] Jackson, Letters, p. 81.

from Benjamin Rush, his experience as an army officer, his opportunity to read extensively in Jefferson's library while serving as his secretary, and the wide-spread use of home remedies on the frontier, makes it improbable that he obtained from Dr. Saugrain any additional specific items of importance to add to his medicinal armamentarium.

It is interesting to speculate as to whether Dr. Saugrain might have been interested in accompanying Lewis and Clark, or in being invited by them to join the Expedition. He was forty years of age when Lewis and Clark were outfitting the Expedition at Wood River, not much older than John Shields, thirty-five, the oldest man on the Expedition. (Patrick Gass was thirty-three and Captain Clark was thirty years of age.) In view of his interest in travel, and in seeking new knowledge, and of his general hardihood and aggressiveness in coping with the frontier, and the evident advantage of having a doctor accompany the Expedition, it would have been a natural thing for Dr. Saugrain to be tantalized by such a challenge. He certainly would have been a far superior addition to the Expedition than Dr. Patterson of Wheeling. But he said good-bye to the captains and their men at St. Charles on May 21, 1804, and returned to St. Louis to serve his community.

There was still another important medical chapter that Dr. Saugrain was to write into the St. Louis medical community. While at Gallipolis he had treated smallpox with inoculation. He was a widely read man and kept abreast of his profession, and knew of Jenner's vaccine by the time Lewis and Clark came to St. Louis; but there is no indication that he had any of the kine-pox at that time.

It is certain that he knew of vaccination in 1805. A letter from his mother in Paris dated December 30, 1804, to Monsieur Saugrain Vigney, Head Physician at the fort St. Louis

DOCTOR ANTOINE FRANCOIS SAUGRAIN
He provided medical advice and supplies to Lewis while the Expedition was organizing at Camp DuBois.
Courtesy of Mr. Philip von Phul.

DOCTOR SAUGRAIN'S VACCINE ANNOUNCEMENT
In the St. Louis Gazette, May 26, 1809, he advertised that he could provide vaccination for smallpox and would do so to "persons in indigent circumstances."
Courtesy of Missouri Historical Society, St. Louis.

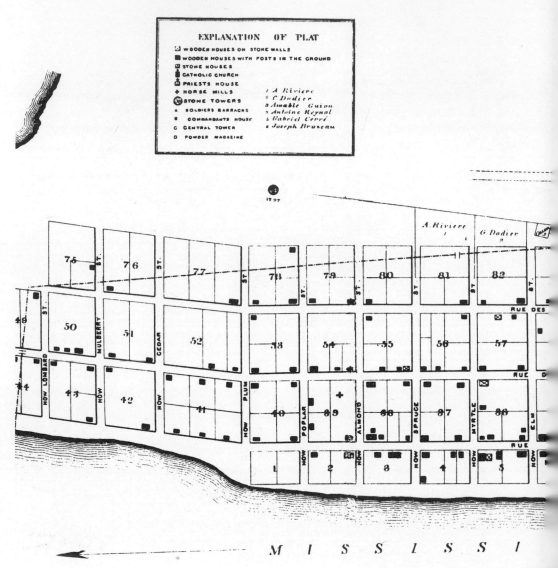

ST. LOUIS IN 1804, as it appeared while Lewis and Clark were
preparing for their Expedition at nearby Wood River Camp.
Courtesy of Missouri Historical Society, St. Louis.

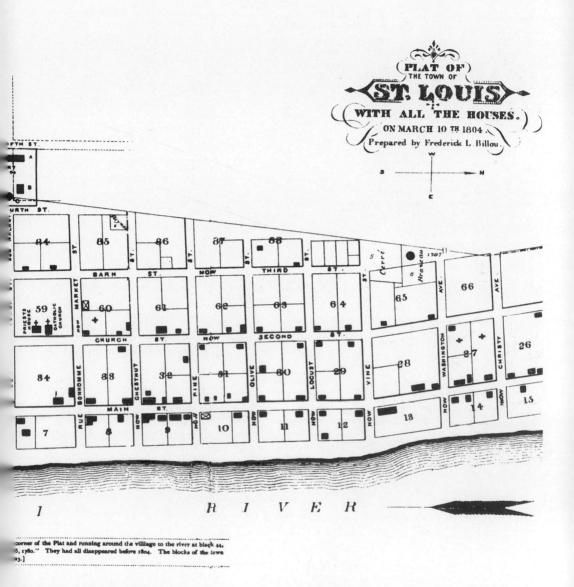

The present-day Jefferson National Memorial Park is bounded by Poplar and Washington streets. The Gateway Arch touches down in the area of blocks seven and nine. Dr. Saugrain's residence was at left in block 50.

THE HOME OF DOCTOR SAUGRAIN

Lewis was probably a frequent visitor here. The home occupied the block between Second and Third, and Gratiot and Lombard streets.

Courtesy of Mr. Philip von Phul.

the Illinois, reads: "Tell me if you are using vaccination. It is quite a success everywhere." [30]

It has been said that Dr. Saugrain obtained his supply of smallpox vaccine from Paris.[31] His own statement in a newspaper account in 1809 was simply: "The undersigned having been politely favored by a friend with the genuine vaccine infection . . . " In view of his great interest in vaccination, as evidenced by his later activity, this certainly could have been one medicine he might have supplied to Lewis and Clark — if he had had any on hand. In view of Lewis' previous

[30] Seen in the Saugrain-Michaux papers at the Mo. Hist. Soc. In this same letter Madame Saugrain writes: "Write me real soon, my dear boy. . . It grieves me to realize that I will not see you or my grandchildren. Let me hear about them and all your family . . . all your brothers and sisters are kissing you. All your family loves you and I do love you above all. Good-bye, my dear boy, write soon to your mother if you love her as much as she loves you. Good-bye again. I kiss you. Your mother Saugrain." There are several more imploring letters from Madame Saugrain to her son, each mentioning that she had received no answer from him. Apparently she died without hearing from him, even though a sister also wrote to him: "We like to read the letters of those whom we love."

I might seem to be treating Dr. Saugrain harshly to follow the above quotation with one from Dr. Benjamin Rush's letter of Nov. 18, 1803, to his son James: "I never knew an instance of a man becoming eminent, respectable, or even wealthy in the profession of medicine who was deficient in punctuality in letter writing. Adieu. From your affectionate though neglected parents." Butterfield, *Letters of Rush*, p. 876.

[31] Mrs. Mary Kennerly Taylor wrote to Mrs. Eva Emery Dye: ". . . during the dreadful small Pox scare among the Indians . . . my Grand Father Saugrain vaccinated them he had sent Paris for the vaccine & he saved the life of hundreds." *See* Dye Mss. in the Oreg. Hist. Soc. The difficulty in shipping live virus makes it improbable that Dr. Saugrain's supply came all the way from Paris, although Jefferson records receiving a live supply from Jenner. Dye used the following dialogue in *The Conquest:*

Dr. Saugrain to Lewis: " 'And have you any kine-pox, for I hear those Omahas have died like cattle in a plague.' " To which Lewis replies: " 'President Jefferson particularly directed me to carry some kine-pox virus, but really, what he gave me seems to have lost its virtue. I wrote him so from Cincinnati, but I fear it will be too late to supply the deficiency.'

"Out of his medicine chest in the corner, the little Doctor brought two tiny vials. 'Sent me from Paris. Carry it, explain it to the Indians, use it wherever you can ——' " Dye, *The Conquest*, p. 159-60.

request for a fresh supply from President Jefferson, he probably would have been glad to have accepted a replenished supply from Dr. Saugrain.

We do know that in 1809 Dr. Saugrain, through an advertisement in the *Gazette,* was informing "such physicians and other intelligent persons as reside beyond the limits of his accustomed practice that he would with much pleasure upon application furnish them with vaccine infection." And to his greater credit, and representative of the ethics of his profession, he also published in the *Gazette* that "persons in indigent circumstances, paupers and Indians will be vaccinated and attended gratis." [32]

Although Dr. Saugrain was not mentioned in the journals when the Expedition returned to St. Louis, as he had been when it left St. Charles, it reasonably can be assumed that he would be among those referred to in the last journal entry, September 25, 1806: "payed some visits of form, to the gentlemen of St. Louis." [33]

Dr. Saugrain lived out the rest of his years in St. Louis, dying on May 19, 1820. He left a legacy of heirs and tradition, and an impress upon the Lewis and Clark Expedition and on the city of St. Louis.[34]

---

[32] St. Louis Gazette, Oct. 26, 1809.

[33] Thwaites, *Journals,* v, p. 395.

[34] The author wishes to inform the reader that the Medcal Hist. Mus. of the St. Louis Med. Soc., 3839 Lindell Blvd., has an excellent replica of Dr. Saugrain's workshop. The reader may also refer to a recent title by Shirley Seiffert, a writer of historical novels of the St. Louis area, on Dr. Saugrain: *The Medicine Man* (Phila: Lippincott, 1971). This was her last novel, and was published posthumously.

BOOK THREE

The Expedition
of
Lewis and Clark

The object of your mission is to explore the Missouri river, & such principal stream of it, as, by it's course & communication with the waters of the Pacific Ocean, may offer the most direct & practicable water communication across the continent, for purposes of commerce.

Jefferson's instructions to Lewis. Thwaites, *Journals*, VII, p. 248

Bold and Farseeing Pathfinders
Who Carried the Flag of the Young Republic
to the Western Ocean and Revealed
an Unknown Empire to the Uses of Mankind

Inscription on Paul Keck's Lewis and Clark Monument at Charlottesville, Virginia

XI

Up the Missouri

The trouble with going up the Missouri in a boat is that you have to take the boat along.[1]

The Corps of Discovery left its winter headquarters at Camp DuBois on May 14, 1804, heading their keelboat[2] and two pirogues directly across the Mississippi River into the mouth of the Missouri, on whose waters they were to live and struggle for many months.[3] There is no notation in Clark's *Field Notes* that trial runs of the keelboat were made prior to the beginning of their voyage (the keelboat, of course, had a good trial run on the Ohio with Lewis, but with very little load compared to its present one; undoubtedly the two captains felt complete confidence in their boats and in their crew).

Clark was the lone captain when the Expedition left Camp DuBois; Lewis remained behind in St. Louis to transact some final business and to conduct the amenities of diplomacy and friendship with the leaders of the St. Louis community. Undoubtedly it was Clark's intention to make a short run with

---

[1] Vestal, The *Missouri*, p. 11

[2] This boat was "fifty-five feet long, drawing three feet of water, carrying a large squaresail and twenty-two oars, a deck of ten feet in the bow, and stem formed a forecastle and cabin, while the middle was covered by lockers, which might be raised so as to form a breastwork in the case of attack." Nicholas Biddle, *History of the Expedition Under the Command of Lewis and Clark* (Philadelphia: Bradford and Inskeep, 1814), I, pp. 2-3. Hereafter cited as Biddle, *History of the Expedition.*

[3] DeVoto gives the length of the Missouri River as 2464.4 miles. DeVoto, *Course of Empire*, p. 425.

the Expedition while waiting for Lewis. On May 13 he recorded in his notes: ". . . all in health and readiness to
set out . . ." *

On the fifteenth the Expedition pulled into St. Charles,
where they expected to be met by Lewis, but he had not
arrived. Clark immediately faced a situation involving the
discipline of his crew: whether to keep the men confined to
bivouac or to "turn them loose on the town" with some admonition. Clark told his men that "the Commanding officer is
full[y] assured that every man of his Detachment will have
a true respect for their own Dignity and not make it necessary
for him to leave St. Charles for a more retired situation." As
might be expected, some of the men did not act with the
decorum desired by their commander. Two days later a
court-martial was held for three of the privates, "to hear and
determine evidences aduced against . . . for being absent last night without leave." These men were tried formally
by their fellows and sentenced "to receive 25 lashes each on
their naked back, but the Court recommended them from
their former Good conduct to the mercy of the commanding
officer . . ." However, another offender, Collins, was sentenced "to receive fifty lashes on his naked back."

This court-martial procedure and method of punishment by
lashing was consistent with Army practices of the time.[4] It is
often thought that Lewis was the main disciplinarian of the

---

* Thwaites, *Journals*, I, p. 16.

4 There were a total of six courts-martial on the Expedition: 1. This one at St.
Charles; 2. Collins and Hall, for stealing whiskey, June 29, 1804. Collins received
100 lashes and Hall received 50; 3. Willard received 100 lashes, 25 each day for
four successive days, for being asleep while on guard duty; 4. Reed, for deserting,
ran the gauntlet four times, and was discharged; 5. Newman, for insubordination,
received 75 lashes; 6. Howard, for climbing over the fence at Fort Mandan, was
to be court-martialed, but there was no further notation regarding the incident. *See*
Thwaites, *Journals*, I, pp. 18-20, 61, 76, 112, 192. There are no further references in
the journals to courts-martial or floggings.

Expedition, but here Clark did not hesitate to impress upon the men that discipline was most essential to the success of the Expedition, and in Lewis' absence promptly proceeded with the court-martial. The months spent at Camp DuBois had been used to emphasize to the men that each man's performance in all regards was important to every other individual. Apparently the occasional floggings and other disciplinary measures used at Camp DuBois had not fully impressed some of the men that the captains meant business.

At St. Charles brothers, Drs. Jeremiah and Seth Millington, supposed to be the first doctors who settled there, were engaged extensively in raising the castor oil bean and manufacturing castor oil. Local St. Charles historical tradition is that "when Lewis and Clark left on their Expedition in 1804 to explore the Louisiana Purchase territory and map an overland route to the Pacific Ocean in making final preparations in St. Charles, they bought a quantity of bottles of Castor Oil to keep their men well." [5] Lewis and Clark were amply supplied with physics for the men of their Expedition, particularly Dr. Rush's "Bilious Pills." Just why they would need to lay in a greater store of physics for the Expedition is hardly explainable, although this was one of the first medications that came to mind when treating anyone for anything in those days.

---

[5] St. Charles *Journal,* April 27, 1967. Charles Clarke states that ". . . castor-oil was obtained from Doctors Jeremiah and Seth Millington. These two American doctors who had arrived in St. Charles in January 1799, were now raising medicinal plants on their farms located above the town." Charles G. Clarke, *The Men of the Lewis and Clark Expedition* (Glendale, Ca: Arthur Clark Co., 1970), p. 33.

Clarke writes in a personal communication: "Of course we now have no way of knowing for sure but I have wondered if that $99 that Drouillard brought over to Captain Clark at St. Charles from Lewis in St. Louis (May 18, 1804 — Thwaites, *Journals,* i, p. 21) could partly be for the castor oil which Clark had discovered could be purchased in St. Charles." Charles Clarke might have found an affirmative answer in the letter Drouillard was bringing to Clark from Lewis, but which was lost.

There is no record to substantiate the story that Lewis and Clark purchased castor oil from the Millington brothers. It is very doubtful that such a purchase was made, even though the product was available. The medical supplies for the Expedition already included an ample supply of cathartics; Cutright quotes an estimate of 1,300 doses of physic in the official drug supply[6] Also, storing supplies of any material in breakable bottles would not be very practical.[7]

While at St. Charles the captains did not note (and may not have had need of it) a shrub which James noted in his travels while in the region of St. Charles: "a shrub . . . much used among the natives, in the cure of Lues venera. They make a decoction of the root, which they continue to drink for some time. It is called the 'blue wool' by the French, and is the Symphoria racemosa of Pursh . . ."[8]

Lewis finally arrived at St. Charles on May 20, accompanied by a coterie of notables of St. Louis, and "found the party in good health and spirits." The following day the captains left St. Charles to proceed on their uninterrupted journey up the Missouri. They faithfully recorded in their journals a description of the landscape, which they greatly admired, and of the wild fowl and deer that were killed by the hunters to supplement their food supply. They described and collected specimens of wild fruits and flowers.

---

6 Paul Cutright, "I Gave Him Barks and Saltpeter," *Great Adventures of the Old West* (New York: Amer. Heritage Pr., 1969), p. 11.

7 Apparently castor oil was not in common use on the frontier. An exception, however, is found in the case of John B. Wyeth, who traveled to Oregon in 1832 and was attacked by yellow fever in New Orleans. A French doctor gave him castor oil, four wine glasses of it in one day, which he assured him would "scare away" the fever. Wyeth wrote: "Its operation was not one-way, but every way. I thought I should have no insides left to go home with." Philip J. Jordan and I. H. Pierce, "Materia Medica from Ohio to California," in Ohio State Medical Jour., Vol. 37, No. 9 (Sept. 1941), pp. 871-875.

8 James, *An Account of an Expedition*, i, p. 73. In Vol. ii, Chapter xii, James has a good account of "Diseases and Medicine Among the Omawhaws."

The first major accident which might have resulted in a
tragedy costing one of the captains' lives occurred on May
23. "Capt. Lewis near falling from the Pinecles of rocks 300
feet he caught at 20 foot." [9] Lewis, pursuing his scientific
activities, was exploring Indian pictographs on the banks of
the Missouri. Fortunately his fall was interrupted at twenty
feet, without injury to himself.

The men were soon getting multiple demonstrations of
what would be demanded of them in sustained and hazardous exertion up the Missouri. Although the river was running at springtime high water, there were still continuous
hazards of submerged and floating trees, shallow sandbars and
rapids, and the danger of collapsing river banks. The willingness and stamina of the men were tested continuously, with
the use of the cordelle [10] to pull the boat while they waded in
water or walked along the shores, and the use of the poles to
steer and push the boat upstream, with some respite occasionally when the wind was right for the use of their square
sail. Log jams, or embarrasses, and submerged logs, or saw-

---

[9] Thwaites, *Journals*, I, p. 27. This "Pinnacle" was commemorated by ceremonies
and placement of a plaque by the Corniela Greene Chapter of the Daughters of the
American Revolution on Oct. 24, 1971.

[10] Chittenden describes the use of the cordelle: "The cordelle was the main
reliance — a long line attached to the top of the mast, which stood a little forward
of the center of the boat. It passed through a ring, which was fastened by a short
line to the bow to help guide the boat, and was drawn by from twenty to forty
men strung along the shore. . .

"It often happened at river crossings and elsewhere that the cordelle could not
be used, and in such cases poles had to be resorted to. These were of various
lengths suited to convenient handling, and were equipped with balls or knobs at
the upper ends to rest in the hollow of the shoulder. To propel the boat by means
of these poles the voyageurs were ranged in single file on each side of the deck
near the bow, facing aft. Planting their poles on the river bottom, pointing down
stream, they pushed steadily against them, at the same time walking towards the
stern along the *passe avant*, a narrow walk some fifteen inches wide on each side
of the cargo box, while the boat, yielding to their pressure, moved ahead." H. M.
Chittenden, *The American Fur Trade of the Far West* (New York, 1935), I, p. 33.

yers,[11] were a continual obstruction to progress and greatly
endangered the boat. Often the winds chilled them and driving rains drenched them. And with all of this they stopped
three times daily to make camp and eat, and often to dry out
their clothes and equipment. The days of training at Camp
DuBois were paying off.

The detachment orders of May 26 indicate the routine and
discipline of the crew:

> The Sergt. at the center will command the guard, manage the sails,
> see that the men at the oars do their duty; that they come on board
> at a proper season in the morning, and that the boat gets under
> way in due time; he will . . . attend to the issues of speritous
> liquors; he shall regulate the halting of the batteaux through the
> day to give the men refreshment . . . it shall be his duty also
> to post a centinel on the bank, near the boat whenever we come
> too and halt in the course of the day, at the same time he will. . .
> reconnoiter the forrest arround the place of landing to the distance
> of at least one hundred paces. when we come too for the purpose
> of encamping at night, the Sergt. of the guard shall post two
> centinels immediately on our landing.

> The day after tomorrow lyed corn and grece will be issued to
> the party, the next day Poark and flour, and the day following
> indian meal and poark; and in conformity to that rotiene provisions
> will continue to be issued to the party untill further orders. should
> any of the messes prefer indian meal to flour they may receive it
> accordingly — no poark is to be issued when we have fresh meat
> on hand.

Waiting for and seeking the hunters became a frequent
occurrence as the Expedition went along. The forward prog-

---

11 "Another dangerous obstruction is a tree becoming undermined and falling
into the river, and the roots fastening themselves on the muddy bottom, while, by
the constant action of the current, the limbs wear off and the body keeps sawing up
and down with great force, rising frequently several feet above the water, and then
sinking as much below. These are called 'sawyers,' & often cause accidents to
unsuspecting navigators." Samuel S. Forman, "Great Heart of the American
Dominion," *Jour. of Amer. Hist.*, I, No. 3, pp. 467-84.

ress of the Expedition never halted, but neither did Lewis abandon the men. A pirogue was often left for a hunter; occasionally other men went back to seek the lost man, or provisions were tied to a tree in an obvious elevated position where they could be found by the man but not reached by animals. The men knew it was their responsibility to catch up with the Expedition, but they also were confident they would not be abandoned.

On June 3 Clark wrote that "I have a bad cold with a Sore throat." His June 5 notation in the journal indicates the extent to which the men depended upon foraging on the landscape: "after jurking the meat killed yesterday (7 deer) . . . my Servent York Swam to the Sand bar to geather Greens for our Dinner, and returned with a Sufficient quantity wild Creases [Cresses] or Tung [Tongue] grass." On June 6 Clark notes that "I am still very unwell with a Sore throat & headake."

Clark noted in his journal on June 10 that he had walked widely and found grapes and wild plums which "hang in great quantities on the bushes," and "great numbers of Deer." Occasionally bears were also being encountered and killed for meat. Any meat above the immediate needs for food was jerked by exposing thin slices of it to the sun for drying — "which is a constant Practice to have all of the fresh meat not used, Dried in this way."

On the sixteenth Clark noted "the Mosquitoes and Ticks are noumerous & bad." This is the first mention of ticks; they were to be encountered throughout the journey without any suggestion of any corpsman developing tick fever.[12]

On June 17 Clark wrote that "The party is much aflicted

---

[12] Also called Rocky Mountain Spotted Fever. There is a good historical accunt about it by Philip A. Kaliseh, "Rocky Mountain Spotted Fever," in *Montana, The Magazine of Western History*, Vol. xxiii, No. 2, pp. 44-55.

with Boils and Several have the Deassentary which I contribute to the water (which is muddy) . . . The Ticks
& Musquiters are verry troublesome." (Lewis brought mosquito nets or "Bier" from Philadelphia.) There are continual
references to mosquitoes and to illnesses of the men, but there
are no descriptions of illnesses which indicate the typical
chills and fever of malaria.

Whitehouse wrote on June 20 that ". . . the watter run
so rappid that the men of the French peirouge Could not
make headway by Roeing Or poleing the(y) had to Jumpd.
out and push her through the water."

The occurrence of boils and dysentery so early in the trip
was a warning of the precarious balance between diet and
infection that would plague the men throughout the journey.
They were living mainly on a high protein diet, and the jerked
meat probably was always contaminated with bacteria. The
meat jerked by themselves probably was cleaner that the meat
and grease which they bought from the Indians and other
traders. Knowledge of bacterial infection was a half-century
in the future. They probably accepted their meat as being
clean and edible unless it was crawling with maggots or so
spoiled as to be repugnant to the nose as well as to the mouth.
The lack of fresh fruit and vegetables also contributed to a
lowered resistance to infection, as did the lack of frequent
bathing and the wearing of soiled and unwashed clothing.
Undoubtedly they developed considerable resistance to these
bacterial infections, but not total immunity, as the future
would show. They were to have repeated and occasionally
almost fatal episodes of intestinal infection.

Sand was to be bothersome to the men, particularly in
crossing the Dakota country. On the twentieth Clark wrote:
"My Servent York nearly loseing an Eye by a man throwing
Sand into it."

On June 29, while encamped at the mouth of the Kansas River, Clark recorded the following: "John Collins Charged with getting drunk on his post this Morning out of whiskey put under his charge as a Sentinal, and for Suffering Hugh Hall to draw whiskey out of the Said Barrel intended for the party." Both were court-martialed, with Collins sentenced to one hundred and Hall to fifty lashes on their bare backs, administered by their fellow men. Nothing is noted in the journals about the suffering of these men either during the flogging, or the care of their wounds, or giving them relief from any of their heavy duties as the Expedition went on with its routine. Their backs must have been swollen and bleeding and raw from the abrasions caused by the lashes. The wearing of clothing next to the skin, or the exposure of the skin to the elements and insects, and the working of muscles under the inflamed skin, must have been extremely painful to them. There is no indication in the journals that special consideration was given to them, or pain-relieving medicines provided for them. Their sentence had been given to them by their comrades, and approved by their captains. They were soldiers; they took their punishment and "proceeded on."

Snakes would be encountered frequently by the men, but not all of them would be poisonous. They wore moccasins and never heavy shoes, and thus it was easy for a snake to sink its fangs into flesh. This occurred first on July 4: "Fields got bit by a snake, which was quickly doctored by bark by Cap. Lewis." Biddle, who edited the first edition of the journals, and who received supplementary information from Clark and Shannon, states that "a poultice of bark and gun-powder was sufficient to cure the wound." In his *Field Notes*, Clark also notes that Fields' "foot swelled much."

Whitehouse recorded further on July 4: "The day mighty hot when we went to toe the Sand (s)calded Our (feet) Some fled from the rope . . . had to put on Our Mockisons."

On July 7 the first bleeding for medical purposes was re-corded: ". . . one man verry sick, Struck with the Sun, [Clark's *Field Notes* identify this man as Frasier]. Capt. Lewis bled him & gave Niter which has revived him much." The temperature had been recorded as ninety-six degrees on June 30. Working in extremely hot weather would affect the men; on July 8, ". . . five men Sick to day with a violent head ake &c." Headache was not recorded as a common com-plaint on the Expedition, and therefore the assignment of this symptom to the hot weather might be correct. In his *Field Notes* of the same date, Clark adds that "Several with Boils," and "the sick man much better."

New detachment orders were issued on July 8 in recogni-tion of the increased necessity to husband the food supply. These orders placed responsibility on three superintendents for the proper use of food and the care of the cooking utensils. This was to assure proper nourishment with no waste.

By July 10 Clark wrote in his *Field Notes* "our men all get-ting well but much fatigued." On July 12 the Expedition delayed their progress for a day, ". . . refreshing our men who are much fatigued," and to conduct a court-martial. The journals recount that Alexander Willard had been guilty of being asleep while serving as a sentinel. "To this Charge the prisoner pleads Guilty of Lying Down, and Not Guilty, of Going to Sleep.

"The Court after Duly Considering the evidence aduced, are of oppinion that the Prisoner Alexdr. Willard is guilty of every part of the Charge exhibited against him . . . do Sentience him to receive One hundred lashes, on his bear back, at four different times in equal proportion. and Order that the punishment Commence this evening at Sunset, and Continue to be inflicted (by the Guard) every evening untill

Completed." And Willard dutifully took the daily lashes inflicted on a back already raw from the preceding floggings.

The journals are replete with references to the beauty and utility of "the prairie" which extended for unending miles back from the river. This permitted supplement of their meat diet with other edibles from the countryside. On July 15 Clark wrote: "I saw Great quantities of Grapes, Plums of 2 kinds, Wild Cherries of 2 Kinds, Hazelnuts and Gooseberries." They also supplemented their diet with "greens" such as lambs-quarter,[13] gathered along the river banks in the way of the pioneers after them. In spite of the availability of varied diet from the countryside, it is probable that more imperative duties prevented the men from gathering enough berries and "greens." It is probable also that these men chose to subsist on an essentially meat diet as is usually true of most hard-working men. This probably accounts for the continued recording of notes like the ones of July 14: "Several men unwell with Boils, Felons &c.;" and of July 17: "Several of the party much inflicted with tumers of different kinds, Som of which is verry troublesom, and difficelt to cure." But there was no reference to poor Willard who, presumably, continued to receive his twenty-five lashes each day until he had received the sentence of one hundred.

On July 18 Clark took time to note: "Saw a Dog nearly Starved on the bank, gave him some meet." Dog meat was to become a frequent and liked source of meat for members of the Expedition before long. Clark was not one of these, and seems to be the only one who did not come to like dog meat. This journal entry of July 18 reflects his kindness to animals and that he preferred to feed rather than to eat dog!

Ordway noted in his journal on July 19 that ". . . we gathered a quantity of cherries at noontime & put into the

---

13 Thwaites identifies this as *Chenopodium album*, a succulent weed.

Whiskey barrel . . ." Ordway does not record if this was a means of preserving the cherries, or of improving the palatability of the cherries or the whiskey! On this same date, Whitehouse records in his journal that he sustained a cut, but the word indicating the location of the cut is not legible; he records that it "was one inch and a half long."

The next day Clark wrote: "It is worthey of observation to mention that our Party has been much healthier on the Voyage than parties of the same number is in any other Situation. Tumers have been troublesom to them all." Clark was noting the healthful effect of moving camps from day to day, as other observers in earlier explorations had recorded before him.

There were times when the weather was intensely hot and the men sought "some Situation . . . Calculated to make our party Comfortable . . . where they Could reeceve the benefit of a Shade," as Clark wrote on July 22, and at the same time lay out their supplies in the sun to be dried. One of the choice and frequent locations for the campsites was on any of the many islands encountered in the river; usually there was firewood, the river water was usually clean, and there was better protection from the Indians.

On July 23 the journal entry says, "one man with a tumor on his breast;" Clark recorded this in his *Field Notes* as "one man with a big riseing on his left breast." On July 26 Clark records one of their first encounters with beaver: ". . . five beaver Cough(t) near the Camp the flesh of which we made use of." On this date Lewis "opened the Tumer of a man on the left breast, which discharged half a point (pint)."

All of the men who kept journals complained continuously of the great number of mosquitoes. On the thirtieth, Clark recorded that "Several men with verry bad Biols," but went on to say that "everything in prime order men in high spirits." Clark wrote in his *Field Notes* that "Sergt Floyd verry unwell a bad cold &c." This was the first mention of Floyd being ill. The next day Floyd confided to his journal: "I am verry Sick and Has ben for Sometime but have Recovered my helth again." Neither Floyd or the captains had recorded previously anything about his being "verry sick;" this also adds to some mystery about the cause of Floyd's death.

The men were getting enough to eat off the land, with turkeys, geese, beaver, fish, deer, berries, and various fruits available to them. Pollution had not yet become a part of the American landscape; Clark wrote on this day: "The air is pure and helthy so far as we can judge."

On August 11 the Expedition reached the great mound where "Black Bird was burried 4 years ago," in an upright position with all of his accoutrements and personal possessions. Clark wrote that "on the Creek & Hills near it [the mound] about 400 of the Mahars Died with the Small Pox."

The Expedition made camp about three miles above the location of the Mahar village and fished a nearby creek: ". . . with Some small Willows & Bark we made a Drag and hauled up the Creek, and Cought 318 fish of different kind i.e. Pike, Bass, Salmon, perch, red horse, small cat, and a kind of perch Called Silver fish. . ." The ponds were covered with "Ducks, Plovers of different kinds." From the same location, Lewis and twelve men caught eight hundred fish on the following day.

August 18, 1804, was a day of contrasting emotions for the corps. A man by the name of Moses Reed had been captured after deserting. Clark writes:

> . . . proceeded to the trial of Reed, he confessed that he "Deserted & stold a public Rifle Shot-pouch Powder & Ball" and requested we would be as favourable with him as we Could consistantly with our Oathes — which we were and only sentenced him to run the Gantlet four times through the Party & that each man with 9 Swichies Should punish him and for him not to be

considered in future as one of the Party . . . Cap L. Birth day the evening, was closed with an extra gill of whiskey and a Dance untill 11 oClock.

The Indians were adversely impressed with the punishment, and tried to intercede with the captains in Reed's favor.

It might seem incongrous to celebrate so joyously the birthday of one of the captains when a man had been so severely punished, but again it must be remembered that such punishment was an army routine for infractions of discipline, and that the punishment was decreed by Reed's fellow members of the corps. In a footnote in Ordway's journal, Quaife states: "In after years Bratton was in the habit of relating to his children that instead of switches the men used their ramrods on the culprit, and that the blows were well laid on, in the fear that anyone showing leniency would incur similar punishment."[14]

The following day the mood of the festivities noting Lewis' birthday was considerably dampened. The journals of August 19 note that ". . . Serjeant Floyd is taken verry bad all at once with a Biliose Chorlick we attempt to relieve him without success as yet, he gets worst and we are much allarmed at his situation, all (give) attention to him." This was the first notation made in the captain's journals about Floyd's illness (although Clark mentioned it in his *Field Notes* on July 30 1804).[15]

However, July 31 Ordway had noted that "Sergeant Floyd

---

[14] Quaife, "The Journals of Lewis and Ordway," p. 112, fns.

[15] Criswell writes that Clark recorded in the journals about the care of Floyd. "Captain Lewis bled him & gave Nitra which has revived him very much." Criswell cites as reference Vol. I, p. 70 of the journals. *See* Elijah H. Criswell, "Lewis and Clark, Linguistic pioneers," in *The Univ. of Mo. Studies*, xv, No. 2 (1940), p. xxxv. But this journal entry is on July 7, 1804, about six weeks before Floyd's terminal illness, and refers to someone else: "One man verry sick, Struck with the Sun, Capt. Lewis bled him & gave Niter which has revived him much." Thwaites, *Journals*, I, p. 70.

had been sick several days but now is Gitting Some better."
Floyd was one of the three sergeants, all of whom kept a
journal. It is natural that Floyd would have noted things about
himself which were not recorded elsewhere. As early as July
11 he wrote: "came to about 12 oclock P.M. for the porpos of
resting on(e) or two days the men is all Sick." The following
day he wrote: "ouer object in Delaying hear is to tak Some
observations and rest the men who are much fategeued. . ."
On July 31, the same date that Sergeant Ordway had first
noted that Floyd was ill, Floyd wrote of himself. "I am verry
Sick and Has ben for Somtime but have Recovered my Helth
again. . ." [16]

Sergeant Patrick Gass wrote on August 15 that "This day
sergeant Floyd became very sick and remained so all night.
He was seized with a complaint somewhat like a violent
cholick." [17] Gass probably meant to indicate that Floyd had
become ill on the nineteenth; he has no journal entries from
the fifteenth until the twentieth.

On Monday, August 20, 1804, Clark wrote: "Sergeant
Floyd much weaker and no better. . . We set out under
a gentle breeze from the s.E. and proceeded on verry well.
Sergeant Floyd as bad as he can be no pulse & nothing will
stay a moment on his Stomach or bowels. Passed two Islands
on the s.s. and the first Bluff on the s.s. Floyd Died with a great

---

[16] Floyd's brief journal was discovered by Thwaites among the papers of Lyman
C. Draper, director of the Wisc. Hist. Soc., in 1893. Floyd's journal is published in
Thwaites, *Journals*, VII. The original Floyd Journal is in the State Hist. Soc. of
Wisc.

[17] The journal of Patrick Gass was the first of all the corps' journals to be published, in Pittsburgh in 1807, by David McKeehan. McKeehan was a teacher who
polished and corrected Gass' prose, and then apparently threw the original away
as it has never been found. What a choice manuscript this must have been in the
language of this colorful sergeant! A bitter controversy developed between McKeehan and Lewis when the latter tried to delay all publication of the unofficial journals of the expedition until the official Journals appeared. *See* Jackson, *Letters*, pp.
399, 408.

deal of Composure, before his death he Said to me, 'I am going away I want you to write me a letter.' We buried him on the top of the bluff ½ Mile below a Small river to which we Gave his name, he was buried with the Honors of War much lamented, a Seeder post with the Name Sergt. C. Floyd died here 20th of august 1804 was fixed at the head of his grave. This Man at all times gave us proofs of his firmness and Determined resolution to doe Service to his Countrey and honor to himself after paying all the honor to our Decesed brother we camped in the Mouth of floyds River about 30 yards wide, a butifull evening."

All the other journalists (Whitehouse, Gass, Ordway) made a similar recording of Floyd's death and burial, all assuring that "he was layed out in the most decent manner possible."

Despite this well-documented death of Sergeant Floyd, one historian wrote regarding the Lewis and Clark Expedition: "This was a labor of love for these men. It had to be, for the material rewards were minimal, and the incredible record of not losing a man of the voyage attests not only to the hardy constitutions and excellent training but to their desire to make the Expedition a success." [18]

Floyd had written in his diary on July 11: "the men is all Sick." Neither Floyd nor the other diarists gave much indication of the nature of the extensive illness of the men, except Clark had written on August 22 regarding the ill-tasting waters of the Missouri: "Capt. Lewis in proveing the quality of those minerals was Near poisoning himself by the fumes & tast of the Cobalt which had the appearance of Soft Isonglass. Copperas & alum is verry pisen . . . Capt. Lewis took a Dost of Salts to work off the effects of the arsenic." Biddle's journal entry made from conference with Clark at

18 Richard E. Oglesby, *Manuel Lisa and the Opening of the Missouri Fur Trade* (Norman: Univ. of Okla., 1963), p. 30.

a later date indicates Clark's continued impression of poisoning from the water: "The appearance of these mineral substances enable us to account for the disorders of the stomach, with which the party had been affected since they left the river Sioux." [19] The men had used freely the water of the Missouri, on which floated a scum; now by dipping deeply and avoiding the scum, they obtained pure water, and their malady soon ceased. Throughout the journey the men had diarrhea very frequently, which was ascribed by themselves to ill tasting water and varied diets.[20]

Brackenridge wrote on his journey up the Missouri in 1811:

> This chief (Black Bird of the Nahas) was as famous in his time amongst all the nations in this part of the world . . . yet, the secret of his greatness was nothing more than a quantity of arsenic, which he had procured from some trader. He denounced death against anyone who displeased him, or opposed his wishes; it is therefore not surprising that he, who held at his disposal the lives of others, should possess unlimited power, and excite universal terror.[21]

Black Bird had been dead for some years, and there is no indication that any succeeding chief possessed arsenic, or that this poison was present in any of the water supplies. Whatever was the cause of Floyd's illness and death, it is most unlikely that it was due to some poison. The most common opinion expressed as the probable cause of Floyd's death is appendicitis. The recordings of the various diarists are compatible with a chronic low-grade appendicitis which became suddenly fulminating and ruptured with ensuing peritonitis.

Lewis' continued gastrointestinal complaints must have

---

[19] Biddle, *History of the Expedition*, i, p. 50.

[20] *See also* notes in Jackson, *Letters*, p. 515.

[21] H. M. Brackenridge, *Views of Louisiana* (Pittsburgh: Spear and Eichbaum, 1814), pp. 229-30.

been of some concern to him after Floyd's recent death with similar, although more violent, symptoms. Clark wrote on August 25 that "Capt. Lewis much fatigued from heat the day it being verry hot & he being in a debilitated state from the Precautions he as obliged to take to prevent the effects of the Cobalt, & Minl Substance which had like to have poisoned him two days ago . . ."

Dillon states that "he [Floyd] might have been suffering from appendicitis, hepatitis, or a malignant diarrhea which, like cholera, was draining away his body's fluids. He may have been afflicted with nothing more than food poisoning caused by some staphylococcus bacteria which tortured the men with painful boils." [22] It is very unlikely that Floyd would have had either cholera or food poisoning without any of the other members of the Expedition being seriously sick — although the above journal entry shows that Lewis did have lingering if not severe gastrointestinal symptoms.

In writing about Floyd's death Jacobs relates that:

Here the party experienced the first serious loss that had befallen them, in the death of one of their number, Sergeant Floyd, who was taken sick on the nineteenth, and died on the twentieth. He was the youngest man of the corps,[23] a Kentuckian by birth, and a distant relative of Capt. Clarke.[24] Being naturally of a delicate constitution he had embarked on this expedition in the hope of acquiring better health, but the exposure superadded to imprudence was too severe, and he had to succumb in spite of all that could be done to saye him. The immediate cause of his death was

---

[22] Dillon, *Meriwether Lewis*, p. 122.

[23] Incorrect; Floyd was not the youngest. Shannon was the youngest member of the corps, being only 19 years of age.

[24] Floyd's sister Nancy married George Rogers, a cousin of Clark. This is probably the reason that Sergeant Floyd's younger brother Nathaniel wrote to his sister Nancy regarding Floyd's death that "Our dear Charles died on the voyage of colic. He was well cared for as Clark was There. . ." *See* Constant R. Marks, "The Life of Sergeant Chas. Floyd," in *Pioneering in the Northwest* (Sioux City: Deitch & Lamar Co., 1924), p. 73.

as follows: He had been amusing himself and carousing at an Indian dance until he became overheated and it being his duty to stand guard that night, he laid himself down on a sandbar of the Missouri, despising the shelter of a tent offered him by his comrade on guard, and was soon seized with the cramp cholic which terminated his life.[25]

This small volume of Jacobs' was published in 1859, eleven years before the death of Patrick Gass; presumably Gass enlarged upon the circumstances of Floyd's death in his reminiscences to Jacobs, providing more information — or opinion — than he had confided directly to his diary.

The revelry in camp the night before Floyd's death, incident to the celebration of Meriwether Lewis' birthday, was recorded by several diarists. Although such an occasion called for a "gill or two" of whiskey, and Cruzatte's fiddle contributed to the dancing and merriment, this hardly merits the portrayal of "carousing at an Indian dance." Also, it is highly improbable that the captains would have permitted one of their sergeants who was due to stand guard to throw "himself down on a sandbar," whether due to carousing or illness, without applying discipline or medical care. On the other hand, perhaps Gass related the true situation to Jacobs, feeling less anguish about Floyd's death after so many years had passed, and thinking there would be less embarrassment to the family in relating the circumstances at this later date.

Jacobs' account also calls for comment when he states in reference to Floyd that he was "naturally of a delicate constitution [and had] embarked on this expedition in the hope of acquiring better health." There is no direct reference in any of the journals, including Clark's *Field Notes* made at Camp DuBois, to indicate that Floyd was the least bit unhealthy or

25 J. G. Jacobs, The Life and Times of Patrick Gass (Wellsburg, Va: Jacob & Smith, 1859), p. 43.

delicate, or that there was any restriction of his regular duties. There had been repeated expressions from the captains that only healthy, strong men were to be enlisted in the corps. Both Patrick Gass and Alexander Willard state that over a hundred men applied but could not pass the examination. This examination may have been made in reference to the men's skills and attitudes rather than their physical condition. There is no record to indicate that these men had any kind of physical examination, and a physician was never in attendance. Only the development of some obvious chronic disease or ailment, such as advanced tuberculosis or a symptomatic hernia, would have been apparent.

Although Floyd was a distant relative of Clark's and a cousin of Sergeant Pryor, it is highly doubtful that he would have been taken along on the Expedition if his health was such as to question his durability, or that the captains and their men would have chosen as a sergeant anyone who was a physical weakling. Journal notes recorded up the Missouri indicate that Floyd had taken his turn hunting with Captain Clark and Drouillard.

Bakeless seems to be impressed with the probability of Jacobs' account when he writes: "Capering too vigorously while dancing with the Indians, Sgt. Floyd returned to camp just in time to go on guard, badly overheated. He flung himself down on a sandbar near the river, refusing the shelter of a tent, and was soon seized with what Sgt. Gass describes as 'the camp colic.' It is just possible that he really had appendicitis." [26] Holman accepts the plausibility of poisoning: "only one of the Expedition died — Sergeant Floyd, and he died on the way west from drinking poisonous water." [27] Ghent

[26] Bakeless, *Partners in Discovery*, p. 123.

[27] Frederick V. Holman, "Lewis and Clark Expedition at Fort Clatsop," in *Oreg. Hist. Qtly.*, Vol. 27 (Sept. 1926), p. 277.

SERGEANT FLOYD'S SKULL
Left: Mr. Carl Wells of the Sioux City Historical
Assn. with the plaster mold, made before reburial
in 1895. Right: Mr. B.R. Diamond, museum director,
holding a piece of board from Floyd's coffin.

MONUMENT TO SERGEANT FLOYD
At Sioux City, Iowa,
viewed from the south.
Courtesy of Dr. V.S. Hinds.

PSORALEA ESCULENTA
Sacagawea ate the tuber of this plant at Great Falls, on which Lewis
blamed her relapse. This photo is of the specimen collected by Lewis,
and remains in the Academy of Natural Sciences, Philadelphia.

ascribes Floyd's death to "natural causes" — an easy, evasive and debatable answer to the questions relating to the sergeant's death.[28]

The notes made by the captains relative to Floyd's illness and death are rather sparse, compared to the extended and discerning notes made by Lewis later when Sacagawea gave birth to her baby at the Mandan villages, and when she was critically ill at the Great Falls in Montana. Clark's statement that "Floyd as bad as he can be no pulse & nothing will Stay a moment on his Stomach or bowels" indicates that he had violent diarrhea and vomiting, which, with the absence of discernible pulse, meant that he was in serious shock.

It is very probable that the court-martial and the celebration of Lewis' birthday in the afternoon and evening two days before may be the reason that the captains' notes were not more detailed, or even that adequate attention was not given to Floyd, perhaps everyone thinking that he had just celebrated too much, as indicated by Jacobs. If Floyd had not been feeling well for some time, and particularly on the evening of the eighteenth, it would have been routine for the captains to have given him "Rush's bilious pills" — which might have ruptured an infected appendix.[29] It also would be unusual for the captains not to have bled their patient, unless "no pulse" was found on the first examination — and it is doubtful that even this finding would have deterred Dr. Rush from using the lancet.

The Boston *Sentinel*, in its issue of July 13, 1805, printed a long article taken from the Kentucky *Gazette*, published at

---

28 W. J. Ghent, *The Early Far West* (New York: Longmans, Green & Co.), p. 89.

29 Thomas Jefferson, who did not hold physicians in very high esteem, but who was quite a "home-spun" medical practitioner himself — much like Lewis' mother — probably would have given Floyd a physic. He wrote: "a dose of salts as soon as they are taken is salutary in almost all cases, & hurtful in none." *See* Edwin M. Betts, *Thomas Jefferson's Garden Book* (Phila: Amer. Philo. Soc., 1944), p. 467.

Lexington, Kentucky, dated June 18, 1805, about Warfington's group returning from the Mandan villages after wintering with the permanent party: ". . . the party have enjoyed perfect health, not one having been sick except the unfortunate young man before mentioned and he was taken off in a few hours by the croup in his stomach." 30

Garver, after lamenting that a physician did not accompany the Expedition, wrote: "If a physician had been along we might now know the cause of Floyd's death — indeed, his life might have been spared." 31 Garver's statement reflects unfamiliarity with the lack of medical knowledge of the time, and an unwarranted trust in the omnipotence of a doctor.

DeVoto writes that "Charles Floyd's death, could not have been prevented. His symptoms suggest a ruptured appendix, which at that period would almost certainly have been fatal anywhere." 32 Will, a medical doctor, concurs that "the probability is . . . that young Floyd died a victim of perforated gangrenous appendix with generalized peritonitis, and the unfortunate sergeant would have fared little better in Philadelphia with Rush and his colleagues in attendance." 33

---

30 Marks, "The Life of Floyd," p. 74.

31 Frank N. Garver, "The Story of Sergeant Charles Floyd," in *Miss. Valley Hist. Assoc. Proc.*, Vol. II (1908-1909), pp. 76-84.   32 DeVoto, *Journals*, p. xlv.

33 Drake Will, "The Medical and Surgical Practice of the Lewis and Clark Expedition," *Jour. of the Hist. of Med. and Allied Sciences*, Vol. 14, No. 3 (1959), p. 287.

The diagnosis of appendicitis, of course, is one which would not have entered the minds of Lewis and Clark. It was not long after the Lewis and Clark Expedition that appendicitis was recognized, but a long time before it was to be treated successfully. Jean Baptiste Lauger-Villernay (1776-1837) reported cases of perforation of the appendix with fatal peritonitis in 1824. "This is said to have resulted in the recognition of appendicitis as a clinical entity." Schmidt, *Medical Discoveries*, pp. 30-31. Brooks recounts interesting historical events in the developing recognition of the entity and treatment of appendicitis. It was not until 1884 that Rudolf Kronlein (1847-1910) diagnosed a case of appendicitis and surgically removed the appendix. In October 1886, Dr. Reginald Fitz (1843-1913) of Boston published his historic paper clearly delineating the symptoms, pathology and treatment of appendicitis; the paper made such an impact in the medical world that appendicitis

Rush certainly would have bled him, but this would have been as futile as the ministrations of Lewis and Clark. Peritonitis was as occult a condition as appendicitis to the medical world of the time, until Laennec [34] first described it.

Sergeant Floyd was the first American soldier to die and be buried west of the Mississippi River. The captains designated the promontory on which Floyd was buried as Floyd's Bluff, and they called the nearby stream Floyd's River. Lewis and Clark had a cedar post erected over his grave which was noted on the hill by travelers who went up the Missouri in succeeding years. Lewis and Clark recorded on September 4, 1806, on their return journey that the grave had been opened by the Indians and left half-covered; they refilled the grave. On this same date, in Biddle's notes,[35] is the following: "4 Sept. 1806. Floyds grave. A chief of one of the Sioux bands encamped near it, lost one of his sons. He had Floyd's grave opened and his son put in with Floyd for the purpose of accompanying him to the other world believing the white man's future state was happier than that of the Savages." [36] Jackson appends

---

was for a time known as Fitz disease. For Fitz' publication *see* Ralph H. Majors, *Classic Descriptions of Disease* (Springfield: Chas. H. Thomas, 1932), p. 654. A remote but expert country doctor, Abraham Groves of Fergus, Ontario, did not divulge to the world until his book was published in 1934 that he had successfully removed an appendix on which he had made a pre-operative diagnosis of appendicitis, in 1883 — and he had the preserved specimen as proof. Dr. Thomas G. Morton (1935-1903) of Philadelphia is usually credited with being the first surgeon to remove the appendix in an operation definitely planned pre-operatively for this purpose. These historical notes about appendicitis are from Stewart M. Brooks, *McBurney's Point* (South Brunswick: A. S. Barnes, 1969).

[34] Rene Laennec (1781-1826) was a French physician. He is also famous as the inventor of the stethoscope for auscultation of the chest. Laennec first described peritonitis without determining its varied etiology, in 1804, while the Expedition was on its way to the Pacific; shortly thereafter, in 1812, James Parkinson (1775-1824), described perforated appendicitis as a cause of peritonitis.

[35] These notes were made by Nicholas Biddle (1786-1844) from direct communication with Clark after the return of the Expedition, preparatory to publishing the first edition of the Journals. The Biddle notes are at the Amer. Philo. Soc. in Phila. *See* Jackson, *Letters*, pp. 497, 545.   [36] *Ibid.,* pp. 541-42.

this note: "It is not clear whether the grave of Floyd was disturbed before Lewis and Clark came back past the site in September 1806, or later." In view of the story of the burial of the Indian boy with Floyd's bones, the question arises about the identification of Floyd's bones when they were moved. The bones listed as having come from Floyd's grave do not include any extra bones, such as three femurs. Without real evidence of some kind, this account of the second body being put into Floyd's grave can be accepted only with extreme skepticism.

When Brackenridge came to Floyd's grave in 1811 he wrote:

> The place of internment is marked by a wooden cross. . . The grave occupies a beautiful rising of ground, now covered with grass and wild flowers. . . Involuntary tribute was paid to the spot, by the feelings even of the most thoughtless, as we passed by. It is several years since he was buried here, no one has disturbed the cross which marks the grave; even Indians who pass, venerate the place and often leave a present or offering near it. Brave, adventurous youth! thou art not forgotten — for although thy bones are deposited far from thy native home, in the desert-waste; yet the eternal silence of the plains shall mourn thee, and memory will dwell upon thy grave! [37]

George Catlin also passed the grave site of Floyd, in 1832. It is not known if he had read Brackenridge's tribute and tried to exceed it, or whether he was just writing in the flowery fullness of the time, but his pen recorded:

> oh, sad and tear-starting contemplation! Sole tenant of this stately mound, how solitary thy habitation; here heaven wrested from thee thy ambition, and made thee sleeping monarch of this land of silence.
> Stranger! oh, how the mystic web of sympathy links my soul to

[37] H. M. Brackenridge, *Journal of a Voyage up the River Missouri in 1811*, in Thwaites, *Early Western Travels*, VI, p. 85.

thee and thy afflictions! I knew thee not, but it was enough; thy tale was told; and I a solitary wanderer through thy land, have stopped to drop familiar tears upon thy grave . . . with streaming eyes I leave thee again, and thy fairyland, to peaceful solitude. My pencil has faithfully traced thy beautiful habitation; and long shall live in the world, and familiar, the name of "Floyd's grave." [38]

In 1833 Maximilian, the prince of Weid, passed the site of Floyd's grave and wrote: "a short stick marks the grave where he is laid and has often been renewed by travellers when the fires in the prairie have distroyed it."[39]

Joseph Nicollet records his passing of the site in 1839: "We stopped for the night at the foot of the bluff on which is Floyd's Grave: my men replaced the signal, blown down by the winds, which marks the spot and hallows the memory of the brave Sergeant, who died there during Lewis and Clark's Expedition.[40]

The Missouri River later cut into the banks to such an extent that Floyd's grave was opened and some of his bones exposed, and some lost. In 1857 the citizens from the new settlement of nearby Sioux City transferred Floyd's remains to a new burial spot.

The new marker placed at the time of the reburial in 1857 gradually rotted away, and a period of disinterest permitted the grave site to be obliterated by vegetation. The grave was

---

[38] *See* frontispiece herein. George Catlin (1796-1872) was an American artist, lawyer, and author who became famous for his writings and paintings of the American Indians. This sketch of Floyd's grave site was used as an illustration in his *North American Indians* (London, 1841, ed.). He also painted a Mandan Medicine Man, plate 64 of Vol. II, and a picture of the "circle of skulls," plate 15, in Vol. I.

[39] Maximilian, Prince of Weid, *Travels in the Interior of North America,* vol. *I,* p. 278 (in *Early Western Travels,* vol. 22. Cleveland, 1905). He took Sacagawea's papoose Baptiste to Europe with him to live and travel for six years.

[40] Joseph Nicollet (1786-1843) was a French explorer on the Missouri and Mississippi rivers. The manuscript of his Journals and reports are in the Library of Congress. *See* Martha Coleman Bray, ed., *The Journals of Joseph N. Nicollet* (St. Paul: Minn. Hist. Soc., 1970).

rediscovered in 1895, and reopened in the presence of nineteen interested individuals. The few bones remaining were collected and sealed in two urns in order to assure their care and preservation.[41] On August 20, 1895, the ninety-first anniversary of Floyd's death, these urns containing his bones were returned to the earth in his last grave site and forever protected by a concrete slab placed over the grave. The Floyd Memorial Association was formed in 1895 to assure the permanent recognition of Floyd's life and his grave site.[42] A combination of federal and state appropriations and community donations made possible the erection of an obelisk monument, one hundred feet high, over the grave. Today's travelers can see it much more easily than the original cedar post which was viewed by the early travelers on the Missouri River. It is hoped that this imposing reminder elicits in our hearts and minds today the appreciation that the men of the Lewis and Clark Expedition felt for their comrade as they erected a simple wooden post in his honor.[43]

This monument has on it a bronze plate with the following inscription:

> This Shaft
> Marks the Burial Place of
> Sergeant Charles Floyd
> a member of the
> Lewis and Clark Expedition.
> He died in his country's service
> and was buried near this shaft,
> August 20, 1804.

Floyd was a cousin of Congressman John Floyd of Virginia, who was also a physician, who introduced the first

---

[41] Wheeler shows a picture of Floyd's skull in his book. Wheeler, *Trail*, I, p. 84. (Before the skull was re-interred, a plaster model was made of it, and this can be seen at the Sioux City Museum. The Sioux City Museum also has an authenticated piece of Floyd's first coffin. See illustration page 235.)

[42] *See* "Report of the Floyd Memorial Association" (Sioux City, 1897).

legislation in Congress to establish the Oregon Territory, and
first used the word "Origon" in official legislation.[44]

By July 10, Clark was writing in his *Field Notes:* "our men
all getting well but much fatigued," and, again, on July 14:
"two men unwell, one with a Felin on his finger." On July 20
he wrote: "George Drewyer Sick," [45] but there is no indication of the nature or seriousness of the illness, or of what
treatment was rendered.

---

[43] Wheeler writes of Floyd's death: "After death had claimed its own we can
realize the gloom which settled o'er each brow as the rude coffin was fashioned;
can see the little procession as it slowly, laboriously climbed the bluff, dug the
narrow cell, Floyd's last earthly home; gently and with loving arms, — for death
softens us all, rough though we may be — lowered all that was mortal of their
friend into the tomb, filled the excavation and sadly retraced their steps to the
boats, leaving the body of their late companion alone in his last long sleep, his soul
in 'the bosom of his Father and his God.' " Wheeler, *Trail,* i, p. 168.

[44] Hulbert writes of Dr. John Floyd: "in as true a sense as the words are cus-
tomarily used, Dr. Floyd may now be said to become, as Professor Bourne called
him, 'The Father of Oregon.' His interest in the Far West, aroused by the life-story
of his cousin, was enhanced by his friendship with William Clark — if, indeed, this
may not have explained Charles Floyd's very participation in the Columbia expedition. This interest drew him toward all who knew the West or were dreaming that
way, particularly to Senator T. H. Benton, who had written essays on the subject
as early as in 1819. At Brown's Hotel in Washington he also met the noted Astor-
ians, Ramsey Crooks and Russell Farnham with whom he and Senator Benton spent
many hours in conversation. If the latter has emphasized the American claims to
the Northwest, it was for Floyd to press upon Congress the problem of occupation.
Years of 'claiming' the Columbia country had resulted in little; projects for occupation were more to the point because, inevitably, discussions of them would spread
abroad information which would make immigration probable — namely of soils,
climate and economic opportunity. Thus the work of Floyd in echoing in Congress
the call of the Columbia makes his stand out significantly as the first promoter of
American expansion thither. That his labors produced no immediate results is not
so important as the fact that he began laying before the American people the desir-
ability of that land from the immigrant's standpoint. For, in the end, it was soil
qualities which sounded the call which was answered by hundreds who finally
poured into the Willamette Valley; and it was the occupation of the valley in
Professor Turner's opinion, which provided the potential force that ultimately
brought the peaceful secession of Great Britain from the country south of the 49th
parallel." Archer Butler Hulbert, *Where Rolls the Oregon* (Denver: The Stewart
Comm. of Colo. and the Denver Pub. Lby., 1933), pp. 42-43.

[45] Osgood, *Field Notes of Clark,* pp. 78, 82.

J. Field seems to have been the first man of the Expedition to have killed a buffalo, on August 23. This was to be a new and plentiful source of food for the men. They were to learn, as did an army of trappers and frontiersmen after them, that they never tired of buffalo meat, and that the tongue, liver and marrow bones, along with the "rump," were the prime edible portions of this animal. However, when food was scarce, all the meat of the animal would be eaten, and even the bones were sucked clean of their marrow.

On August 26 Shannon and Drouillard were sent out to find some lost horses, and Shannon joined the horses — lost again! Clark wrote in his journal of August 27 that "G Drewyer [Drouillard] came up and informed that he could neither find Shannon nor horses, he had walked all night — we Sent Shields & J. Fields back to look for Shannon and the horses." On the twenty-eighth Clark recorded that Shields and Field had not been able to find Shannon but "that Shannon had the horses ahead and that they Could not overtake him This man not being a first rate Hunter, we deturmined to Send one of the men in pursuit of him with some Provisions."

The captains had added reason to be concerned about Shannon because they were now in the land of the Sioux. Shannon reappeared in two weeks — a cause for rejoicing matched only by the previous despair. The disappearance of Shannon from time to time was to be a matter of concern with the captains.[46] In view of Clark's note, it might rightfully be wondered why one as young and as poor a hunter as Shannon was enlisted in the corps. Shannon proved resourceful, though — he killed a rabbit with a stick of wood fired from his gun!

The Expedition got its first taste of dog meat on August 29, although some individuals of the Expedition may have eaten it at a previous time. Clark recorded that "A Fat Dog was

[46] Wheeler, *Trail*, II, p. 108.

presented as a mark of their [the Indian chiefs'] Great respect for the party of which they partook hartily and thought it good and well flavored." They were to become quite used to this meat before their return home, some of the men even preferring it to elk meat.[47]

The men could never be sure of what meat would be available to them from day to day. Therefore, when opportunity presented itself they killed more animals than they could eat at the time, and preserved the remainder. Clark wrote on September 8 that they "jurked the meat Killed to day Consisting of 2 buffalow, one large Buck Elk, one Small, 4 Deer 3 Turkeys & a Squirel."

By mid-September they were no longer plagued by excessively hot weather; the rainy season was upon them, so that on the sixteenth Lewis noted that they delayed a couple of days "in order to dry our baggage which was wet by the heavy showers of rain which had fallen within the last three days." During this stay they noted a "small species of white oak . . . loaded with acorns of an excellent flavor."

Clark wrote on September 19: "I hurt my hands and feet last night." [48] He doesn't mention how the injury occurred, but it probably was the result of a fall. It probably was not severe, as he doesn't mention it again, and he was able to write.

There had been very little mention of boils for some time, but on September 21 Clark wrote: "one frenchman [one of

[47] Cox writes in his Astoria Journal: "Mr. Holmes gave us a plentiful dinner of roast pork, roast dog, fowl, ham fish, wine and rum. . . The idea of eating so faithful an animal without even the pleas of necessity, effectually prevented any of us joining in this part of the feast; although, to do the meat justice, it really looked very well roasted." Later, when Cox's table was not so bountiful, he wrote: "As our provisions were nearly consumed, we were obliged to purchase twenty dogs from them (the Indians). It was the first time I had eaten any of the flesh of this animal and nothing but stern necessity could have induced me to partake of it." Cox, The Columbia River, pp. 32-33, 127.

[48] Osgood, Field Notes of Clark, p. 141.

the voyageurs] I fear has got an abscess on his they [thigh].
he Complains verry much we are makeing every exertion to
reliev him." Probably the "exertion" consisted of hot fomen-
tations, poultices, pain medication (probably laudunum) and
rest. "Physician" Clark added a progress note on September
24, to the effect that "the French Man who had for Some time
been Sick, began to blead which allarmed him. . ." This
would have pleased Rush — it would have been evidence that
this was nature's way of treating such a condition! Clark does
not record what was done to stop the hemorrhage — if anything.

September 29 the Expedition met the Sioux Indians, who
were to present one of the most serious obstacles to passage
up the river. There was considerable bluffing on both sides,
with the captains maintaining a cautious guard, and keeping
their guns loaded and ready. Some of the braves tried to hold
onto the pirogues, and even succeeded in boarding the keelboat. The Indians knew that they were no match with their
bows and arrows, even though they greatly outnumbered the
white men. The show of strength and fearlessness made possible by the discipline of the entire corps finally controlled the
threatening Indians, and the Expedition "proceeded on."

Spurious editions of the Lewis and Clark Expedition, published in London and in Philadelphia in 1807 and later, contained very little pertinent information and were based mainly
on Lewis' letter to Jefferson from the Mandans and Jefferson's
report to Congress. The author let his imagination loose when
he wrote, relative to the captains' subduing the Sioux Indians:

> The treatment we have received from the Indians, during nearly
> three years that we were with them was very kind and hospitable;
> except the ill treatment we received from the Sioux tribe, who
> several times made attempts to stop us; and we should have been
> massacred, had we not terrified them from their murderous inten-
> tion, by threatening them with the small-pox in such a manner as

would kill the whole tribe. Nothing could be more horrible to them, than the bare mention of this fatal disease. It was first communicated to them by the Americans, and it spread from tribe to tribe with an unabated pace, until it extended itself across the continent.

This same language is in the several spurious editions, indicating copying, although the page numbers vary.[49]

The above statement is entirely fictitious. Lewis was irate enough at the Sioux that he certainly would not have hesitated to record such a consideration if it had been in his mind. Lewis and Clark had no one along who had active smallpox, and thus no one who could have given them the disease. It is highly doubtful that Lewis would have conjured up such a bluff. It was certainly contrary to the intention of Jefferson and himself, as evidenced by Jefferson's having Lewis bring along some kinepox to vaccinate the Indians. None of the true journals mentions threatening the Indians with smallpox. This appears to be entirely a fabrication.[50]

On September 26, while with the Sioux, Ordway wrote that ". . . [the Indians] Gave Capt Lewis Some fine Soup made of what they call white apples. they sent all the party Some fat Buffaloe meat cooked and some dryed and pounded fine. the marrow of the Buffalow Bones, mixed together, which Eat Verry well . . . they killed Several dogs and

---

[49] The London 1809 edition has the quotation on page 25, and the 1809 Philadelphia edition has it on page 36. The 1812 Baltimore edition has the same quotation on page 40, and the 1813 Baltimore edition has it on page 35. The wording is the same in all. The official Biddle edition of the Journals was not published until 1814, in Philadelphia.

It is fair to note that the spurious 1809 edition states in the introduction, page vi: "The small-pox had raged, when little or no communication was held with them [the Indians]. Provisions are already made to introduce vaccine inoculation among them, which will prevent those horrible ravages that are mentioned in the course of this work."

[50] Wheeler thinks that this smallpox scare "seems to come from some member of the Lewis and Clark Party," but he does not offer any reason for this opinion. Wheeler, Trail, pp. viii-ix.

cooked them in a decent manner to treat our people with."
Clark records on the same day: "I saw & eat Pemitigon
[pemmican] the Dog, Groud potatoe made into a Kind of
homney, which I thought but little inferior." This same day
Clark also recorded that "one man verry sick on board with
a Dangerass Abscess on his Hip."

The beginning of October was to see the Expedition in the
area of the Ricaree Indians, who were generally warlike people, but who gave the captains no trouble on this occasion.
The Expedition was able to keep itself well supplied with
meat from the countryside — deer, elk, and buffalo were available to them. Clark records on October 6 that they "Saw
Gees, Swan, Brants, & Ducks of Different Kinds . . .
great numbers of Prarie hens, I observe but fiew Gulls or
Pleover. . ." He also noted that they found three kinds of
squash growing in the Ricaree village. On October 9 Clark
recorded that "Several hunters Came in with loades of meat
. . . I have a Slite Plursie this evening verry cold. . ."
On October 10 Ordway recorded that the Indians gave them
corn, beans, dried pumpkin and squashes, and he added:
"Some of their women are verry handsome & clean . . ."

The Ricaree Indians were more of a sedentary tribe, with
a land culture similar to that of the Mandan Indians. Clark
describes them thusly: "Those people are Durtey, Kind, pore,
& extravigent. pursessing national pride, not beggarley recive
what is given with great pleasure, Live in warm houses. . ."
Clark's note of October 12 is a lengthy one, and among other
things he notes that "a curious custom with the Souix as well
as the rickeres is to give handsom squars to those whome they
wish to Show some acknowledgements to. The Seauex we got
clare of without taking their squars, they followed us with
Squars two days, The Rickores we put off dureing the time we

were at the Towns but 2 (handsom young) Squars were sent
by a man to follow us, they came up this evening, and pur-
sisted in their civilities."

The thirteenth was truly an unlucky day for John Newman.
He had been a very good member of the corps, but too much
alcohol loosened his tongue and he made derogatory remarks
about the captains which the latter considered to be mutinous.
The entire charge, the court-martial and the execution of the
sentence is herewith quoted in full for several reasons. This
was the fourth and most serious court-martial that would be
required for the entire journey. It also reaffirmed to the men
that discipline had to be maintained, and the men acknowledged this by being rather severe on their court-martialed
comrades. Whatever language Newman used, it was certainly
of a kind that the captains considered to be disrespectful,
which they could not tolerate if they were to maintain command of the crew.

> In conformity to the above order the Court martial convened
> this day for the trial of John Newman, charged with "having
> uttered repeated expressions of a highly criminal and mutinous
> nature; the same having a tendency not only to distroy every prin-
> ciple of military discipline, but also to alienate the affections of the
> individual composing this detatchment to their officers, and dis-
> affect them to the service for which they have been so sacredly and
> solemnly engaged." The Prisonar plead not guil[t]y to the charge
> exhibited against him. The court after having duly considered the
> evidence aduced, as well as the defence of the said prisonor, are
> unanimously of opinion that the prisonor John Newman is guilty
> of every part of the charge exhibited against him, and do sentence
> him agreeably to the rules and articles of war, to receive seventy-
> five lashes on his bear back, and to be henceforth discarded from
> the perminent party engaged for North Western discovery; two-
> thirds of the Court concurring in the sum and nature of the
> punishment awarded. the commanding officers approve and con-

firm the sentence of the court, and direct the punishment take place tomorrow between the hours of one and two P.M.[51]

The following day the Expedition stopped on a sandbar and after lunch administered the seventy-five lashes to Newman. He also was demoted to a laborer on a pirogue and relieved of his arms.

The entire corps seems to have regretted the court-martial and subsequent punishment of Newman. Quaife observes in an extensive footnote that the other diarists make scant reference to the court-martial, indicating their displeasure; he interprets this as meaning they had high respect for Newman and were reluctant to recount an unpleasant situation about him.[52] Gass and Ordway, who were members of the court, and who kept journals, hardly mention it; Whitehouse even says: "Nothing else extra ordinary hapened this day." That the men were very unhappy about Newman's plight is also indicated by Clark recording that "two-thirds of the Court concurring in the sum and nature of the punishment awarded," which is considerably less than the unanimous verdicts rendered regarding the other court-martials.

As with other punishments inflicted as the result of courts-martial, no mention was made in subsequent notes by any of the diarists regarding the condition of the punished individual. Newman served his captains and his fellow corpsmen

---

[51] Probably this court-martial with its specific charges brought forth sharp memories to Captain Lewis. While serving in the Army under General "Mad Anthony" Wayne he was court-martialed with similar charges placed against him on Nov. 6, 1795. He, like Newman, apparently got too familiar with the available liquor supply with the result that he was charged with conduct unbecoming an officer and disturbing the peace and using provocative language. Lewis pled not guilty and the verdict sustained him. Unlike poor Newman, he not only received no lashes on his bare back, but was reassigned to a unit under Capt. William Clark, his future co-leader of the Corps of Discovery. Of such uncertain turns of the wheel of fortune is interesting history made!

[52] Quaife, "The Journals of Lewis and Ordway," p. 153.

faithfully during the rest of the journey to the Mandan village, and during their 1804 winter stay with the Mandan Indians. He was very desirous of continuing on the rest of the journey, but Lewis, a stern disciplinarian, was adamant and Newman was sent back down the river to St. Louis with Corporal Warfington the next spring. Lewis agreed with Tilton that ". . . discipline is of the first consequence. Without it, there can be neither health nor comfort in an army." [53] In 1812, corporal punishment was ordered discontinued by the army.[54]

However firm he might be in demanding discipline, Lewis was also fair, and when he made recommendations for rewards for members of the Expedition to Secretary Dearborn after their return, he included a generous recommendation for Newman. Lewis wrote: "The conduct of this man previous to this period (mutiny), had been generally correct; and the zeal he afterwards displayed for the benefit of the service, was highly meritorious." [55]

Clark recorded on October 19: ". . . all the Streems falling from the hills or high lands so brackish that the water can't be Drank without effecting the person making use of it as Globesalts [Glauber's salts] . . ." [56]

The days were getting shorter and colder. On October 21 Lewis wrote: "a verry Cold night wind hard from the N.E.

---

[53] Tilton, *Economical Observations*, p. 34.

[54] May 16, 1812, Congress repealed the act: "as authorizes the infliction of corporeal punishment, by stripes of lashes, be, and the same hereby is repealed." *Military Laws and Rules and Regulations for the Army of the United States*, War Dept., Nov. 1814. I am indebted to Col. Robert H. Fechtman, Chief, Hist. Services Div., Dept. of the Army, Wash., D.C. for the additional information: "However, an Act of 2 March 1833 revived flogging as a form of punishment for deserters. This provision remained in effect until abolished by an Act of 5 Aug. 1861.

See also John D. McDermott, "Crime and Punishment in the United States Army," *Jour. of the West*, Vol. VII, No. 2 (April 1968), pp. 246-255.

[55] Jackson, *Letters*, p. 365-66.

[56] Osgood, *Field Notes of Clark*, p. 163.

Some rain in the night which frosed as it fell   at Day light it began to Snow . . ." On the following day Clark wrote that "last night at 1 oClock I was violently and Suddenly attacked with the Rhumetism in the neck which was so violent I could not move Capt. (Lewis) applied a hot Stone raped in flannel which gave me some temporey ease. We Set out early, the morning Cold . . . my Neck is yet verry painfull at times Spasms." By October 24 Clark was improved: "I am something better of the Rhumitism in my neck," and the next day he recorded that "R. Fields with the Rheumatism in his neck, P. Crusat with the Same complaint in his Legs — the party other wise is well, — as to my self I feel but slight Simptoms of that disorder at this time."

By the twenty-sixth Clark's rheumatism was bad again so that he could not accompany Captain Lewis to the Arikara village to confer with the chiefs. Clark wrote the following day that the chiefs were displeased with him because "my indisposition provented my eating," but he satisfied them with an explanation.

During the last few days of October the men were in the Mandan villages, receiving numerous gifts of food from them, including corn, beans, squashes, and meat. The captains explored the land about and between the Mandan villages for the most advantageous place to locate their winter quarters. There was not enough timber around the higher Mandan villages to permit them to build a fort and provide them with firewood so they dropped down a few miles to the lower Mandan village. On November 2, 1804, they chose the site of their winter residence, and began the construction of Fort Mandan.

Clark wrote on November 3: "A fine morning . . . we commenced building our cabins."

XII

At Fort Mandan

Generally helthy except Venerials Complaints which is very Common amongst the natives and the men Catch it from them.
William Clark [1]

It was during the last days of October when the captains brought their Expedition among the Mandan Indians, with whom they planned to spend the winter. They were well-informed about these Indians, from stories which had been brought back down the Missouri by traders, and also from information which the agents of the British and French fur trappers had reported.[2] It was known that these Indians were

---

[1] Thwaites, *Journals,* I, p. 279.

[2] The captains had available to them the report of Jean-Baptiste Truteau who had led a small expedition up the Missouri in 1794, for the Missouri Company. This report provided much information about the various tribes on the Missouri, including their mores and morals; thus Lewis and Clark knew what health problems to anticipate, particularly in regard to "the venerial."

"The Panis, Mandanes, Ricaras and Bigbellies, are somewhat more than ordinarily indifferent as to their women. — No such sentiment as jealousy ever enters their breasts. They give this reason for it, that when a man dies he cannot carry women with him to the regions of the dead; and that they who quarrel, fight, and kill each other about the possession of a woman, are fools or mad-men. They are so firmly convinced of this, that many of them take a pride in treating some of the considerable men among them with their youngest and handsomest women. So true is this, that husbands, fathers and brothers, are importunate with the white men who visit them, to make free with their wives, daughters and sisters, particularly those who are most youthful and pretty; and in consideration thereof accept a few baubles or toys. Indeed both the girls and married women are so loose in their conduct, that they seem to be a sort of common stock; and are so easy and accessible that there are few among them whose favours cannot be bought with a little vermillion or blue ribbon. The consequence of these libertine manners is the venereal disease. This is very frequent among them; but the Indians cure it by

sedentary, although sending hunting parties far out on the prairie for buffalo meat and hides. The Mandans had developed considerable expertise in raising vegetables, including beans, squash and corn, which they ate fresh and also dried and stored in caves under their lodgings. They preserved their meat in a variety of ways: fileting and drying it, pounding it with berries to make pemmican, and taking advantage of the natural refrigeration of the cold winters by hanging their meat high in trees or enclosing it within a stockade to keep the wild animals from it.

Lewis and Clark expected to find the Mandan Indians larger and fairer than any they had seen so far. They had heard of the stories about the Welsh Indians who lived in the interior somewhere up the Missouri River, supposedly lighter skinned because of dilution by a lost tribe of Norsemen who had come to the North American continent and made their way inland.[3]

Lewis and Clark provided white civilization with the best record of the construction of the Mandan houses. These were made of eight to ten foot portions of trees erected vertically

decoction [concoction] of certain roots. I have seen some that were rotten with it, cured in six months." J. B. Truteau, Remarks on the Manners of the Indians Living High up the Missouri, quoted in A. Nasatir, Before Lewis and Clark (St. Louis: Historical Documents Found., 1952), p. 258.

[3] See letter of Jefferson to Lewis dated Jan. 22, 1804, in which Jefferson refers to these legendary Indians. Jackson, Letters, p. 165. Also see Whitehouse Journal note of Sept. 6, 1805 (Thwaites, Journals, VII, p. 150), which indicates that these Welsh Indians were on the minds of all the members of the expedition: "we take these Savages to be the Welsh Indians if there be any such from the language. So Capt. Lewis took down the names of everry thing in their Language, in order that it may be found whether they are or whether they Sprang or origenated first from the welsh or not." (The Expedition was now in the Rocky Mountains, among the Flathead Indians, but the Welsh Indians, like the Northwest Passage, were still on everyone's mind.) For accounts of the Welsh Indians' story and the continued romanticism attending it, see Gene Jones, "The Mandan Indians, Descendants of the Vikings," Real West, IX, No. 47 (1966), p. 31; David Williams, "John Evans' Strange Journey," Amer. Hist. Rev., Vol. LIV (Jan.-April, 1949), pp. 277-95; De Voto, The Course of Empire, pp. 470-72.

in a circle, from which long timbers sloped upward to the center, leaving a small central opening for the exit of smoke. The timbers were covered with twigs and then sod. This made a remarkably dry and warm enclosure. The horses and dogs were kept within the same building, occupying one side, while the people slept on elevated platforms on the other side. Fires for warmth and cooking were built in the middle, so that the smoke could rise directly upward to the central aperture. At times the interior probably resembled a smokehouse. A very handy pantry was provided by digging an opening in the floor, and then enlarging it to a wider space which was lined with grass, in which baskets of vegetables were stored.

Sergeant Ordway wrote: "we dug a vault 100 yds abo[ve] the huts in order to make or keep the place healthy." This is the only specific reference in the journals about latrine arrangements — undoubtedly it was expected that whoever read the journals would understand the usual army procedure.

Gass was the main carpenter; most of the men, except the hunters, were busy with the construction of the cabins. There had been times when all of the men, despite their specialties and inclinations, had to be watermen, but now they were needed as carpenters. Undoubtedly those who were more expert with the tools did the main work of erecting the cabins, and the other men had the jobs of falling and trimming the trees. On November 11, Clark records that "Two men cut themselves with an ax," but gives no further detail as to who the victims were, the seriousness of the cuts, or the treatment given.

More important to the future of the Expedition was another bit of information recorded by Clark on November 11: "two Squars of The Rock mountains, purchased from the Indians by a frenchmen came down   .   .   ." This was the first mention of Sacagawea and Charbonneau. Sacagawea always was

treated as a squaw, but none of the men of the Expedition
demanded that she labor as did the squaw written about by
Clark on November 12: "the Big white principal Chief of the
lower Village of the Mandans came Down, he packd about
100 lb. of fine meat on his squar for us." Clark recorded on
this same date that "maney years ago they [the Mandans]
lived in Several Villages on the Missourie low down the Smallpox distroyed the greater part of the nation and reduced them
to one large village and Some Small ones."

Ice began to run in the river and the weather became colder
and more stormy. Game was scarce near the Mandan villages,
and therefore some of the men had to be excused from building the cabins in order to obtain meat. Ordway records on
November 13: "Capt Lewis retorned with his party towards
evening much fatigued. they got fast on a Sand bar & had to
be out in the water abt 2 hours. the Ice running against their
legs. their close frooze on them. one of them got 1 of his
feet frost bit. it hapned that they had Some whiskey with them
to revive their Spirits." This is one of the very few times when
any of the men of the Expedition sustained frostbite. There
is no record of treatment given to this man nor of any chronic
ill effects which the man suffered.

Clark had become concerned about the delay of Lewis and
his men returning from the hunt and he noted that "we are
compelled to use our Pork which we doe Spearingly for fear
of some falur in precureing a Sufficiency from the woods."

On November 16 the men were able to move into their huts;
although they were not finished, they protected them against
the severe weather. Ordway wrote on this same date: "raised
a provision & Smoak house 24 feet by 14 f," and added on
November 19: "all the meat we put up on poles in the Roofs
of our meat & Smoak houses."

Clark recorded on the nineteenth the results of a hunting expedition: "our Perogue of Hunters arrive with 32 deer, 12 Elk & a Buffalow, all this meat we had hung up in a Smoke house, a timeley supply." He also wrote on this date that the men moved into their huts, and on the following day he recorded that "Cap Lewis & my Self moved into our hut."[4] On November 21 Clark wrote: "G D [George Drouillard] hurd his hand verry bad   all the party in high Spirits."

Very little is recorded about how the men were protected against the elements before they moved into their cabins, but undoubtedly they continued with their army routine of using tents, and warming themselves and cooking their meals with fires. Working and hunting in cold wet weather contributed to the repeated recordings in the journals that several men had bad colds, and "one man Shields with rhumitism." The men had better protection when they moved into their "huts," each one with a fireplace. The heat was retained and the wind diverted by pressing mud between the logs.

The usual routine of afflictions such as colds, boils, pleurisy and rheumatism changed on November 29 to an orthopedic complaint: "Sergeant Pryor in takeing down the mast put his Sholder out of Place, we made four trials before we replaced it. . ."[5] Many well-trained future physicians would expe-

---

[4] Lewis gives the date of the completion of the cabin, "so far as to put ourselves under shelter," as Nov. 21. (See Lewis' letter to his mother, Jackson, *Letters*, p. 222.)

[5] The classical Kocher method of reduction published in textbooks of orthopedics describes a series of four maneuvers. Pryor was to develop a recurrent dislocation of the shoulder. There are two more journal entries about future dislocations: July 11, 1805, at the Great Falls portage ("it was replaced immediately") and the next time on Dec. 11, 1805, at Fort Clatsop. The shoulder seems to have bothered Pryor in future years, as indicated by a letter written by Capt. Clark in 1827 on behalf of Pryor for a position with the Indian Agency; this letter requests that consideration be given to "his being disabled by a dislocation of his shoulder." Jackson, *Letters*, p. 646. Apparently the shoulder was not adequately immobilized the first time, permitting the capsule and ligaments to heal with a redundancy that permitted easy redislocation. Subsequent reductions are usually more easily accomplished than is the initial dislocation; no mention is made of special maneuvers to obtain a reduction. Mention is made of Pryor having pain for a day or two.

rience similar prolonged and frustrating efforts in reducing a dislocated shoulder. Clark did not write a clinical description of the dislocation which led him to make the diagnosis. However, the patient usually knows when the shoulder dislocates and when it is properly reduced. It would be interesting also if Clark had described the manipulation which was used to get the shoulder reduced during the "four trials." Orthopedic surgeons generally agree that one of the most important requirements in reducing a discolated shoulder in a young, well-muscled individual is adequate relaxation. There is no reference in Clark's note about using whiskey or opium, two drugs which were used extensively before the advent of anesthetics, to induce relaxation. Gass' account of Pryor's dislocated shoulder simply states that "we went to unrig the boat, and by an accident one of the sergeants had his shoulder dislocated."

Ordway writes on December 7 that "2 of our men Got their feet frost Bitten & one Got his Ear frost bitten this day by being exposed in the praries." On the same day Clark noted in his journal that it was "1d. below 0, three men frost bit badly to day."

It was rapidly getting colder. Clark's journal mentions on December 8 that "the Thermometer Stood at 12d below 0 — which is 42d below the freesing point." Nevertheless Clark led a group of fifteen men on a buffalo hunt and returned with eight buffalo and one deer. He reported that "this day being Cold Several men returned a little frost bit, one of [the] men with his feet badly frost bit my Servents [York] feet also frosted & his P---s a little, I felt a little fatigued haveing run after the Buffalow all day in Snow many Places 18 inches Deep . . . two men hurts their hips verry much in Slipping down."

Apparently York's afflictions were minor and temporary,

without any permanent disability. He had been a special attraction for the Indian maidens of all the tribes, but he reached
the pinnacle of his activity in the Mandan villages due to the
sexual promiscuity of the Mandan women, condoned and even
urged and arranged for by their husbands.[6] That York was not
permanently disabled by his frostbite is attested to by the fact
that in future years his kinky-haired progeny were traceable
among the Indian tribes contacted by the Expedition all the
way to the Pacific.[7]

That all of the frostbitten men were not seriously afflicted
is shown by Clark's journal entry of December 10: "The men
which was frost bit is getting better." He also recorded in the
same journal entry that Lewis had spent a cold, disagreeable
night in the snow with one small blanket.

The men were very fortunate to be housed in their cabins
with the fireplaces completed before the most severe weather
arrived. On December 12, Lewis was writing that the thermometer was —38°: "the weather is So Cold that we do not
think it prudent to turn out to hunt in Such Cold weather, or
at least untill our Consts. are prepared to under go this Climate." On the same day Ordway was writing in his journal
that "our Rooms are verry close and warm So we can keep

---

[6] In writing about the venereal infection of the men obtained from the Mandan
women, Larsell seems to misread the journals. He writes that ". . . on January
14 (1805), Clark writes of sending Sergeant Pryor and five men with some Indians
to hunt several men who had become infected." Olaf Larsell, *The Doctor in Oregon*
(Portland: Oreg., Hist. Soc., 1947), p. 52. Compare with Thwaites: "This morning
early a number of Indians men women children Dogs &c. &c. passed down on the
ice to joine those that passed yesterday, we sent Sergt Pryor and five men with
those indians to hunt (Several men with the Venereal cought from the Mandan
women)." Thwaites, *Journals*, I, p. 248.

[7] Bakeless says that "Negro blood was traceable among the Mandans as late as
1889." Bakeless, *Partners in Discovery*, p. 176. *See also* the letter from Gerard to
Eva Emory Dye on Nov. 1, 1889, in Dye Mss. at the Oreg. Hist. Soc: "York's progeny were traceable for years afterward among many tribes along the Missouri and
in the mountains of Idaho, where their kinky hair can still be detected. . .
Negro blood was traceable among the Mandans as late as 1889."

ourselves warm and comfortable." He added that the "Sentinel who stood out in the open weather had to be relieved every hour all this day."

On December 17, 1804, Clark recorded the lowest temperature of any time on the Expedition: ". . . about 8 oClock PM. the thermometer fell to 74° below the freesing pointe" [−42°]. During this extremely cold weather with the ground continually covered with snow and the river covered with ice, the men could supplement their diet only with the generous but sparse gifts of corn from the Indians, and by dipping into their store of flour and other food materials which they had brought with them up the Missouri.

The medical practice of Lewis and Clark among the Indians was to serve them repeatedly in diplomacy and in bartering with the Indians. On December 21, Clark wrote: ". . . a Womon brought a Child with an abscess on the lower part of the back, and offered as much Corn as she could Carry for some Medison, Capt. Lewis administered &c."

A constant exchange of gifts and favors went on between the men of the Expedition and the Indians. The Indians were particularly fond of blue beads, whiskey, vermillion paint, and they particularly appreciated iron instruments which were made and given to them by the blacksmiths of the Expedition (Shields, Bratton and Willard).

Clark wrote on December 22: "A number of Squars & men Dressed in Squars Clothes Came with Corn to Sell. . ." Biddle's Notes state: "Among the Minitarees if a boy shows any symptoms of effeminacy or girlish inclinations he is put among the girls, dressed in their way, brought up with them, & sometimes married to men." [8]

There are entries in the journals indicating that the Indians at times presented the white men with food without demanding trade. Clark writes on December 23 that ". . . the

[8] Jackson, *Letters*, p. 531; *see also* Thwaites, *Journals*, I, p. 239.

little Crow loadd his wife & Sun with Corn for us . . .
she made a kittle of boiled Cimnins, beens, Corn & Choke
Cheries with Stones, which was palitable. . ."

An indication of the supplies brought from St. Louis, and
used to supplement their meat diet, is given by Gass' entry
in his diary on December 24: "Flour, dried apples, pepper
and other articles were distributed in the different messes to
enable them to celebrate Christmas in a proper and social
manner." Clark wrote on Christmas Day that ". . . The
men merrily Disposed, I give them all a little Taffia and permitted 3 Cannon fired, at raising Our flag, . . . Danceing
. . . Continued untill 9 oClock P.M. when the frolick ended."

The journals contain many references to the questionable
friendliness of the Mandans; in fact, the captains had evidence of plotting on the part of the Mandans with other
Indians to exterminate them, or at least turn them back down
the Missouri. LeBorgne, the one-eyed Mandan chief was particularly hostile. [9] There is also ample evidence that the attitude and duplicity of the Mandan Indians and their neighbors
were abetted, even instigated, by the British operating in the
same area. The fact that the Louisiana Territory now belonged to the United States made very little difference in the
cut-throat methods of the fur trade. Lewis was very suspicious
of the intentions and the activities of the British; his suspicions
were perhaps a little exaggerated, undoubtedly an attitude
acquired from having lived with President Jefferson, who was
an unapologetic Anglophobe.

In spite of the above circumstances, the Mandan Indians
manifested an almost continuous friendliness in day-by-day
living with the Americans. Ordway writes in his journal on
December 30: "they Brought us corn & Beans Squasshes, also
a Some of their kind of Bread which they make of pearched

---

[9] Biddle, *History of the Expedition*, p. 146.

corn and beans mixed together & made in round balls. they
have a Sweet kind of corn which they Boil considerable of it
when it is in the milk & drys it which they keep through the
winter Season."

The most eventful happening of the New Year was the buffalo dance. This was a traditional ritual of supplication to
bring the buffalo near to the Mandan village. The buffalo
meat was used for food, their hides for clothing, and their
bones were used for receptacles, pounding instruments, war
clubs, needles and a variety of other purposes. In the spring
of 1805 the buffalo were slow to make an appearance; therefore, soon after the first of the year, the chiefs and medicine
men decided that it was necessary to stage their traditional
buffalo dance.

On January 5, 1805, Clark wrote:

> a Buffalow Dance (or Medeson) [Medecine] for 3 nights passed
> in the 1st Village, a curious Custom the old men arrange them-
> selves in a circle & after Smoke [ing] a pipe which is handed them
> by a young men, Dress [ed] up for the purpose, the young men
> who have their wives back of the Circle go [each] to one of the
> old men with a whining tone and request the old man to take his
> wife (who presents [herself] necked except a robe) and-(or Sleep
> with her) the Girl then takes the Old Man (who verry often can
> scarcely walk) and leades him to a convenient place for the busi-
> ness, after which they return to the lodge; if the old man (or a
> white man) returns to the Lodge without gratifying the Man &
> his wife, he offers her again and again; it is often the Case that
> after the 2d. time without Kissing the Husband throws a new robe
> over the old man &c. and begs him not to dispise him & his wife
> (We Sent a man to this Medisan Dance last night, they gave him
> 4 Girls) all this to cause the buffalow to Come near So that they
> may kill them.[10]

---

[10] In Biddle's two-volume edition of the Journals, the first account of the Buffalo
dance, Latin was used for the "lurid" portions of the description. *See* Biddle, *History of the Expedition*, II, pp. 150-51.

The "untiringly zealous" participation of the young men of the Expedition not only in rituals such as the buffalo dance, but in clandestine and forthright bartering arrangements, contributed to the men being more afflicted with venereal disease while at the Mandan village than at any other time during the Expedition.[11] The confinement during the winter months, and the persistent offering of the Indian men to trade the favors of their mothers, wives, sisters, and daughters for the trinkets of the white men, contributed to the constant reinfecting of the Indians and the white men. Biddle's notes state: "The wom[en] afflicted with both sorts of vl [venereal?] which were given to the men."[12]

It is evident that there was no embarrassment on the part of the men to conceal their venereal infections; in fact, they probably lightly accepted such infections as a routine part of their soldierly activities. There are no notations in the journals that the captains required their men to report their venereal diseases, as is now required in the armed forces. The captains probably expected a high proportion of their personnel to be afflicted with venereal diseases, as indicated by the list of medical supplies. To have confined the men in such a way as to make contact with the Indian women impossible would

[11] *See* DeVoto, *Op. Cit.*, p. 616. "It is not within my province to determine whether or how far Lewis and Clark shared the evening pleasures of the men which the Journals freely record. The folklore may be mentioned, however, and there is a lot of it. The West is well stocked with people who claim to have descended from Lewis and women of most tribes the expedition met, and they are not unknown in the East. I have corresponded with gentlemen in Virginia and Florida who have elaborate genealogical charts which convince them, and have talked with a number of professed descendants in the West. Curiously, I have met no one who claims Clark as an ancestor. But literature long ago filled the gap, bestowing on him a love affair with Sacajawea which, on no evidence, has steadily gained ground even in histories."

See also "What are the Facts?" an account of a Chopunnish half-breed son of William Clark, in *Montana, Magazine of Western History*, Vol. v, No. 3 (Summer, 1955), pp. 36-37.   [12] Jackson, *Letters*, p. 521.

have caused more discipline problems — and probably would have been ineffective.

But the captains were not totally unconcerned about the men's venereal diseases. Lewis had brought along from Philadelphia one Clyster Syringe and "four Penis do [ditto]" — four of this item compared to only "three Best Lancets" to be used for all the bleeding to be done for almost all afflictions. They also brought with them two pounds of "Ung. (Mercuriale [Mercury salve]." Mercury was also used in the pill form as calomel (mercurous chloride). Mercury had been the universal staple for the treatment of syphilis for centuries, and continued to be until the recent advent of antibiotics. Tilton recorded that mercury was the specific remedy for syphilis.[13]

In 1821, James Hamilton wrote about the powers of mercury in controlling syphilis: "Notwithstanding all the hazards resulting from the use of mercury, there can be no doubt that it has certain medicinal virtues, the most remarkable of which is the power of curing the diseases occassioned by the Syphilitic virus."[14]

There are very few notes in the journals about the symptoms of the men who contracted syphilis. Apparently the captain-physicians were concerned only with the acute stages, although they mention re-infection and chronic symptoms.[15]

---

[13] Tilton, *Economical Observations*, p. 57.

[14] James Hamilton, *Observations on the Use and Abuse of Mercurial Medicines* (New York: Bliss & White, 1821), p. 27.

[15] There are three stages to the typical untreated case of syphilis: the primary stage of a red papule (a chancre) on the area of contact, a secondary stage of skin eruption of a pox (Will is incorrect in calling the pox the primary stage; *see* Will, "Westering Physicians," p. 11); and a tertiary stage which appears later (sometimes many years later) and is characterized by neurological involvement such as *tabes dorsalis*. Syphilis has been one of mankind's serious and persistent diseases, although not as fatal nor as contagious as several other diseases. Its origin is not certain, but it became prominently recognized after Columbus' return to Italy. The word syphilis comes from Syphilus, the name of a shepherd infected with the disease in the psalm of Fractarius (1530), in which the word first appears. In the

Nothing is known of the health or activities of the men following their discharge from the Expedition that would indicate that they had tertiary syphilis. It might be assumed, therefore, that the captains did a reasonably good job of treating their men who had venereal diseases. No details are recorded in the journals about the procedures used, such as the frequency of application of the mercurial ointment, except to use salivation as an indication of saturation; undoubtedly they followed instructions given to Lewis verbally by Dr. Rush, and perhaps by Dr. Saugrain. The two captain-physicians had one advantage that is universal with all army physicians: they had a captive clientele!

Hamilton does not discuss the required dosage of mercury. However, he does caution that "if the individual be robust, sixteen or twenty ounces of blood should be drawn from the man before any preparation of mercury be exhibited." Vigorous purging was also used in preparation for medicating with mercury. There is no indication in the journals that such preparatory treatment was a part of the practice of the captain-physicians. Dr. Benjamin Rush did not include syphilis among the extensive list of indications for bleeding, and he did not include reference to syphilis in his ten rules of health care for the Expedition.

On January 10, 1805, Clark recorded: "last night was excessively Cold. the Murkery this morning Stood at 40° below

---

fifteenth century it reached epidemic proportions in Europe. It was not until 1905 that Fritz Schaudinn (1817-1906) discovered the causal organism, the *spirochaeta pallida*. In 1906 August von Wasserman (1866-1925) described his laboratory test on the blood. William Cockburn (1669-1739) described gonnorrhea in 1713 in his article on "The Symptoms, Nature, Cause and Cure of a Gonorrhea," but he thought that gonorrhea and syphilis were the same disease. Lewis and Clark recognized them as separate diseases, but, of course, knew nothing of the bacteriology of either. It was not until 1879 that Albert Neisser (1855-1916) discovered the gonococcus as the causal organism of gonorrhea. For both syphilis and gonorrhea the use of antibiotics has replaced older treatments.

0 which is 72° below the freesing point, we had one man out last night, who returned about 8 oclock this morning." He had probably shared a tepee somewhere!

The captains' health care included attention to the Indians as well as to their own men. On January 10, Clark also wrote that "about 10 o'Clock the boy about 13 years of age Came to the fort with his feet frosed and had layed out last night without fire with only a buffalow Robe to Cover him . . . we had his feet put in cold water and they are Comeing too." It appears from Ordway's note of the same day that the Indians had abandoned this boy as dead.

The severe cold weather continued, but the men had to risk hours of exposure outside the warmth of the fort in order to acquire wood and meat. On January 13, "Mr. Chabonee (our inturpreter) and one man that accompanied him to Some loges . . . returned, both frosed in their faces." Whitehouse wrote in his journal on January 14, that "I got my feet So froze that I could not walk to the fort;" Ordway states that Shannon reported Whitehouse's condition and said that he could not walk and that he would need a horse to get back to the fort. The horse was sent to bring Whitehouse, and examination, according to Gass, showed that "his feet were not so bad as we had expected." (On the fourteenth, Clark placed in parentheses, as if of little importance: "Several men with the Veneral Cought from the Mandan women.") The men continued to have frequent complaints about the trauma to their feet from the ice and snow. It is surprising that there were not more complaints of injury to the feet; probably the men's feet were continually sore, but it was considered too commonplace to mention in the journals.

On January 26 Clark wrote: "one man taken violently Bad with Plurisie. Bleed & apply those remedies Common to that disorder." Clark did not mention what those remedies were, but they probably included purging and greasing the chest as well as bleeding. The next day he recorded: "I bleed the man with the Plurisy to day & Swet him, Capt. Lewis took off the Toes of one foot of the boy who got frost bit Some time ago." [16] Probably the necrotic tissue had demarcated in the two weeks since his toes were frozen, and probably the amputations done by Lewis consisted of plucking loose the dead tissue, possibly disarticulating the joints, and possibly having to sever tendons. The raw, tender areas were then permitted to granulate over with new tissue. Undoubtedly Clark was following the general routine of medical treatment of the day and probably Rush's instructions specifically when he bled his patient

---

[16] Mackenzie also describes an occasion when he was called on to use his surgical technique and which reflects how all frontier captains were called upon to minister to health needs: "On my arrival here last fall, I found that one of the young Indians had lost the use of his right hand by the bursting of a gun, and that his thumb had been maimed in such a manner as to hang only by a small strip of flesh. Indeed, when he was brought to me, his wound was in such an offensive state, and emitted such a putrid smell, that it required all the resolution I possessed to examine it. His friends had done every thing in their power to relieve him; but as it consisted only in singing about him, and blowing upon his hand, the wound, as may be well imagined, had got into the deplorable state in which I found it. I was rather alarmed at the difficulty of the case, but as the young man's life was in a state of hazard, I was determined to risk my surgical reputation, and accordingly took him under my care. I immediately formed a poultice of bark, stripped from the roots of the spruce-fir, which I applied to the wound, having first washed it with the juice of the bark: this proved a very painful dressing: in a few days, however, the wound was clean, and the proud flesh around it destroyed. I wished very much in this state of the business to have separated the thumb from the hand, which I well knew must be effected before the cure could be performed; but he would not consent to that operation, till, by the application of vitriol, the flesh by which the thumb was suspended, was shrivelled almost to a thread. When I had succeeded in this object, I perceived that the wound was closing rather faster than I desired. The salve I applied on the occasion was made of the Canadian balsam, wax, and tallow dropped from a burning candle into water. In short, I was so successful, that about Christmas my patient engaged in an hunting party, and brought me the tongue of an elk: nor was he finally ungrateful. When he left me I received the warmest acknowledgments, both from himself, and the relations with whom he departed, for my care of him. I certainly did not spare my time or attention on the occasion, as I regularly dressed his wound three times a day, during the course of a month." *See* Mackenzie, *Through North America*, pp. 137-38.

for pleurisy. The next day Clark could write: ". . . the man Sick yesterday is getting well." On the twenty-eighth, Clark also recorded that "Mr. Jessome our interpiter was taken verry unwell this evening . . ." Clark gives no information about the nature of Jessome's "unwellness" but on the following day he records that he gave him a "Dost of Salts."

Clark wrote on January 29, 1805, that "we are now burning a large Coal pit, to mend the indians hatchets, & make them war axes, the only means by which we percure Corn from them." Lewis wrote on February 6 about the particular importance of the blacksmiths to the Expedition: "the blacksmiths take a considerable quantity of corn today in payment for their labour the blacksmiths have proved a happy resou[r]ce to us in our present situation as I believe it would have been difficult to have devised any other method to have procured corn from the natives."

Clark continued very successfully in his role as the chief physician to the Expedition. On January 31, he states that "George Drewyer [Drouillard] taken with the Pleurisy last evening Bled & gave him Some Sage tea, this morning he is much better." On this same day Clark recorded: "Sawed off the boys toes." Presumably this was the same Indian boy who had toes removed from "one foot" on the twenty-seventh. Probably both feet were frozen, and the boy lost some or all of the toes from both feet. But did Clark really *saw* off the toes? A surgical saw was not listed in the medical kit. (Maybe he used one of the two handsaws in the general supplies! There was a "saw-set" as well as "Sergecal instruments Hosp.") Sawing would indicate amputation through the metatarsals, instead of disarticulation of the toes. Such surgery probably would have required cauterization to stop the bleeding, which is not mentioned. Any such surgery would require frequent progress dressings not mentioned in the journals.

Clark's rather casual and brief note is puzzling. Whatever the details of the treatment, Clark was to write on February 23 that "The father of the Boy whose feet were frozed near this place, and nearly Cured by us, took him home in a Slay."

Though Jessaume improved after he was given the dose of salts, Clark records on February 2 that "our interpeter Still unwell," and also that "one of the wives of the Big belley interpetr Sick." Charbonneau was the interpreter from the Big Belly or Minitaree Indians; Clark does not say if Sacagawea was the wife who was ill.

Clark headed a hunting expedition of eighteen men in −18° weather because the meat supply was running low, and because they wanted to build up a supply to prepare for "our voyage in the spring of the year." This probably meant pounding it into pemmican because there was not enough warm sunshine to jerk it.

On February 11, 1805, occurred one of the momentous medical events of the Lewis and Clark Expedition: Clark noted that Sacagawea "delivered a fine boy." The journals do not record just when Lewis and Clark decided to take Sacagawea with them, but it was soon after meeting her, and she was pregnant then.

They knew that her pregnancy would be terminated before the Expedition departed the Mandan villages in the late spring. Clark had recorded previously how he was concerned enough about Sacagawea that he ordered his servant to take some soup to her when she was ill. Several previous journal entries had recorded the captains' recognition of the fact that Sacagawea had come from the Shoshone or Snake Indians, near the Rocky Mountains. Probably they were keeping fairly close watch on her as she approached her time of delivery. When that time arrived, it was Lewis who gave attention to her, as Clark was away on a hunting trip.

Lewis recorded the event of February 11, 1805:

about five Oclock this evening one of the wives of Charbono was
delivered of a fine boy. it is worthy of remark that this was the first
child which this woman had boarn, and as is common in such cases
her labour was tedious and the pain violent; Mr. Jessome informed
me that he had freequently administered a small portion of the
rattle of the rattlesnake, which he assured me had never failed to
produce the desired effect, that of hastening the birth of the child;
having the rattle of a snake by me I gave it to him and he administered two rings of it to the woman broken in small pieces with
the fingers and added to a small quantity of water. Whether this
medicine was truly the cause or not I shall not undertake to determine, but I was informed that she had not taken it more than
ten minutes before she brought forth   perhaps this remedy may
be worthy of future experiments, but I must confess that I want
faith as to its efficacy.

It is to Lewis' credit that although he had grown up hearing
all sorts of tales about health care, and had witnessed almost
universal belief in them, he demonstrated the attitude of the
true scientist: doubt, but willingness to investigate.

The young mother was destined to be a real contributor to
the success of the Expedition, and a greatly publicized heroine. Her new infant son was called Baptiste. This young man
made the longest papoose journey on record, going with his
mother from the Mandan village to the Pacific and back.
When he reached manhood, he traveled in Europe for six
years with his benefactor, Maxmillian of Weid, after which he
returned to the United States. He lived out a long and useful
life, including service on the Santa Fe Trail and in California.
He died on the way to the gold rush in Montana, and is buried
in Danner, Oregon.[17] He is the only member of the Expedition
who returned to Oregon, and the only one buried in Oregon
soil.

There is no mention in the journals of Sacagawea or her
baby having any post-partum complications. Lewis and Clark

17 See Irving W. Anderson, "J. B. Charbonneau, Son of Sacajawea," Oreg. Hist.
Soc. Qtly., Vol. LXXI, No. 13 (Sept. 1970), pp. 247-68.

and the other journalists gave very little attention to the subject of parturition among the Indians; particularly, they did not mention complications.

After his return from the hunting trip, Clark recorded that he had broken through the ice, and that the uneven ice had blistered the bottoms of his feet, and that walking was painful to him. "Several Men being nearly out of Mockersons," they determined to return to the fort. Clark was happy to report the results of his hunting expedition: "forty Deer, three buffaloe bulls, & sixteen Elk, most of them were so meager that they were unfit for uce." The fact that the meat was "meager" is probably the reason for Clark writing on February 18 that "our Store of Meat is out today."

On February 28, Clark wrote that "two men of the NW compy. arrived with letters . . . also a Root and a top of a plant, presented by Mr. Haney,[18] for the Cure of Mad Dogs Snakes &c., and to be found and used as follows viz: this root is found on the high lands and asent of the hills, the way of useing it is to scarify the part when bitten to chu or pound an inch or more if the root is Small, and applying it to the bitten part renewing it twice a Day. the bitten person is not to chaw nor Swallow any of the Root for it might have contrary effect." [19] Lewis gives a more "dressed up" descrip-

[18] Hugh Henney was a British fur trader for the North West Company, stationed on the Assinboine River. Lewis and Clark first met him when he came to Fort Mandan on Dec. 16, 1804.

[19] Coues discusses and speculates on the identity of this anti-venomous plant: "But what was the specific for these afflicted creatures? The relation is universal tradition in the west; I have heard it around the camp-fire from the British to the Mexican boundary; and everybody knows the plant, except the botanists. Coues, *History of Lewis and Clark*, i, pp. 347-48.

Coues was a medical doctor, but not a botanist. Paul Cutright, a biologist and an authority on Lewis and Clark, thinks that the snake-bite plant was *Echinacea angustifolia*, the Narrow-leafed Purple Cone-flower. *See* Paul Cutright, *Lewis and Clark: Pioneering Naturalists* (Urbana, 1969), pp. 122, 273, and 408. Cutright cites Melvin Randolph Gilmore's "Uses of Plants by the Indians of the Missouri River Region," *Thirty-third Annual Rept. of the Bur. of Amer. Ethnology, 1911-12*

tion of this plant's use in his letter of March 5, 1805, from Fort Mandan to Thomas Jefferson.[20] Lewis also sent a specimen of this plant to Jefferson; the invoice included "a specimen of a plant, and a parsel of its roots, highly prized by the natives as an efficatious remidy in the cure of the bite of the rattle snake, or mad dog."[21] There is no evidence that Jefferson had it analyzed. He did, however, send it along with other things to William Hamilton;[22] in a letter to Hamilton, he mentions a plant without a label, but adds, "I believe it is a plant used by the Indians with extraordinary success for curing the bite of the rattle snake & other venomous animals."

Clark's journal entry of March first, 1805, is a typical description of the daily business of the men: "I am ingaged in Copying a Map, men building perogus, makeing Ropes, Burn-

---

(Wash: G.P.O.), p. 131. Gilmore states: "This plant was universally used as an antidote for snake bite and other venomous bites and stings and poisonous conditions. A variety of *Echinaceas* are used now as garden flowers, commonly called Coneflower." In his extensive and detailed article of 101 pages, Gilmore does not list any of the several plants mentioned by Coues except *Astragulus Caroliniana*, and the only medicinal value he assigns to it is that of a febrifuge. Thus it is most probable that Cutright is correct.

20 "FORT MANDAN MARCH 5, 1805. This specimen of a plant [H.] common to the prairies in this quarter was presented to me by Mr. Hugh heney a gentleman of rispectability and information who has resided many years among the natives of this country from whom he obtained the knowledge of its virtues. Mr. Haney informed me that he had used the root of this plant frequently with the most happy effects in cases of the bite of the mad wolf or dog and also for the bite of the rattle snake he assured me that he had made a great number of experiments on various subjects of men horses and dogs particularly in the case of madness where the symptoms were in some instances far advanced and had never witnessed it's failing to produce the desired effect. the method of using it is by external application, to half an ounce of the root finely pulverized, add as much water as is necessary to reduce it to the consistency of a common poltice and apply it to the bitten parts, renewing the dressing once in twelve hours. in cases of the bite of the mad dog where the wound has healed before the symptoms of madness appear, the bitten part must be lacerated or sca[r]efyed before the application is made. the application had always better be made as early as possible after the injury has been sustained. I have sent herewith a few pounds of this root, in order that experiments may be made by some skillful person under the direction of the P[h]ilosophical society of Philadelphia." Jackson, *Letters*, p. 220.

21 Jackson, *Letters*, p. 235.   22 *Ibid.*, p. 172.

ing Coal, Hanging up meat & Makeing battle axes for Corn."
The making of canoes and ropes indicated that the men were
anticipating the coming of spring and their departure. Clark
recorded a favorable omen on March 3: "A large flock of
Ducks pass up the River," and two days later, he recorded the
thermometer to be forty above zero.

On March 6, "one man Shannon Cut his foot with the ads
[adze] in working at the perogue." On March 7 one of the
chiefs "Visited us with a Sick child, to whome I gave Some of
rushes' pills." Clark says he gave "Some pills;" if he gave more
than one of Dr. Rush's potent cathartics this child certainly
had an adequate dose! A few days later a man and his wife
brought a sick child to Clark who recorded that "I administer
for the Child."

The weather rapidly ameliorated during the latter part of
March. The men freed their boats from the melting ice and
repaired them. They dried out and restored their baggage,
both for the Expedition to the west and for the men who were
returning to St. Louis. They repeatedly tested their firearms to
prove that they were in excellent condition. They had kept
their supplies of powder in sealed lead canisters coming up
the Missouri and had stored it in their dry cabins during the
winter. The meat supply had been replenished by the better
hunting afforded by the recent improvement in the weather.

On March 30, Clark was able to write: ". . . all the
party in high Sperits they pass but fiew nights without
amuseing themselves danceing possessing perfect harmony
and good understanding towards each other, Generally helthy
except Venerials Complaints which is verry Common amongst
the natives and the men Catch it from them." This note would
indicate that the men had come through the winter without
dietary deficiencies or chronic pulmonary ailments. Apparently Pryor was suffering no chronic complaints or disability
from his dislocated shoulder. That the men had come through

the confinement of their wintering at Fort Mandan with "perfect harmony and good understanding towards each other" augured well for the future of the Expedition. Clark wrote to his brother-in-law, Major William C. Croghan, on April 2: "Our party has enjoyed a great share of health and are in high spirits." [23]

On March 31, 1805, Lewis had written a long and reassuring letter to his mother, stating in part: "For myself individually I [enjoy] better health than I [have] since I commenced my [voyage. The] party are now in [good] health and excellent sperits, [are at]tatched to the enterp[rise and] anxious to proceed; not a whisper of discontent or murmur is to be heared among them, but all act in unison, and with the most perfect harmony." [24]

In a letter dated on the day of the Expedition's departure from Fort Mandan, April 7, 1805, Lewis wrote to Jefferson:

Since our arrival at this place we have subsisted principally on meat, with which our guns have supplied us amply, and have thus been enabled to reserve the parched meal, portable soup, and a considerable portion of pork and flour, which we had intended for the more difficult parts of our voyage. If the Indian information can be credited, the vast quantity of game with which the country abounds through which we are to pass leaves us but little to apprehend from the want of food.

As to myself, individually I never enjoyed a more perfect state of good health, than I have since we commenced our voyage. My inestimable friend and companion, Capt. Clark, has also enjoyed good health generally. At this moment, every individual of the party are in good health, and excellent sperits, zealously attached to the enterprise, and anxious to proceed; not a whisper of discontent or murmur is to be heard among them; but all in unison, act with the most perfect harmoney, with such men I have every thing to hope, and but little to fear.[25]

---

[23] Jackson, *Letters*, p. 230.   [24] *Ibid.*, p. 224.
[25] *Ibid.*, pp. 231-34.

XIII

To the Gates of
the Rocky Mountains

Fortunately for us our men are healthy.   William Clark [1]

Clark had made an entry in his journal on January 7, 1805, that ". . . from the best information, the Great Falls is about (eight-hundred) miles nearly West." The Great Falls was a landmark destination for the captains; when it was reached they knew they would be "way West" — nearing the western end of the Missouri and approaching the Rocky Mountains. But the captains had no definite idea about the distance from the Great Falls to the mouth of the Columbia. And they certainly had no idea of the ruggedness of the Rocky Mountains or the suffering they would endure while passing through them, or they might not have started west from the Mandan villages in such high spirits.

April 7, 1805 — the momentous date on which the Corps of Discovery left Fort Mandan and headed into the unknown West, and on the same day Captain Lewis "dismissed the barge and crew" for St. Louis. These were the voyageurs who helped bring the Expedition up the Missouri, and who took the keelboat with collected specimens back to St. Louis, under the command of Corporal Warfington.[2]

---

[1] Thwaites, *Journals,* III, p. 218.

[2] Corp. Richard Warfington and several men accompanied Lewis up the Missouri for the explicit purpose of returning to St. Louis from the Mandan Villages in the spring of 1805 to carry messages and materials collected by the Expedition. He and his men left for St. Louis on the day that the permanent party left for the

For some unexplained reason the journals do not relate any health care attention of these men on the way up the Missouri and at Fort Mandan, although they surely had their share of illness and accidents. It is not believable that the captains would have considered them unworthy of care and mention, when they cared for and recorded health care of Indians on many occasions.

Lewis was an infrequent diarist compared to Clark, but he made a lengthy and eloquent entry in the journal on their departure from the Mandans on April 7, giving an indication of what the published journals might have been like if Lewis had lived to put his impress on them:

> Our vessels consisted of six small canoes, and two large perogues. This little fleet altho' not quite rispectable as those of Columbus or Capt. Cook, were still viewed by us with as much pleasure as those deservedly famed adventurers ever beheld theirs; and I dare say with quite as much anxiety for their safety and preservation. we were now about to penetrate a country at least two thousand miles in width, on which the foot of civilized man had never trodden; the good or evil it had in store for us was for experiment yet to determine, and these little vessells contained every article by which we were to expect to subsist or defend ourselves. however, as the state of mind in which we are, generally gives the colouring to events, when the imagination is suffered to wander into futurity, the picture which now presented itself to me was a most pleasing one. enterta[in]ing as I do, the most confident hope of succeeding in a voyage which had formed a da[r]ling project of mine for the last ten years,[3] I could not but esteem this moment of my departure as among the most happy of my life. The

West. However, in a sense he and his men were still members of the Expedition until they reached St. Louis on June 1, 1805. His pay was seven dollars a month.

[3] This statement of Lewis' gives support to the probability that Lewis and Jefferson had shared their dream for many years. Lewis had applied to Jefferson to lead an expedition which Jefferson was proposing to the American Philosophical Society in 1792. Lewis was only 18 years old then, and Andre Michaux, an erstwhile French botanist, was chosen to lead the abortive expedition. This application by Lewis probably was not forgotten by Jefferson.

party are in excellent health and sperits, zealously attached to the enterprise, and anxious to proceed; not a whisper or murmur of discontent to be heard among them, but all act in unison, and with the most perfict harmony.[4]

Spring was coming rapidly; on April 9 Clark noted "great numbers of Brant [wild geese] flying up the river, the Maple & Elm has buded & cotton and arrow wood beginning to bud," and the following day Lewis wrote that "the geese are now feeding in considerable numbers on the young grass which has sprung up in the bottom prairies." Both he and Clark recorded that the mosquitoes were troublesome.

On the eleventh they were having their first meat in several days. ". . . . a comfortable dinner on a venison stake and beavers tales with the bisquit which had got wet on the 8th inst. by the accident of the canoe filling with water . . ." Lewis describes the extensive snow-like coverage of the banks and hills in which they were passing. This white material "tastes like a mixture of common salt and glauber salts . . . and had a purgative effect."[5] The following day Lewis recorded that they "found a great quantity of small onions in the plain where we encamped."

A near-tragedy occurred on April 13, which Lewis describes:

> . . . this accedent was very near costing us dearly. beleiving this vessell [a perogue] to be the most steady and safe, we had embarked on board of it our instruments, Papers, medicine and the most valuable part of the merchandize . . . we had also embarked on board ourselves, with three men who could not swim and a squaw with a young child, all of whom, had the perogue

---

[4] The last part of this journal entry is very similar to the composition of Lewis' letters of Mar. 31, 1805, to his mother, Lucy Marks, and of Apr. 7, 1805, to Jefferson.

[5] Thwaites states that "it consists largely or mainly of sulfate of soda." Thwaites, *Journals*, i, p. 295.

overset, would most probably have perished, as the waves were high, and the perogue upwards of 200 yards from the nearest shore.

Charbonneau "in this state of alarm" let go of the steering, and the perogue went more out-of-control, being righted only with difficulty. It is doubtful if loss of some of the medicines would have meant much difference to the future health of the men, except that it would have been unfortunate if they had lost any of the "eyewash" which would be used for diplomatic purposes with the Indians on the return journey through the Rocky Mountains. The captains' evaluation of the medicines is shown by having stored them on the pirogue considered to be "the most steady and safe." It is interesting to note that the pirogue contained "three men who could not swim;" with all the care that the captains used in sorting out and accepting men who were healthy and capable of managing the demands of the frontier, it seems ridiculous that the ability to swim was not a requisite of every member of the Expedition.

The men were beginning to find a few beaver, of which Lewis wrote "the men prefer the flesh of this animal, to that of any other which we have, or are able to procure at this moment. I eat very heartily of the beaver myself, and think it excellent; particularly the tale, and liver. . ."

On April 18 Clark recorded "I concluded to walk thro' the point about 2 miles and take Shabono, with me, he had taken a dost of Salts." Apparently because of the expected results of the medication, Clark thought that Charbonneau better not be confined to the boat!

The upper Missouri River was rather placid, and the men were making good time with their boats with the use of a sail, and needing comparatively little use of the oars and pole. There is no mention of serious health problems, the only complaint being that "the Buffaloe, Elk and deer are poor at this

season, and of cours are not very palitable, however our good
health and apetites make up every necessary deficiency, and
we eat very heartily of them." When four buffalo calves were
killed, they were "found very delicious." Lewis added that
"I think it equal to any veal I ever tasted."

By the last of April the Expedition was in the region of
the Yellowstone River and the prairie winds were whipping
"immence quantities of sand" from bars of the river "in such
clouds that you were unable to discover the opposite bank of
the river in many instances . . . so penitrating is this
sand that we can not keep any article free from it; in short we
are compelled to eat, drink, and breath it very freely." Lewis
blamed this driving sand for one of their new complaints:
"Soar eyes is a common complaint among the party."

Game was becoming far more plentiful; Lewis wrote on
April 27 that "game was very abundant and gentle" and he
then added a remark which deserves the approbation of every
conservationist, and was in keeping with Indian practices:
"we only kill as much as is necessary for food." He believed
that "two good hunters could conveniently supply a regiment
with provisions."

Undoubtedly the men were glad to be out on the trail again,
free from the monotony and confinement of Fort Mandan.
Traveling was easy, the weather was good, there was plenty
of game, and the countryside was a-blooming. Surprisingly,
on May 2, the men experienced another touch of winter with
one inch of snow, the thermometer at 28°, and ice freezing on
the oars. Clark wrote: "a verry extraordernarey climate, to
behold the trees Gree & flowers spread on the plain, & Snow
an inch deep."

The first record of illness on the way West was that of John
Shields' rheumatism, although many of the men probably had
venereal hangovers from the Mandan women. Lewis was

called on May 4 to treat Joseph Field for the most serious
acute illness that had developed since the Expedition left
Fort Mandan. He records "Joseph Fields was very sick today
with a disentary had a high fever I gave him a doze of Glauber
salts, which operated very well, in the evening his fever
abated and I gave him 30 drops of laudnum."

On May 5 Clark and Drouillard killed a large brown bear
which was divided among the men, and the fat boiled and
"put in a cask for future use."

On May ninth, Lewis describes one of the delicacies of the
frontier:

> Capt C. killed 2 bucks and 2 buffaloe, I also killed one buffaloe
> which proved to the best meat, it was in tolerable order; we saved
> the best of the meat, and from the cow I killed we saved the
> necessary materials for making what our wrighthand cook Char-
> bono calls the *boudin (poudingue) blanc,* and immediately set
> him about preparing them for supper; this white pudding we all
> esteem one of the greatest del[ic]acies of the forrest, it may not be
> amiss therefore to give it a place. About 6 feet of the lower extrem-
> ity of the large gut of the Buffaloe is the first mo[r]sel that the
> cook makes love to, this he holds fast at one end with the right
> hand, while with the forefinger and thumb of the left he gently
> compresses it, and discharges what he says is not good to eat, but
> of which in the s[e]quel we get a moderate portion; the mustle
> lying underneath the shoulder blade next to the back, and fillets
> are next saught, these are needed up very fine with a good portion
> of kidney suit [suet]; to this composition is then added a just pro-
> portion of pepper and salt and a small quantity of flour; thus far
> advanced, our skilfull opporater C———o seizes his recepticle,
> which had never once touched the water, for that would intirely
> distroy the regular order of the whole procedure; you will not for-
> get that the side you now see is that covered with a good coat of
> fat provided the anamal be in good order; the operator sceizes the
> recepticle I say, and tying it fast at one end turns it inward and
> begins now with repeated evolutions of the hand and arm, and a
> brisk motion of the finger and thumb to put it what he says is *bon
> pour manger*; thus, by stuffing and compressing he soon distends

the recepticle to the utmost limmits of it's power of expansion, and
in the course of it's longtudinal progress it drives from the other
end of the recepticle a much larger portion of the [blank space in
MS] than was prev[i]ously discharged by the finger and thumb of
the left hand in a former part of the operation; thus when the sides
of the recepticle are skilfully exchanged the outer for the iner, and
all is compleatly filled with something good to eat, it is tyed at the
other end, but not any cut off, for that would make the pattern too
scant; it is then baptised in the missouri with two dips and a flirt,
and bobbed into the kettle; from whence, after it be well boiled it
is taken and fryed with bears oil untill it becomes brown, when
it is ready to esswage the pangs of a keen appetite or such as
travelers in the wilderness are seldom at a loss for.

On Friday, May 10, Lewis recorded one of the most precise
prescriptions that either one of the captains used during all
the months of the Expedition. He wrote "Boils and impos-
thumes have been very common with the party   Bratton is
now unable to work with one on his hand; soar eyes continue
also to be common to all of us . . .   for the imposthume I
use emmolient poltices, and for soar eyes a solution of white
vitriol and the sugar of lead in the proportion of 2 grs. of the
former and one of the latter to each ounce of water."

The boil on his hand was to be only a part of Bratton's
trouble. On the following day he was permitted to walk on
shore, and came running back to the river out of breath. He
had shot a grizzly bear through the lungs, but the bear continued to chase Bratton for half a mile before he succumbed.
The bear was butchered, and about eight gallons of oil was
rendered and put in kegs for future use.

Lewis came to know and value the choke cherry in many
ways. He brewed himself a concoction of it to drink when he
was ill; probably he learned the use of the choke cherry from
his mother. Lewis describes in detail many ways the Indians
use the choke cherry as food; mainly preparing it as a sort of
pemmican.

The steady and strenuous performance of the men and the good luck which often saved them, was taken note of many times by the captains. On May 14 several of the men almost lost a battle with a grizzly bear that required several shots to kill him; and Charboneau, who Lewis described "cannot swim and is perhaps the most timid waterman in the world" lost his head while steering a pirogue and almost lost the boat, too — the pirogue which contained instruments, merchandise and medicines. As Charboneau was "crying to his god for mercy," Cruzatte threatened to shoot him if he didn't grab hold of the rudder. In contrast to the performance of her husband, Sacagawea calmly retrieved many articles from the water. Besides Charboneau, two other men on this pirogue could not swim. Whitehouse wrote that "the Medicine spoiled or damaged very much."

Whitehouse wrote on the next day that several men went out hunting while the merchandise was being dried and aired, and "killed one buffaloe 7 Deer and 4 beaver."

As well as being physician to the men of the Expedition, Lewis was called upon to play the role of veterinarian when his dog was bit by a beaver: "one of the party wounded a beaver, and my dog as usual swam out to catch it; the beaver bit him through the hind leg and cut the artery; it was with great difficulty that I could stop the blood; I fear it will yet prove fatal to him." Clark mentions this incident briefly and states that the dog was "near bleading to death."

Ordway noted on May 25 that "the air of this country is pure & healthy [and] the water of the Missourie fine and cool." On the same day Whitehouse records that "Gibson one of the hunters putt one of his Shoulders out of place today but got it back in again." There is no further comment from Whitehouse or the other journalists to indicate how Gibson got his shoulder "out," nor how he got it reduced, nor if he reduced it by himself or with the assistance of others. It is possible that instead of the shoulder being completely dislocated it was subluxated, and that with self-manipulation it easily reduced. Neither of the captains recorded Gibson's shoulder dislocation in their journals.

Again and again the men's health and life were preserved by good luck. On May 29 a buffalo rampaged through the sleeping camp, greatly exciting everyone but hurting no one — although there were several "near misses." Lewis wrote that "my dog saved us by causing him [the buffalo] to change his course a second time . . . leaving us by this time all in an uproar with our guns in o[u]r hands enquiring of each other the ca[u]se of the alarm."

The Missouri became more shallow in places, with wide rapids almost exposing the rocks, and the stream became more tortuous in its windings. The work and endurance of the men is described by Lewis in his journal entry of May 31:

> The men are compelled to be in the water even to their armpits, and the water is yet very could . . . they are one fourth of their time in the water, added to this the banks and bluffs along which they are obliged to pass are so slippery and the mud so tenacious that they are unable to wear their mockersons, and in that situation draging the heavy burthen of a canoe and walking acasionally for several hundred yards over the sharp fragments of rocks . . . their labour is incredibly painfull and great, yet those faithfull fellows bear it without a murmur.

Poor Charbonneau! When he accompanied Drouillard to hunt for meat they encountered a grizzly bear which almost caught Drouillard, and "it also pursued Charbono who fired his gun in the air as he ran." Charbonneau then hid in some thick bushes and Drouillard brought the bear down with a shot through the head. It was fortunate that in these multiple encounters with the grizzlies not one of the men lost his life. They did not possess guns with the firepower of a modern rifle, and their guns were not repeaters; it took a minute or so to prime and fire their muzzle-loaders. It is a wonder that their trembling hands got their guns loaded and aimed steadily. One or two shots were rarely enough; in fact, some times it took as many as six shots well placed in the vital parts of the bear to bring it down.

On June 3 Lewis again recorded the pitiful endurance of the men:

> Those who have remained at camp today have been busily engaged in dressing skins for cloathing, notwithstanding that many of them have their feet so mangled and bruised with the stones and rough ground over which they passed barefoot, that they can scarcely walk or stand; at least it is with great pain they do either. for some days past they were unable to wear their mockersons; they have fallen off considerably, but notwithstanding the difficulties past, or those which seem now to mennace us, they still remain perfectly cheerfull.

On June 4 Lewis wrote of the "great abundance of prickly pears which are extreemely troublesome; as the thorns very readily perce the foot through the Mockerson; they are so numerous that it requires one half of the traveler's attention to avoid them." Two days later Lewis recorded: "it continues to rain and we have no shelter and uncomfortable nights without rest is the natural consequence."

Good luck again smiled on the Expedition and prevented loss of life on June 7, 1805, when Lewis again slipped off a ledge, this time accompanied by Windsor, whose escape was even closer. Lewis recorded in his journal on June 7:

> It continued to rain almost without intermission last night and as I expected we had a most disagreable and wrestless night. our camp possessing no allurements, we left our watery beads at an early hour and continued our rout down the river. It still continues to rain the wind hard from N.E. and could. the grownd remarkable

slipry. . . In passing along the face of one of these bluffs today
I sliped at a narrow pass of about 30 yards in length and but for
a quick and fortunate recovery by means of my espontoon I should
been precipitated into the river down a craggy pricipice of about
ninety feet. I had scarcely reached a place on which I could stand
with tolerable safety even with the assistance of my espontoon
before I heard a voice behind me cry out god god Capt. what
shall I do on turning about I found it was Windsor who had
sliped and fallen ab[o]ut the center of this narrow pass and was
lying prostrate on his belley, with his wright hand arm and leg
over the precipice while he was holding on with the left arm and
foot as well as he could which appeared to be with much difficulty.
I discovered his danger and the trepedation which he was in gave
me still further concern for I expected every instant to see him
loose his strength and slip off; altho' much allarmed at his situation
I disguised my feelings and spoke very calmly to him and assured
him that he was in no kind of danger, to take the knife out of his
belt behind him with his wright hand and dig a hole with it in the
face of the bank to receive his right foot which he did and then
raised himself to his knees; I then directed him to take off his
mockersons and to come forward on his hands and knees holding
the knife in one hand and the gun in the other. this he happily
effected and escaped . . . we had reserved and brought with
us a good supply of the best peices [of deer meat], we roasted and
eat a hearty supper of our venison not having taisted a mo[r]sel
before during the day; I now laid myself down on some willow
boughs to a comfortable nights rest, and felt indeed as if I was
fully repaid for the toil and pain of the day, so much will a good
shelter, a dry bed, and comfortable supper revive the sperits of the
w[e]aryed, wet and hungry traveler.

The first week of June saw the Expedition passing westward from the Marias River which Lewis named after a lady
friend back home, Miss Maria Weed. This river was believed
to be the true Missouri by all the men except the captains. It
was good sized, and its apparent northernly source did in-
trigue the captains, who still had the Northwest Passage on

their minds. There was no one to help them make a decision; they were beyond where white men had previously ventured west. This was not Sacagawea's territory, and she could be of no help here. It was the captains' own reasoning that kept them on the true Missouri, rather than leading the Expedition up the Marias.

Clark wrote on June 9 that "Capt. Lewis a little unwell to day & take salts &c . . . in the evening the party amused themselves danceing and Singing Songes in the most social manner." In spite of the sore feet, Whitehouse wrote cheerfully on this date that "towards evening we had a frolick. the officers gave the party a dram, the fiddle played and they danced late &c."

On June 10 the men constructed a cache, in which they deposited "1 Keg of flour, 2 Kegs of parched meal, 2 Kegs of Pork, 1 Keg of salt, some chissels, a cooper's Howel, some tin cups, 2 Musquets, 3 brown bears skins, beaver skins, horns of the bighorned anamal, a part of the men's robes clothing and all their superfluous baggage of every discription, and beaver traps." Clark recorded that "Sahcahgagwea our Indian woman was verry sick I blead her;" the illness was not described and no estimate was made of the amount of blood removed.

Lewis was still too ill on June 11 to pursue a side exploration on which he was leading some men; he wrote:

This morning I felt much better, but somewhat w[e]akened by my disorder. at 8 A.M. I swung my pack, and set forward with my little party . . . I determined to take dinner here, but before the meal was prepared I was taken with such violent pain in the intestens that I was unable to partake of the feast of marrowbones. my pain still increased and towards evening was attended with a high fever; finding myself unable to march, I determined to prepare a camp of some willow boughs and remain all night. having brought no medecine with me I resolved to try an experiment with some simples; and the Choke cherry [6] which grew abundantly in the bottom first struck my attention; I directed a parsel of the small twigs to be geathered striped of the leaves, cut into pieces of about 2 Inches in length and boiled in water untill a strong black decoction of an astringent bitter tast was produced; at sunset I took a point [pint] of this decoction and ab[o]ut an hour after repeated the d[o]ze by 10 in the evening I was entirely releived from pain and in fact every symptom of the disorder forsook me; my fever abated, a gentel perspiration was produced and I had a comfortable and refreshing nights rest.

Sacagawea did not improve, so that on June 11 Clark bled her again: "the indian woman verry sick, I blead her which appeared to be of great service to her."

On June 12 Lewis was improved, so that he could write: "This morning I felt myself quite revived, took another portion of my decoction and set out at sunrise." That evening he wrote: "altho' the sun had not yet set I felt myself somewhat w[e]ary being weakened I presume by late disorder; and therfore determined to remain here during the ballance of the day and night, having marched about 27 Miles today. . ." On this same date, Ordway, who was with the main party, wrote that "several rattle Snakes has been seen by the party today one man took hold of one which was in a bunch of bushes as he was taking along the towing line, but luckley escaped being bit . . . our Intrepters wife verry Sick."

Clark wrote in more detail on June 12 about Sacagawea: "The enterpreters wife verry sick so much so that I move her into the back part of our covered part of the Peroque which is cool . . . one man have a fellon riseing on his hand   one other with the Tooth Ake has taken cold in the Jaw. . ."

---

[6] Choke cherry: *Prunus Virginia* (Cutright), here used as an astringent. For general use of the choke cherry, see Scully, *Treas. of Herbs*, p. 26. Many early travelers to the west mention the use of the choke cherry. Townsend notes of it: "tolerable eating, somewhat astringent;" see Thwaites, *Early Western Travels*, xxi, p. 249.

The Expedition was approaching the Great Falls in Montana. They had heard of the Great Falls from many Indians and trappers. Lewis with a few men proceeded ahead, and therefore viewed the falls before Clark, on June 13. Today the Missouri River is crossed with a power dam so that the original grandeur of the falls is lost; enough is still visible, however, so that it is not hard to join with Lewis in admiring them as a "truely magnificent and sublimely grand object."

Back at the lower camp, Clark was still very concerned about his patient, Sacajawea, and wrote on June 14:

> a fine morning the Indian woman complaining all night and excessively bad this morning. her case is somewhat dangerous. two men with the Tooth ake 2 with Tumers, & one man with a Tumor & a slight fever . . . three men with Tumers went on shore and stayed out all night one of them killed 2 buffalow, a part of which we made use of for brackfast.

On June 15 Clark's patient was worse; he wrote:

> our Indian woman sick & low spirited—I gave her the bark and apply it exteranely to her region which revived her much . . . the men in the water from morning untill night hauling the cord & boats walking on sharp rocks and round sliperery stones which alternately cut their feet & throw them down, notwithstanding all this dificuelty they go with great chearfulness, aded to those dificuelties the rattle snakes are inumberable & require great caution to prevent being bitten.

Lewis wrote on the same day: "when I awoke from my sleep today I found a large rattlesnake coiled on the leaning trunk of a tree under the shade of which I had been lying at the distance of about ten feet from him. I killed the snake. . ." The men were to encounter rattlesnakes from here to the Hood River, Oregon, and were most fortunate that not one of the Expedition was bitten.

Lewis returned to the lower camp at the foot of the Great

Falls on June 16 to join Clark and give attention to Sacagawea:

about 2 PM I reached the camp found the Indeen woman extremely ill and much reduced by her indisposition. this gave me some concern as well for the poor object herself, then with a young child in her arms, as from the consideration of her being our only dependence for a friendly negociation with the Snake Indians on whom we depend for horses to assist us in our portage from the Missouri to the columbia river . . . I found that two dozes of barks and opium which I had given her since my arrival had produced an alteration in her pulse for the better; they were now much fuller and more regular. I caused her to drink the mineral water altogether . . . when I first came down I found that her pulse were scarcely perceptible, very quick frequently irregular and attended with strong nervous symptoms, that of twitching of the fingers and leaders of the arm; now the pulse had become regular much fuller and a gentle perspiration had taken place; the nervous symptoms have also in a great measure abated, and she feels herself much freer from pain. she complains principally of the lower region of the abdomen, I therefore continued the cataplasms of barks and laudnumn which I had previously used by my fried Capt. Clark. I believe her disorder originated principally from an obstruction of the mensis in consequence of taking could.[7] I determined to remain at this camp to make some celestial observation and restore the sick woman. [Clark added the following on June 16:] the Indian woman verry bad & will take no medisin what ever, untill her husband finding her out of her sences, easyly provailed on her to take medison, if she dies it will be the fault of her husband as I am now convinced. . .

Lewis' testimony above should put at rest any doubt about

---

[7] Will suspects that Sacajawea's illness was due to chronic pelvic inflammatory disease. See Will, "The Medical and Surgical Practice of the Lewis and Clark Expedition," p. 290. Her history as a captive-slave among the diseased and licentious Mandans lends probability to this diagnosis; if so, it probably was gonorrheal in nature.

Beard comments on the attention that the Captain-physicians gave to Sacajawea: "The medical observations of both leaders are exceptional, but some of the 'bedside notes' of Captain Lewis are so extraordinary as to do credit to a Dieulafoy or an Osler." Beard, "The Medical Observations and Practice of Lewis and Clark," p. 507.

why the two captains brought Sacagawea along. They could
not expect that Charbonneau would be of any value to them
as a guide, and very little assistance to them as an interpreter
among western Indians. They knew from their first meeting
with Sacagawea that she was of the Snake nation, and they
knew that the Snakes or Shoshones resided in the Rocky
Mountains. Charbonneau had another Snake wife and it
would seem reasonable that, if any Snake squaw would have
been acceptable, they would have taken the one without the
papoose. Sacagawea must have impressed them as being particularly competent. Otherwise it would seem most unreason-
able that these men who had and would continue to endure
so much would take into their party a sixteen-year-old mother
with a papoose. Although Sacagawea was probably Charbonneau's favorite squaw, he had at least two and maybe three
wives and probably would have been satisfied with various
tent-mates who were easily available along the trail. It seems
a reasonable conclusion that the two captains definitely
wanted Sacagawea, and that Charbonneau was the appendage who was just taken along — although he was a useful
"hand" on the Expedition.

Captain Lewis' notes of June 16 are impressive because
they are made by a non-medical man. His recording of the
patient's complaints, his physical examination of her, the medication employed, and his genuine concern about her probably would not be exceeded by any physician of his time.
The patient Sacagawea was indeed dangerously ill; she had a
barely perceptible and irregular pulse and muscle twitching.
These physical findings indicate a loss of body fluids and electrolytes, particularly a calcium-potassium imbalance, caused
by pernicious vomiting and diarrhea. When such a chemical
imbalance develops in a patient today it is usually treated
with intravenous fluid containing the required electrolytes.

Such knowledge and equipment were not possessed by the captains. It was fortunate that Sacagawea could drink and retain the mineral water which Lewis thought would be beneficial for her. Cutright conjectures, probably correctly, that the vital minerals were thus restored to her.[8] Cutright also points out that the repeated bleedings could have dehydrated Sacagawea; however, her thirst stimulated drinking of the mineral water.

Fortunately Lewis could write on June 17 that "the Indian woman much better today; I have still continued the same course of medicine; she is free from pain clear of fever, her pulse regular, and eats as heartily as I am willing to permit her of broiled buffaloe well seasoned with pepper and salt and rich soope of the same meat; I think therefore that there is every rational hope of her recovery." The fact that Lewis now expressed hope of recovery indicates the despair that the two captains had felt about Sacagawea's life. In the near future she was to find her Shoshone tribesmen, with her brother now the chief; and by helping the captains procure horses, she in turn helped save their lives.

On the seventeenth Whitehouse, who was working with the men at the portage, wrote that "we had Some difficulty in gitting them (the canoes) up the rapids to day, as well as a dangerous job. one canoe turned upside down in a bad rapid, & was near drowning the 2 men which was in hir."

Lewis wrote an optimistic progress report the following day: "The Indian woman is recovering fast she set up the greater part of the day and walked out for the fi[r]st time since she arrived here; she eats hartily and is free from fever or pain. I continue same course of medecine and regimen except that I added one doze of 15 drops of the oil of vitriol[9]

---

8 Cutright, "Barks and Saltpeter," p. 23.

9 Today sulphuric acid is used mainly in manufacturing processes; in the time of

today about noon."

On June 19 Sacagawea had a relapse, from an overindulgence of eating, in Lewis' opinion. He wrote:

> . . . the Indian woman was much better this morning she walked out and gathered a considerable quantity of the white apples [10] of which she eat so heartily in their raw state, together with a considerable quantity of dryed fish without my knowledge that she complained very much and her fever again returned. I rebuked Sharbono severely for suffering her to indulge herself with such food he being privy to it and having been previously told what she must only eat. I now gave her broken dozes of diluted nitre untill it produced perspiration and at 10 P.M. 30 drops of laudnum which gave her a tolerable nights rest. . .

The next day Lewis noted that Sacagawea was quite free from pain and fever and "appears to be in a fair way for recovery, she has been walking about and fishing."

It was fortunate that Sacagawea's illness occurred while the Expedition was relatively stationary at the portage of the Great Falls. If she had become ill while the Expedition was "proceeding on" she probably would have been unable to travel, and the Expedition would have had to halt until she recovered. This would have meant a loss of precious time. It must have been evident to the captains that the considerable illness of several members, and the great effort required by the portage, did not present good prospects.

Lewis and Clark it was used medicinally as a tonic and astringent when given in small doses. Here the desired effect was as a tonic and astringent. Lewis does not specify the dosage that he used. It was certainly contraindicated to give Sacagawea a dosage that would produce more vomiting. This incident indicates that the captain-physicians must have possessed a very reliable idea of the proper dosage of their medicines.

[10] Cutright, "Barks and Saltpeter," identifies this as *psoralea esculenta*. It is not poisonous. Bradbury stated that John Colter of the Lewis and Clark Expedition, who later discovered the Yellowstone Park, subsisted on the *Psoralea esculenta* when he made his famous escape from the Blackfeet Indians. *See* Vinton, *Colter*, p. 91.

The Expedition had to portage some eighteen miles [11] around the several portions of the Great Falls, unloading all of their material, constructing wooden axles and wheels to carry their pirogues reloaded with their baggage and supplies over rough terrain of sharp rocks and prickly pears. Over this terrain the men walked with moccasins or bare feet, sustaining bruises and cuts and tortured by the one-half inch spines of the prickly pear.[12]

Clark had explored ahead to determine the best route for the portage. The men began on June 21, 1805, to take their supplies overland up Portage Creek. Lewis noted on the twenty-second that "the prickly pears were extreemly troublesome to us sticking our feet through our mockersons." On the same date Ordway wrote that "it must of course be a healthy country. we all enjoy good health as yet." This would indicate that Sacagawea had fully recovered; in fact, Lewis was to

[11] Thwaites gives the distance as 18¼ miles. Thwaites, *Journals*, ii, p. 183; Coues gives the distance as 17¾ miles. Coues, *History of Lewis and Clark*, ii, p. 392, n. 9; Wheeler states the same distance as Coues. Wheeler, *Trail*, i, p. 326. *See also* Larry Sill, "The Great Portage," in *We Proceed On*, vol. I, no. 4, pp. 6-9.

[12] *Opuntia Missouriensis*. The prickly pears were becoming more numerous. Today they can be seen all over the ground in the portage area, rising three to six inches high and holding numerous sturdy spikes one-half to one inch long. To barely touch the point of one of these spikes with the tip of the finger makes it inconceivable that the men of the expedition could "all go on with cheerfulness" step after step on these cacti.

Lewis and Clark were not the only ones who suffered from prickly pears; they were troublesome to others as well. Cox relates a painful experience in his journal: ". . . while riding a short distance ahead of the men, my horse happened to stand on a bunch of the prickly pears, which pained him so much that he commenced plunging and kicking, and ultimately threw me into a cluster of them. My face, neck, and body were severely pierced; and every effort to rise only increased the painfulness of my situation, for wherever I placed my hands to assist in raising my body they came in contact with the same tormenting thorns. In fact I could not move an inch; and to add to my disaster, I observed three rattlesnakes within a few feet of my head. The men . . . with considerable difficulty disentangled me from my painful situation . . . I immediately hailed the canoes, and resumed my old place on board, firmly resolved never again to ride while a prickly pear was visible." Cox, *The Columbia River*, p. 90.

record on June 24 that "the Indian woman is now perfectly recovered."

Clark portrayed the tortures of the portage on June 23:

the men mended their mockersons with double soles to save their feet from the prickley pear, (which abounds in the Prairies,) and the hard ground which in some & maney places [is] so hard as to hurt the feet verry much, the emence number of Buffalow after the last rain has trod on the flat places in such a manner as to leave it uneaven, and that has tried [dried] and is worst than frozen ground, added to those obstructions, the men has to haul with all their strength wate & art, maney times every man all catching the grass & knobes & stones with their hands to give them more force in drawing on the Canoes & Loads, and notwithstanding the coolness of the air in high presperation and every halt, those not employed in reparing the course, are asleep in a moment, maney limping from the soreness of their feet some become fant for a fiew moments, but no man complains all go chearfully on. to state the fatigues of this party would take up more of the journal than other notes which I find scerely time to set down.

On June 25 Field again was chased by a grizzly bear, but escaped over the edge of a river bank. Lewis wrote that "this man has been truely unfortunate with these bear, this is the second time he has narrowly escaped from them." Lewis recorded on this day ". . . The party prepare their baggage for an early start in the morning after which such as were able to shake a foot amused themselves in dancing on the green to the music of the violin which Cruzatte plays extreemly well."

The mosquitoes had bothered the men of the Expedition almost all the way along the journey except in the winter months, and they did not relent during the three weeks of the portage. These pestiferous mosquitoes probably made the men grateful that the prickly pear could not fly! It may also be that the men of the Expedition brought "ague" to these mosquitoes from the Ohio and Mississippi valleys.

On June 26 Lewis wrote:

> Whitehouse much heated and fortiegued and drank a very hearty draught of water and was taken almost instantly extreemly ill. his pulse were full and I therefore bled him plentifully from which he felt great relief. I had no other instrument with which to perform this opperation but my penknife, however it answered very well.

The following day Whitehouse could write that "I feel Some better but not able to go back to the lower Camp So I remain with Capt. Lewis."

Undoubtedly Lewis' pen knife served as well in performing this venesection as would his lancet, if he had had it with him. As a frontiersman, he kept his knife razor-sharp. As any surgeon knows, a sharp knife is safer than a dull one; it can be more easily controlled and does not make a bruising cut. The main danger of venesection was infection, and this could occur from an unsterilized lancet as well as an unsterilized knife. Probably Lewis had used his knife many times to skin and dress animals, and for eating — the knife was an all-purpose instrument of frontiersmen, including its use for fighting.

Grizzly bears continued to bother the men, particularly at night, so that Scannon, Lewis' dog, was in a "constant state of alarm . . . barking all night." Lewis no longer let a lone man go out hunting because of his concern that he would not have a chance of survival if attacked by one of the grizzlies.

On June 29 a near tragedy occurred when Clark and Charbonneau and Sacagawea were caught in a ravine during a flash flood and hail storm, from which they barely escaped as the torrents of water came at them. Hailstones also punished the men; Clark wrote that some of the hailstones "was 7 Inches in circumfrence & waied three ounces."[13] The backs of the men were bruised and bleeding. It is not surprising that Clark recorded the next day that the "Men complain of being sore this day dull and lolling about."

On July 1 Clark wrote that "one man verry unwell, his legs & thies broke out and Swelled." July 2 was a day of rejoicing in spite of their fatigue and sore feet — on this day they completed their portage.

On July 3 Lewis anticipated the coming shortage of buffalo meat and what that would mean to the Expedition. He recorded: "some hunters were sent out to kill buffaloe in order to make pemecon [14] to take with us and also for their skins which we now w[a]nt to cover our baggage in the boat and canoes when we depart from hence. the Indians have informed us that we should shortly leave the buffaloe country after passing the falls; this I much regret for I know when we leave the buffaloe that we shal[l] sometimes be under the necessity of fasting occasionally. and at all events the white puddings will be irretrievably lost and Sharbono out of imployment."

On Independence Day, 1805, Lewis made an extended note as befitted the occasion:

[we] have concluded not to dispatch a canoe with a part of our men to St. Louis as we had intended early in the spring. we fear also that such a measure might possibly discourage those who

13 Laroque reported a similar severe hail storm on July 2, 1805, when he was exploring in the region of present-day North Dakota: ". . . at sunset there was a hail storm so violent that I have seen nothing similar before, the pieces of hail were of the size of the yolk of a hen's egg and some were as large as the egg even." Ruth Hazlitt, "The Journal of Francois Antoine Laroque," *Sources of Northwest History*, No. 20, *The Frontier*, xiv, Nos. 3 and 4, and xv, No. 1 (Missoula: State University of Montana, 1934).

14 Pemmican: an Indian food made of pounded and dried meat, usually buffalo or deer, with oil and berries added and dried into cakes. It was a concentrated and highly nutritious food, easily stored and transported. The white men soon adopted its use, especially for travel and to supplement when fresh meat was not available. Its use was very much like that of the portable soup carried by the Expedition.

would in such case remain, and might possibly hazzard the fate of the expedition. we have never once hinted to any one of the party that we had such a scheme in contemplation, and all appear perfectly to have made up their minds to suceed in the expedition or purish in the attempt. we all beleive that we are now about to enter on the most perilous and difficult part of our voyage, yet I see no one repining; all appear ready to me[e]t those difficulties which await us with becoming fortitude . . . our work being at an end this evening, we gave the men a drink of Sperits, it being the last of our stock, and some of them appeared a little sensible of it's effects the fiddle was plyed and they danced very merrily untill 9 in the evening when a heavy shower of rain put an end to that part of the amusement tho' they continued their mirth with songs and festive jokes and were extreemly merry untill late at night. we had a very comfortable dinner, of bacon, beans, suit dumplings & buffaloe beaf &c. in short we had no just cause to covet the sumptuous feasts of our countrymen on this day.

On July 7, 1805 Lewis wrote very much as the physician. It is particularly interesting that he was aware of the term "intermitent fever" and that he had certain ideas of treatment for it: "Capt. Clarks black man York is very unwell today and he gave him a doze of tartar emettic [15] which operated very well and he was much better in the evening. this is a discription of medecine that I never have recourse to in my practice except in cases of the intermittent fever."

According to Lewis note of July 11, Bratton was unable to work for several days "in consequence of a whitlow [16] on one of his fingers; a complaint which has been very common among the men." This is a very painful condition, and fre-

---

[15] Tartar emetic is a white salt compound of potassium, antimony, oxygen, carbon and hydrogen which is soluble in water. As the name implies, it was used medically mainly as an emetic, and also as an expectorant and diaphoretic. It is rarely used today in medical practice.

[16] Whitlow: a paronychia or felon; an infection of the end of a finger or toe, around and under the nail, and may extend deep to the bone.

quently requires the removal of a portion or of all the nail.
It is somewhat unusual that the men should have this condition very often, inasmuch as their fingers were scoured thoroughly by the elements. However, they probably used very
little soap, and were not always well-nourished, and the
fingers became infected from the many boils which afflicted
them. Clark describes Bratton's trouble as "a tumer riseing on
his finger." Clark also records that the "Musquetors verry
troublesom, and in addition to their torments we have a Small
Knat [17] which is as disagreeable." On July 11 Sergeant Pryor
dislocated his shoulder again. Lewis writes that "it was replaced immediately and is likely to do him but little injury; it
is painfull to him today." Actually, dislocation of the shoulder
is a very serious injury, and is fraught with the possibility of
future problems if not carefully managed. There is the danger
of protecting the shoulder too much and developing an ad-
hesive capsulitis with stiffness and weakness, or of being
active too early, permitting the tissues to heal stretched out
so that recurrent dislocation can occur easily. Chronic recurrent dislocation of the shoulder today usually requires a surgical repair.

On the same day that Pryor dislocated his shoulder, Whitehouse committed his own troubles to his journal: "I walked
a Short distance in the plains today . . . and trod on a
verry large rattle Snake. it bit my leggin on my legg I shot it.
it was 4 feet 2 Inches long, & 5 Inches & a half round."

Lewis noted on July 15:

the prickly pear is now in full blume and forms one of the beauties
as well as the greatest pests of the plains. the sunflower is also in
blume and is abundant. this plant is common to every part of the

---

[17] Coues identifies this as the buffalo-gnat, a species of Simulium; Coues, *History
of Lewis and Clark,* II, p. 226.

Missouri from its entrance to this place . . . we eat an immensity of meat. it requires four deer, an elk, and a deer or one buffalo to supply us plentifully twenty-four hours. [On the 16th he wrote:] here for the first time I ate of the small guts of the buffalo cooked over a blazing fire in the Indian stile without any preperation of washing or other clensing and found them very good.

Lewis noted on July 17 that the Indians who did not cultivate maize made use of the sunflower seed for bread and to thicken their soup. "they most commonly first parch the seed and then pound them between two smooth stones untill they reduced it to a fine meal." Lewis considered that mixing of the sunflower meal with marrow grease provided a very "pallatable dish."

Clark complained on July 19 that "my feet is verry much brused & cut walking over the flint, & constantly stuck full [of] Prickley pear throns, I puled out 17 by the light of the fire to night   Musqutors verry troublesom." Fortunately a good supply of mosquito "biers" was brought along to protect the men at night, but this did not help them when they were trying to do their work in the daytime. The following day Clark wrote again of the agony of the prickly pear: "my man York nearly tired out, the bottoms of my feet blistered . . . the feet of the men with me So Stuck with Prickley pear & cut with the Stones that they were Scerseley able to march at a Slow gait this after noon."

Fortunately the men were eating well. There were only a few buffalo now, but there were deer, elk, and goats, and there were "emence quantities of Sarvice buries,[18] yellow, red, Purple & black currents ripe and Superior to any I ever tasted particularly the yellow & purple kind. Choke Cheries are Plenty; Some Gooseburies."

---

[18] Service berries, used as food extensively by the Indians, often to make bread.

Lewis wrote in his journal entry of July 19 "we are almost
suffocated in this confined valley with heat . . . this evening we entered much the most remarkable cliffs that we
have seen. the cliffs rise from the waters edge on either side
perpendicularly to the hight of (about) 1200 feet. every
object here wears a dark and gloomy aspect. the tow[er]ing
and projecting rocks in many places seem to tumble on us.
The river appears to have forced its way through this immense body of solid rock for the distance of five and three-
fourths Miles . . . from the singular apperance of this
place I call it the Gates of the Rocky Mountains."

XIV

To the Pacific Ocean

*we . . . mixd a little portable soup with Snow water and lay
down contented.* Joseph Whitehouse [1]

The men were traversing easier terrain than they had on
the portage, and moving the boats by water was considerably
less exertion than moving them on land. Nevertheless the
Missouri was tortuous and tricky, with shoals and shallows,
and the banks lined for the most part with willows and other
brush. And the commanders, who were pushing to get over
the Rocky Mountains before the snow fell, permitted the men
little time to recover from the strains and bruises of the portage. July 22 Clark wrote: "I opened the bruses & blisters of
my feet which caused them to be painfull   dispatched all the
men to hunt in the bottom for Deer, deturmined my Self to
lay by & nurs my feet. haveing nothing to eat but Venison and
Currents, I find my Self much weaker than when I left the
Canoes and more inclined to rest & repose to day." Rarely did
one of the captains favor himself with "rest & repose;" rather,
they were always in the vanguard, and gave needed assistance to the hunters, rowers, and cooks when some member
was ill or added effort was needed. On this day Lewis took
time to eulogize the "pleasantly flavored" wild onions they
found on an island.

---

[1] The first portion of the Whitehouse Journal is published in Thwaites, *Journals*,
vii, and this quotation is from page 157. The original journal is in the Newberry
Lby. in Chicago.

Lewis wrote on July 24: "our trio of pests still invade and obstruct us on all occasions, these are the Musquetoes eye knats and prickley pears, equal to any three curses that ever poor Egypt laiboured under, except the Mahometant yoke. the men complain of being much fortiegued. their labour is excessively great. I occasionally encourage them by assisting in the labour of navigating the canoes, and have learned to push a tolerable good pole in their fraize [phrase]."

Charbonneau had had very little illness or any physical affliction since the Expedition left the Mandan village, although presumably he was participating in the regular work of the Expedition, as demanded by the captains when they hired him. On July 25 Lewis noted that "Charbono gave out, one of his ankles failed him and he was unable to proceede any further." There is no mention of illness; he may have sprained his ankle or the excessive work may have exhausted him.

It was on this day that the vanguard led by Captain Clark reached the Three Forks of the Missouri. Here they rested to permit the men (especially Capain Clark) to recuperate, to make clothes, and most importantly, to explore and determine which one of the three forks was the proper one for them to take. They named the Three Forks the Jefferson, the Gallatin and the Madison. They properly chose the Jefferson, and "proceeded on."

One of the "trio of pests" mentioned above continued to plague the men: the prickly pears. The journals record on July 26 (Lewis) that "these penetrate our mockersons and leather legings and give us great pain untill they are removed. my por dog suffers with them excessively, he is constantly binting and scratching himself as if in a rack of pain . . . Capt. C. was so unwell that he had no inclination to eat." Clark's note of July 26 is much briefer, presumably because

he was too ill to do much writing. He did not take time to
mention that he had saved Charbonneau from drowning
(which Lewis records). Clark had left Charbonneau and one
of the men (Field) who had sore feet and proceeded to explore the region of the three forks. It was after he returned
to Charbonneau and Field that the rescue occurred. It was
fortunate for Charbonneau (who could not swim) that he
had not ventured into the river while Clark was absent.

Captain Clark continued to be very ill, probably in part
because he persisted in his physical output. He developed
a high fever and chills and aching which might have been due
to ague, but their continuance indicates infection. There have
been no specific recordings of chills with fever until now, such
as Lewis mentioned in his journal down the Ohio.[2] The aching
in his muscles could have been due to his strenuous physical
activity; on the twenty-seventh he records "the men are in
a continual state of their utmost exertion to get on, and they
begin to weaken fast from this continual state of violent exertion." Clark's chills and fever may have been due to infection
from the bruises and prickly pear punctures on his feet. It is
remarkable that Clark took time to make a journal entry on
the twenty-seventh, even a brief one: "I was verry unwell all
last night with a high fever & akeing in all my bones. My
fever &c. continus . . . I continue to be verry unwell
fever verry high, take 5 of rushes pills & bathe my feet & legs
in hot water." Even with his use of heroic doses of medicine,
it is very doubtful that Dr. Rush would have prescribed fifty
grams each of calomel and jalap, the probable amount of each
medicine in "5 of rushes pills."

Clark's illness was of considerable concern to all members
of the Expedition; Whitehouse, Ordway, and Gass all mention it in their journal entries of the twenty-eighth. Also, they

2 Quaife, "The Journals of Lewis and Ordway," p. 47.

all mention that all members of the party are greatly fatigued
and have lame, sore feet. They were continuing to eat well,
the hunters bringing in plenty of meat. Whitehouse wrote
that "I am employed makeing the chief part of the cloathing
for the party." Lewis confided to his journal his worry about
the illness and exhaustion of the men and also his concern
about locating the Snake Indians or being lost "within the
bosom of this wild and mountainous country."

Clark used his pen very little on the twenty-eighth, but
Lewis recounts more of Clark's illness: "My friend Capt. Clark
was very sick all last night but feels himself somewhat better
this morning since his medicine has opperated." Clark could
now rest some while the Expedition reconnoitered at the
three forks. Lewis writes that he "had a small bower or booth
erected for the comfort of Capt. C. our leather lodge when
exposed to the sun is excessively hot." The Expedition was
encamped "precisely on the spot" where Sacagawea had been
captured five years before.

The next day Lewis could write: "Capt. Clark is much
better today, is perfectly clear of fever but still very languid
and complains of a general soarness in all his limbs. I prevailed on him to take the barks which he has done and eate
tolerably freely of our good venison."

Although the men were still in the low country, having not
yet reached the foothills of the Bitterroot Mountains, game
began to be less plentiful. Lewis recorded on July 31:

> nothing killed today and our fresh meat is out. when we have a
> plenty of fresh meat I find it impossible to make the men take
> any care of it, or use it with the least frugallity, tho' I expect that
> necessity will shortly teach them this art. the mountains on both
> sides of the river at no great distance are very lofty. we have a
> lame crew just now, two with tumers or bad boils on various parts
> of them, one with a bad stone bruise, one with his arm accidently

dislocated but fortunately well replaced,[3] and a fifth has streigned his back by sliping and falling backwards on the gunwall of the canoe. the latter is Sergt. Gass. it gives him great pain to work in the canoe in his present situation, but he thinks he can walk with convenience, I therefore scelected him as one of the party to accompany me to-morrow, being determined to go in quest of the Snake Indians. I also directed Drewyer and Charbono to hold themselves in readiness. Charbono thinks that his ankle is sufficiently recovered to stand the march but I entertain my doubts of the fact; he is very anxious to accompany me and I therefore indulge him.

Lewis' diary entry of August 1 relates his own physical status, which is probably an indication of how most of the crew were doing: "to add to my fatiegue in this walk of about 11 miles I had taken a doze of glauber salts in the morning in consequence of a slight desentary with which I had been afflicted for several days; being weakened by the disorder and the opperation of the medecine I found myself almost exhausted before we reached the river." Lewis was hardly following the best medical practice by giving himself a physic when he already had dysentery, the most pronounced symptom of which is usually diarrhea.

The captains do not give much note of Clark's birthday on August the 1st. But Whitehouse writes: "at noon Capt. Clark killed a mountain Sheep . . . we got it and dined eairnestly on it. it being Capt. Clark's buthday he ordered Some flour gave out to the party.[4]

The following day Lewis was much improved — perhaps prescribing a physic for diarrhea cured the affliction quickly. He was able to join with the men in feasting "sumn[ptuously] on our wild fruit" — they had found currants, gooseberries and service berries. But the other captain was ailing; Clark

---

[3] Could this be Pryor again with a recurrent dislocation?

[4] Clark became 35 on this day; this was the life expectancy at that time.

wrote on August 2 that "I have either got my foot bitten by Some poisonous insect or a tumer is riseing on the inner bone of my ankle which is painfull." Whitehouse on the same date records that he has a pain in his shoulder but does not give the reason.

On August 3 Clark used his orthopedic knowledge to observe that there was "indian sign" in the area. He wrote "in my walk I saw fresh track which I took to be an indian from the Shape of the foot as the toes turned in."

Day by day the advance was becoming more difficult. Ordway wrote on August 5 that in places the water "falls nearly 3 feet in the length of the canoe, but with hard labour we draged them over." On the same day Lewis recounts that Drouillard "missed his step and had a very dangerous fall, he sprained one of his fingers and hirt his leg very much. in fifteen or 20 minutes he was able to proceed . . . Capt. Clarks ankle is extreemly painfull to him this evening; the tumor has not yet mature, he has a slight fever. The men were so much fortiegued today that they wished much that navigation was at an end that they might go by land."

From the condition of the men with their injuries and illness and strenuous labor at this stage, it is difficult to imagine that they were to endure even more arduous labor in getting over the Rocky Mountains, particularly when hunger to the point of near starvation was added to their problems.

And their troubles and increased labor were just beginning. On August 6 Lewis wrote:

> . . . one of their canoes had just overset and all the baggage wet, the medicine box among other articles . . . Whitehouse had been thrown out of one of the canoes as she swing in a rapid current and the canoe had rubed him and pressed him to the bottom as she passed over him and had the water been 2 inches shallower must inevitably have crushed him to death . . . Whitehouse is in much pain this evening with the injury one of

his legs sustained from the canoe today at the time it upset and swing over him. Capt. Clarks ankle is also very painfull to him. . .

On August 8 Sacagawea recognized Beaverhead Rock, a landmark of her country and her people. Lewis' journal entry of August 8 recorded Clark's continued suffering with the abscess on his ankle: "t(h)e tumor on Capt. Clarks ankle has discharged a considerable quantity of matter but is still much swolen and inflamed and gives him considerable pain." There is no note that Clark incised the tumor, or bled himself; apparently he chose to suffer the pain of waiting for the abscess to rupture spontaneously. This indeed must have given him extreme pain walking for miles on rough terrain. The brave and sturdy captain writes on August 9 about the "rageing fury of a tumor on my anckle muscle."

The hunters were being dispersed widely and for long hours because "game of every kind scerce (Clark)." Ordway writes on August 10 that "we have now to live on poor venison & goat or antelopes which goes hard with us as the fatigues is hard." Whitehouse also writes of the "poor venson & goat meat," and adds that "as our fatigues (are) hard we find that poor meat alone is not Strong diet, but we are content with what we can git."

Anyone who has traveled along the upper portions of the Beaverhead River approaching Beaverhead Rock, can understand the difficulty of these men in trying to make headway up the shallow winding stream, with a thick expanse of low brush hanging from the banks. On August 12 Lewis recorded "as we had killed nothing during the day we now boiled and eat the remainder of our pork, having yet a little flour and parched meal. . ." This pork had left St. Louis fifteen months before! "this morning Capt. Clark set out early. found the river shoally, rapid, shallow, and extreemly difficult. the

men in the water almost all day. they are geting weak soar
and much fortiegued; they complained of the fortiegue to
which the navigation subjected them and wished to go by
land   Capt. C engouraged them and passifyed them. one of
the canoes was very near overseting in a rapid today. they
proceeded but slowly."

The Expedition was getting deeper into Sacagawea's country, and the hopes and expectations of the captains were increasing that they would soon meet some of the Shoshone
Indians. Although Clark was in the forefront of the Expedition
during much of the long journey, leading with a small group
for the purpose of exploration and hunting and locating campsites, Lewis, as the commanding officer, chose to take the lead
at certain important times. It was Lewis who advanced first
to see the Great Falls; it was now Lewis who went on ahead
seeking to make contact with the Indians.

Lewis and his men plodded on, climbing up Lemhi pass,
and near its summit they drank from the small trickle of water
which they supposed to be the origin of the Missouri River.
MacNeal straddled this tiny stream "and thanked his god he
had lived to bestride the mighty and heretofore deamed end-
less Missouri."

On the western side of Lemhi Pass they made contact with
the Shoshone Indians, which was a successful, friendly greet-
ing due to Lewis' diplomacy. This diplomacy was further
tested when he had to prevail upon Cameahwait to lead his
braves back over Lemhi pass to meet Clark and the rest of the
party. Lewis' situation was desperate; he and his men, to
prove their good intention to the Indians that they were not
being led into a trap, gave their rifles to them with instructions
to shoot them if they proved dishonest. Lewis most certainly
would not have used this tactic with any of the Indian tribes
on the Missouri. The offer of trade by Lewis, and his assur-

ance that a woman accompanied Clark (a sign of peace), gave weight to his argument.

The main part of the Expedition under Clark was making its final strenuous effort to nudge the loaded canoes up the last miles of shallow water. They knew that when they could no longer go forward on water, the baggage would have to be carried by the men, necessitating many relays, or be carried horseback — and they had no horses.

August 13, 1805, was a notable day for Lewis in two regards: he met and communicated with some of Sacagawea's people; and he had his first taste of Pacific salmon: "an indian called me into his bower and gave me . . . peice of a fresh salmon roasted . . . which eat with very good relish."

The men were soon to face another problem: an increasing shortage of food. The Shoshone Indians were always half starved, because of the lack of game in the high mountains where they hid because they did not have guns to protect themselves when on buffalo hunting trips in the plains. It had been five years ago on one of these hazardous expeditions for meat that Sacagawea had been captured. The Expedition, whose own food supplies were dwindling, was to get little in the way of provisions from the Shoshone Indians. The deprivations of the Indians is reflected in Lewis' note of August 14 "we had nothing but a little flour and parched meal to eat except the berries with which the Indians furnished us."

Clark, in the rear with most of the party and at a lower elevation, was more fortunate with his food supply. He could write on this same date that "the river near the mountain is one continued rapid, which requres great labour to push & haul the Canoes up . . . I checked our interpreter for Striking his woman at their Dinner. The hunters Jo. & R. Fields killed 4 Deear & a antilope, I killed a fat Buck in the evening, Several men have hurt themselves pushing up the Canoes. I am oblige to (use) a pole occasionally."

The following day, August 15, Lewis remained with the Indians, sharing hunger and a little food with them, while waiting for Clark and the rest of the party to come up. Clark wrote on this date that "the men Complain much of their fatigue and being repetiedly in the water which weakens them much perticularly as they are obliged to live on pore Deer meet which has a Singular bitter taste . . ."

The starvation of the Shoshone Indians, even during the summer months, is shown graphically by Lewis' entry of August 16:

I sent Drewyer and Shields before this morning in order to kill some meat as neither the Indians nor ourselves had any thing to eat . . . he (a young Indian) had come to inform us that one of the whitemen had killed a deer . . . when they arrived where the deer was which was in view of me they dismounted and ran in tumbling over each other like a parcel of famished dogs each seizing and tearing away a part of the intestens which had been previously thrown out by Drewyer who killed it; the seen was such when I arrived that had I not have had a pretty keen appetite myself I am confident I should not have taisted any part of the venison shortly. each one had a peice of some discription and all eating most ravenously. some were eating the kidnies the melt and liver and the blood runing from the corners of their mouths, others were in a similar situation with the paunch and guts but the exuding substance in this case from their lips was of a different discription. one of the last who att[r]acted my attention particularly had been fortunate in his allotment or reather active in the division, he had provided himself with about nine feet of the small guts one end of which he was chewing on while with his hands he was squezzing the contents out the other. I really did not untill now think that human nature ever presented itself in a shape so nearly allyed to the brute creation. I viewed these poor starved divils with pity and compassion   I directed McNeal to skin the deer and reserved a quarter, the ballance I gave the Chief to be divided among his people; they devoured the whole of it nearly without cooking.

It is surprising and amusing that Lewis' gastronomy could be repelled by the scene which he described but in which he did not participate, in view of his previous enjoyment of the white puddings prepared by Charbonneau.

On August 18, 1805, Lewis celebrated his second birthday while on the Expedition; this again put him in a philosophical mood:

> This day I completed my thirty first year, and conceived that I had in all human probability now existed about half the period which I am to remain in this Sublunary world. I reflected that I had as yet done but little, very little, indeed, to further the hapiness of the human race, or to advance the information of the suceeding generation. I viewed with regret the many hours I have spent in indolence, and now soarly feel the want of that information which those hours would have given me had they been judiciously expended. but since they are past and cannot be recalled, I dash from me the gloomy thought, and resolved in future, to redouble my exertions and at least indeavour to promote those two primary objects of human existence, by giving them the aid of that portion of talents which nature and fortune have bestoed on me; or in future, to live for mankind, as I have heretofore lived for myself.

Lewis was wrong on both accounts. He did much to increase the happiness of the American portion of the human race and to contribute information to succeeding generations. He was also wrong in his estimate of life expectancy; he was to die at thirty-five, on October 10, 1809.

Lewis gives a detailed description of the sexual mores of the Shoshones, with considerable reference to the presence of syphilis and gonorrhea among them. He wrote on August 19:

> the chastity of their women is not held in high estimation, and the husband will for a trifle barter the companion of his bead for a night or longer if he conceives the reward adiquate; tho' they are not so importunate that we should caress their women as the siouxs were. and some of their women appear to be held more sacred

than in any nation we have seen. I have requested the men to give
them no cause of jealousy by having connection with their women
without their knowledge, which with them, strange as it may seem,
is considered as disgracefull to the husband, as clandestine connec-
tions of a similar kind are among civilized nations. to prevent this
mutual exchange of good officies altogether I know it impossible to
effect, particularly on the part of our young men whom some
months abstanence have made very polite to those tawney damsels.
no evil has yet resulted and I hope will not from these connec-
tions . . . I was anxious to learn whether these people had
the venerial, and made the enquiry through the interpreter and his
wife; the information was that they sometimes had it but I could
not learn their remedy; they most usually die with it's effects. this
seems a strong proof that these disorders bothe ganaraehah [gon-
orrhea] and Louis Venerae are native disorders of America.[5] tho'
these people have suffered much by the small pox which is known
to be imported and perhaps those other disorders might have been
contracted from other indian tribes who by a round of communications might have obtained from the Europeans since it was
introduced into that quarter of the globe. but so much detatched
on the other ha[n]d from all communication with the whites that
I think it most probable that those disorders are original with
them.

The captains busied themselves in making friends with the
Shoshones, gaining information, bartering for horses, and ar-
ranging for scouts. Horses were the prime requisite; probably
Lewis and Clark would have found their way west by follow-

---

[5] This remark by Lewis shows that he differentiated between syphilis and
gonorrhea and that he was conversant with the argument about whether syphilis
originated in Europe or America. The medical writings of the time seem to rou-
tinely differentiate between these two diseases, but there also was much medical
assumption that they were manifestations of the same disease. Benjamin Bell
(1749-1806) is said to have been the first to have differentiated between the two
diseases, in 1793. In 1838 Phillippe Ricord (1799-1889) delineated syphilis into
the primary, secondary and tertiary stages. He also helped to demonstrate the
separate identities of gonorrhea and syphilis. His demonstrations depended upon
inoculations, as the bacteriology of these diseases was not to be established for
many years: gonorrhea in 1879, syphilis in 1905.

ing some Indian road, but they needed horses to carry all of the baggage. There was some traffic of Pacific coast Indians across these mountains to secure buffalo; and, in reverse, Indians traveled west to get salmon.

While among the Shoshone Indians the men of the Expedition enjoyed their first taste of salmon. On August 22 Lewis recounted that "late in the evening I made the men form a bush drag, and with it in about 2 hours they caught 528 very good fish, most of the large trout." The next day Lewis recorded that their store of provisions was growing too low to give the Indians any more; fortunately the hunters brought in some deer. Lewis stated that "our stock of provision is now so low that it would not support us more than ten days."

Lewis and Clark finally obtained thirty horses from the Shoshone Indians, with the great help of Sacagawea, whose brother Cameahwait had become chief of a tribe during her absence. The captains employed a Shoshone guide, Toby, to take them along the Nez Perce trail to the North, where they were advised that they could find a continuing trail to the Columbia. This was rough country, but not as rough as they were to encounter beyond Lolo Pass which they now approached.

On August 24 Lewis wrote of their departure from the Shoshone camp:

> I had now the inexpressible satisfaction to find myself once more under way with all my baggage and party. an Indian had the politeness to offer me one of his horses to ride which I accepted with cheerfulness as it enabled me to attend better to the march of the party. I had reached the lower part of the cove when an Indian rode up and informed me that one of my men was very sick and unable to come on. I directed the party to halt . . . and rode back about 2 Miles where I found Wiser very ill with a fit of the cholic. I sent Sergt. Ordway who had remained with him for some water and gave him a doze of the essence of Pepper-

mint and laudinum which in the course of half an hour so far
recovered him that he was enabled to ride my horse and I proceeded on foot and rejoined the party . . . I gave the Indians
who were absolutely engaged in transporting the baggage, a little
corn as they had nothing to eat.

On the same date Clark recorded "Brackfast on buries
(I sliped & bruised my leg verry much on a rock) the party
had killed several phesents and caught a fiew Small fish on
which they had Subsisted in my absence . . . nothing to eate
but Choke Cherries & red haws, which act in different ways
So as to make us Sick." Gass described their situation as "poor
and uncomfortable enough . . . supperless went to rest
for the night." Health references to Weiser and Clark on
the twenty-fourth were the first since August 8, although the
journals comprise 95 printed pages during these days — the
captains were concerned about locating and bartering with
the Shoshones, and perhaps gave little thought to the relatively minor health problems of their men.

Lewis' lucky star still hovered over him: a shot fired by
Frazier (August 25) ricocheted when he was shooting at a
duck and barely missed Lewis. He was not to be so lucky the
next year when Cruzatte accidentally fired and didn't miss.

The durability of the Indian squaw and her lack of concern
about childbirth is shown in Lewis' journal entry of August
26:

one of the women who had been assisting in the transportation of
the baggage halted at a little run about a mile behind us, and sent
on the two pack horses which she had been conducting by one of
her female friends. I inquired of Cameahwait the cause of her
detention, and was informed by him in an unconcerned manner
that she had halted to bring fourth a child and would soon overtake us; in about an hour the woman arrived with her newborn
babe and passed us on her way to the camp apparently as well as
she ever was . . . I have been several time informed by those

who were conversant with the fact, that the Indian women who are pregnant by whitemen experience more difficulty in childbirth than when pregnant by an Indian.[6]

On the same date Clark wrote, "not one mouthfull to eate untill night as our hunters could kill nothing." They were beginning to complain about their "retched Situation." Clark wrote that he was weak from having mainly salmon to eat, and "my flesh I find is declineing."

Whitehouse noted on September 3: "Some of the mountains was So Steep and rockey that Several of the horses fell back among the rocks and was near killing them . . . we Camped after a disagreeable days march of only 11 miles with much fatigue and hunger as nothing has been killed this day only 2 or 3 fessents, and have no meat of any kind. Set into raining hard at dark So we laid down and Slept, wet hungry and cold." Clark wrote this day "we met with a great misfortune, in haveing our last Th[er]mometer broken by accident."

On September 4 Ordway wrote that "we had nothing but

---

[6] Clark gives another example of the strength and endurance of the Indian women when he records an incident while returning over Tillamook Head from collecting whale blubber on January 9, 1806: ". . . on the steep decent of the Mountain I overtook five men and Six women with emence loads of the Oil and blubber of the Whales . . . one of the women in the act of getting down a Steep part of the Mountain her load by Some means had Sliped off her back, and She was holding the load by a Strap which was fastened to the mat bag in which it was in, in one hand and holding a bush by the other, as I was in front of my party, I endeavored to relieve this woman by takeing her load untill She could get to a better place a little below, & to my astonishment found the load as much as I could lift and must exceed 100 lbs. . . ."

Mackenzie relates a similar observation: "The Indians . . . consider the fate of the woman in labour as among the most trifling occurrences of corporal pain to which nature is subject. . . It is by no means uncommon in the hasty removal of their camps from one position to another, for a woman to be taken in labour, to deliver herself in her way, without assistance or notice from her associates in the journey, and to overtake them before they complete the arrangements of their evening station, with her newborn babe on her back." Mackenzie, *Voyages Through North America*, p. 141.

a little pearched corn to eat, the air on the mountains verry chilly and cold. our fingers aked with the cold . . . our hunter killed a deer on which we dined. our guide and the Indian who accompanied him eat the verry guts of the deer. The snow over our mockasons in places." Gass wrote on September 5 that "the indian dogs are so hungry and ravinous, that they eat 4 or 5 pair of our mockasons last night."

September 9, a good day for the Expedition — they killed three deer and several ducks. On this same day they reached a stream (Lolo Creek) which came into their river from the west, and their guide indicated they were to follow this creek. Lewis wisely decided to give the horses and men a rest before attempting the mountains, appropriately calling this camp "Traveler's Rest." The rest was enhanced by a better food supply: they killed four deer and some ducks. This was a great respite from their diet of service berries and choke cherries. Rested and fed, they were now ready to approach their most grueling ordeal: crossing the Rocky Mountains — crossing before winter caught them.

On the thirteenth the Expedition reached Lolo Pass, and camped near today's Packer Meadows. Unfortunately the guide Toby did not keep them on the high ridge trail they had come to at Lolo Pass, but took them down a rugged trail into the Lochsa valley. Ralph Space [7] believes that Toby took them down to the river because he came to this area to fish, and had

---

[7] Ralph Space of Orofino, Idaho was raised near Weippe. He worked for the Forest Service for 39 years. He first traveled the Lolo Trail in 1924 in charge of a mapping party, and served his last nine years as Supervisor of the Clearwater National Forest. He located several Lewis and Clark campsites not previously identified, set aside the Lewis and Clark Grove, identified and named Whitehouse Pond for Whitehouse, who mentioned it in his diary, and had the name of Hungry Creek reapplied to that stream. He has guided many Lewis and Clark authors along the exact route taken by Lewis and Clark, which covers much rougher terrain than the present Lolo Trail road. Mrs. Chuinard and I traveled the trail of Lewis and Clark in Idaho with Mr. Space in the summer of 1966.

not become acquainted with the high ridge trail beyond Lolo Pass. The Indians and animals used the high ridges for travel because they were free of the underbrush which grew thickly along the river banks.

The Expedition reached the floor of the Lochsa valley on September 14, near the present day Powell Ranger Station, and camped "opposit a Small Island" which can still be seen. They were becoming accustomed to the problems of traveling by horse-packing, after having done most of their previous traveling by boat, but the worst was yet to come. These men from the eastern part of the United States had not the slightest conception of the massiveness of the Rocky Mountains, and of the great physical demands necessary to traverse them. Lewis wrote later of the Expedition's trials "within the bosom of this wild and mountainous country" and stated that ". . . to one acquainted with them it would have seemed impossible to have escaped." They had "supped" and "dined" well from the countryside most of the time they were traveling, but now they would find no game on the barren ridges where the trail would take them, nor forage for the horses, and but little water for the men and beasts. At their river camp on the Lochsa on the fourteenth they were so ravenous that they killed a colt for food, and named the nearby stream Colt Killed Creek. Ordway wrote in his journal on this day: "had nothing to eat but Some portable Soup we being hungry for a fat colt which eat verry well at this time." On the 15th the tired and hungry Expedition had to climb the steep walls of the Lochsa valley to the trail on the high ridge. They moved on downstream about four miles from their Colt Killed Camp before starting the difficult climb to the trail 4,000 feet above them.[8] This climb was one of the most difficult physical trials of the entire journey. The gravel was so loose on the steep and

---

[8] Thwaites, *Journals*, III, p. 67, note.

winding trail that the men and horses could find only uncertain and precarious footing. The horse carrying Clark's desk rolled several feet down a steep hill breaking the desk against a tree, but not harming the horse. They reached the top near present day Spring Mountain. They were cold and wet, half starved and weak. Each diarist records their duress in uncomplaining but pitiful language. Whitehouse wrote: "we marched on top of this mountain untill after dark in hopes to find water, but could not find any . . . but found plean[ty] of Snow . . . we melted what we wanted to drink and made or mixd. a little portable Soup with snow water and lay down contented." Gass adds that they had a handful of parched corn to go with the soup. Ordway, on the other hand, states that "we drank a little portable Soup and laid down without any thing else to Satisfy our hunger." Clark recorded that they cooked "the remns. of our Colt & make our Supe . . . nothing killed today except 2 Phests."

In their beginning struggles on September 15 along the ridge trail, and without food to assuage their hunger and fatigue, Lewis brought forth his portable soup which he had transported all the way from Philadelphia. This was the first time they used portable soup, and it supplemented the small remainder of their colt meat; this was a significant meal, composed of the combination that was to keep them from starving and to get them through these rugged mountains. Portable soup, contained in lead canisters and brought safely without spilling or spoiling from Philadelphia, was to become a necessary but not very palatable means of sustaining the men on several future occasions when they might otherwise have starved.

Clark wrote on September 16:

> I have been wet and as cold in every part as I ever was in my life, indeed I was at one time fearfull my feet would freeze in the thin

Mockirsons which I wore, . . . proceded on . . . and
built fires for the party agains[t] their arrival which was at Dusk,
verry cold and much fatigued, . . . men all wet cold and
hungary. Killed a Second Colt which we all Suped hartily on and
thought it fine meat.

The men awoke with surprise on this day because they were
covered with snow. Whitehouse wrote: "we mended up our
mockasons. Some of the men without Socks raped rags on
their feet." There was about 6 inches of total snow fall that
day.* Then men had been delayed one, and possibly two days,
by their digression into the Lochsa valley; they might have
been well ahead of the storm, or subjected to very little of it,
if they had proceeded directly along the ridge trail from Lolo
Pass. Evening found them camping in a thicket for protection
but still with only portable soup to eat. Gass writes that they
traveled 15 miles that day over "the most terrible mountains
I have ever beheld."

The seventeenth of September was warmer, but this caused
the snow to melt so that water covered the men's moccasins.
The hunters found only a few pheasants, which Clark writes,
"compelled us to kill Something, a Coalt being the most
useless part of our Stock, he fell a Prey to our appetites."

By September 18 the men were about to come out of the
high mountains (Clark sighted the Camas Prairie from Sher-
man Peak), but were still traversing rough territory. Ordway
wrote: "the Mountains continues as fer as our eyes could
extend," and as if he had not said it impressively enough, he
added, "they extend much further than we expected." Lewis
wrote that "we dined and suped on a skant proportion of
portable soupe, a few canesters of which, a little bears oil and
about 20 lbs. of candles form our stock of provision, the only

---

* This was an early and unusual snowfall which caught the Expedition. See
Stephen E. Ambrose, "Snow Conditions on the Lolo Trail: Some Comparisons,"
We Proceed On, Vol. IV, No. 1, pp. 12-14.

resources being our guns & packhorses." Clark gave the name of "Hungery Creek" to the location of the camp. Whitehouse ended his journal entry of the day: "we Suped on a little portable Soup and lay down."

The following day Gass wrote that "the men are becoming lean and debilitated, on account of the scarcity and poor quality of the provisions on which we subsist." And Whitehouse adds: "the most of the party is weak and feeble Suffering with hunger." Lewis wrote that "several of the men are unwell of the disentary. brakings out, or irruptions of the Skin, have also been common with us for some time." The men were suffering from malnutrition and thus were susceptible to infection. They were in the early stages of starvation,[9] and yet they must try to remain strong enough to do what they so frequently recorded: "proceed on." Providence occasionally intervened, as on the occasion when Clark found a stray horse, which they used for food.

Clark usually was ahead of the main party with two men, scouting the way and hunting. On September 20 he came to the Nez Percé Indians. He wrote:

> . . . those people gave us a Small piece of Buffalow meat, Some dried Salmon beries & roots in different States, Some round and much like an onion which they call Pas she co [quamash,[10] the bread of cake is called Pas-shi-co] Sweet, of this they make bread & Supe they also gave us, the bread made of this root all of which we eate hartily . . . They call themselves Cho-pun-nish or Pierced Noses — I find myself very unwell all evening from eating the fish and roots too freely.

Whitehouse wrote pathetically "we eat a fiew peas & a

---

[9] Mirsky thinks that the men had scurvy at this time. *See* Mirsky, *The Westward Crossings*, p. 318.

[10] The Quamash or Camas *(Camassia)* is a bulbous plant with a beautiful blue flower, which grows in moist places. It is usually dug in the early summer months. It is cooked in various ways, often being made into bread. It may be eaten raw. Like the potato, it can be stored and will keep well through the winter.

little greece which was the verry last kind of eatables of any kind except a little portable Soup. We then load up our horse and Set out." Ordway wrote that the group was half starved and very weak. All journals express gratitude for the wild horsemeat which Clark had hung along the trail for them.

Clark was very ill on September 21 "and puke which relive me." Lewis and his men were gratified to kill a few pheasants and a prairie wolf and to find a few crawfish which "enabled us to make one more hearty meal, not knowing where the next was to be found I find myself growing weak for the want of food and most of the men complain of a similar deficiency, and have fallen off very much." But the party was descending into lower country and on September 22 the hunters brought in three deer — truly a feast for these starving men. Clark's hip was bruised badly in an escapade with a horse.

The men were able to buy salmon and Camas roots and bread from the Nez Percé Indians: they were so ravenously hungry that they overate and made themselves sick. Clark wrote on September 24 "several 8 or 9 men sick, Capt. Lewis sick all Complain of a Lax & heaviness at the stomack, I gave Rushes Pills to several . . . Capt. Lewis scercely able to ride on a jentle horse which was furnished by the Chief, Several men So unwell that they were Compelled to lie on the Side of the road for Some time others obliged to be put on horses. I gave rushes Pills to the Sick this evening."

The overeating of the new food may have had something to do with the men's gastrointestinal complaints, but it is very probable that the food was infected with some organism that contributed to their violent illness. Clark repeated on September 25 that Lewis was very sick. Whitehouse attributed the dysentery to the change of climate as well as the diet. Clark gave his patients "Some Salts and Tarter emetic." Gass noted in his journal that "Captain Clarke gave all the sick a dose of

Rush's Pills to see what effect they would have" — probably Clark, by now, was certain "what effect they would have!"

Clark recorded on the 26th: "Capt. Lewis still verry unwell, Several men taken Sick on the way down, I administered Salts, Pils Galip [jalap] Tarter emetic, &c. I feel unwell this evening." Whitehouse wrote: ". . . men Sick with the relax . . ." The Expedition was now out of the high mountains and following the Clearwater River, and looking for good trees from which to hollow out canoes.

Clark records on September 27 that all of the men who were able to work had started building five canoes. Some of the men were too ill to work, and some of those who tried to work were too weak and ill to continue. On this same day, Clark adds "Capt. Lewis very sick nearly all the men sick," and Gass wrote that "game is very scarce, and our hunters unable to kill any meat. we are therefore obliged to live of fish and roots that we procure from the natives." Clark wrote on the following day "Our men nearly all Complaining of their bowels, a heaviness at the Stomach & Lax."

Lewis was very ill for several days, but by October 1 Clark could write that he was "getting much better," and "nothin to eate except a little dried fish which the men complain as working of them as a dost of Salts." Gass wrote on this same date that "all the men are now able to work; but the greater number are very weak." Dried fish and roots comprised their main diet, but "we kill a horse for the men at work to eate . . ." The roots "give the men violent pain in their bowels." Clark's note of October 4 gives an indication of how sick Lewis was; he states that "Capt. Lewis Still Sick but able to walk about a little."

The men began buying dogs for food; on October 5 Gass stated that "we have some Frenchmen who perfur dog-flesh to fish." But the main staple continued to be dried roots and dried fish which they obtained from the Indians. Clark was not very happy about the roots; he wrote on October 5 "Capt. Lewis & myself eate a Supper of roots boiled, which filled us so full of wind, that we were scercely able to Breathe all night feel the effects of it." The following day he recorded that he had been ill all night with a pain in the stomach and bowels because of the diet. Clark was still "verry unwell" on October 7, but still felt obliged to attend to everything.

Ordway wrote on October 7 that "we put the other three canoes in the River got them in readiness and loaded them about 3 oClock P.M. we Set out on our journey to descend the river." After weeks of intense physical effort and starvation crossing the Lolo Trail, it was a joyful relief to be able to "proceed on" by water transportation, on the beautiful Clearwater River. For the time being they were free of the poles and tow ropes, and of pack horses and hiking, and were gliding on their way to the Columbia River and the Pacific Ocean — but one canoe overturned in a rapids, hurting Thompson and endangering several men who could not swim. The revival of the physical condition and the spirits of the crew is reflected in Whitehouse's journal entry of October 9: "after dark we played the fiddle and danced a little" — the first time in many weeks. Clark wrote this day: "Lewis recovering fast."

In order to obtain meat it became necessary for the men to rely on dogs. Clark confided to his journal that "all the Party have greatly the advange of me, in as much as they all relish the flesh of dogs, Several of which we purchased of the nativs for to add to our store of fish and roots &c." Ordway's note of October 24 shows that the dog diet was varied a bit: "we bought a number of fat dogs, crambries and white cakes of root bread." Clark also noted that the afflictions of the Indians "are but fiew and those fiew of a s(c)rofelous nature.[11] they make great use of Swetting."

On October 11 Clark described one of the universal health treatments of the Indians, the sweathouse. His journal entry for that date states:

> We set out early and proceeded on passed a rapid at two miles, at 6 miles we came too at Some Indian lodges and took brackfast, we purchased all the fish we could and Seven dogs of those people for Stores of Provisions down the river   at this place I saw a curious Swet house underground, with a Small whole at top to pass in or throw in the hot Stones, which those in[side] threw on as much water as to create the temperature of heat they wished . . .

The captains greatly appreciated the friendliness and help of the Nez Percé or Chopunnish Indians who agreed to keep the captains' horses for them and who befriended them in other ways. Clark described them as "Stout likely men, handsom women, and verry dressey in their way." They did not have such a high opinion of the Indians they later saw along the Columbia River; those Indians were filthy, unfriendly, thieving and flea-ridden. The men kept to their canoes as much as possible, chancing rapids in order to save the time it would take to make a portage. This resulted in overturning some of the canoes, with threat to the lives of the men who could not swim. Wood became almost as scarce an article as food, and often had to be purchased from the Indians, in order to cook their food and dry out their clothes and equipment.

The party had brought their canoes down the Clearwater River to the Snake and on October 16, 1805, the current of the Snake River swept them out into the broad Columbia.

---

11 Scrofula: tuberculosis of the lymph glands, sometimes with systemic involvement with abcesses and fistulae. Rarely seen today among people with adequate diet and medical care.

They had become better nourished with the proteins of fish and dog meat, and there is no mention by any of the diarists of skin infections plaguing the men at this time. Gass mentioned that dog fare "we find strong wholesome diet," and Clark recorded that "we purchased forty dogs for which we gave articles of little value." The captains recorded that sore eyes were prevalent among these Indians, which they attributed to the reflection of the sun on the water while fishing.

Indian women brought salmon to the captains and cooked it for them by putting hot stones in a basket of water with the fish. They then served the fish "neetly" on a platter of rushes. Clark went to unusual length to describe these Indian women of the Columbia: "(they) only ware a truss or pece of leather tied around them at their hips and drawn tite between ther legs and fastened before So as bar[e]ly to hide those parts which are so sacredly hid & s[e]cured by our women."

On October 18 the men sighted Mt. Hood and on the following day Mt. Adams but mistook it for Mt. St. Helens. Breakfast, lunch, and dinner were all monotonously composed of dog, fish, and roots; although they were on the Columbia, "the fish being very bad, those which was offered to us, we purchased forty dogs . . ." Occasionally they had interesting and delicious variants in their diet, such as roasted acorn and "some excellent beer of the *Pasheco quarmash* bread of roots which was verry good."[12] This was a production of John Collins.

The men spent considerable time exploring the vaults and skeletal remains of the Indian burial grounds on the Memaloose Islands, where old skeletons were stored along with recently "raped" bodies, along with sacrificial and ceremonial trinkets and possessions of the deceased. These islands were

[12] *See* note 10, above in this chapter.

mentioned by future travellers for the stench emanating from them.

On October twenty-second the men were approaching Celilo Falls, the tortuous rapids where the Columbia thundered through the mountains with great force. On the banks Clark noted how the Indians pounded and dried their salmon and piled it in layers — "thus preserved those fish may be kept Sound and sweet Several years." The Indians were reluctant to sell their good fish, and the men of the Expedition had to be content mainly with poor dog meat. However, they must have obtained a good supply of dried fish as Clark would write on November 29, at the mouth of the Columbia: "our diet at this time and for several days past is the dried pounded fish we purchased at the falls boiled in a little salt water."

Celilo Falls [13] was a great fishing place for the Indians until The Dalles Dam was completed in 1959. When the salmon runs came to the falls, the Indians would stand on the banks and on springboards projecting from the rocks, and harpoon the salmon in the air as they jumped at the falls. When the Expedition was portaging around the falls, the salmon were not running, and the Indians were not too busy. The men were greatly annoyed by their thieving and their fleas.

Although eating as many dogs as they could purchase, the Expedition probably made little dent in the flea population of the Indian villages around the falls. But they made an extra effort to depopulate the fleas: Clark wrote on October 26 that "The flees which the party got on them at the upper & great falls, are very troublesom and difficult to get rid of, particularly as the me[n] have not a Change of Clothes to put on, they strip off their clothes and kill the flees, during which time they remain nakid . . . One man giged a Salmon-

---

[13] Clark drew a very accurate map of Celilo Falls, included in Thwaites, *Journals*, III, opposite p. 158.

trout which we had fried in a little Bears oil . . . and I think the finest fish I ever tasted."

Clark put three empty canoes through the short narrows; "the only danger in passing thro the narrows was the whorls and swills [swells] arriseing from the Compression of the water, and which I thought by good Stearing we could pass down Safe, accordingly I deturmined to pass through this place notwithstanding the horrid appearance of this agitated gut swelling, boiling & whorling in every direction . . . I sent by land all the men who could not Swim."

The portage around the Celilo Falls was not as strenuous and prolonged as that around the Great Falls in Montana. It was completed in five days — a hazardous, strenuous five days. On October 26 the Expedition had collected itself below the falls and reloaded and rested and made necessary repairs, and were on their way again down the Columbia. Two days later the Expedition was confronted with the long rapids of the Cascades. These rapids were formed by rock which, according to Indian legend, had collapsed into the river from a natural bridge which crossed the Columbia River at this site (The Bridge of the Gods).[14] These long rapids are now inundated by Bonneville Dam.[15] At the lower end of the rapids Clark noticed evidence of tidewater, and also noted a large "Beaten" (Beacon) Rock. He estimated the height of this rock at eight hundred feet above water level; his estimate was

---

[14] F. N. Balch wrote an interesting novel partially based on this legend, *The Bridge of the Gods* (Chicago: A. C. McClung & Company, 1890). An equally interesting book is Leonard Wiley's *The Granite Boulder* (Portland, Oreg., 1970), in which he relates the tragic life of Balch, and his abandonment and subsequent recovery of the manuscript of the novel, whose multiple printings testify to its continued popularity.

[15] Constructed in 1938. Named after Benjamin L. E. deBonneville (1796-1878), who was an American army officer. He led army and fur-trading expeditions in the West. *See* Washington Irving, *The Adventures of Captain Bonneville, U.S.A., in the Rocky Mountains and the Far West* (N.Y: G. P. Putnam & Company, 1852).

about one foot short! — another example of Clark's remarkable appraisal of geographic distances.

Signs of the white man's traffic were seen more frequently below the Cascade rapids, such as copper kettles, steel implements and other items obtained from traders who touched along the Northwest Pacific Coast. Clark wondered if this "traffick" was "with white people who are either settled or visit the mouth of this river," but concluded that it must be the latter.

Although the men were still buying dogs for their meat diet, they were now getting more deer and fowl. From the Indians on Wappato Island,[16] they bought bushels of roots, also known as wappato. The wappato grew abundantly on the low, inundated portion of this island. The squaws waded into the water and loosened the roots with their toes and gathered them in baskets as they floated to the top. These roots were used in various ways: roasted, in bread or in soup. The men of the Expedition preferred the wappato to the camas of the Weippe Prairie.

On November 1, Clark wrote a very uncomplimentary description of the Indians below the falls:

The Indians on these waters do not appear to be sickly, sore eyes are common and maney have lost their eyes, some one and many both, they have bad teeth . . . They are rather small high cheeks, women small and homely, many of them have sweled legs, large about the knees owing to the position in which they set on their hams, They are nearly necked only a piece of leather tied about their breech and a small robe. They are durty in the extreme both in their cooking and in their houses . . . Their noses are all Pierced . . . all the women have flat heads pressed almost to a point at top. The[y] press the female childrens heads between 2 bords when young . . . This . . . is considered as a great mark of buty . . .

16 Now known as Sauvies Island, after Laurent Sauve, a French Canadian of one of the Hudson's Bay Company farms. The story of this island is recounted in Omar C. Spencer, *The Story of Sauvies Island* (Portland: Binfords & Mort, 1950).

Now that they were on the western side of the Cascades, they were to endure rains such as they had never experienced before. Clark wrote on November 5 "we are all wet and cold and disagreeable, rain continues & encreases."

On November 7 Lewis described the Indian women below the falls whose clothes "hang with their ends pendulous from the waist, the whole being of Suff[i]cent thickness when the female Stands erect to conceal those parts usually covered from familiar view, but when she Stoops or places herself in any other attitude this battery of Venus is not altogether impervious to the penetrating eye of the amorite." Clark put it more simply: ". . . the Tosels seperate."

In addition to the increased rainfall which made it almost impossible for the men ever to be dry and warm, they encountered an increasing size of waves and a higher tide as they descended the Columbia, which posed problems they had not encountered previously in their water travel. On November 8 Clark wrote:

> the swells continued high all the evening & we are compelled to form an Encampment on a Point scercely room suffioient for us all to lie clear of the tide water. hills high & with a steep assent, river wide & at this place too salt to be used for Drink. We are all wet and disagreeable, as we have been continually for several days past. . . The swells were so high and the canoes roled in such a manner as to cause several to be verry sick. Reuben, fields, Wiser McNeal & the Squar wer of the number.

Thus seasickness is a new complaint. The "swells" also contributed a new threat to the safety of the canoes and the men; for those who could not swim it was much more of a hazard to be thrown into this giant River of the West than had been true in the more shallow rivers they had boated in the previous months.

On November 9 Clark's journal entry recounts the troubles with the high tide:

the Strictest attention by every individual of the party was scercely
sufficient to Save our Canoes from being crushed by those mon-
sterous trees maney of them nearly 200 feet long and from 4 to 7
feet through. our camp entirely under water dureing the hight of
the tide, every man as wet as water could make them all the last
night and to day all day as the rain continued all day. . . The
Water of the river being too Salt to use we are obliged to make use
of rain water. Some of the party not accustomed to Salt water had
made too free a use of it on them it acts as a pergitive.

The Expedition had been astonished at the ruggedness and
bigness of the Rocky Mountains; they were now experiencing
the ruggedness and bigness of the mighty Columbia. And
with all the water and trees around them, good drinking water
and dry wood were scarce. And with all the vastness of the
West, these unfortunate men were pinnioned into an uncom-
fortably narrow space along the banks of the tidewater
Columbia.

The steep banks and the gigantic trees extending to the
water edges and the increasing size of waves made a real
problem for the men to find a place to camp. November 11
was equally tormenting to the men:

A hard rain all the last night, dureing the last tide the logs on
which we lay was all on float . . . most tremendious waves
brakeing with great violence against the Shores, rain falling in
torrents, we are all wet as usial — and our Situation is truly a disagreeable one; the great quantities of rain which has loosened the
Stones on the hill Sides; and the Small stones fall down upon us,
our canoes at one place at the mercy of the waves, our baggage in
another; and our selves and party Scattered on floating logs and
Such dry Spots as can be found on the hill sides, and crivicies of
the rocks.

And yet, Clark wrote on the following day "Fortunately for
us our men are health."

It is a wonder that these men were not sick unto death from
malnutrition and exposure. Only young hardy individuals pre-

viously conditioned physically and mentally could have endured. There is no mention of illness or injury of any member
of the Expedition after the notation of Lewis' "recovering
fast" from his gastric symptoms on October 9 until November
15, when one man developed a "violent cold cought by lying
in wet clothes." It may have been that the captains failed to
record some health problems when they were so occupied
striving against the elements.

The Expedition was now on the wide estuary of the Columbia, but not yet at the ocean. The high waves made it difficult
to "proceed on," and the men had to delay until the storm
subsided. The wet weather rapidly rotted the leather clothing
and robes, and fresh skins were not being obtained due to a
lack of game. The weather was very adverse to drying skins,
even if they had been able to obtain them.

On November 16 Clark recorded an upper respiratory infection: "one man sick with a violent cold caught by lying in
his wet clothes, several nights." It is miraculous that every
member of the Expedition did not die of pneumonia.

The severe rain and wind and waves held the party prisoner
in a very exposed position, unable to get around a "blustering
Point." [17] A break in the weather finally permitted them to
proceed; they were now in view of the ocean although this
was difficult to discern from the wide estuary. Lewis explored
on the Washington side around the mouth of the Columbia
for a satisfactory camp but such could not be found, there
being too much exposure to the wind and rain, too little fuel,
and no evidence of deer or other meat to eat.

On November 18 Clark recorded the pitiful health of the
Chinook Indians: "I saw 4 womin and Some children one of
the women in a desperate Situation, covered with sores scabs
& ulsers no doubt the effects of venereal disorders which Several of this nation which I have Seen appears to have. . . ."

[17] Point Ellice.

The Journals are replete with entries of the deplorable skin afflictions of the Indians of the lower Columbia region.

Despite his desperate situation, Clark continued to write extensively. On November 21, he stated in part,

> . . . Several Indians and squars came this evening I beleave for the purpose of gratifying the passions of our men, Those people appear to view sensuality as a necessary evill, and do not appear to abhore this as crime in the unmarried females. The young women sport openly with our men, and appear to receve the approbation of theer friends & relations for so doing maney of the women are handsom. . . Pocks & venereal is common amongst them. I saw one man & one woman who appeared to be all in scabs & several men with the veneral their other Disorders and the remides for them I could not lern. . .

On November 23 Clark recorded "This nation [the Clatsops] is the remains of a large nation destroyed by the Small pox or Some other (disease) which those people were not acquainted with." On November 24 Whitehouse mentions one reason for choosing to winter near the ocean: "on account of making Salt, which we are nearly out of at this time, & the want of it in preserving our Provisions for the Winter, would be an object well worth our attention."* This is the only reference by any journalist of using salt for any purpose other than seasoning food.

The party unanimously agreed to abandon their camp on the north (now Washington) shore and move across to the south (now Oregon) side. Clark wrote on November 24: "Being now determined to go into Winter quarters as soon as possible, as a convenient Situation to precure the Wild animals of the forest which must be our dependance for Subsisting this Winter . . . They [the natives] generaly agree that the Most Elk is on the Opposit Shore, and that the greatest

---

* From the recently discovered copy of the second part of Whitehouse's Journal, Newberry Library. All future references to Whitehouse's account are from this source.

numbers of Deer is up the river at Some distance above
. . . added to [this] a convenient Situation to the Sea
coast where We Could make Salt, and probility of Vessels
comeing into the Mouth of Columbia . . ." Once the
decision was made to move to the south bank of the Columbia,
reconnoitering was necessary to locate a favorable site. This
was found by Lewis a few miles up the Netul River (now,
properly, called the Lewis and Clark River) on a rise of land
which would make them safe from the tides, and far enough
from the ocean to be protected from the severity of the winds
and yet close enough that salt could be evaporated from the
ocean water. Clark was not too happy about the prospect of
spending the winter on the ocean shore. On November 24 he
commented: "Salt water I view as an evil in as much as it is
not helthy."

Clark's temperament usually did not succumb to despair,
but after moving to a temporary exposed site on the south
bank of the Columbia he wrote feelingly on November 28:
"O! how disagreeable is our Situation dureing this dreadfull
weather." And he added "we are all wet bedding and stores,
haveing nothing to keep ourselves or stores dry, our Lodge
nearly worn out, and the pieces of sales & tents so full of holes
& rotten that they will not keep anything dry. . ."

On the thirtieth he wrote: "Several men Complain of a
looseness and griping which I contribute to the diet, pounded
fish mixed with Salt water, I derect that in future that the
party mix the pounded fish with fresh water. The squar gave
me a piece of bread made of flour which She had reserved for
her child and carefully Kept untill this time, which has unfortunately got wet, and a little Sour. this bread I eate with
great satisfaction, it being the only mouthfull I had tasted for
Several months past. my hunters killed three Hawks, which
we found fat and deliciious."

XV

At Fort Clatsop

We would have Spent this day the nativity of Christ in feasting, had we anything wither to raise our Sperits or even gratify our appetites. William Clark, December 25, 1805

Everyone was in favor of finding a more suitable location for their winter quarters, one less exposed to the ocean and with more opportunities for good hunting. Lewis and several men had been reconnoitering the south side of the Columbia, and reported favorably about the prospects there. All members of the Expedition, including York and Sacagawea,[1] were permitted to vote their first and second choices for a winter location. The great majority voted to "cross and examine" the site chosen by Lewis; there was some interest in wintering at the Sandy River and the falls (Celilo).[2]

The Expedition fought its way up river through high waves and around dangerous points of land to Pillar Rock (which still stands just off the Washington coast), where the water was not so rough and a group of islands afforded protection for a crossing. On November 26, 1805, the Expedition landed "at a Indian village of 9 large houses on an emence." In his second draft in the journals Clark describes it as "a handsom elivated Situation   .   .   ." This is the site of present-day Knappa, Oregon.

---

[1] The first suffragette vote in the Oregon country! Sacagawea was in favor of a place with plenty of "Potas" (this was probably present-day Sauvie's Island where she had dug wappato on the way west.) The Oregon Suffragettes who used Sacagawea as a rallying symbol failed to mention that their heroine had voted in the

Clark was still not happy with the ocean and again he wrote that he could not call the ocean Pacific ". . . . as I have not Seen one pacific day Since my arrival in this vicinity, and its waters are forming and petially [perpetually] breake with emenc waves on the sands and rockey coasts, tempestuous and horiable."

The men were out of food except for dried fish which they had purchased at the falls of the Columbia. Their clothes were rotting on them. The elk they had expected to find evaded the hunters. Clark and many of the men became wretchedly ill from eating the dried fish boiled in salt water. On December 3 Clark wrote: "I am still unwell and can't eate even the flesh of the Elk," but it revived the spirits of the men. Clothing and supplies remained wet from "this dredfull wind and rain."

Lewis moved ahead with a few men to search for a suitable place for winter quarters, and his delay in returning to the main party caused Clark to ". . . fear Some accident has taken place in his craft or party . . . 1000 conjectures has crouded into my mind respecting his probable situation & safety." But Lewis had found a good "situation" and had killed six elk and five deer — this heartened the party and they pushed on to arrive on December 7 at the site on the Netul (now Lewis and Clark) River where they were to build their Fort Clatsop. They immediately started preparing for winter, sending out the hunters to get meat and hides, felling timber to build their cabins, and Clark blazed a trail to the ocean where a cairn was to be built to evaporate the ocean water for salt.[3]

Oregon country one hundred years before — in the U.S. Army! Thwaites, *Journals,* III, p. 246-47.   [2] *Ibid.*

[3] The salt cairn is located near the north end of the seawall at Seaside, Or., on Lewis and Clark Way. For an account of identifying its location, see *Proc. of the Oreg. Hist. Soc. for 1900,* pp. 16-23. The following information about the salt cairn is provided by the Seaside Chamber of Commerce: "The Oregon Historical Society established the site in 1900, through the testimony of Jenny Michel of

Clark records the sick call for December 11: "sergeant Pryor unwell from a dislocation of his left sholder, Gibson with a disentary, Jo. Fields with biles on his legs, & Werner with a Strained Knee." Pryor's continuing shoulder ailment probably indicates that the primary reduction was not followed with proper management, something that Lewis and Clark could hardly be expected to know.

Coues comments about his recurrent dislocation of the shoulder:

> Sergeant Pryor's case is peculiar. I hardly see how he could have got into the way of slipping his humerus out of its socket so easily and so often as his shoulder is said to be "dislocated" in this work; nor is this luxation so readily reduced as it seems to have been done on several occasions. I imagine the sergeant displaced the tendon of the long head of the biceps from the bicipital groove on the first instance, by an unlucky wrench, and was afterward liable to recurrence of this accident from slighter causes. It is a rare affection; I have treated such cases.[4]

It is appropriate for Coues to comment on Pryor's affliction inasmuch as he was an army surgeon. In fact, Coues would have been a very proper one to write the medical history of the Lewis and Clark Expedition. However, in this instance Coues' comments are not correct; recurrent dislocation of the shoulder is not uncommon, and occurs particularly in those individuals who are not properly cared for after the reduction of a primary dislocation. It is possible to have afflictions of the long head of the biceps tendon as the cause of chronic shoulder conditions, including the dislocation of it as mentioned

Seaside, who was born in that vicinity in 1816 and died in 1905. Her Clatsop Indian mother remembered seeing the white men boiling water at the site, and pointed out the place to her when she was a young girl. The fence and sidewalk were constructed by the Great Northern and Spokane, Portland and Seattle Railways more than 40 years ago. The Lions Club of Seaside reconstructed the actual cairn according to specifications in the Lewis and Clark diaries supplied by the Oregon Historical Society."

[4] Coues, *History of Lewis and Clark*, II, p. 733.

by Coues. However, chronic dislocations and subluxations of
the head of the humerus are far more common than those
of the biceps tendon.

The weather continued to be wet and cold, and the fleas
continued to bite — a combination which prevented comfort
day and night. This resulted in the men vigorously and en-
thusiastically pursuing the building of the cabins. It was soon
necessary to construct a "meathouse" because of the great
supply of elk which the hunters were bringing in. Drouillard
and Shannon brought in eighteen elk one day.

Their fort when completed would consist of two rows of
cabins facing each other with pointed log pickets and a gate
closing the space between them. The entire "fort" comprised
a space fifty feet square. An exact duplicate of the fort was
reconstructed at the Sesquicentennial observance of the Lewis
and Clark Expedition; this was made possible by Clark having
recorded the specifications in his journal,[5] with designations
about who occupied each room and a floor design.

Clark was grateful for the "streightest & most butifullest
logs" which they could split for flooring and roofing. Their
clothes and leather tents were falling apart, which Clark
recorded on December 14: "scerce one man in camp can bost
of being one day dry Since we landed at this point, the Sick
getting better, my man York Sick with Cholick & gripeing."

On December 16 Clark wrote:

> rained all the last night we covered our selves as well as we could
> with Elk skin, & set up the greater part of the night, all wet I lay
> in the wet verry cold, the 5 men who stayed out all night joined
> me this morning Cold & wet. . .   The winds violent Trees fall-
> ing in every direction, whorl winds, with gusts of rain Hail &
> Thunder, this kind of weather lasted all day, Certainly one of the
> worst days that ever was! . . .   Several men complaining of
> hurting themselves carry[ing] meat, &c.

[5] Thwaites, *Journals*, III, p. 268.

Whitehouse noted on this date that "The Man that was sick (George Gibson) got much better."

They were now well fed, but were constantly wet and cold. Although they were working desperately to get the cabins completed so that they could be dry and warm, Clark writes on December 18, "the men being but thinly dressed, and no shoes causes us to doe but little." On the 19th Whitehouse made an entry in his journal: "Serjeant Ordway was very sick, but the Men in general continue in good health, notwithstanding the bad weather & hardships that they undergo." Ordway's being very sick was not mentioned by any other journalist, indicating that many incidents relating to health and other things were not noted in the journals. By December 22 they had one row of huts covered and were "Dobbing" mud in the cracks; the "Punchin" floor and bunks were also completed in these cabins. Clark writes that Sergeant Ordway and Gibson and York and several others had boils and bruises of different kinds.

On December 23 the two captains moved into their unfinished "hut," and the following day most of the men were under cover. Although they were getting plenty of meat, it spoiled rapidly; they did not have the freezing weather and snow to preserve their meat as they did at Fort Mandan. They were visited on the twenty-fourth by an Indian Chief and his squaw, who "offered a woman to each of us which we also declined acepting of, which despleased the whole party verry much — the female part appeared to be highly disgusted at our refuseing to axcept of their favours &c."

Christmas Day 1805 was one of pathetic happiness for the men of the Expedition. All of them were housed in their new cabins, dry and warm, and they had plenty of Elk meat. Clark wrote of this Christmas day: "our Diner concisted of pore Elk, so much Spoiled that we eate it thro' mear necessity, Some Spoiled pounded fish and fiew roots."

In a note of poignant appreciation Whitehouse wrote: "We had no ardent sperits of any kind among us; but are mostly in good health, a blessing, which we esteem more, than all the luxuries this life can afford, and the party are all thankful to the Supreme Being, for his goodness towards us, hoping he will preserve us in the same, & enable us to return to the United States again in safety. We have at present nothing to eat but lean Elk meat & that without Salt but the whole of our party are content with this fare."

On December 27 the captains dispatched some men along the trail which Clark had blazed to the location of the salt cairn; this was located approximately fifteen miles from Fort Clatsop and "within one hundred paces of the Ocin," according to Clark. The first detail of men included Joseph Field, Bratton and Gibson, taking with them "5 of the largest Kittles." Willard and Wiser accompanied them to carry the heavy kettles. Clark wrote of some food given to them by an Indian chief: "Those roots and berries are timely and extreamly greatfull to our Stomacks, as we have nothing to eate but Spoiled Elk meat . . ."

On December 29 Clark noted that "the Chin-nook womin are lude and carry on sport publickly the Clotsop and others appear deffident, and reserved." Biddle's 1814 edition describes the morals and cleanliness of the Indians:

Yet all these decorations are unavailing to conceal the deformities of nature and the extravagance of fashion; nor have we seen any more disgusting object than a Chinnok or Clatsop beauty in full attire. Their broad flat foreheads, their falling breasts, their ill shaped limbs, the awkwardness of their positions, and the filth which intrudes through their finery; all these render a Chinnook or Clatsop beauty in full attire, one of the most disgusting objects in nature.[6] Fortunately this circumstance conspired with the low

---

[6] Cox uses superlatives in describing the Chinook women: "Then the women, — Oh ye gods! With the same (as the men) auricular, olfactory and craniological

diet and laborious exercise of our men, to protect them from the
persevering gallantry of the fair sex, whose kindness always exceeded the ordinary courtesies of hospitality. Among these people,
as indeed among all Indians, the prostitution of unmarried women
is so far from being considered criminal or improper, that the
females themselves solicit the favours of the other sex; with the
entire approbation of their friends and connexions. The person is
in fact often the only property of a young female, and is therefore
the medium of trade, the return for presents, and the reward for
services. In most cases, however, the female is so much at the dis-
posal of her husband or parent, that she is farmed out for hire.
The Chinnook woman, who brought her six female relations to
our camp, had regular prices, proportioned to the beauty of each
female; and among all the tribes, a man will lend his wife or
daughter for a fish-hook or a strand of beads. To decline an offer
of this sort is indeed to disparage the charms of the lady, and
therefore gives such offence, that although we had occasionally to
treat the Indians with rigour, nothing seemed to irritate both sexes
more than our refusal to accept the favours of the females. On one
occasion we were amused by a Clatsop, who having been cured
of some disorder by our medical skill, brought his sister as a
reward for our kindness. The young lady was quite anxious to
join in this expression of her brother's gratitude, and mortified that
we did not avail ourselves of it, she could not be prevailed on to
leave the fort, but remained with Chaboneau's wife, in the next
room to ours, for two or three days, declining all the solicitations
of the men, till finding, at last, that we did not relent, she went
away, regretting that her brother's obligations were unpaid.[7]

   The little intercourse which the men have had with these women
is, however, sufficient to apprise us of the prevalence of the

---

perculiarities, they exhibited loose hanging breasts, short dirty teeth, skin saturated
with blubber, bandy legs, and a waddling gait; . . . this covering (their
short dresses) in calm weather, or in an erect position, served all the purposes of
concealment; but in a breeze, or when indulging their favourite position of squatting, formed a miserable shield in defence of decency: and worse than all, their
repulsive familiarities rendered them objects insupportably odious. . ." Cox,
Adventures on the Columbia, p. 112.

   [7] This paragraph justifies Dr. Rush's statement that "But the infamy of the
Indian character is completed by the low rank to which they degrade their
women." Quoted by Goodman, *Rush,* p. 291.

venereal disease, with which one or two of the party had been so
much afflicted, as to render a salivation necessary.[8] The infection
in these cases was communicated by the Chinnook women. The
others do not appear to be afflicated with it to any extent; indeed,
notwithstanding this disorder is certainly known to the Indians on
the Columbia, yet the number of infected persons is very incon-
siderable. The existence of such a disorder is very easily detected,
particularly in the men, in their open style of dress; yet in the
whole route down the Columbia, we have not seen more than two
or three cases of gonorrhoea, and about double the number of lues
venera.[9] There does not seem to be any simples which are used
as specifics in this disorder,[10] nor is any complete cure ever ef-

Clark records on December 28 of 1805 that his servant York
was "verry unwell from violent colds and strain," and that
"pete Crusat sick with a violent cold." Although meat continued to be plentiful, Clark wrote that "we are now liveing
on spoiled Elk which is extremely disagreeable to the smel. as
well as the taste . . .   I derected sinks to be dug. . ."
Ordway confirmed in his journal that the men "dug 2 sinques."
This last statement showed that the old army routine was
followed while in stationary camps.

As on all special occasions and when his time permitted,

---

[8] This reference to salivation indicates that the Captains were following the
established practice of administering mercury for the treatment of syphilis until
the patient salivated.

[9] The use of the term "lues venera" reflects the captains' army training; this is
the term used in the army at the time of Lewis and Clark. *See* Ashburn, *Medical
Dept.*, p. 11. At one time Lues and gonorrhea were not differentiated by medical
doctors. The use of this term also indicates that the captains clearly distinguished
between gonorrhea and syphilis (lues). Biddle says in his notes only that
". . . lues which is excessively bad on Sea Coast. . ." Jackson, *Letters*, p.
506.

[10] This is in contrast to the quite universal practice of the Indians of North
America, who used a variety of medicinal plants in the treatment of venereal
disease. *See* Vogel, *American Indian Medicine*, pp. 210-13.

fected.[11]

[11] Biddle, *History of the Expedition*, II, p. 134-36.

Lewis waxed loquacious in his journal entry of January 1, 1806. He looked forward "in the anticipation of the 1st day of January 1807, when in the bosom of our frends we hope to participate in the mirth and hilarity of the day . . . at present we were content with eating our boiled Elk and wappetoe, and solacing our thirst with our only beverage pure water."

The men carried their fleas with them into their new quarters, so that Lewis wrote on January 2 that "we are infestd with sworms of flees already in our new habitations." On January 3 he noted that:

> our party from neccessity having been obliged to subsist some lenth of time on dogs have now become exrteemly fond of their flesh; it is worthy of remark that while we lived principally on the flesh of this anamal we were much more healthy strong and fleshey than we had been since we left the Buffaloe country. for my own part I have become so perfectly reconciled to the dog that I think it an agreeable food and would prefer it vastly to lean Venison or Elk [12] . . . Sent Sergt. Gass and George shannon to the salt-makers who are somewhere on the coast to the s.w. of us. . .

Clark's journal entry from this day was the same, the captains often copying verbatim from each other, except that Clark wrote in relation to the dog meat "as for my own part I have not become reconciled to the taste of this animal as yet."

---

[12] Dog meat was used considerably by white men on the frontier, usually as a necessity at first, then sometimes as a matter of preference to other meat. Ross Cox, a clerk for Hudson's Bay Company at Astoria, wrote: "Mr. Holmes gave us a plentiful dinner of roast pork, roast dog, fowl, ham, fish, wine, and rum. . . The idea of eating so faithful an animal without ever the plea of necessity, effectually prevented any of us from joining in this part of the feast, although, to do the meat justice, it really looked very well when roasted. . . The islander (Hawaiian) esteem it the greatest luxury they possess. . ." Later, the "plea of necessity" caused Cox to write: "As our provisions were nearly consumed, we were obliged to purchase twenty dogs from them [the Indians]. It was the first time I had eaten any of the flesh of this animal, and nothing but stern necessity could have induced me to partake of it." Cox, *The Columbia River* (Stewart Edition), pp. 32-33, 127.

On January 5 the Indians brought a quantity of whale blubber to the captains. Lewis wrote: "I had a part of it cooked and found it very pallitable and tender, it resembled the beaver or the dog in flavour . . . it is a fact that the flesh of the beaver and the dog posses a very great affinity in point of flavor." Although Clark did not care for dog meat he made a journal entry of his own similar to Lewis' philosophical note about meat in general: "as to the species of meat I am not very particular, the flesh of the dog the horse and the wolf, having from habit become equally formiliar with any other, and I have learned to think that if the chord be sufficiently strong, which binds the soul and boddy together, it does not so much matter about the materials which compose it."

Ordway wrote on the same date that "2 men came from the Salt Camp with about two gallons of salt." Lewis noted that these men informed him that they could obtain from three quarts to a gallon of salt per day.[13] The men had been without salt for a few weeks, and they greatly relished its addition to their diet; however, Lewis wrote that "my friend Capt. Clark was indifferent to its use."

The elk meat was made more palatable to them with the addition of salt, which put considerable demand on the salt makers. Lewis wrote, "with the means we have of boiling the salt water we find it a very tedious opperation, that of making salt, not with standing we keep the kettle boiling day and night. we calculate on three bussels lasting us from hence to our deposits [14] of that article on the Missouri."

---

[13] Dr. Saugrain (*see* Chapter x) records in his diary, written on a trip down the Ohio River in 1788: "A great quantity of salt is made here (near Lexington, Kentucky, at Blue Lick) by evaporating the water. It takes as many as 1000 gallons to make a bushel of it. They evaporate the water in kettles." Kennerly, *Persimmon Hill,* p. 130. Thus the technique of evaporating water to get salt was probably familiar to Clark and the "nine young men from Kentucky." A more sophisticated way of obtaining salt from "saline springs" is described by James, *Account of an Expedition,* p. 90.

The captains heard from the Indians about a stranded whale. On January 6 Captain Clark and several men set out to find the whale and purchase meat and blubber. Sacagawea insisted that she be taken along, observing that she had traveled all the way with the Expedition and had not yet seen the ocean. Her wish was granted. Clark led his party to the salt cairn, then south over Tillamook Head to where the whale was lying by a creek on a sandy beach. Clark named this creek Ecola — the Chinook word for whale.[15] He thanked providence that the whale had come to be eaten by them, instead of them being swallowed by the whale, as happened to Jonah.

When Clark and his party returned on January 10 from their visit to the whale, Lewis observed that they "were not able to procure more blubber than about three hundred lb. and a few gallons of the oil."

The main meat supply came from the elk,[16] and Drouillard was the only hunter who was consistently successful in bringing down this animal. Clark wrote of him: "I scercely know how we Should Subsist, I believe but badly if it was not for the exertions of this excellent hunter." Some days several elk and perhaps a deer or two were shot; on these days the men would eat heartily and perhaps somewhat wastefully. This led Lewis to issue the fresh meat sparingly, jerking the rest of it to be used during lean times.

The diet of the men was occasionally supplemented with

[14] Refers to caches made on the way west. Cache is a French word meaning "hidden." A cache was made by digging a hole which was enlarged underground, then lined with poles and grasses, and covered with dirt and debris to remove all markings. The caches on the Missouri were at Great Falls and the Marias River.

[15] The name Ecola was replaced with the Elk Creek name by early settlers. In 1974 the Oregon Geographic Names Board officially renamed this stream Ecola Creek at the request of the Oregon Lewis and Clark Trail Committee.

[16] These elk are named after Theodore Roosevelt; see Paul Cutright, *Theodore Roosevelt the Naturalist* (N.Y: Harper & Brothers, 1956), p. 85. Mr. Don Holm, Wildlife Editor of the *Portland Oregonian,* assures me that today's elk in the Northwest are the Roosevelt elk.

native roots which the Indians gathered and sold or traded to them. Lewis particularly mentions "the root of the thistle . . . is more shugary than any fruit or root that I have met with in uce among the natives; the sweet is precisely that of the sugar in flavor." He also mentions that the natives eat the roots of ferns, one of which is much like wheat dough when roasted, and another edible root which Lewis describes as "The root of the rush." Lewis also describes the use of a purple berry which the Indians call "Shal-lun;" [17] the natives ate these berries raw, or dried them in the sun or in sweating kilns, or pounded them and baked them in large loaves which were used as bread.

Lewis wrote on January 27, 1806: "Goodrich has recovered from the Louis Veneri [lues veneris] which he contracted from an amorous contact with a Chinnook damsel. I cured him as I did Gibson last winter by the uce of murcury." On January 31 Clark discovered that McNeal "had the pox, [18] gave him some medicine." There is no indication from the journals that the captains held daily sick call. How often they did not know of some affliction of the men, or failed to record a note in their journals about some illness or accident, is a matter of conjecture; in Lewis' entry of the 27th he refers to curing Gibson of syphilis the previous winter, but it had not been recorded initially. Clark noted that the smallpox had destroyed a great number of the Clatsop nation, this disease having passed through them about five years previously. [19]

---

[17] *Gaultheria Shallon,* usually called salal.

[18] This indicates that McNeal had not reported the first stage of his syphilis, the chancre, and that Clark knew of his infection only when he erupted with pox — the second stage.

[19] Robert Haswell, an officer on the Columbia Rediviva of Capt. Gray's voyage of 1788 (Capt. Gray's first visit to Oregon), noted in his log on Aug. 11, 1788, that of some Indians who brought their canoes alongside "two or three of our visiters were much pitted with the small pox." T. C. Elliott, "Haswell's Log of the Sloop Washington — 1788," *Oreg. Hist. Soc. Bull.,* Vol. 29, No. 2 (June, 1928), pp. 165-89.

The winter months at Fort Clatsop were dreary and repetitious: rainy weather, hunting, clothes-making, salt-making, and a little buying and trading with the Indians. Bargaining with the Indians was very restricted by the captains because of the dwindling supply of trade articles. As the future revealed, the two captains were to depend more and more on their practice as physicians as a method of diplomacy to obtain their needs from the Indians.

Some fanciful assumptions have been written into the novelized histories of the Lewis and Clark Expedition. Wilson, in his biography of Lewis, writes, "John Shields, the lyrical Welshman, acquired whooping cough [this was while the Expedition was at Fort Clatsop], and became for that reason the most conspicuous member of the corps. There could be no real doubts as to his whereabouts or his occupation, which was coughing." [20] There is no description in any of the journals of any illness that suggests whooping cough, which is a disease mainly afflicting children, and no mention of any corpsman having a peculiar cough; in fact, Shields is never mentioned at any time during the stay at Fort Clatsop as having a health problem of any kind.

The captains busied themselves with writing more fully in their journals from the notes they had made along the trail. Lewis gave special attention to the natural history of the area. Clark spent a considerable portion of his time in putting together the segments of maps which he had made since they left the Mandan villages. The supply of clothes was replenished from the elk hides. Clark enjoyed the whale blubber, but "on this food I do not feel Strong, but enjoy tolerable health." On February 7 Clark wrote "This evening we had what I call an excellent supper it consisted of a marrow-bone,

[20] Charles Morrow Wilson, *Meriwether Lewis of Lewis and Clark* (N.Y: 1934), p. 172.

a piece of brisket of boiled Elk that had the appearance of a little fat on it. This for Fort Clatsop is liveing in high stile, and in fact fiesting."

February 9 was a day of health complaints among the crew at the salt works: Willard cut his knee badly with his tomahawk (Gass wrote that "he could hardly walk"), Bratton was "very unwell," and Gibson was so ill he could not sit or walk alone. The hunters became more successful and Lewis was able to record that they had a supply of dried meat to last a month.

The men at the salt works continued to have problems; Lewis wrote on February 15:

> about 3 P.M. Bratton arrived from the salt works and informed us that Sergt Pryor and party were on their way with Gibson who is so much reduced that he cannot stand alone and that they are obliged to carry him on a litter. Bratton himself appears much reduced with his late indisposition but is now recovering fast. . . We are much pleased in finding him by no means as ill as we had expected. we do not consider him in danger by any means, tho' he has yet a fever and is much reduced. we believe his disorder to have orriginated in a violent cold which he contracted in hunting and pursuing Elk and other game through the swam[p]s and marshes . . . he is nearly free from pain . . . we gave him broken dozes of diluted nitre and made him drink plentifully of sage tea, had his feet bathed in warm water and a 9 P.M. gave him 35 drops of laudanum.

The following day Lewis gave considerable attention to his patients:

> Bratton is still very weak and complains of a pain in the lower part of his back when he moves . . . I gave him barks. Gibson's fever still continues obstenate tho' not very high; I gave him a doze of Dr. Rush's which in many instances I have found extreemly efficatious in fevers which are in any measure caused by the presence of boil. the nitre has produced a profuse persipiration this evening and the pills operated late at night his fever after which abated almost entirely and he had a good night's rest.

Lewis continued his medical practice the next day:

continue the barks with Bratton, and commenced them with Gibson his fever being sufficiently low this morning to permit the uce of them. I think therefore that there is no further danger of his recovery. at 2 P.M. Joseph Fields arrived from the Salt works and informed us that they had about 2 Kegs of salt on hand which with what we have at this place we suppose will be sufficient to last us to our deposits of that article on the Missouri. we there[fore] directed a party of six men to go with Fields in the morning in order to bring the salt and kettles to the fort.

The condition of Bratton and Willard continued to be refractory to the captain-physicians' efforts; Bratton's condition particularly fluctuated from day to day. On February 19 Clark "gave Bratten 6 of Scotts pills which did not work him. he is very sick and complains of his back." This is the first mention of Scott's pills. There is no mention of "Scotts pills" in the list of drugs which Lewis brought with him from Philadelphia. Clark notes that the pills "did not work him," indicating that the pills were a physic. It might be considered that Clark used the name of Scott as a misnomer for Rush, but this would not likely be true of Lewis, who knew Rush well. There were no Dr. Scotts listed in Philadelphia or St. Louis at the time, nor any advertisement of a proprietary drug bearing the name of Scott. Possibly the captains and their men added a few personal medicines to the official supply.

On February 19, Whitehouse, who was going with six men to the "Salt works" wrote of the exposure which the men accepted as a part of the expected routine: "We crossed a Creek, which took us middle deep, which benumbed & chilled the party very much. We came to an Old deserted Indian hut, in which we made a fire."

On February 20 Lewis records that "Bratton has an obstenate cough and pain in his back and still appears to be geting weaker. McNeal from his inattention to his disorder has become worse" — this indicates that Lewis expected McNeal to medicate himself with a mercury ointment; or did he re-infect himself with another "amorous damsel"? Clark recorded on the same date that "Batten has an obstinate cough and pain in his back and still appears to be getting weaker . . . Willard has a high fever and complains of a pain in his head and a want of appetite."

On February 21 the salt makers returned with their equipment, having evacuated the salt camp. Lewis writes that "our stock of salt is now about 20 Gallons; gave Willard and bratton each a doze of Scott's pills; on the former they operated on the latter they did not. Gibson still continues the barks three times a day and is on the recovery fast." Now it is Lewis who uses the name "Scott's pills"; the use of this name by both captains indicates the possibility that they really possessed such an item. The captains many times copied verbatim from each other in order to bring their journals up to date, but Clark had administered Scott's pills on the nineteenth and Lewis on the twenty-first. On this latter date Clark writes: "Gave Willard a dose of Scots pills; they opperated very well." Lewis and Clark both mention Scott's pills again on March 3. The journals mention Scott's pills only on three occasions.[21]

Dr. Scott's pills remain an enigma, but inquiry has produced some interesting information. With both captains mentioning them on different days, it is not probable that the name Scott was used by mistake; therefore, further conjecture as to how and when one of the captains could have purchased

---

[21] From the captains' remarks regarding them, Scott's pills were a physic. As mentioned, the medical supplies also included several other cathartics; therefore, it was unnecessary for the Expedition to have added more of the same. Dr. Scott's cast iron pills are mentioned in a verse published in 1861, and may refer to the same Dr. Scott; many patent medicines served early Americans for the half-century from 1805 to 1860. *See* James Harvey Young, *The Toadstool Millionaires* (Princeton University Press, 1961), p. 93.

Dr. Scott's pills led to the awareness that Lewis spent six weeks at Pittsburgh. A Dr. Hugh Scott was living in Pittsburgh when Lewis was there with time on his hands, fretfully waiting completion of his keel-boat. Dr. Scott had come to Pittsburgh in 1800 and set himself up as a "Physician and Apothecary," and had been recommended highly to prescribe drugs for the U.S. Command Station at Detroit.[22] He was serving as postmaster of Pittsburgh in 1803, while Lewis was there. It is probable that Dr. Scott became aware of Lewis' army activities in this frontier town and that they spent some time together, and that health problems of the Expedition were discussed. A natural consequence would be for the good army doctor to provide Lewis with some pills for purging — something to which doctors and patients alike were addicted. If this Dr. Hugh Scott did provide the purgative pills used at Fort Clatsop, it is too bad that Lewis did not give him the credit — he mentions other doctors in his Ohio journal who had little, or less, cause to have their name recorded in the annals of the Expedition.*

From the Rocky Mountains west the captains were in the midst of a plentiful supply of one of the world's most used and most effective cathartics: the bark of the cascara sagrada tree.[23] There is no indication from the journals that the cap-

---

[22] I am indebted to Mr. Joseph G. Smith, Dir. of Comm. Services, Hist. Soc. of Western Pa., Pittsburgh, for this information about Dr. Hugh Scott. Mr. Smith also informs me that the Pittsburgh Post Gazette and the Pittsburgh Weekly Gazette of 1803 do not contain advertisements for Dr. Scott's pills, although many other pills are advertised.

* For a more detailed discussion of Dr. Scott's pills see Chuinard, "A Medical Mystery at Fort Clatsop," We Proceed On, Vol. III, No. 2, pp. 8-9.

[23] Rhamns pushiana. Scully writes of this tree: "This age-old remedy grows on the sides and at the base of the Rocky Mountains. The early Spanish settlers learned from the Indians of its superlative medicinal properties and named it cascara sagrada, the 'sacred bark. . . They learned of other herbs that the Indians combined with it as a purgative and found that, alone, it was an excellent cure for constipation.' " Scully, A Treasury of Herbs, p. 133.

tains knew of its use as a cathartic among the Indians at the time of the Expedition, but the Northwest Indians of later years did use it for catharsis. Apparently Lewis encountered this "shrub" on the return journey on May 29, 1806,[24] and preserved a specimen, but did not ascribe to it any medicinal properties.

On February 22 Lewis wrote that "we had not had so ma[n]y sick at one time since we left Wood River. The general complaint seems to bad colds, and fever, something I believe of the influenza." He mentions "Gibson, Bratton, Sergt. Ordway, Willard and McNeal are all on the recovery."

Hugh Hall is seldom mentioned in the journals, and almost never in regard to illness or injury, but on March 6 he is listed among the injured. Lewis records that he "had his foot and ankle much injured yesterday by the fall of a large stick of timber; the bones were fortunately not broken and I expect he will be able to walk again shortly." This diagnosis was made without X-ray[25] of course; undoubtedly it was made because of a lack of deformity and the absence of intolerable pain with weight-bearing. Lewis also mentioned: "Bratton is now weaker than any of the convalessants."

Clark's entry of March 7 states that:

Bratten is much worse to day he complains of a violent pain in the small of his back, is unable in consequence of it to set up. we gave him one of our flannel shirts. I applied a bandage of flanel to the part and rubed it well with some volatile linniment which was prepared with sperits of wine, camphire, castile soap, and a little laudinum. he felt himself better in the evening at which time I repeated the linniment and bathed his beet [feet], to restore circulation which he complained of in that part.

---

[24] See Cutright, Pioneering Naturalists, p. 416.

[25] Wilhelm Roentgen (1845-1923) did not describe the use of x-rays to show bones until 1895.

Gass had a complaint which he thought important enough to commit to his journal; on March 7 he wrote: "among our other difficulties we now experience the want of tobacco, and out of 33 persons composing our party there are but 7 who do not make use of it; we use crabtree bark as a substitute." The following day, March 8, Bratton was much better, with only a little pain in his back. McNeal and Goodrich had recovered from their venereal infection, and Clark directs them to discontinue the use of mercury.

Bratton's improvement was very brief; on March 9 he was again complaining of his back being very painful. Lewis wrote: "I conceive this pain to be something of the rheumatism. we still apply the liniment and flannel; in the evening he was much better."

While describing the various fish in the area, Lewis wrote on March 12: ". . . the shell fish are the clam, perrewinkle, common mussle, cockle, and a specie with a circular flat shell." Was the latter the crab? Probably not, from Clark's later description.[26] As these shell fish were known to Lewis and Clark, why did they not use them? Fort Clatsop was away from the beach, but there was lots of trading of other edibles by the Indians with the white men. On March 15 Clark wrote: "The Clams of this coast are very small;" but Clark was describing a species of mussels.[27] The men of the Expedition roamed the beaches and obtained general information and salmon from the Indians. Why did they not have clams and crabs when they were constantly in need of food? [28]

[26] Thwaites, *Journals*, IV, pp. 160, 173.

[27] *Ibid.*, p. 173.

[28] This question was put to Mr. George E. Phebus, Supervisor, Processing Laboratory, Dept. of Anth. of the Smithsonian Inst., who answered: "I think several points may be involved. First, I believe that the economy of the Chinookan Indians, including the Clatsops, was not geared to a continuous exploitation of the nearby maritime resources. Their cultural tradition was riverine and apparently focused heavily upon salmon, (particularly dried, smoked, etc.) plant products and inland

Clark had noted in his journal on December 10th that he had encountered Indians walking on the beach looking for fish — "this was Conclusive evedance to me that this small band [of Indians] depended in some measure for their winters subsistence on the fish which is thrown on shore and

mammals. Additionally, I believe, their culture was already rapidly changing if not, in part, disappearing before the arrival of Lewis and Clark. This I think was directly attributable to the new 'Trade economy' (initially with ships). In other words, the Clatsops probably never did exploit the maritime ecology to a maximum degree and once they became tied up in trade they would have had little time or desire to continue to any degree.

"Secondly, and possibly of greater importance is the fact that the beach line south of the Columbia mouth has filled dramatically since the time of Lewis and Clark and before. The nearly entire area of present Seaside was once a deep bay much like that at current Nehalen or Willappa. This ancient bay of 1000-3000 years ago provided an immense source of maritime products for the early inhabitants of the North Coast. This is the source of the tremendous shell deposits mentioned by Mr. Drucker. [Mr. Robert M. Drucker of Astoria participated with Mr. Phebus in doing archeological investigations for the Smithsonian Institute.]

"By the time of Lewis and Clark, nearly all of the bay had filled in and I suspect the beach was only about 50 feet or less from its present location.

"Also, I have been told and have read that the abundant Razor clam population of today in no way resembles the condition along the North Coast prior to the construction of the jetties which are directly responsible for the immense beaches in which this clam flourishes. The rather small percentage of Razor clam in the prehistoric sites at Seaside substantiates this point, I believe.

"I also believe that the Lewis and Clark party was not particularly in tune with maritime products and their availability; the Clatsops were not themselves harvesting richly from the sea due to several factors; and the natives do not appear to have been overly concerned with the welfare of Lewis and Clark's party beyond the aspect of trade.

"A final comment would be simply that during the time of the year of the Lewis and Clark visit (winter), the weather does not really permit the extensive harvesting of maritime resources which does occur starting about mid-April.

"The clams (?) adhering to the rocks were undoubtedly mussels — strongly suggesting the party's ill acquaintance with maritime products. Some crab remains (claws) do occur in the prehistoric middens at Seaside."

The explanation offered by Dr. Phebus that there were no local clam and crab sand beaches around the estuary until the jetties were built is suggested by evidence that these shellfish were used by Indians elsewhere. Robert Haswell writes in his log of the Columbia during Capt. Gray's visit in Tillamook Bay on Aug. 14, 1788, that the Indians came alongside in canoes ". . . each canoe brought with them large quantities of berries and crabs ready boiled."

left by the tide." Clark told Biddle "Saw no oysters on the
Pacific Ocean." [29] And, apparently, neither Clark or the Indians saw crabs left by the tide as it left fish for the Indians —
and as it leaves crabs in "crab holes" today.

On March 12 Clark wrote in his journal: "Our party are
now furnished with 358 par of Mockersons exclusive of a
good portion of Dressed leather, they are also provided with
shirts overalls capoes of dressed Elk skins for the homeward
journey." They had made use of the elk in much the same way
as the Indians: for food and clothing.

The weather was changing to the better in March, and the
men were getting eager to be on their way.[30] However, the
captains knew from information given to them by the Rocky
Mountains Indians on the way west that they would not be
able to return east before the latter part of May or early June.

Clark wrote on March 15:

We were visited this Afternoon in a canoe 4 feet 2 I. wide by
De-lash-hel-wilt a Chinnook Chief his wife and six women of his
Nation, which the Old Boud his wife had brought for Market.
this was the same party which had communicated the venereal to
several of our party in November last, and of which they have
finally recovered. I therefore gave the men a paricular charge with
rispect to them which they promised me to observe . . .
Bratten is still very weak and unwell.

Lewis commented regarding the Chinnook women: "I be-

---

[29] Jackson, *Letters*, p. 520.

[30] Lewis and Clark were about to leave Fort Clatsop and its miserable weather.
They were not destined to see the springtime in the northwest, as did Franchere,
whose diary entry of April 12, 1811, describes an Oregon landscape unfamiliar, and
perhaps unbelievable, to the two captains: "We landed at the bottom of a small
bay, where we formed a sort of encampment. The spring . . . was already
far advanced, the foliage was budding, and the earth was clothing itself with
verdure; the weather was superb and all nature smiled. We imaged ourselves in
the garden of Eden, the wild forests seemed to us delightful groves, and the leaves
transformed to brilliant flowers." Franchere, *Narrative of a Voyage*, p. 102.

lieve notwithstanding every effort of their wining graces, the men have preserved their constancy to the vow of celibacy which they made on this occasion to Capt. and myself."

Lewis wrote on March 18 that "Drewyer was taken last night with a violent pain in his side. Capt. Clark blead him. Several of the men are complaining of being unwell. it is truly unfortunate they should be sick at the moment of our departure." Perhaps Drouillard's abdominal pain made Lewis think of Floyd's fatal illness.

Before leaving Fort Clatsop Clark described the custom of head-flattening practiced by the Indians of the lower Columbia:

> the most remarkable trait in their physiognomy is the peculiar flatness and width of the forehead which they artificially obtain by compressing the head between two boards while in a state of infancy, and from which it never afterwards perfectly recovers . . . I have observed the head of maney infants after this singular bandage had been dismissed, at about the age of 11 or 12 months, that were not more than two inches thick about the upper part of the forehead and reather thiner still higher from the top of the head to the extremity to the nose is one streight line. this is done in order to give a greater width to the forehead, which they must admire.[31]

---

[31] Kane also gives a vivid description of the head-flattening procedure: "The Chinooks and Cowlitz Indians carry a custom of flattening the head to a greater extent than any other of the Flat head tribes. The process is as follows: — The Indian mothers all carry their infants straped to a piece of board covered with moss or loose fibers of sea bark, and in order to flatten the head they place a pad on the infant's forehead, on the top of which is laid a piece of smooth bark, bound on by a leathern band passing through holes in the board on either side, and kept tightly pressed accross the front of the head, — a sort of pillow of grass or cedar fibers being placed under the back of the neck to support it. this process commences with the birth of the infant, and is continued for a period of from 8 to 12 months, by which time the head had lost its natural shape and acquired that of a wedge: the front of the skull flat and higher at the crown giving it a most unnatural appearance.

"It might be supposed, from the extent to which this is carried that the operation would be attended with great suffering to the infant, but I have never heard the

Lewis wrote on the 19th: ". . . the large or apparently swolen legs particularly observable in the women are obtained in a great measure by a cord tied around the ankle."

The Expedition had been stationed at Camp DuBois for five months and at Fort Clatsop for about three and one-half months. There were no descriptions of illnesses suggesting malaria, although this disease was endemic on the Columbia, and Lewis knew its manifestations from personal experience. Early journals of travel in the Oregon country reveal the presence of malaria at a later date.[32]

The men were ready to get on their way, except for two persistent invalids. Lewis wrote on March 20: "our sick men Willard and Bratton do not seem to recover; the former was taken with a violent pain in his leg and thye last night. Bratton is now so much reduced that I am somewhat uneasy with rispect to his recovery; the pain of which he complains most

---

infants crying or moaning, although I've seen the eyes seemingly starting out of the sockets from the great pressure. But, on the contrary, when the lashings were removed, I have noticed them cry until they were replaced. From the apparent dullness of the children while under the pressure I should imagine that a state of torpor or insensibility is induced, and the return to consciousness occasioned by its removal must be naturally followed by the sense of pain.

"This unnatural operation does not, however, seem to injure the health, the mortality amongst the Flathead children not being perceptibly greater than amongst other indian tribes; nor does it seem to injure their intellect. On the contrary, the Flatheads are generally considered fully as intelligent as the surrounding tribes, who allow their heads to preserve the natural shape, and it is from amongst the round heads that the Flatheads take their slaves, looking with contempt upon the white for having round heads, the Flathead being considered as a distinguishing mark of freedom." Paul Kane, *Wanderings of an Artist* (Rutland, Vt., 1858), pp. 123-24.

Townsend also has an interesting account of head flattening. *See* John K. Townsend, *Narrative of a Journey Across the Rocky Mountains,* pp. 175-77.

[32] "The epidemic ague . . . which has swept away great numbers of the natives, and proved an annual scourge to the whiteman, commenced, according to the best authorities, in 1830. Before that time it had never been known in the country, not even a single case." Townsend recounts the use of quinine and the ingenious trial of the native dogwood (Cornus Nuttali). *Ibid.,* pp. 241-42.

seems to be seated in the small of his back and remains obstinate. I believe that it is the rheumatism with which they are both afflicted." Clark apparently thought that their illness was due to want of proper food and added that "I expect when we get under way we shall be much more healthy. it has always had that effect on us heretofore." This last observation has been a constant experience of the armies of the world.

Clark probably expressed the feeling of all the men as they were getting ready to leave: "Altho' we have not fared sumptuously this winter and spring at Fort Clatsop, we have lived quite as comfortably as we had any reason to expect we should. . ."

XVI

Return Journey

. . . The army was always more healthy when in motion, than in fixed camps. James Tilton

I expect when we get under way that we shall be much more healthy. it has always had that effect on us heretofore. Meriwether Lewis [1]

March 23, 1806 — The captains and their men said goodbye to Fort Clatsop and turned their canoes against the current of the Columbia. They gave the fort to Chief Coboway of the Clatsops in appreciation for his friendly help. The personnel of the Expedition was still intact as it was when it left Fort Mandan. All were in comparatively good health except Bratton, who was so disabled with his back affliction that he could not do any work. Their food supply was "meager," and their merchandise for trading with the Indians was almost exhausted. There had been some speculation that President Jefferson would have a ship available to transport some of them home by sea. But the captains had long ago decided that they needed all of the men for the homeward journey — they were now a compact group, all needing each other.* And so, even though the memory of the arduous and hazardous de-

---

[1] Tilton, *Economical Observations*, p. 33. Thwaites, *Journals*, IV, p. 194.

* See E. G. Chuinard, "Thomas Jefferson and the Corps of Discovery: Could He Have Done More?" *Amer. West*, Vol. XII, No. 6, pp. 4-13. Lewis wrote on July 4, 1805, at Great Falls: "We have conceived our party sufficiently small and therefore have concluded not to dispatch a canoe with a part of our men to St. Louis as we had intended . . ." Thwaites, *Journals*, II, p. 209.

mands of the westward trip was still fresh in their minds, they faced the homeward journey with eagerness.

Travel going up the river was slower than coming down, and the Expedition spent more time with the Indians. Ordway wrote on March 24 "the Cathlah-mah village is the dirtiest & Stinkenest place I ever Saw." Again they experienced the problems of the high tide; Ordway wrote on March 26 that he twice had to carry his blankets to higher ground in order to avoid the rising tide. Their diet became more varied; dogs and wappato roots became more available to them. On March 29 Clark could write that Willard was quite well and Bratton much stronger.

Lewis wrote on March 30: "those people (Indians) are fond of cold, hot, & vapor baths of which they make frequent uce both in sickness and in health and at all seasons of year. they also have a very singular custom among them of bathing themselves all over with urine every morning."

The party was having trouble obtaining enough food to live on as they proceeded upriver, and information that the Indians above The Dalles were dying of hunger added to their concern and made them double their effort at hunting and rationing their food. On April 6 they halted to build scaffolds and collect firewood to dry an unexpected bounty of meat. They placed this dried meat in "shaved Elk Skins."

On April 8 Gass records that "some of the men are complaining of rheumatick pains; which are to be expected from wet and cold we suffered last winter, during which from the 4th of November 1805 to the 25th of March 1806, there were not more than 12 days in which it did not rain, and of these but six were clear."

Clark wrote on this same day:

I observed an Indian woman who visited us yesterday blind of an eye, and a man who was nearly blind of both eyes. the loss of sight I have observed to be more common among all the nations inhabiting this river than among any people I ever observed. they have almost invariably sore eyes at all stages of life. the loss of an eye is very common among them; blindness in persons of middle age is by no means uncommon, and it is almost invariably a concammitant of old age. I know not to what cause to attribute this prevalent deficientcy of the eye except it be their exposure to the reflection of the sun on the water to which they are constantly exposed in the occupation of fishing.

It is doubtful if the sun caused any eye trouble other than intermittent photophobia. The eye trouble of the Indians was probably from a variety of causes, including glaucoma, trachoma, gonorrheal infections and near-sightedness. These diseases produced blindness in a large number of them.

The main object of the captains at this time was to get back to the Nez Percé Indians to secure their horses and prepare to get over the Rocky Mountains.[2] Their main delay was at the Cascades and The Dalles. Here the portage was uphill, and the unloaded boats had to be pulled upward through the torrents of water; this was accomplished with the loss of only one boat. The thieving Indians had to be watched closely; even so, some articles were stolen. Lewis was particularly exasperated with the theft of his dog Scannon, which he retrieved by threatening to shoot some of the Indians. Above The Dalles food continued scarce, and the scarcity of wood for cooking and warmth was again a problem.

[2] The captains again missed the entrance to the Multnomah (Willamette) River, about which the Indians had informed them on their way west; both times they passed on the opposite side of three small islands which obscured its mouth. When they were told by the Indians that they had missed the Multnomah River again, Clark dropped back from their camp near the Sandy River with six corpsmen and York, and with the help of an Indian guide, briefly explored the river up to the site of present-day Portland. It is interesting to conjecture that if Clark had known about the Willamette Falls being only a few miles above Portland, whether he might have pushed on to see them; the distances indicated to him by the Indians had been deceptive.

By the time the men were at The Dalles they were relying on dogs for their main meat supply. Lewis confided to his journal on April 13: "the dog now constitutes a considerable part of our subsistence and with most of the party has become a favorite food; certain I am that it is a healthy strong diet, and from habit it has become by no means disagreeable to me, I prefer it to lean venison or Elk, and it is very far superior to the horse in any state."

Ordway wrote on April 15 that "Capt Lewis & Clark went on a small high Island to see a large burying ground they saw seven large sepulchers made of wood in a square form and by appearence is nearly a hundred persons piled in one on another with their robes Sowed round them, and all their heads down the River." This was Sepulchre Island, one of the burying grounds of the Klickitat Indians. For years future travelers would note and describe the smell when this island was passed. It is now almost covered by the waters behind the Bonneville Dam.

On April 18 Clark recorded an incident where their medical practice was a diplomatic aid:

> . . . I dressed the sores of the principal Chief gave some small things to his children and promised the chief some Medicine for to cure his sores. his wife who I found to be a sulky Bitch and was somewhat efflicted with pains in her back. this I thought a good oppertunity to get her on my side giveing her something for her back. I rubed a little camphere on her temples and back, and applyed worm flannel to her back which she thought had nearly restored her to her former feelings. this I thought a favourable time to trade with the chief who had more horses than all the nation besides. I accordingly made him an offer which he excepted and sold me two horses . . . as I had not slept but very little for the two nights past on account of mice & Virmen with which those indian houses abounded. . .

Bratton spent much of his travel up the Columbia River

lying in a canoe. Frequent notes were not made about his condition, but on April 20 Lewis wrote: "I had a load made up for seven horses, the eighth Bratton was compelled to ride as he was yet unable to walk . . . these people have yet a large quantity of fish on hand yet they will not let us have any but for an exorbitant price. we purchased 2 dogs and some shappellel from them."

Clark wrote on April 24 that "most of the party complain of their feet and legs this evening being very sore. it is no doubt caused by walking over the rough stone and deep sand after being accustomed to a soft soil. my legs and feet give me much pain. I bathed them in cold water from which I experienced considerable relief." The following day Gass concurred regarding the condition of the men's feet: "The men in general complain of their feet, being sore; and the officers had to go on foot to permit some of them to ride."

While among the Walla Walla Indians Clark wrote one of his best medical accounts, on April 28:

. . . they brought several disordered persons to us for whome they requested some medical aid. one had his knee contracted by the Rhumitism . . . another with a broken arm &c. to all of whome we administerd much to the gratification of those pore wretches, we gave them some eye water which I believe will render them more essential sirvice than any other article in the medical way which we had it in our power to bestow on them sore eyes seam to be a universal complaint among those people; I have no doubt but the fine sands of those plains and the river contribute such to the disorder. The man who had his arm broken had it lossely bound in a piece of leather without any thing to surport it. I dressed the arm which was broken short above the wrist & supported it with broad sticks to keep it in place, put [it] in a sling and furnished him with some lint bandages &c. to Dress it in future.

Lewis recorded Clark's treatment humorously in his casual

spelling: "Cap C Splintered the arm of the man which was broke."

This fracture "which was broken short above the wrist" was probably the one described by Abraham Colles, the Dublin surgeon, eight years later, and which today is usually designated as Colles' fracture. If the Lewis and Clark journals had been published promptly, this fracture might have been designated in medical literature as a Clark fracture. Neither Clark nor Colles had the advantage of x-ray demonstration of the exact nature of the fracture.[3]

On April 29 the Expedition camped on the Walla Walla River about one mile from its entrance to the Columbia. Clark recorded purchase of

> a store of 12 dogs for our voyage thru the plains. . . Several [of the Walla Walla Indians] applyed to me to day for medical aide, one a broken arm another inward fevers and several with pains across their loins, and sore eyes. I administered as well as I could to all. in the evening a man brought his wife who was verry unwell the effects of violent coalds was placed before me. I did not think her case a bad one and gave such medesene as would keep her body open and raped her in flannel.

Clark takes first prize for his interesting if not accurate spelling! He continues: "left some simple medesin to be taken. we also gave some Eye water 1 G(rain) of Ela v V. & 2 grs. of Sacchm Stry to an ounce of water and in that perportion."[4]

---

[3] Claude Pouteau of l'Hotel Dieu of Lyons, France, first described this fracture in 1783. This French publication was not recognized in the English speaking medical world for many years. The Colles fracture still is often referred to as the Pouteau fracture in French medical literature in Canada.

[4] Having been tutored by Dr. Rush, Lewis might have used a prescription found in *Rush's Quack Recipe Book:* For two quarts of eye-water: "Take one ounce of white vitriol and four scruple of sugar of lead. Infuse them in two quarts of snow melted (or springwater). Bathe the eyes with it 3 or 4 times a day and shake it every time before you use it. This is Wm. Alden's famous Recipe." Probably Clark did as well in treating the Indians' eye problems as did Rush for his son. On November 25, 1803, Rush wrote to his son James at Princeton: "I am sorry to hear

By the first of May, the Expedition was leaving the Walla Walla Indians, and immediately thereafter they had eaten all of their dried fish and dogs. Lewis wrote on May 2, "we made but a scant supper and had not anything for tomorrow." The following day Ordway wrote "made 28 miles this day, having nothing to eat bought the only dog the Indians had with them." Gass recorded the same comments and added that "we can kill no game in these plains."

On May 4 Lewis wrote that they halted for breakfast which was made of a couple of lean dogs, purchased with difficulty, and "a few large cakes of half cured bread made of a root which resembles the sweet potatoe, with these we made some soope and took breakfast." On this date he also wrote of a custom of the Nez Percé Indians in the treatment of their women during the time of the menses: "at all these lodges of the Chopunnish I observe an appendage of a small lodg with one fire which seems to be the retreat of their women in a certain situation . . . the men are not permitted to approach this lodge within a certain distance and if they have anything to convey to the occupants of this little hospital they stand at the distance of 50 or 60 paces and throw it towards them as far as they can and retire."

The medical practice of the two captains continued to afford them the only means of obtaining provisions from the Indians. Lewis wrote extensively on May 5 regarding this aspect of their journey while on the Kooskooskee (Clearwater) River:

> we passed an indian man [who] gave Capt. C. a very eligant grey mare for which he requested a phial of eyewater which was accordingly given him. while we were encamped last fall at the

that your eyes are diseased. Take a little physic, and abstain from eating meat and butter for a few days. Wash them at the same time frequently with cold water. When the inflammation is a little reduced, wash them in a solution of a scruple of sugar of lead in a common sized teacupful of water of green tea." *See* Butterfield, *Letters of Rush*, ɪɪ, p. 877.

entrance of the Chopunnish river Capt. C. . . . gave an indian man some volitile linniment to rub his k[n]ee and thye for
a pain of which he complained . . . the fellow soon after
recovered and has never ceased to extol the virtues of our medicines and the skill of my friend Capt. C. as a phisician. this
occurrence added to the benefit which many of them experienced
from the eyewater we gave them about the same time has given an
exalted opinion of our medicine. my friend Capt. C. is their
favorite phisician and has already received many applications. in
our present situation I think it pardonable to continue this desep-
tion for they will not give us any provision without compensation
in mercandize and our stock is now reduced to a mere handfull
. . . we had several applications to assist their sick which we
refused unless they would let us have some dogs or horses to eat.
a man [Chief] whose wife had an absess formed on the small of
her back promised a horse in the morning provided we would
administer to her accordingly Capt. C. opened the absess introduced a tent and dressed it with basilicon; (Capt. C. soon had
more than 50 applications) I prepared some dozes of the flour of
supher and creem of tarter which were given with directions to be
taken on each morning. [Clark wrote] those two cures has raised
my reputation and given those nativs an exolted oppinion of my
skill as a phi[si]cian.

Perhaps Doctors Lewis and Clark reached the acme of their
professional stature when they recorded, in defense of their
dispensing "eyewash" to the Indians that "we take care to give
them no article which can possible injure them." A great and
ancient precept for any practitioner of the healing arts is that
if one can not be sure of doing good, at least one should be as
certain as possible to do no harm.

Clark's medical practice continued throughout almost the
whole day of May 6: ". . . we received a second horse for
medecine & pro(s)cription to a little girl with the rhumitism
whome I had bathed in worm water, and anointed her a little
with balsom capivia (balsam Capaiboe) . . . I was bus-
ily imployed for several hours this morning in administering

eye water to a crowd of applicants. we once more obtained a plentiful meal, much to the comfort of all the party."

The Nez Percé (Chopunnish) Indians who lived in the area of what is now southwest Washington and adjacent Idaho greeted the returning explorers with their previous friendliness and help, although there was a problem in rounding up all the horses which the Expedition had left here the year before. These Indians provided the near-starving men with fat horses for food, without charge, and "a few roots of cows of which we made soape." Lewis wrote on May 10: "This is a much greater act of hospitality than we have witnessed from any nation or tribe since we have passed the Rocky Mountain," and could add "our men . . . have their s[t]omachs once more well filled with horsebeef and mush of the bread of cows." In return the two captain-physicians did all they could to care for the health problems of the natives. On May 11 Lewis wrote:

> many of the natives apply to us for medical aid which we gave them cheerfully so far as our skill and store of medicine would enable us. schrofela, ulsers, rheumatism, soar eyes, and the loss of the uce of their limbs are the most common cases among them. the latter case is not very common but we have seen th[r]ee instances of it among the Chopunnish. it is a very extraordinary complaint. a Chief of considerable note at this place has been afflicted with it for three years, he is incapable of moving a single limb but lies like a corps in whatever position he is placed, yet he eats heartily, digests his food perfectly, injoys his understanding, his pulse are good, and has retained his flesh almost perfectly, in short were it not that he appears a little pale from having lain so long in the shade he might well be taken for a man in good health. I suspect that their confinement to a diet of roots may give rise to all those disorders except the rheumatism & soar eyes, and to the latter of these, the state of debility incident to a vegetable diet may measureably contribute.

Ordway mentions on this date that "in evening we fiddled

and danced a while." This fiddling and dancing was a common release-recreation therapy used by these tired men, and often served as a friendly amusement to the Indians.

Lewis wrote on May 12 that "it was agreed between Capt. C. and myself that he should attend the sick as he was their favorite phisician . . ."

The captains had to hold their Expedition at "Camp Chopunnish"[5] from May 13 till June 10 while impatiently waiting for the snow to melt sufficiently to permit them to cross the Rocky Mountains. They were disturbed about the difficulty in accumulating food supplies to carry them over the mountains, correctly anticipating that the travel would be more difficult on the return journey because of tramping through the snow, and because the snow might also serve to obliterate the trail. They could not expect to kill much game along the high trail, and snow would make it almost impossible to obtain forage for their horses. Although the men never relished portable soup, they would be glad to have it in the high mountains on the return journey. In places the snow was so deep and packed so firmly that it provided help in traveling by covering rocks and fallen timber. Lewis' concern to get over the mountains early enough to be able to return home the same year prompted him to lead the Expedition into the mountains against the advice of the Nez Percés. They were forced with great disappointment to store much of their supplies and turn back to a lower camp (which they called Camp

---

[5] Wheeler writes: "After Forts Mandan and Clatsop, Camp Chopunnish and vicinity was the place to which the expedition remained the longest, after leaving Wood River, and here they were, perhaps, more happily circumstanced, all things considered, than at any other point. They were in a beautiful valley, the hunting was fairly good, there were plenty of fat horses and nutritious roots to be had and at reasonable prices, and they were among the finest lot of Indians, the most intelligent and manly, that they met in all their journeyings. The latter had all the hospitality of the Shoshoni, with a much higher order of intelligence and nobility. Wheeler, *Trail*, ii, p. 268.

Chopunnish after the Chopunnish, or Nez Perces) and wait another three weeks for favorable weather. This waiting time had the advantage of permitting the men to rest, and the captain-physicians to give better attention to the health problems of the Indians and the corpsmen.

All of the required health care was not directed toward the Indians. Lewis wrote on May 15 that "Frazier, J. Fields and Wiser complain of violent pains in their heads, and Howard and York are afflicted with the cholic. I attribute these complaints to their diet of roots (to) which they have not been accustomed . . ." The captains were also called upon to be veterinarians: "Several of the horses which were gelded yesterday are much swolen particularly those cut by Drewyer, the others bled most but appear much beter today than the others." Lewis had written of the castration procedure done by the Indians on May 14: "One of the indians present offered his services on this occasion. he cut them without tying the string of the stone as is usual, and assures us that they will do much better in that way; he takes care to scrape the string clean from all adhering veigns before he cuts it. we shall have an opportunity of judging whether this is a method preferable to that commonly practiced. . ." Apparently this method was preferable — Lewis was to lose one of his horses castrated by Drouillard because of infection. He records having to shoot the horse on June 2, and states "I have no hesitation in declaring my beleif that the indian method of gelding is preferable to that practised by ourselves."

Ordway recounted on May 14 how the Expedition ingeniously solved the problems of hunger and mean horses: "we eat several of our stud horses as they have been troublesome to us." And again on the sixteenth he wrote, "we eat two more of our unruly stud horses . . . killed two deer."

The importance of the captains' medical services in diplom-

acy and trading is emphasized by Lewis' note of May 21 that
"each man's stock in trade amounts to no more than one awl,
one Knitting pin, a half an ounce of vermillion, two nedles, a
few scanes of th[r]ead, and about a yard of ribbon; a slender
stock indeed with which to lay in a store of provision for that
dreary wilderness."

The captain-physicians' practice had been mainly among
their own men and the Indians, but they were now called
upon to act as pediatricians to Sacagawea's very sick child,
who had a large abscess on his neck. Lewis wrote on May 22,
1806: "Charbono's Child is very ill this evening; he is cuting
teeth, and for several days past has had a violent lax, which
having suddonly stopped he was attacked with a high fever
and his neck and throat are much swolen this evening. we
gave him a doze of creem of tartar and flour of sulpher and
applyed a poltice of boiled onions to his neck as warm as he
could well bear it." Clark wrote that the little boy "is dangerously ill." — and indeed he was; good doctoring, good mother's
care, and good luck saved this little fellow for an interesting
saga all his own.

The next day Lewis recorded that

the Creem of tartar and sulpher operated several times on the
child in the course of the last night, he is considerable better this
morning, tho' the swelling of the neck has abated but little; we
still apply pol[t]ices of onions which we renew frequently in the
course of the day and night, at noon we were visited by 4 indians
who informed us they had come from their village on Lewis's river
at the distance of two days ride in order to see us and obtain a
little eyewater, Capt. C. washed their eyes and they set out on
their return to their village. our skill as phisicians and virtue of
our medicines have been spread it seems to a great distance.
I sincerely wish it was in our power to give releif to these poor
aff[l]icted wretches.

Sacagawea's child showed no real improvement the next
day, and Lewis wrote: "The child was very wrestless last

night; it's jaw and the back of its neck are much more swolen
than they were yesterday tho' his fever has abated considerably. we gave it a doze of creem of tartar and applyed a fresh
poltice of onions."

May 24 was an important day in the medical care of a
chronically ailing member of the Expedition. William Bratton
had been continuously ill since he returned to Fort Clatsop
from the salt cairn. It had been necessary to transport him by
canoe and horseback, because walking was too painful for
him. Lewis wrote on May 24:

> William Bratton still continues very unwell; he eats heartily digests
> his food well, and has recovered his flesh almost perfectly yet is so
> weak in the loins that he is scarcely able to walk, nor can he set
> upwright but with the greatest pain. we have tried every remidy
> which our engenuity could devise, or with which our stock of
> medicines furnished us, without effect. John Sheilds observed that
> he had seen men in a similar situation restored by violent sweats.
> Bratton requested that he might be sweated in the manner pro-
> posed by Sheilds to which we consented. Sheilds sunk a circular
> hole of 3 feet in diamiter and four feet deep in the earth. he
> kindled a large fire in the hole and heated well, after which the
> fire was taken out a seat placed in the center of the hole for the
> patient with a board at bottom for his feet to rest on; some hoops
> of willow poles were bent in an arch crossing each other over the
> hole, on these several blankets were thrown forming a secure and
> thick orning of about 3 feet high. the patient being striped naked
> was seated under this orning in the hole and the blankets well
> secured on every side. the patient was furnished with a vessell of
> water which he sprinkles on the bottom and sides of the hole and
> by that means creates as much steam or vapor as he could possibly
> bear, in this situation he was kept about 20 minutes after which he
> was taken out and suddonly plunged in cold water twise and was
> then immediately returned to the sweat hole where he was con-
> tinued three quarters of an hour longer then taken out covered up
> in several blankets and suffered to cool gradually. this experiment
> was made yesterday; Bratton feels himself much better and is
> walking about today and says he is nearly free from pain.

DeVoto states regarding Bratton's illness: "the symptoms and the nature of the cure suggest an inflamation or a strain of the sacroiliac joint." [6] In a footnote he adds "one of the medical men I have consulted rejects this diagnosis, and suggests that Bratton's weakness and backache resulted from the severe abdominal infection suffered at the camp of the Salt makers." [7] Probably DeVoto's diagnosis is more accurate than that of his phantom physician friend. Lewis and Clark showed in their notes regarding the illnesses of Sergeant Floyd and Sacagawea that they could recognize abdominal symptoms and findings and directed treatment to the abdomen. There is no record of Bratton having nausea and vomiting. It is ridiculous to think that the captains would record Bratton as having pain in his back, and treat his back, if his condition was intra-abdominal.

Other diagnoses which are more reasonable than that of an intra-abdominal condition include a herniated inter-vertebral disc, and an infection of a intervertebral disc with osteomyelitis of the adjacent vertebral margins. Bratton did not have a herniated disc syndrome as it is recognized today, on the basis of symptoms described by the captains; a herniated disc is possible without leg symptoms, although this is atypical. The presence of fever is consistent with a diagnosis of an intervertebral disc infection, and the prolonged severe disability and the spontaneous recovery (disregarding the sweathouse as a cause of the cure) is consistent with this diagnosis.

The following day, May 25, Sacagawea's baby was "more unwell than yesterday . . . we gave it a doze of creem

---

[6] DeVoto, *Journals*, p. 314.

[7] Brown also suggests that Bratton had intra-abdominal trouble: "William Bratton . . . came very near dying of an ailment which modern medical men believe was a severe abdominal infection combined with sacroiliac pain." D. Alexander Brown, *The Great Adventure* (Gettysburg, 1970), p. 20. Perhaps Brown picked up this opinion from DeVoto.

of tartar which did not operate, we therefore gave it a clyster in the evening." Bratton, however, was improved. The apparently paralyzed chief was brought to the captains, and they proposed to treat him as they did Bratton. They could not follow through with this treatment because he was unable to sit upright in the sweat hole. Palliative treatment consisted of giving him some horse mint. Lewis conjectured "I am confident that this would be an excellent subject for electricity and much regret that I have it not in my power to supply it." This reference to electricity indicates that Lewis had become conversant with the electrical experimentations of Benjamin Franklin [8] while he was in Philadelphia, and perhaps talked

[8] Benjamin Franklin's versatile interests and abilities included many medical subjects. He invented bifocal glasses and the flexible urinary catheter, and wrote intelligently about the common cold. See William Pepper, M.D., The Medical Side of Benjamin Franklin (Philadelphia, 1911), pp. 31-32. In Pepper's book are recorded several letters in which Franklin related the use of electricity in the treatment of paralytic cases. Franklin wrote the following letter to Sir John Pringle (British physician, 1707-1782) regarding the use of electricity: "Sir — in compliance with your request, I send you the following account of what I can recollect relating to the effects of electricity in paralytic cases, which have fallen under my observation. Some years since, when the newspapers made mention of great cures performed in Italy and Germany, by means of electricity, a number of paralytics were brought to me from different parts of Pennsylvania, and the neighboring provinces, to be electrised. which I did for them at their request. My method was, to place the patient first in a chair, on an electric stool, and draw a number of sparks from all parts of the effected limb or side. Then I fully charged two six gallon glass jars, each of which had about three square feet of surface coated; and I sent the stroke commonly three times each day. The first thing observed, was an immediate greater sensible warmth in the lame limbs that had received the stroke, than in the others; and the next morning the patients usually related that they had in the night felt a pricking sensation in the flesh of the paralytic limbs; and would sometimes shew a number of small red spots, which they supposed were occasioned by those prickings. The limbs, too, were found more capable of voluntary motion and seemed to receive strength. A man, for instance, who could not the first day lift the lame hand from off his knee, would the next day raise it four or five inches, the third day higher; and on the fifth day was able, but with a feeble languid motion to take off his hat. These appearance gave great spirits to the patients, and made them hope a perfect cure; but I do not remember that I ever saw any amendment after the fifth day; which the patients perceiving, and finding the shock pretty severe, they be-

with Dr. Franklin about the possible clinical use of it. Lewis records on May 26 that "the Clyster given the Child last evening operated very well. it is clear of fever this evening and is much better, the swelling is considerably abated and appears as if it would pass off without coming to a head. we still continue fresh poltices of onions to the swolen part." The following day Sacagawea's son was much better, though the swelling on the side of his neck "I believe will terminate an ugly imposthume [an abscess] a little below the ear." This may indicate that the little boy had either an external abscess on the side of the neck, or mastoiditis.[9] There is no information about this boy's future life to indicate that he had chronic drainage or impairment of hearing, which often occur as sequels to an acute mastoiditis.

These days of illness were the most difficult times of health

came discouraged, went home, and in a short time relapsed; so that I never knew any advantage from electricity in palsies that was permanent. And how far the apparent temporary advantage might arise from the exercise in the patient's journey, and coming daily to my house, or from the spirits given by the hope of success, enabling them to exert more strength in moving their limbs, I will not pretend to say. Perhaps some permanent advantage might have been obtained, if the electric shocks had been accompanied with proper medicine and regimen, under the direction of a skillful physician. It may be, too, that a few great strokes, as given in my method, may not be so proper as many small ones; since, by the account from Scotland of a case, in which two hundred shocks from a phial were given daily, it seems that a permanent cure has been made. As to any uncommon strength supposed to be in the quantity of surface of glass coated; so that my shocks from those large jars must have been much greater than any that could be received from a phial held in the hand. I am, with great respect, sir. Your most obedient servant, B. Franklin."

Franklin had performed his famous experiment of drawing electricity from the sky with a kite and key in 1752.

The use of electricity for therapeutic purposes gained a wide following very rapidly. Dr. Archibald Currie of Richmond in 1800 offered "to The Faculty his 'electrical machine for medical purposes,' designed to treat paralysis, blindness, deafness and apparently any disease that hithertoo had been thought incurable." Quoted from Blanton's *Medicine in Virginia*, p. 336.

9 Coues thinks the baby may have had the mumps. Coues, *History of Lewis and Clark*, III, p. 823.

care for Sacagawea's infant; no doubt he was near death at times as indicated by the captains concerned notes in their journals. And throughout these days as with every day along the journey, Sacagawea had to provide the routine sanitary care of the baby; even though she contributed many things to the Expedition, care of the infant was her own particular responsibility. The captains and the other diarists do not relate anything about what Sacagawea did for routine sanitary care of little Pomp. She probably followed the usual custom of Indian mothers who mainly used the skin of various animals as diapers and filled these with absorbent materials such as cattail fuzz. The Mandan, Hidatsa and Arikara Indians, from whom Sacagawea probably learned a mother's techniques, used moss in the diapers. The skin diapers were cared for by routine washing. No doubt Sacagawea was a busy mother during the days of Pomp's severe illness, and his recovery must be attributed to her mother's care and his endurance and natural resistance, as well as to the prescriptions of the captain-physicians.

The men were waiting impatiently for reports that the snows had receded enough to permit them to get over the mountains. They were still disturbed about the difficulty in accumulating food supplies to carry them over the mountains; they could not expect to kill much game along the high trail, and snow would make it almost impossible to obtain forage for their horses. All along the return journey they had hoped the salmon run would catch up with them, but in this they were to be disappointed.

On June 5, 1806, Clark wrote: "We gave the Indian Chief another sweat to-day, continuing it as long as he could bear it, in the evening he was vary languid but still (continued) to improve in the use of his limbs. the Child is recovering fast. I applied a plaster of sarve (salve) made of the rozen of the long leafed pine, Beaswax and Bears oil mixed, which has subsided the inflomation entirely, the part is considerably swelled and hard." Where did Clark get the "Beaswax"? There is no listing of this item among any of the supplies, medical and otherwise, procured by Lewis from the Schuylhill Arsenal in Philadelphia. Was the beeswax obtained along with other medical items supposed to have been supplied by Dr. Saugrain in St. Louis? Or did the captains procure it from a "bee tree," as did other frontiersmen? Whitehouse gives the only clue; while at Fort Clatsop he wrote on March 9, 1805, "Several of the Natives came to the fort. They brought with them Some Small fish, Bees Wax &ca. to trade with us."[10]

Lewis wrote on June 8 of the patients' continued improvement: "The sick Chief is fast on the recovery, he can bear his weight on his legs, and has acquired a considerable portion of strength. the child is nearly well;[11] Bratton has so far recovered that we cannot well consider him an invalid any longer, he has had a tedious illness which he boar with much fortitude and firmness." Bratton indeed fully recovered — he served in the War of 1812 and fathered ten children.[12] On June 11 Lewis complained that the quamash root "is pallateable but disagrees with me in every shape I have ever used it."

On June 18, poor Potts was in trouble again. Lewis wrote: "we had not proceeded far this morning before Potts cut his leg very badly with one of the large knives; he cut one of the large veigns on the inner side of the leg; I found much difficulty in stoping the blood which I could not effect untill

[10] From unpublished portion of Whitehouse journal seen at the Newberry Lby., Chicago. For an account of this journal see Cutright, "Whitehouse," pp. 146-47.

[11] Little Pomp was the only member of the Expedition to return to Oregon, where he died and is buried. See Anderson, "Charbonneau," pp. 247-64.

[12] See biographical sketch of William E. Bratton in Clarke, The Men of the Lewis and Clark Expedition, p. 43.

I applyed a tight bandage with a little cushon of wood and tow on the veign below the wound." The above notes reveal Lewis' knowledge of anatomy and treatment for hemorrhage — he applied pressure on the vein below the laceration. Ordway wrote in his diary that "Lewis Sowed up the wound and bound it up." There is no mention in the list of medical supplies of surgical needles or sutures. If Lewis did suture the wound he probably used regular darning needles and thread — and very dirty they would have been, as nothing at that time was known about bacteriology and sepsis. Potts probably developed infection, both a cellulitis and phlebitis, as indicated by Lewis' journal entry of June 22: "Pott's legg is inflamed and very painfull to him. we apply poltice of roots and Cows.

Lewis recorded an accident of Colter's on June 18: "Colter's horse fel with him in passing hungry creek and himself and horse were driven down the creek a considerable distance rolling over each other among the rocks. fortunately (he) escaped without injury or the loss of his gun."

On June 24 the captains again started to take their Expedition over the mountains and by the twenty-sixth they were again back at their point of farthest advance where they had stored some of their baggage nine days previously. They frankly acknowledged that they would be hopelessly lost without the Nez Percé guides. However, Lewis became concerned about one of the guides, writing on June 25, "We collected our horses readily and set out at an early hour this morning. one of our guides complained of being unwell, a symptom which I did not much like as such complaints with an indian is generally the prelude to his abandoning any enterprize with which he is not well pleased. we left them at our encampment and they promised to pursue us in a few hours." Lewis was gratified a little later to find that his concern was unwarranted. Clark wrote "our guides overtook us. indians continue with us and I beleive are disposed to be faithfull to their engagements. Cap. L. gave the si(ck) indian a buffaloe robe he having no other covering except his mockersons and a dressed Elk skin without the hair."

By the twenty-seventh Lewis could write that "Potts's legg which has been much swolen and inflamed for several days is much better this evening and gives him but little pain. we applyed the pounded roots and leaves of the wild ginger from which he found great relief."

On June 29 the men were well down out of the snow, and they found that the hunters who preceded them had left them a deer, and they also came to a hot spring in which they indulged themselves with warm baths.

On June 30 Lewis had another accident which might have cost him his life. He notes in his journal: ". . . this morning on the steep side of a high hill my horse sliped with both his hinder feet out of the road and fell, I also fell off backwards and slid near 40 feet down the hill before I could stop myself such was the steepness of the declivity; the horse was near falling on me in the first instance but fortunately recovers and we both escaped unhirt. . ."

The Expedition arrived back at Traveller's Rest, in good hunting country. Clark paid farewell to the mountains: "Decended the mountain to Travellers rest leaveing these tremendious mountains behind us, in passing of which we have experienced cold and hunger of which I shall ever remember . . . our food was horses of which we eate three." On the following day the hunters brought in thirteen deer — too much to eat in one day, so most of it was "fleeced and exposed in the sun on poles to dry."

On the way west Lewis and Clark had become informed about Indian roads which led directly east and west between

Lolo Pass and the Great Falls. They formulated definite plans while at Fort Clatsop that on the return journey they would divide the Expedition's men at Traveller's Rest and Lewis would take the Indian road toward Great Falls and explore the Marias River while Clark would take the main portion of the Expedition overland to the head of Jefferson River where their canoes had been cached. These canoes were to be used by Sergeant Ordway and nine men to descend the Missouri River and join Lewis at the Great Falls. This left Clark with ten men; they crossed overland from Three Forks to the Yellowstone River. On this trip Clark and his men went through what is now Bozeman Pass, which was pointed out to Clark by Sacagawea. Sergeant Pryor with Shannon, Windsor, and Hall were designated by Clark to take the horses overland to the Mandan village to be used as barter to induce some of the Mandan chiefs to accompany the Expedition back to St. Louis. This left five of the men along with Charbonneau, Sacagawea and Baptiste under the direction of Clark to descend the Yellowstone River, where the captains hopefully expected to bring the entire corps together again.

It is interesting that Lewis used medical reasons to make up the small contingent of men who would go with him. He writes on July 2 that "Goodrich and McNeal are both very unwell with the pox which they contracted last winter with the Chinook women. This forms my inducement principally for taking them to the falls of the Missouri where during an interval of rest they can use the mercury freely." Ordway mentioned on July 2 that "2 Invalleeds in going to the falls to Stay their untill the party comes down with the canoes." The "2 Invalleeds," of course, were Goodrich and McNeal. They undoubtedly medicated themselves with a mercury salve. These two men seem to have been the main ones with continuing trouble with "the veneral," although on January 14,

1805 Lewis recorded "several" men "with the Venereal cought from the Mandan women." On January 27, 1806, Goodrich was recorded as having the "Louis veneri" and four days later McNeal was noted to have "the pox." These were undoubtedly fresh infections as the skin eruptions would not be due to an infection contracted a year before, and Lewis assigns the infection to the "Chinook women." Lewis states Goodrich was cured with mercury "as was Gibson." These are the only men of the Expedition who were specifically mentioned as having syphilis, but it is very improbable that the venereal census was so low, since none of the diarists admit to having the disease!

On July 3, 1806, Lewis wrote in his journal: "I took leave of my worthy friend and companion Capt. Clark and the party that accompanied him. I could not avoid feeling much concern of this occasion although I hoped the seperation was only momentary." Lewis had nine men and five Indians with him. He went northeast along the Hellgate and Blackfoot rivers and dropped down to Great Falls along the Sun River. He then went east a few miles to pick up the Marias River, the mouth of which they had explored on the way west. On this trip he crossed from the Hellgate to the Sun River via what is now known as the Lewis and Clark Pass. Clark never saw this pass; there are many other passes both explorers traversed and which could have been more appropriately named for both of them.

All components of the divided corps were again in buffalo country, and were also able to find deer, so that food was plentiful. By July 11 Lewis and his men had reached the region of the White Bear islands above the portage of the Great Falls. Here they made bull boats out of buffalo hides and willow strips and crossed the river, swimming their horses with them. When they opened the cache on the thirteenth,

Lewis was greatly disappointed to find that high water had flooded it and destroyed much of his equipment, particularly "all my specimens of plants." Almost everything was damaged, but many things were partly salvageable. Lewis notes that "the stoper had come out of a phial of Laudinum and the contents had run into the drawer and distroyed a gre[at] part of my medicine in such a manner that it was past recovery."

Wheeler attributes to good luck a great portion of the success of the Expedition.[13] This good luck is well exemplified in the repeated encounters with grizzly bears. Many times one or two men of the Expedition would wander off alone, or be sent on a specific mission. On July 15, Lewis sent McNeal on horseback to inspect a cache. When McNeal came upon a grizzly bear and was thrown by the frightened horse directly in front of the bear, he clubbed the bear with his gun, breaking it, then climbed a tree and waited for the bear to leave in order to save himself. He found his horse and returned safely to camp.

Lewis and his companions were getting back into mosquito country. On the fifteenth Lewis wrote: "the musquetoes continue to infest us in such manner that we can scarcely exist; for my own part I am confined by them to my bier at least ¾ths of my time. my dog even howls with the torture he experiences from them, they are almost insupportable, they are so numerous that we frequently get them in our thr[o]ats as we breath."

On July 18 Lewis and Drouillard and the two Field brothers were making their way overland to the Marias River, leaving the rest of their party at the upper end of the falls to await the arrival of Sergeant Ordway with the men who would separate from Clark at the three forks of the Missouri (while Clark went up the Gallatin River and cut across

13 Wheeler, *Trail*, i, p. 46.

through Bozeman Pass to the Yellowstone). Lewis was now in the country of the Blackfeet Indians, the most ferocious of all the red men. He was hoping that the upper reaches of the Marias River might afford some connection with the Saskatch-ewan and perhaps a better portage to the Pacific Ocean than they had already traversed. They were also getting north of the buffalo country; they soon consumed their meat reserve, and had to get along with pigeons and "cows."

On July 26 Lewis saw a large band of horses on a hill, and his spy glass revealed Indians among them. He knew that he was outnumbered, and that these few Indians and horses might be only a small part of a larger hunting party. Lewis again had to demonstrate his sagacity and diplomacy with the Indians:

> this was a very unpleasant sight, however I resolved to make the best of our situation and to approach them in a friendly manner . . . the Indians soon asked to smoke with us . . . as it was growing late in the evening I proposed that we should remove to the nearest part of the river and encamp together . . . I took the first watch tonight and set up untill half after eleven; the indians by this time were all asleep, I roused up R. Fields and laid down myself; . . . this being done I feel into a profound sleep and did not wake untill the noise of the men and the indians awoke me a little after light in the morning.

Under the date of July 27 Lewis continues his description of the encounter with the Indians. The Indians were trying to get away with their firearms:

> R. Fields as he seized his gun stabed the indian to the heart with his knife the fellow ran about 15 steps and fell dead . . . I reached to seize my gun but found her gone, I then drew a pistol from my holster and terning myself about saw the indian making off with my gun I ran at him with my pistol and bid him lay down my gun which he was in the act of doing when the Fieldses re-turned and drew up their gun to shoot him which I forbid as he did not appear to be about to make any resistance or commit any

offensive act, he droped the gun and walked slowly off, . . . as soon as they found us all in possession of our arms they ran and indeavored to drive off all the horses . . . I called to them . . . that I would shoot them if they did not give me my horse and raised my gun, one of them jumped behind a rock and spoke to the other who turned arround and stoped at the distance of 30 steps from me and I shot him through the belly, he fell to his knees and on his wright elbow from which position he partly raised himself up and fired at me, and turning himself about crawled in behind a rock which was a few feet from him. he overshot me, being bearheaded I felt the wind of his bullet very distinctly. not having my shotpouch I could not reload my piece and . . . therefore returned leasurely towards camp . . . my design was to hasten to the entrance of Maria's River as quick as possible in the hope of meeting with the canoes and party at that place having no doubt but that they [the Indians] would pursue us with a large party . . . after refreshing ourselves we again set out by moonlight and traveled leasurely, heavy thunderclouds lowered arround us on every quarter but that from which the moon gave us light. we continued to pass immence herds of buffaloe all night as we had done in the latter part of the day. we traveled untill 2 OCk in the morning having come by my estimate after dark about 20 ms. we now turned out our horses and laid ourselves down to rest in the plain very much fatiegued. . .

It is doubtful if a more impressive scenario has ever been written for a western thriller than what happened to Lewis and his men on July 28. Lewis records it thusly in his journal:

I slept sound but fortunately awoke as day appeared . . . I was so soar from my ride yesterday that I could scarcely stand, and the men complained of being in a similar situation however I encouraged them by telling them that our own lives as well as those of our friends and fellow travellers depended on our exertions at this moment . . . I . . . told them that . . . if we were attacked in the plains . . . that the bridles of the horses should be tied together and we would stand and defend them, or sell our lives as dear as we could . . . we heared the report of several rifles very distinctly on the river to our right, we quickly repared to this joyfull sound and on arriving at the bank

of the river had the unspeakable satisfaction to see our canoes
coming down. we hurried down from the bluff on which we were
and joined them . . . Wiser had cut his leg badly with a
knife and was unable in consequence to work. we descended the
river opposite to our principal cash which we proceeded to open
. . . the gunpowder corn flour poark and salt had sustained
but little injury the parched meal was spoiled or nearly so . . .
we encamped late but having little meat I sent out a couple of
hunters who soon returned with a sufficient quantity of the flesh
of a fat cow.

However exhausted Lewis may have been following his
long ride to get away from the Blackfeet, he did not have a
chance to rest. He wrote on July 29: "Shortly after dark last
evening a violent storm came on from N.W. attended with rain
hail Thunder and lightning. Which continued the greater part
of the night. No(t) having the means of making a shelter
I lay in the water all night."

The men were now back in good hunting and eating country. On July 31 they killed fifteen Elk and fourteen deer. Not
until August 2 did Lewis halt his party to rest and dry their
supplies and animal hides. On August 3, twenty-five deer fell
under the guns of the two Field brothers. The men were
coasting rapidly down the Missouri, with no mishaps except
a close escape for Willard when he was thrown from a canoe.
They reached the entrance of the Yellowstone on August 7;
here Lewis found evidence that Captain Clark had arrived
before him.

After separating from Lewis at Traveller's Rest, Clark went
southeast to hit the Yellowstone River. At this time Sacagawea
definitely was helpful as a guide, pointing out to Clark what
is now Bozeman's Pass. On the very first day of Clark's sep-
aration from Lewis, July 3, he writes that "Jo: Potts very
unwell this evening owing to rideing a hard trotting horse:
I gave him a pill of opiom which soon releve(d) him."

Clark did not forget the 4th of July. He wrote: "This being the day of the decleration of Independence of the United States and Day commonly celebrated by my Country I had every disposition to selebrate this day and therefore halted early and partook of a Sumptious Dinner of a fat Saddle of Venison and Mush of Cows (roots) after Dinner we proceeded on. . ." On July 5, Clark wrote that his trunk got wet and several articles got wet, "also an osortment of Medicine. . ." On the 8th Ordway "lay down to sleep fatigued, rideing upwards of 40 miles this day. And nothing to eat this evening but the head of a goat or antelope which the party had droped on the road."

Clark and his men got along very well without undue accidents until July 18. Clark's journal entry of this day states that:

Shabono was thrown from his horse to day in pursute of a Buffaloe, the ho[r]se unfortunately steping into a Braroe hole fell and threw him over his head. he is a good deel brused on his hip sholder & face. . . Gibson in attempting to mount his horse after Shooting a deer this evening fell and on a Snag and sent it nearly [two] inches into the Muckeler part of his thy. he informs me this snag was about 1 inch in diameter burnt at the end. this is a very bad wound and pains him exceeding. I dressed the wound.

Ordway was having his troubles on the same date, writing that "the Musquetoes and Small flyes are verry troublesome. my face and eyes are Swelled by the poison of those insects which bite verry severe indeed." He adds that "we make fires of buffaloe dry dung to make Smoaks & C."

The following day Gibson's wound was very painful; Clark

. . . rose early and dressed Gibsons wound he slept but very little last night and complains of great pain in his Kne and hip as well as his thy . . . conclude to take Gibson in a litter if he is not able to ride on down the river untill I can find a tree Sufficiently large [for making a canoe] . . . had the strongest and

jentlest Horse Saddled and placed Skins & blankets in such a
manner that when he was put on the horse he felt himself in as
easy a position as when lying. this was a fortunate circumstance as
he could be much more at ease than in a litter . . . I proceeded
on about 9 miles, and halted to let the horses graze and let Gibson
rest. his leg become So numed. from remaining in one position, as
to render [it] extreemly painfull to him. I derected Shields to . . .
hunt for some Wild Ginger for a Poltice for Gibson's wound.

Surely Clark gave Gibson some opium to lessen his pain.

On July 20 things were looking up: "Sergt. Pryor dressed
Some Skins to make him Clothes. Gibsons wound looks well.
I dressed it. The horses being fatigued and their feet very
Sore, I shall let them rest a fiew days. during which time the
party . . . will dress their skins and make themselves
clothes to ware, as they are nearly naked." Gibson continued to improve so that Clark could write on July 21: "I am
in great hope that it will get well in time for him to accompany Sgt. Pryor with the horses to the Mandans." Gibson did
not improve sufficiently to go with Pryor, who took Shannon,
Windsor and Hall with him. They literally "went to sleep on
the job," permitting the Crow Indians to steal the remainder
of their horses. They were now afoot and alone; but the ingenious men made themselves two bullboats [14] and floated on

---

[14] Clark describes the making of the bullboats from buffalo bulls killed by Shannon: "2 Sticks of 1¼ inch diameter is tied together so as to form a round hoop of
the size you wish the canoe, or as large as the Skin will allow to cover, two of those
hoops are made one for the top or brim and the (other) for the bottom the deabth
you wish the canoe, then Sticks of the same size are crossed at right angles and
fastened with a throng to each hoop and also where each Stick crosses each other.
then the Skin when green is drawn tight over this fraim and fastened with throngs
to the brim or outer hoop so as to form a perfect bason. one of those canoes will
carry 6 or 8 Men and their loads. Those two canoes are nearly the same size 7 feet
3 inches diameter and 16 inches deep 15 ribs or cross Sticks in each. Sergt. Pryor
informs me that the cause of his building two Canoes was for fear of one meating
with some accedent in passing down the rochejhone a river entirely unknown to
either of them by which means they might loose their guns and ammunition and
be left entirely destitute of the means of precureing food. he informed me that they

down the Yellowstone to join Clark.

Gibson was able to walk by July 30. This apparently had been a deep and jagged wound, and he, like Lewis later with his gunshot wound, was most fortunate not to develop a deep infection.

Clark and his crew were making good time, having only the problems that could be expected of frontiersmen of their time; he writes on August 3: "last night the Musquetors was so troublesom that no one of the party Slept half the night. for my part I did not sleep one hour. Those tormenting insects found their way into My beare and tormented me the whole night. They are not less noumerous or troublesom this morning. . ."[15]

The mosquitoes continued to cause suffering and inconvenience. Clark wrote on August 4: "the child of Shabono has been so much bitten by the Musquetors that his face is much puffed up & Swelled," and again he writes that "the Musquetors was so noumerous that I could not keep them off my gun long enough to take sight. . ."[16] A drenching rain

passed through the worst parts of the rapids and Shoals in the river without takeing a drop of water, and waves raised from the hardest winds dose not effect them." Thwaites, *Journals*, v, p. 326.

[15] A century later, a student of the Lewis and Clark Expedition was having similar trouble with mosquitoes. Eva Emory Dye, author of *The Conquest*, while researching her story, wrote to her husband in Oregon City from Madison, Wisc., on July 10, 1902: "The mosquitoes here are something terrible. I am all bit up, have to bind rags wet in ammonia on to get any comfort. They bite right thro ones clothes. And it swells into great lumps." From the Dye Mss., Oreg. Hist. Soc.

[16] Antoine Tabeau also recorded a similar annoyance from the mosquitoes when he was a resident trader among the Arikaras in 1804: "During the whole day the boats were enveloped as in a cloud [of mosquitoes] and the *engages*, who were compelled by the extreme heat to keep the body naked, were covered with blood and swellings. Often our hunters not being able to endure them, returned at full speed to throw themselves into the boats. What is more they could not aim their weapons when covered with these insects." Annie Heloise Abel, *Tabeau's Narrative of Loisel's Expedition to the Upper Missouri River* (Norman: Univ. of Ok. Press, 1939), p. 63.

"which wet us all" drove the mosquitoes away "which is a joyful circumstance to the party."

On August 8, Clark was surprised to have Pryor and his men come "floating down the river in two canoes." The sergeant had to explain his predicament and the loss of horses to his Captain.

The Expedition had eaten wolf meat on several occasions during the journey, and found it not too unpalatable. Sergeant Pryor did not feel too well toward this animal, however: ". . . the night after the horses had been stolen a Wolf bit Sergt. Pryor through the hand when asleep, and this animal was so vicious as to make an attempt to seize Windsor, when Shannon fortunately Shot him. Sergt. Pryers had has nearly recovered." (Clark, August 8.)

When Clark brought his canoes out of the Yellowstone into the Missouri he thought that Lewis and the other men must surely be ahead of them, so pushed on; however, Lewis was behind them.

The Expedition had traversed the Rocky Mountains and what is now the State of Montana on both the outward and return trips. Nowhere in the journals are there any recordings that would indicate that they were bothered by ticks or afflicted with the symptoms of Rocky Mountain Spotted Fever, or tick fever. It may be that the men did not differentiate ticks from the lice and "vermin" that they constantly described as infesting the Indian villages. They had a variety of illnesses of which febrile symptoms are common, but there is no description of illness suggesting the classical signs and symptoms of Rocky Mountain Spotted Fever.[17]

---

[17] Rocky Mountain Spotted Fever was first reported in Idaho and Montana in the 1890s. It is a serious febrile illness which may be fatal. It is characterized by headache, chills, fever and by small red spots which appear on the extremities in the fourth day, thus its name. Howard Ricketts isolated the causative organism, the Rickettsia rickettsi, in 1959. It is conveyed by the woodtick Derenacentor Andersoni in the West, which becomes active in the spring and summer. Although called

The journals show that Lewis nearly lost his life on several occasions, in falls, with Grizzly bears, and Blackfeet Indians. But the most serious accident occurred when he was almost home. On August 11, 1806, he writes in his journal:

. . . jus[t] opposite to the birnt hills there happened to be a herd of Elk on a thick willow bar and finding that my observation was lost for the present I determined to land and kill some of them accordingly we put too and I went out with Cruzatte only. we fired on the Elk I killed one and he wounded another, we reloaded our guns and took different routs through the thick willows in pursuit of the Elk; I was in the act of firing on the Elk a second time when a ball struck my left thye about an inch below my hip joint, missing the bone it passed through the left thye and cut the thickness of the bullet across the hinder part of the right thye; the stroke was very severe; I instantly supposed that Cruzatte had shot me in mistake for an Elk as I was dressed in brown leather and he cannot see very well; under this impression I called out to him damn you, you have shot me, and looked towards the place from whence the ball had come, seeing nothing I called Cruzatte several times as loud as I could but received no answer; I was now pre-swaded that it was an indian that had shot me as the report of the gun did not appear to be more tham 40 paces from me and Cruz-atte appeared to be out of hearing of me; in this situation not knowing how many indians there might be concealed in the bushes

Rocky Mountain Spotted Fever, it occurs in areas throughout the United States. The laboratory in Hamilton, Missouri, in which Ricketts did his work is now a museum. Dr. William Jellison, who is in charge of this museum, answered an inquiry from me as follows: "The Lewis and Clark Journals as I read them make no mention of any disease that could have been spotted fever. Their return trip through this valley would have been in the tick and spotted fever season. If any one contracted it he would have been seriously ill and possibly have died. There is no definite history of spotted fever in the Indians but some legends indicate they know about it. I think it is possible spotted fever was not present here in 1806, in the Bitter Root Valley."

Two interesting and informative articles about Rocky Mountain Spotted Fever: Louise Fenner, "It Can Be Deadly," *Montana Outdoors*, Vol. III, No. 1 (Jan.-Feb. 1972), p. 32; Philip A. Kalisch, "Rocky Mountain Spotted Fever: The Sickness and the Triumph," *Montana, Magazine of Western History*, Vol. XXIII, No. 2 (Apr. 1973), pp. 44-55.

I thought best to make good my retreat to the perogue, calling out as I ran for the first hundred paces as loud as I could to Cruzatte to retreat that there were indians hoping to allarm him in time to make his escape also; I still retained the charge in my gun which I was about to discharge at the moment the ball struck me. when I arrived in sight of the perogue I called the men to their arms to which they flew in an instant . . . I told them to . . . return & give them battle and releive Cruzatte if possible who I feared had fallen into their hands; the men followed me as they were bid and I returned about a hundred paces when my wounds became so painfull and my thye so stiff that I could scarcely get on; in short I was compelled to halt and ordered the men to proceed and if they found themselves overpowered by numbers to retreat in order keeping up a fire. I now got back to the perogue as well as I could and prepared my self with a pistol my rifle and air-gun being determined as a retreat was impracticable to sell my life as deerly as possible. in this state of anxiety and suspense I remained about 20 minutes when the party returned with Cruzatte and reported that there were no indians nor the appearance of any; Cruzatte seemed much allarmed and declared if he had shot me it was not his intention, that he had shot an Elk in the willows after he left or seperated from me. I asked him whether he did not hear me when I called to him so frequently which he absolutely denied. I do not beleive that the fellow did it intentionally but after finding that he had shot me was anxious to conceal his knowledge of having done so. the ball had lodged in my breeches which I knew to be the ball of the short rifles such as that he had, and there being no person out with me but him and no indians that we could discover I have no doubt in my own mind of his having shot me. with the assistance of Sergt. Gass I took off my cloaths and dressed my wounds myself as well as I could, introducing tents of patent lint into the ball holes, the wounds blead considerably but I was hapy to find that it had touched neither bone nor artery . . . my wounds being so situated that I could not without infinite pain make an observation [of the elk meat] I determined to relinquish it and proceed on . . . as it was painfull to me to be removed I slept on board the perogue; the pain I experienced excited a high fever and I had a very uncomfortable night.[18]

Gass writes very little of Lewis' accident, considering all the things this explosive corpsman might have written about Cruzatte.

Ordway describes Lewis' gunshot wound:

Peter Cruzatte a frenchman went out with Capt Lewis they Soon found a gangue of Elk in the thicket. Capt Lewis killed one and cruzatte killed two, and as he still kept fireing one of his balls hit Capt Lewis in his back side and the ball passed through one Side of his buttock and the ball went out of the other Side of the other buttock and lodged at his overalls which wounded him bad. he instantly called to peter but Peter not answering he Supposd it to be Indians and run to the canoes and ordered the men to their armes. they were in readiness in a moment and Capt Lewis atempd to go back for battle but being faint the men perswaded him not to go himself but the party run out found Cruzatte and he had Seen no Indians then peter knew that it must have been him tho an exidant. we dressed the wound [and] prepared a place for him to lay in the white perogue.

On the day after the bullet wound Lewis recorded:

my wounds felt very stiff and soar this morning but gave me no considerable pain. there was much less inflamtion than I had reason to apprehend there would be. I had last evening applyed a poltice of peruvian barks. at 1 P.M. I overtook Capt. Clark and party and had the pleasure of finding them all well. as wrighting

---

18 Dunlop writes an erroneous account of this accident despite Lewis' own recording of it: "Lewis, hunting where the Yellowstone meets the Missouri, accidentally shot himself in the left thigh." *See* Richard Dunlop, "The Doctors Who Helped Tame the West," *Today's Health,* Vol. 41, No. 12, pp. 44-47, 66-68.

A similar careless gunshot wound in the leg by a fellow frontiersman, rendering it necessary to carry the victim in a litter, was described by Cox: "The wound was dressed with friar's balsam and lint, the ball extracted the next day; and in about a month afterwards he was able to walk." Cox, *The Columbia River,* p. 78. Note the use of lint to pack the wounds of both men. Friars balsam is a tincture (alcoholic solution) of benzoin, borax, aloes, and talc balsam; or tincture of benzoin compound. It is used for abrasions, ulcers, blisters and open wounds. It is often spoken of as "new skin" when used by athletes. It comes from balsamic resin of styrax benzoin, a South American plant.

in my present stituation is extreemly painfull to me I shall desist untill I recover and leave to my fri[e]nd Capt. C. the continuation of our journal.

On the day following the shooting, Lewis caught up with Clark, who wrote:

. . . at Meridian Capt. Lewis hove in Sight . . . I found him lying in the Perogue, he informed me that his wound was slight and would be well in 20 or 30 days this information relieved me very much. I examined the wound and found it a very bad flesh wound the ball had passed through the fleshy part of his left thy below the hip bone and cut the cheek of the right buttock for 3 inches in length and the debth of the ball.

Gass confirmed the status of things on August 12: "Capt. Lewis is in good spirits, but his wounds stiff and soar. We proceeded on and at 10 oclock overtook Capt. Clarke and his party, all in good health . . . and now, (thanks to God) we are all together again in good health, except Capt. Lewis and his wound is not dangerous."

Ordway recorded on August 14 that "Capt Lewis fainted as Capt Clark was dressing his wound, but Soon came too again." Perhaps Clark could cleanse and pack the wounds more thoroughly than Lewis could. The other diarists do not mention that Lewis fainted. On this same day Gass wrote that "the inhabitants of all the villages appeared very glad to see us, and sent us presents of corn, beans, and squashes;" the men were now getting back into civilization. They also met parties of trappers going up the Missouri, "who gave our party as much whiskey as they could drink." Perhaps this helped relieve Lewis' discomfort!

Lewis continued to improve, although he had to lie in the pirogue very quietly for a few days, being unable to tolerate weight and motion of the thigh muscles. Again fortune blessed Lewis and the Expedition: infection did not develop even though the bullet had gone through dirty clothing and Lewis kept packing it with "lint."

Lewis certainly deserves to be complimented for his agility in packing lint in a wound in his back side while lying in a pirogue and without the assistance of mirrors! Nothing was known about antisepsis or asepsis. Most certainly the wound and the lint would be contaminated, and perhaps the infection was pushed deeper by Lewis' daily packing of the wound.

It is almost certain that Lewis did not develop a profound infection, because on August 19 Clark could write "Capt. Lewis'es wounds are heeling very fast, I am much in hope of his being able to walk in 8 or 10 days . . . the hunters which was sent out this morning killed 4 Elk & 12 deer near the river. . ." Clark wrote, after some squaws stretched a piece of leather over some sticks: "under this piece of leather I slept dry, it is the only covering which I have had Sufficient to keep off the rain Since I left the Columbia."

On August 22 Clark wrote "rained all the last night every person and all our bedding wet . . . I am happy to have it in my power to Say that my worthy friend Capt. Lewis is recovering fast, he walked a little today for the first time. I have discontinued the tent in the hole the ball came out." Use of the "tent" for packing is a good medical procedure so long as sterile technique is followed; the purpose is to keep the outer portion of the wound open so that it will heal from the bottom outward and not enclose a pocket of infection.

The next day Clark wrote of Lewis' wounds: "the hole in his thy where the ball passed out is closed and appears to be nearly well. The one where the ball entered discharges very well." This notation indicates clearly that Lewis had infection — probably the two captains accepted this as "laudable pus."

On the twenty-sixth Clark could note some progress in his

patient: "Capt. L. is Still on the mending hand he walks a
little. I have discontinued the tent in the hole where the ball
entered, agreeable to his request he tells me that he is fully
convinced the wound is suffeciently heeled for the tents to be
discontinued."

Lewis became a little too enthusiastic about his recovery,
and spent two very uncomfortable days from prolonged hiking. This brought about some remission of his progress, so
that Clark wrote on August 30, "Capt. Lewis is mending
slowly. . ."

The Expedition was moving rapidly downstream, and was
beginning to meet trappers going upstream — all moving with
an eagerness to get home or to get to the beaver country. On
September 3 Clark writes of meeting a Mr. Airs and his party:
"This Gentleman received both Capt. Lewis and myself with
every mark of friendship he was himself at the time with a
chill of the agu on him which he has had for Several days."
This reference to ague shows that the captains were familiar
with this omnipresent disease; the Expedition is almost home
and there has been no mention of any members of the Expedition having it — but surely many of them did!

On September 4 the Expedition passed Floyd's Bluff where
they had buried the only deceased member of their Expedition. Clark writes "at meridian we came too at Floyds Bluff
below the Enterance of Floyds river and assended the hill,
with Capt. Lewis and Several men, found the grave had been
opened by the nativs and left half covered. we had this grave
completely filled up . . . and proceeded on."

On September 9 Clark wrote, perhaps prematurely, about
Lewis' improvement: "My worthy friend Cap Lewis has entirely recovered his wounds are heeled up and he can walk
and even run nearly as well as ever he could, the parts are yet
tender." September 14 was a happy day; the returning ex-

plorers met men going up the river who gave them whiskey and food. Clark writes that "our party received a dram and Sung Songs untill 11 oClock at night in the greatest harmoney."

The Expedition met Captain John McCallan and his party ascending the Missouri River on September 17; Clark wrote:

> . . . we met a Captain McClellin . . . an acquaintance of my friend Capt. Lewis was Somewhat astonished to see us return . . . this Gentleman informed us that we had been long since given out [up] by the people of the U S Generaly and almost forgotton, the President of the U. States had yet hopes of us; . . .

The men had had very little trouble with their eyes since they left the sand of the northern plains and the gleaming snow of the mountains. On the eighteenth Clark noted "J. Potts complains very much of one of his eyes which is burnt by the Sun from exposeing his face without a cover from the Sun. Shannon also complains of his face & eyes &c." The next day Clark again notes the trouble with the eyes:

> a very singular disorder is takeing place amongst our party that of the Sore eyes. three of the party have their eyes inflamed and Sweled in Such a manner as to render them extreamly painfull, particularly when exposed to the light, the eye ball is much inflaimed and the lid appears burnt with the Sun, the cause of this complaint of the eye I can't [account] for. from its' sudden appearance I am willing to believe it may be owing to the reflection of the sun on the water.

The following day he wrote: ". . . three of the party was unabled to row from the State of their eyes." Clark's account sounds like several of the men had infectious conjunctivitis; certainly the reflection of the sun on the water should not be so troublesome after months of summer traveling on the rivers.

Ordway wrote on September 21, "towards evening we

arrived at St Charles fired three rounds and Camped at the
lowere end of the Town. the people gathered on the bank and
could hardly believe that it was us for they had heard and had
believed that we were all dead and were forgotten." On
September 23, 1806, the captains and their men arrived at
St. Louis. The men were received joyously — and the captains
were entertained by the leading townspeople. Clark wrote on
the twenty-fifth, "paid some visits of form, to the gentlemen
of St. Louis. In the evening a dinner & a Ball." Under the
same date, but apparently the next day, he wrote, "a fine
morning, we commence wrighting &c."

The captains and their men were home again. They had
much to tell, the most important of which was that they had
accomplished their mission while *only one man died.*

XVII

Retrospect

*We concieve it to be a signal proof of the wisdom and attention
with which you have conducted the expedition, that but one man
has been lost to your country.* Clark to Citizen's of Fincastle. [1]

It is almost two centuries since Lewis and Clark and their
Corps of Discovery made their remarkable exploration, and
returned safely home. During this journey they endured hardships day after day that stagger the imagination of those who
follow in their path today with all the conveniences of modern
travel. These sturdy men traveled twenty miles a day over
grueling country of rivers and mountains much more formidable than they had ever seen before, facing the fiercest
variations of the elements in winter and summer, rustling
their food from an unknown and changing countryside, sup-
ping bountifully on buffalo tongue and marrowbones or din-
ing in near-starvation on roasted dog and portable soup.
A time of complete rest and repose was unknown to them;
they worked while their eyes could see; they slept fighting
mosquitoes or out in the open with rain pouring on them.
Day after day they unpacked their messes to eat what they
could divide among them, and repacked to "proceed on."
They made their own clothes from the animals that they
killed for food, and these raiments served them as body covering day and night — except when removed for occasional

---

[1] Jackson, *Letters,* p. 359.

bathing and picking off fleas and ticks. The "proceeding on" rarely stopped to care for disease or accidents. Many of the men and both of their captains barely survived fatal diseases and escaped fatal accidents. Unbalanced diets and near-starvation were a continuous serious threat to their survival.

Jefferson was a great humanitarian in many ways; he wanted a government with laws that protected every citizen from predators. The first draft of the Declaration of Independence used the phrase "Life, Liberty, and Property." It was Jefferson who changed this phraseology to "Life, Liberty, and the Pursuit of Happiness." He was also interested in his fellow men having every opportunity for good health. If it had occurred to him, Jefferson might well have accepted the words "Life, Liberty and the Pursuit of Health," and such would have been compatible with his extensive writings on this subject.

It is a tribute to Jefferson that he was aware of the dangers to the life and health of the men of the Lewis and Clark Expedition, and that he did not permit unbridled enthusiasm at the prospect of his dream coming to fruition to blind him to the sober aspects of the enterprise. Jefferson had a comprehensive concept of the part that he had played, and was continuing to play, in the Expedition; he wrote of "the peculiar part I have had in the designing and execution of this expedition." [2] He also made reference to "the risk of valuable lives," [3] and he called the Expedition "perilous." [4] In his letter of January 13, 1804, to Lewis, Jefferson once again shows his constant concern for the safety of the men: ". . . assure all your party that we have our eyes turned on them with anxiety for their safety and the success of their enterprize." [5]

---

[2] Thwaites, *Journals,* i, p. xlvii.   [3] *Ibid.*
[4] Jackson, *Letters,* p. 21.   [5] *Ibid.,* p. 163.

Jefferson sought in many ways to provide assistance and instruction for Lewis in the health care of the men of the Expedition.

Lewis and Clark were equally and constantly concerned with the health of their men. Day after day the captains gave attention to the health needs of the men and made comprehensive journal notes about illnesses and accidents, as well as the treatment used. They walked so that ill men could ride; they bathed their men's feet in warm water [6]— "imposing no privation unshared by themselves;" [7] they shared the messes with the men, often cooking for them; and Lewis "learned to push a tolerable pole." [8] Whitehouse wrote of "the humanity shown at all times by them [the captains] to those under their command." [9] Both Lewis and Clark repeatedly expressed gratification in their journal notes and letters to Jefferson and their relatives, regarding the good health of their men. (An important thing in their favor was that they were on the move much of the time; and yet, they survived the hard sedentary winters at Fort Mandan and Fort Clatsop without disproportionate health problems.)

The return of Lewis and Clark and their men to St. Louis on September 23, 1806, must have given this frontier village the most exciting occasion of its young history. Lewis found time to write to Jefferson on this same day: "Sir, It is with pleasure that I announce to you the safe arrival of myself and party at 12 OClk. today at this place with our papers and baggage. . . The whole of the party who accompanyed me from the Mandans have returned in good health, which is not I assure you, to me one of the least pleasing considerations

---

[6] Thwaites, *Journals*, iv, p. 143.

[7] Coues, *History of Lewis and Clark*, p. v.

[8] Thwaites, *Journals*, ii, p. 266.

[9] Cutright, "The Journal of Private Whitehouse," *Bull. of Mo. Hist. Soc.*, p. 160.

of the Voyage." [10] On this same day Clark wrote to his brother George Rogers Clark:

> Dureing our passage over these mountains we suffered everything which hunger, cold and fatigue could impose; . . . we found that we could not subsist on those articles [roots and dried salmon] and almost all of us grew sick on eating them. we were obliged therefore to have resource to the flesh of horses and dogs as food to supply the dificiency of our guns which produced but little meat as game was scarce in the vicinity of our camp on the Kooskooske . . . while we remained here I was myself sick for several days . . . and my friend capt. Lewis suffered serious indisposition. . . We left Fort Clatsop on the 27th of March We have not lost a man since we left the Mandans a circumstance which I assure you is a pleasing consideration to me."[11]

There was no rapid transit, no telegraph, no telephone, no television to convey from the captains to their Commander-in-Chief the word of their return within a few seconds or even a few days. It was not until October 26 that Jefferson could respond to Lewis from Washington: "I recieved, my dear sir, with unspeakable joy your letter of Sep. 23 announcing the return of yourself, Captain Clarke, & your party in good health to St. Louis. The unknown scenes in which you were engaged & the length of time without hearing of you had begun to be felt awfully." [12] Indeed Jefferson could be happy. The method of purchasing the Louisiana Territory and the apparent disappearance of Lewis and Clark provided reasons for his enemies to be picking at him constantly. Therefore, return of the captains and their men, with much to report, was the answer to Jefferson's detractors. Jefferson would be interested, of course, in learning all the details of the Expedition's journey from Lewis and Clark; but the greatest news and satis-

10 Jackson, *Letters,* pp. 319, 324.
11 *Ibid.,* pp. 325, 329. Clark's error; they left the Fort on the 23rd.
12 *Ibid.,* p. 350.

faction was to know of their safe return. Jefferson wrote also on October 26 to Meriwether's brother, Dr. Reuben Lewis: "I have the pleasure to inform you of his safe arrival in St. Louis." He did not write to his son-in-law Thomas Mann Randolph until November 3, because he was "taken with the autumnal fever so as to be unable to write."[13] Even the President of the United States was not immune to the ague!

A grateful country welcomed the return of the captains with proper accolades. On their journey to Washington, tribute was paid to them by the citizens of Fincastle:

> Sentiments of esteem and gratitude induce us to offer you our sincere congratulations, upon your safe return to the bosom of your country. During your absence upon the perilous & laborious service, we have reflected with deepest solicitude, on the dangers which you must necessarily encounter; our anxiety for your safety, and that of the party under your command, is now happily terminated.
>
> We concieve it to be a signal proof of the wisdom and attention with which you have conducted the expedition, that but one man has been lost to your country. This fact will afford to future travellers the most salutary instruction. It will teach them, that, discoveries [apparently the most difficult] may be effected without the effusion of human blood.[14]

Clark replied: "Those sentiments of esteem and solicitude for our personal safty expressed in your affectionate address has excited in me the livelyest sencibility. . . To respect the rights of humanity has and ever will be the leading principal of my life, and no reflection is more pleasing to me than that of effecting the objects we had in view with the effusion of so small a portion of human blood." And then this great and humble captain of the Corps of Discovery added: "Gentlemen we ought to assign the general safety of the party to a singular interposition of providence, and not to the wisdom of those who commanded the expedition."[15]

---

[13] *Ibid.*   [14] *Ibid.*, pp. 358-59.   [15] *Ibid.*

It was appropriate for Clark to thank the "interposition of providence" for the health and safety of the men. But many factors contributed to the success of the Expedition. Wheeler recognized that a generous amount of good luck also had been helpful. DeVoto states that ". . . intelligence was a principle reason for the success of the expedition . . . both were men of intelligence, of distinguished intelligence. The entire history of North American exploration contains no one who could be called their intellectual equal." DeVoto also paid tribute to the type of men recruited and their organization and discipline at Camp DuBois. He added: "unquestionably military organizations and military discipline added effectiveness to the wilderness techniques and so helped to explain the success of the expedition." [16]

Coues wrote that "The discipline of the party was perfect." [17] The importance of this quotation is emphasized by the statement of Cutbush that "discipline and exercise are intimately connected in the preservation of the health of troops. . ." [18] Certainly the men had both exercise and discipline! The commanders and the men had army discipline ingrained in them; without it, they would not have succeeded. The corps presented a combination for which there is no greater promise of success: leadership and disciplined ability. The captains picked the right men, and they used them to the fullness of their capabilities, and never misused them.

The accomplishment of the Lewis and Clark Expedition is brought into more impressive relief by the disastrous performance of the Wilson Price Hunt overland party of the Astor expedition ten years later. Of this Hunt party Coues wrote: "The hardships and sufferings of an undisciplined mob which

16 DeVoto, *Journals,* pp. xliv, xlv.
17 Coues, *History of Lewis and Clark,* p. v.
18 Cutbush, *Preserving the Health,* p. 18.

straggled across the continent were terrible; some deserted, some went mad, some were drowned or murdered, and the survivors reached Astoria in a pitiful plight, in separate parties at different times." [19] Lewis and Clark had shown them the way several years before. The tragedy of the Hunt party was caused by the lack of discipline under firm leadership. Unquestionably discipline — fair discipline — was a paramount factor in the success of the Lewis and Clark Expedition. [20] Newman deserves sympathy and admiration for his demonstrated repentance for his minor "mutiny," but Lewis' firm insistence of dismissal of Newman from the permanent party is also understandable as the wise and necessary course of a commander responsible for the success of the Expedition, success which could come only from unquestioned loyalty and dedication — and discipline; floggings were no longer required after the Expedition left Fort Mandan for the West.

Chittenden has written of the Lewis and Clark Expedition: "This celebrated performance stands as incomparably the most perfect achievement of its kind in the history of the world." [21] Elliott Coues states that "the story of this adventure stands easily first and alone. This is our national epic of exploration." [22] The success of the Expedition can be attributed to the planning of Jefferson and the execution of the two

[19] Elliott Coues, ed., *New Light on the Early History of the Greater Northwest: The Manuscript Journals of A. Henry and David Thompson* (New York: Francis P. Harper, 1897), II, p. 842, n.

[20] Discipline is still a prime requisite of health care, whether in army or civilian life. The need for physicians, ancillary personnel, hospitals, and the costs of all these would be greatly reduced if the public would discipline itself in regard to automobile driving, over-eating, alcohol consumption, careless accidents, adherence to health programs and advice. Lewis and Clark had the authority of army discipline, but civilians must rely on self-discipline. Benjamin Franklin wrote: "Want of care does more damage than want of knowledge" — all the modern health knowledge, and the means to pay for it, is not enough; the patient, too, must care.

[21] Chittenden, *The American Fur Trade*, I, p. 81.

[22] Coues, *History of Lewis and Clark*, I, p. v-vi.

captains. They were true leaders and commanders. They met
and solved every emergency, and most remarkable of all, they
found time to place on paper one of the most interesting and
informative records of exploration. Intelligence, discipline,
good luck, dedicated men — all of these things were wrapped
together in two superb captains.

Lewis and Clark admirably provided a foremost example
of the statement of Tilton that "the health, hardihood, and
efficiency of an army depend very much, if not entirely, upon
the wise and prudent conduct of the commanding officers."
They completely fulfilled the expectations and responsibilities
placed upon them for the health care of the men. They lived
and served during a time when the medical practices of the
trained medical graduate, the medical apprentice, the army
doctor, colonial and frontier home remedies, and Indian medicine all melted together into a potpourri of health care practice. It is a tribute to the human race that out of the morass of
the health care of the nineteenth century we have evolved so
rapidly to the health care of today. It is also a tribute to Lewis
and Clark that from out of this morass they chose and applied
their health care as well as they did — indeed as well as any
medical doctor of the time would have done.

The two captains gave their men better personal attention
in regard to health problems than was rendered by the Revolutionary War doctors, and their journal entries constituted
better clinic notes than were kept in the hospitals during the
Revolutionary War. Today we might be amused at some of
the medicines used by Lewis and Clark, but "real" doctors
used the same drugs. A physician today, fatigued by long
hours and uncertain demands, can rightfully marvel at the
attention given to the health needs of the men by their captains, and can admire even more the regularity and astuteness
of their "clinic notes," made under such trying conditions.

Both Lewis and Clark demonstrated their ability as natural physicians, and a dedication to their patients unsurpassed by the noblest examples of a humane profession.

Will appraised the medical capacities of Lewis and Clark with high regard: "Undoubtedly Lewis and Clark possessed not only extraordinary common sense but also the medical knowledge common to most educated men of the time, particularly to those who had served as military officers and had seen military physicians at work." [23] Cutright also has generous praise for the medical abilities of Lewis and Clark:

> In assessing the competence of Lewis and Clark as medical practitioners, it is reasonable to say that if either had subsequently studied medicine, he would have distinguished himself. Lewis, from what we know of him, would have come nearer being the astute discerning diagnostician. Clark certainly would have had much the better bedside manner. The one incontrovertible fact about the medical practice of these two men is that in 28 months, and traveling some 8,000 miles in a land of parched sands, rampaging rivers, and unpredictable savages, they had lost but one man, and the best medical brain of the day, even the eminent Dr. Rush, could probably not have saved him. Thomas Jefferson, we are convinced, made no mistake in entrusting the health and welfare of the party to these two resourceful, clear-headed scions of our American frontier. In fact, considering the low state of medicine in the world at that time, who can conscientiously insist that the expedition would have fared better in the hands of a qualified doctor than in those of Meriwether Lewis and William Clark? [24]

Captains Lewis and Clark admirably fulfilled all of the responsibilities given to them by Thomas Jefferson. They traversed the Missouri River and sought a portage to the Columbia. They made detailed records of the many Indian tribes, and diplomatically handled the problems between the tribes and between the Indians and themselves. They de-

---

[23] Will, "Medical Practice," p. 297.
[24] Cutright, *Pioneering Naturalists*, p. 344.

scribed the terrain of their journey, noting landmarks with such vivid descriptions that they are easily discernible today. They commented on the agricultural and mineral potential of the land. They noted favorable sites for trading posts and forts, and envisioned population centers as far west as the Willamette Valley. The fur trade was the biggest stimulus for the British-American competition for the trans-Mississippi West, but Lewis and Clark brought back a record of much more potential wealth. They described many animals and plants never seen before by white men, with such accuracy and detail that articles and books are still appearing which show high regard for their work as naturalists. They interpreted information which had been provided for them by Jefferson from multiple sources, and with keen insight picked their way astutely through the geography of the plains and the mountains.[25] The Lewis and Clark Expedition assured that there would be no delay in gaining knowledge about the Louisiana Territory, which had just been purchased, and by doing this it also assured the territorial bridge to the Oregon Country. Lewis and Clark fulfilled abundantly and magnificently the dreams and the directives of their Commander-in-Chief. Their abilities and personalities and the discipline they exercised assured their leadership, and their men followed devotedly. They were an organized, perfectly functioning unit, even when they were divided on their return journey.

And with all these things, the medical aspects played an important, and at times a determining part in the success of the Expedition. Probably the specifics from the medicine chest, except in the case of mercury for syphilis, did not do

25 John L. Allen, "Lewis and Clark on the Upper Missouri: Decision at the Marias," *Montana, Mag. of Western History*, Vol. xxi, No. 3 (Summer 1971), pp. 2-17. Also, in more detail, the same author's book, *Through the Garden*, Univ. of Illinois Press, 1975.

the men as much good as the reassurance gained from the loyal attention of their captain-physicians. Disease, injuries, malnutrition and climate combined to exact from the captains a constant attention to the health of the men. This devoted attention to their health care probably contributed more than anything else to eliciting a responsive discipline from the men. And the captains' health services to the Indians played an important part in their diplomatic success in dealing with them.

Much has been written about the natural genius of the captains, of their unusual versatility of interests and abilities, of their natural qualities of leadership, of their exemplary cooperation and mutual respect. But if their men could tell us, they might well point out that their captains were also their physicians, promptly responding with concern to their every need, ministering to them with that admixture of specifics and devotion which has always denoted the true physician. Like Dr. Rush, they bled and purged; but also, like him, they gave of themselves in devoted attention to their charges. Perhaps they gained their acme of professional stature when in desperation they gave eye water profusely to the Rocky Mountain Indians as inducement for their friendly help, but said "We take care to give them no particle which can possibly injure them."

In completing his instructions to Lewis before he left Washington, Jefferson wrote: ". . and bring back your party safe." This the captains did, and in no small part this happy result was consummated because, in addition to all their other responsibilities, Lewis and Clark served their men as physicians across the continent.[26]

[26] These last two paragraphs are from the author's address to the Friends of the Library of Oreg. St. Univ., at Corvallis, Oreg., Apr. 28, 1965.

Appendices

Appendix I

Jefferson's Medical Books

The Library of Congress includes Jefferson's Monticello library, and from this is listed below only those medical books published before or while Lewis lived at Monticello, thus having these books available for his study.

Jefferson acquired more medical books at later dates, some held at the Library of Congress. James A. Bear, Jr., Curator of the Jefferson Memorial Foundation informed the author: "The only other catalogues of Jefferson's later libraries are the Poor Sale Catalogue listing books in the Monticello library after 1815 that were sold after Jefferson's death and the Leavitt Catalogue listing books from the Poplar Forest (Jefferson's other home) library also sold after Jefferson's death." Although listing medical books acquired after 1803 would serve to reflect Jefferson's medical interests, they would not be ones available to Lewis for study, and thus not germane to the Lewis and Clark Expedition.

It is interesting that the copy of the Poor (Nathaniel P. Poor, auctioneer) Catalogue which Mr. Bear sent to me has on it the signature of " 'Rich' Rush, Secy of the Treasury." Richard Rush was the son of Dr. Benjamin Rush. He also served as minister to England and to France.

Of special note are the several books and pamphlets dealing with vaccination.

SURGERY:
1. Mauriceau, Francois. *Maladies des Femmes Grosses.* 1681
2. LaForest. *L'Art de Soigner Les Piedes.* 1782
3. Bell, Benjamin. *A System of Surgery.* 1791
4. Bell, John. *Discourses on the Nature and Cure of Wounds.* 1795

MEDICINE:
1. Cabanis, Pierre Jean Georges. *Du Degre de Certitude de la Medicine.* 1803

2. Lemery, Nicolas. *Dictionnaire des Drogues Simples.* 1716
3. Quincy, John *Quincey's Dispenatory.* 1749.
4. *Edinburgh New Dispensatory.* 1791
5. Salmon, William. *Phylaxa Medicina.* 1688
6. *New Pharmacopoeia of the Royal College of Physicians of London.* 1788
7. Fuller, Thomas. *Pharmacopoeia Extemporanea.* 1714
8. *Pharmacopoeia Londinensis.* 1711
9. Baume, Antoine. *Elements de Pharmacie Theorique et Pratique.* 1784
10. Cullen, William. *Materia Medica.* 1789
11. Blankaart, Steven. *Blancardi Lexico Medicum.* 1717
12. Blankaart, Steven. *The Physical Dictionary.* 1715
13. Quincy, John. *Quincey's Medicinal Dictionary.* 1749
14. Hippocrates. *Opera.* 1595
15. Hippocrates. *Opera Omnia.* 1665
16. Celsus, Aulus Cornelius. *Celsus de re Medica.* 1592
17. Aretaeus. *Opera.* 1603
18. Mercurialis, Hieronymus. *Murcurialis.* 1598
19. Boerhaave, Hermann. *Institutiones Medicae.* 1734
20. Shaw, Peter, *A New Practice of Physic.* 1738
21. Brookes, Richard. *An Introduction to Physic and Surgery.* 1763
22. Brookes, Richard. *The General Practice of Physic.* 1763
23. Riverius, Lazarus. *The Practice of Physick.* 1663-78
24. Gorraeus, Joannes. *Ioannis Gorraei Medici Parisiensis Opera.* 1622
25. Strother, Edward. *Euodia.* 1718
26. Dover, Thomas. *The Ancient Physician's Legacy to His Country.* 1733
27. Tissot, Samuel. *Ouvrages Divers Latin et Francais.* 1769-1785
28. Tissot, Samuel. *Advice to the People in General.* 1768
29. Buchan, William. *Domestic Medicine.* 1786.
30. [Flowerden, Joseph.] *A Compendium of Physic, and Surgery.* 1769
31. Astruc, Jean. *Diseases Incident to Children.* 1746
32. Cullen, William. *First Lines of the Practice of Physic.* 1784
33. Darwin, Erasmus. *Zoonomia.* 1797
34. [Brown, John.] *Elements of Medicine.* 1797
35. Tazewell, William. *Vade-Mecum Medicum.* 1798
36. Sanctorius, Santorius. *Medicina Statica.* 1723-4.

37. Boerhaave, Hermann. *Aphorismi.* 1744
38. Harvey, William. *Opera.* 1737
39. *Sydenhami Opera.* 1716(?)
40. Sydenham, Thomas. *Sydenham's Works.* 1705
41. Mead, Richard. *The Medical Works of Richard Mead, M.D.* 1775
42. Pitcairne, Archibald. *The Whole Works of Dr. Archibald Pitcairn.* 1715
43. Chrestien, Jean Andre. *de la Methode Iatroliptrice.* 1803
44. *Family Companion for Health.* 1729
45. Hill, Sir John. *The Old Man's Guide to Health and Longer Life.* 1771
46. Daignan, Guillaume. *Tableau des Varietes de la vie Humaine.* 1786
47. Adair, James Makittrick. *Medical Cautions.* 1787
48. Adair, James Makittrick. *A Philosophical and Medical Sketch of the Natural History of the Human Body and Mind.* 1787
49. Peale, Charles Willson. *On the Means of Preserving Health.* 1803
50. Wainewright, Jeremiah. *A Mechanical Account of the Non-Naturals.* 1708
51. *Trattati Fisici del Cocchi.* 1762
52. Cocchi, Antonio. *Del Matrimonio Ragionamento.* 1762
53. Short, Thomas. *Discourses on Tea, Sugar, Milk,* . . . 1750
54. Floyer, Sir John and Edward Baynard. *The History of Cold Bathing.* 1706
55. Fontana, Felice. *Traite sur les Poisons.* 1781
56. Valentin, Louis. *Traite de la Fievre Jaune d'Amerique.* 1803
57. Berthe, Jean Nicolas. *Precis Historique de la Maladie d'Andalousie de 1800.*
58. MacBride, David. *Experimental Essays.* 1764
59. College of Physicians of Philadelphia. *Facts and Observations on the Pestilential Fever of Philadelphia.* 1798
60. McClurg, James. *Experiments Upon the Human Bile.* 1772
61. *Medical Observations.* 1758
62. Mandeville, Bernard. *The Hypochondriack and Hysterick Diseases.* 1730
63. Millar, John. *Observations on the Change of Public Opinion in Religion, Politics and Medicine.* 1803
64. *Onania.* 1730
65. Hunter, John. *A Treatise on the Venereal Disease.* 1786

66. Turner, Daniel. *A Discourse Concerning Gleets*. 1729
67. Liger, Charles Louis. *A Treatise on the Gout*. 1760
68. Warner, Ferdinando. *A Full and Plain Account of the Gout*. 1768
69. Cadogan, William. *A Dissertation on the Gout*. 1771
70. Falconer, William. *Observations on Dr. Cadogan's Dissertation on the Gout*. 1772
71. Cullen, William. *Lecture on the Gout*. 1770
72. Pfeiffer, Goerge. *An Inaugural Dissertation on the Gout*. 1791
73. Mease, James. *Dissertation on the Rabies*. 1792
74. Woodhouse, James. *Dissertation on the Persimmon Tree*. 1792
75. Rodgers, John R.B. *Dissertatio Medica*. 1785
76. Stokes, William. *Tentamen Medicum Inaugurale*. 1793
77. Bracken, Henry. *The Traveller's Pocket Farrier*. 1744
78. Gibson, William. *The Farrier's Dispensatory in Three Parts*. 1726
79. Waterhouse, Benjamin. *A Prospect of Exterminating the Small-Pox*. 1800
80. Waterhouse, Benjamin. *A Prospect of Exterminating the Small-Pox, Part II*. 1802
81. La Societe de Medicine. [Several tracts] 1801-1803
82. *Address of the Royal Jennerian Society, for the Extermination of the Small-Pox*. 1803
83. Lettsom, John Coakley. *Observations on the Cow-Pock*. 1801
84. *Report from the Committee of the House of Commons on Dr. Jenner's Petition, Respecting His Discovery of Vaccine Inoculation*. 1802
85. *The Report on the Cow-Pock Inoculation*. 1803
86. Valentin, Louis. *Resultats de l'Inoculation de la Vaccine*. 1802
87. Coxe, John Redman. *Practical Observations on Vaccination*. 1802
88. Aikin, Charles Rochemont. *A Concise View of All the Most Important Facts . . . Concerning the Cow-Pox*. 1801
89. Boyveau-Laffecteur, Denys. *Observations sur l'Histoire et les Effets du Rob Anti-Syphilitique de Sieur Boyveau Laffecteur*. 1781
90. Dupau, Jacques. *Observations sur l'Usage des Vegetaux Exotiques*. 1782
91. Beddoes, Thomas. *Observations on the Nature and Cure of Calculus*. 1797
92. Rush, Benjamin. *Medical Inquiries and Observations*. 1796
93. Young, Joseph. *A New Physical System of Astronomy*. 1800

94. Barnwell, William. *Physical Investigations & Deductions.* 1802
95. Fothergill, Anthony. *A New Enquiry into the Syspension of Vital Action.* 1795
96. *Pamphlets Medical.* 1800
97. Rush, Benjamin. *Three Lectures Upon Animal Life.* 1799
98. Mease, James. *Observations on the Arguments of Professor Rush.* 1801
99. Barton, Benjamin Smith. *Collections for an Essay Towards a Materia Medica of the United States.* 1798
100. *Waterhouse on Kine-Pox.* 1800
101. *First Report of the Vaccine Pock Institution.* 1800
102. Hardie, James. *An Account of the Malignant Fever.* 1799
103. Rush, Benjamin. *Observations Upon the Origin of the Malignant Bilious.* 1799
104. *Tracts in Medicine.* 1802
105. Rush, Benjamin. *Six Introductory Lectures.* 1801
106. Rush, Benjamin. *An Inquiry Into the Effects of Ardent Spirits.* 1790(?)
107. Vaughan, John. *A Concise History of the Autumnal Fever.* 1803
108. Sinclair, Sir John. *An Essay on Longevity.* 1802
109. Vaughan, John. *The Valedictory Lecture Before the Philosophical Society of Delaware.* 1800

ANATOMY:
1. Noguez, Pierre. *l'Anatomie du Corps de l'Homme en Abrege.* 1726
2. Cheselden, William. *The Anatomy of the Human Body.* 1763
3. Cocchi, Antonio. *Dell' Anatomia.* 1745
4. Winslow, Jakob Benignus. *Anatomical Exposition.* 1756
5. Cuvier, Georges. *Lecons d'Anatomie Comparee.* 1800
6. Lassus, Pierre. *Essai ou Discours Historique et Critique sur les Decouvertes Faites en Anatomie.* 1783
7. Descartes, Rene. *l'Homme de Descartes.* 1677
8. Bell, John and Sir Charles. *The Anatomy of the Human Body.* 1802-04
9. Hunter, John. *The Natural History of the Human Teeth.* 1778

Appendix II

Letter from Thomas Jefferson to Dr. Caspar Wistar, June 21, 1807[1]

We know, from what we see and feel, that the animal body in it's organs and functions is subject to derangement, inducing pain, and tending to it's destruction. In this disordered state, we observe nature providing for the reestablishment of order, by exciting some salutary evacuation of the morbific matter, or by some other operation which escapes our imperfect senses and researches. She brings on a crisis, by stools, vomiting, sweat, urine, expectoration, bleeding, etc., which, for the most part, ends in the restoration of healthy action. Experience has taught us, also, that there are certain substances, by which, applied to the living body, internally or externally, we can at will produce these same evacuations, and thus do, in a short time, what nature would do but slowly, and do effectually, what perhaps she would not have strength to accomplish. Where, then, we have seen a disease, characterized by specific signs or phenomena, and relieved by a certain natural evacuation or process, whenever that disease recurs under the same appearances, we may reasonably count on producing a solution of it, by the use of such substances as we have found produce the same evacuation or movement. Thus, fulness of the stomach we can relieve by emetics; disease of the bowels, by purgatives; inflammatory cases, by bleeding; intermittents, by the Peruvian bark; syphilis, by mercury; watchfulness, by opium; etc. So far, I bow to the utility of medicine. It goes to the well-defined forms of disease, and happily, to those the most frequent. But the disorders of the animal body, and the symptoms indicating them, are as various as the element of which the body is composed. The combinations, too of these symptoms are so infinitely diversified, that many associations of them appear too rarely to establish a definite disease; and to an unknown disease, there cannot be a

---

[1] A. A. Liscomb and A. E. Bergh, *The Writings of Thomas Jefferson*, xi (New York, 1903), pp. 242-48.

known remedy. Here then, the judicious, the moral, the humane physician should stop. Having been so often a witness to the salutary efforts which nature makes to re-establish the disordered functions, he should rather trust to their action, than hazard the interruption of that, and a greater derangement of the system, by conjectural experiments on a machine so complicated and so unknown as the human body, and a subject so sacred as human life. Or, if the appearance of doing something be necessary to keep alive the hope and spirits of the patient, it should be of the most innocent character.

One of the most successful physicians I have ever known has assured me, that he used more bread pills, drops of colored water, and powders of hickory ashes, than of all other medicines put together. It was certainly a pious fraud. But the adventurous physician goes on, and substitutes presumption for knolege. From the scanty field of what is known, he launches into the boundless region of what is unknown. He establishes for his guide some fanciful theory of corpuscular attraction, of chemical agency, of mechanical powers, of stimuli, of irritability accumulated or exhausted, of depletion by the lancet and repletion by mercury, or some other ingenious dream, which lets him into all nature's secrets at short hand. On the principle which he thus assumes, he forms his table of nosology, arrays his diseases into families, and extends his curative treatment, by analogy, to all cases he has thus arbitrarily marshalled together. I have lived myself to see the disciples of Hoffman, Boerhaave, Stahl, Cullen, Brown, succeed one another like the shifting figures of a magic lantern, and their fancies, like the dresses of the annual doll-babies from Paris, becoming, from their novelty, the vogue of the day, and yielding to the next novelty their ephemeral favor. The patient, treated on the fashionable theory, sometimes gets well in spite of the medicine. The medicine therefore restored him, and the young doctor receives new courage to proceed in his bold experiments on the lives of his fellow creatures.

I believe we may safely affirm, that the inexperienced and presumptuous band of medical tyros let loose upon the world, destroys more of human life in one year, than all the Robinhoods, Cartouches, and Macheaths do in a century. It is in this part of medicine that I wish to see a reform, an abandonment of hypothesis for sober facts, the first degree of value set on clinical observation, and the lowest on visionary theories. I would wish the young practitioner, especially, to have deeply impressed on his mind, the real limits of his art, and that when the state of his patient gets beyond these, his office is to be watchful, but quiet spectator of the operations of nature, giving them fair play by a well-regulated regimen, and by all the aid they can derive from the excitement of good spirits and hope in the patient. I have no doubt that some diseases not yet understood may in time be transferred to the table of those known. But, were I a physician, I would rather leave the transfer to the slow hand of accident, than hasten it by guilty experiments on those who put their lives into my hands. The only sure foundations of medicine are, an intimate knolege of the human body, and observation on the effects of medicinal substance on that. The anatomical and clinical schools, therefore, are those in which the young physician should be formed. If he enters with innocence that of the theory of medicine, it is scarcely possible he should come out untainted with error. His mind must be strong indeed, if, rising above juvenile credulity, it can maintain a wise infidelity against the authority of his instructors, and the bewitching delusions of their theories. You see that I estimate justly that portion of instruction which our medical students derive from your labors; and, associating with it one of the chairs which my old and able friend, Doctor Rush, so honorably fills, I consider them as the two fundamental pillars of the edifice. Indeed, I have such an opinion of the talents of the professors in the other branches which constitute the school of medicine with you, as to hope and believe, that it is from this side of the Atlantic, that Europe, which has taught us so many other things, will at length be led into sound principles in this branch of science, the most important of all others, being that to which we commit the care of health and life.

Appendix III

Clark's List of Questions[1]

[1804]

Inquiries relitive to the *Indians* of Louisiana.*

1st.   *Physical History and Medicine*

What is their state of Life as to longivity?

At what age do both sexes usially marry?

How long do the Women usially succle their Children?

What is the diet of their Children after they wean them?

Is polygamy admited among them?

What is the state of the pulse in both sexes, Children, grown persons, and in old age, by feeling the Pulse Morning, Noon, & Night &c.?

What is their most general diet, manner of cooking, and manner of eating; and how do they preserve their provisions?

What time do they generally consume in sleep?

What are their *acute* dis-eases?

Is rheumatism, Pluricy, or *bilious fevers* known among them? & does the latter ever terminate in a vomiting of *black matter?*

What are their chronic diseases — are palsy, apoplexy, Epilepsy, Madness, the goiture (or Swelled Neck) and the Venereal disease known among them?

What is their mode of treating the *Small pox* particularly?

Have they any other disease amongst them, and what are they?

What are their remidies for their different diseases?

Are artificial discharges of blood used among them?

In what manner do they generally induce evacuation?

Do they ever use Voluntary fasting?

---

1 Thwaites, *Journals*, VII, p. 283.

* Clark actually meant this to refer to all Indians encountered on the course of the Expedition.

What is the nature of their baths, and at what time of the day do they generally use them?

At what age do their women begin and cease to menstruate?

2nd.   *Relative to Morrals*

What are the Vices most common among the Indians?

Do they ever resort to Suicide under the influence of their passions, particularly love?

Is murder common among them, and do their Laws punish it by Death?

Are the lives of the wife and Children subject to the Capprice of the husband, and father, and in the case of the murder by him of either do their Laws punish the Culprit with Death?

Can the Crime of Murder be paliated by pecuniary Considerations?

Do they use any liquor or Substitute to promote intoxication, besides ardent spirits?

Are they much attached to spiritous liquors, and is intoxication deemed a Crime among them?

Have they any and what are the *punishments* of which their usuages admit of — for either Crimes?

3rd.   *Relative to Religion*

What affinity is there between their religious ceremonies and those of the ancient Jews?

Do they use animal sacrifises in their worship?

What are the principal objects of their worship?

Do they Consider *Mannatoe* or the *good Spirit* & *Michimannatoe* or the *bad Spirit* as two distinct powers, neither haveing the power of Controling the other?

Do they ever petition the *good Spirit* to interfere with his power to avert or relieve them from the evils which the *bad Spirit* meditates or is practicing against them?

Do they sacrifice or petition the *bad Spirit* in order to avert the pernicious design which they may conceive he has formed against them?

How do they dispose of their dead?

And with what ceremonies do they inter them?

Do they ever use human sacrifices in any case?

Do they Mourn for their disceased friends and what [is] their cerimony on such occasions?

4th. *Traditions or National History*

From what quarter of the earth did they emigrate as related to them by their ancisters?

What the cause of their removal and the circumstancies attending their peregrination?

With what savage nations have they formed strict allyance, or those of offensive and *Defensive* war?

Have they any Monuments to perpetuate national events or the memory of a distinguished Chief — and if so what are they?

5th. *Agriculture and Domestic economy*

Do they obtain by the Cultivation of the soil their principal mantainence?

What species of grain or pulse do they cultivate?

What are their implements of husbandry, and in what manner do they use them?

Have they any domestic anamals & what are they?

Do their men engage in agriculture or any other domestic employments?

How do they prepare their culinary and other domistic utensils and what are they?

At what time do they usually relinquish their hunt and return to their village?

What are the esculent plants, and how do they prepare them?

What are those that are Commonly used by them?

In what form and of what materials are their Lodges, or *Houses* usially built?

Of what does the furniture of those lodges Consist, for the accomidation of the necessary avocations of human life *eating Drinking & Sleeping?*

What materials compose, and in what form do they erect their temporary tents?

Do more that [than] one family inhabit the same lodge and in such case, is the furniture of the lodge considered as the common property of the inhabitants of it?

6th. *Fishing & Hunting*

Do those furnish their principal employment?

Do their [women?] participate in the fatigues of either?

How do they persue, and how take their game?

What are the employments used for those purposes — how prepare
& in what manner do they use them?

How do they preserve, and how prepare the Skins & furs of their
games when taken for raiment or for Market?

7th. *War*

What is the cerimony of declareing war, and making peace; or forming alliancies?

What the cerimony of setting out and the return of the war party?

Do their women ever accompany them on those th[e]ir hostile ex-
perditions?

At what season of the year do they usially go to war?

In what manner are those war parties organised?

What is their Disipline and regulations by which they are governed?

Do they burn or torture their prisoners?

Do they eat the flesh of their prisoners?

Do they ever adopt their Prisoners as members of their Nation?

What are their implements of war, how do they prepare and how use
them?

8th. *Amusements*

Have they any and what are they?

Do they with a view to amusement only make a feist.

Do they play at any games of risk, & what are they?

Have their women any games particularly to themselves, or do they
ever engage in those common to the Men?

Do they ever dance and what is the cerimony of their Dance?

Have they any music, and what are their musical instruments?

9th. *Clothing Dress* & *Orniments*

What garments do their dress usially Consist, in both Sexes?

What are the shapes & materials of those garments?

In what manner are they worn?

What orniments do they use to decorate their person?

Do they use paints of Various Colours on the surface of their skins,
and what are the most usial colours thus used?

Do they *tattoe* (or scarify) their bodys and on what parts?

Do they imprint with the aids of a sharp pointed instrument and som
colouring matter any figures on their skins: and what are the part
of the body on which they are usially imprinted?

Which are the usial figures?

Customs & Manners Generally

In what particularly do they differ from those nations in our neighborhood?

Have they any & what are their festivals or feasts?

What is the cerimony of reciving a stranger at their Village?

When publickly recived at the Lodge of the Chief of the Village is
there any Cerimony afterwords necessary to your admission in any
other Lodge?[2]

---

[2] Jackson says, "The basis of this list is one supplied by Dr. Benjamin Rush
perhaps with additional material from Dr. Caspar Wistar and Dr. Benjamin Smith
Barton. Jackson, *Letters*, pp. 157-61.

Bibliography

There have been extensive writings about the contributions of Lewis and Clark to geography, mineralogy, agriculture, commerce and national expansion. Many excellent books have been written about the Lewis and Clark Expedition, from the first Biddle-Allen two volume 1814 edition to the Thwaites eight volume edition, and there have been several editions in English and foreign languages. The Coues four volume edition of 1893 was very scholarly but was soon overshadowed by the more extensive Thwaites work, published at the time of the Lewis and Clark Centennial in 1904. The Thwaites edition included everything; the journal entries were maintained in the quaint phraseology and phonetic spelling of the journalists. Lewis and Clark and the other journalists very responsibly carried out Jefferson's instructions to record everything about the Indians, the landscape, the climate, the vegetation, the minerals and the commercial aspects. The recording of detailed and dependable observations made by these men under all sorts of trying situations is nothing less than remarkable.

Following the publication of the Thwaites journals, there have been many books dealing with the special aspects of the Expedition: Paul Cutright's *Pioneering Naturalists;* R. D. Burroughs' *The Natural History of the Lewis and Clark Expedition;* Criswell's *Lewis and Clark: Linguistic Pioneers;* and Donald Jackson's *Letters and Documents of the Expedition.* Several books have also been written about the members of the Expedition, such as Richard Dillon's *Meriwether Lewis,* Grace Hebard's *Sacajawea,* M. O. Skarsten's *George Drouillard,* and Grace Johnson's *Colter's Hell.* Sergeant Patrick Gass published his journal in 1807, and this was followed by J. G. Jacobs' *The Life and Times of Patrick Gass* in 1859. Charles G. Clarke has recently published *The Men of the Lewis and Clark Expedition.* Bernard DeVoto has excerpted the journals with meaningful interpolation, published in one volume. *The Trail of Lewis and Clark* by Olin D. Wheeler, published in two volumes at the time of the centennial celebration, is an excellent book with travel overtones. Albert and Jane Salisbury in *Two Captains West* and Ingvard Eide in the *American Odyssey* have published excellent photographic records of the Expedition. John Bakeless published a scholarly general account of the Lewis and Clark Expedition with a biographical background of the captains. Recently, Gerald S. Snyder for the National Geographic Society has published *In the Footsteps of Lewis and Clark*, a brief and interesting account with beautiful illustrations. Novels, movies and documentaries continue to appear. Many magazine articles have been written through the years, particularly in relation to the role of Sacagawea in the Lewis and Clark Expedition. Monuments and paintings provide perpetual reminders of the personnel and events of the Expedition.

Abel, A. Lawrence, M.D. "Blood-Letting." *JAMA*. Vol. 214, No. 5, Nov. 2, 1970

Adelman, Seymour. "Equipping the Lewis and Clark Expedition." Amer. Philosophical Soc., *Library Bulletin*, Phila: 1945

Allen, John L. "Lewis and Clark on the Upper Missouri: Decision at the Marias." *Montana, The Magazine of Western History*, xxi, No. 3, Summer 1971

———. "An Analysis of the Exploratory Process: The Lewis and Clark Expedition of 1804-1806." *Geographical Review*, Jan. 1972

Anderson, Irving W. "J. B. Charbonneau, Son of Sacajawea." *Oreg. Hist. Soc. Quar.*, lxxi, No. 13, Sept. 1970

Anderson, Sarah Travers Lewis. *Lewises, Meriwethers and their Kin.* Richmond, Va: 1938

Appleman, Roy E. "Lewis and Clark: The Route 160 Years After." *Pacific Northwest Quar.* lvii, No. 1, Jan. 1966

———. "The Lost Site of Camp Wood," *Jour. of the West*, viii, No. 2, April 1968, pp. 270-74

Ashburn, Percy M. *A History of the Medical Department of the United States Army.* Houghton Mifflin Co., N.Y; 1929

Bakeless, John. *Lewis & Clark: Partners in Discovery.* William Morrow & Co., N.Y: 1947

———. "Lewis and Clark's Background for Exploration." *Wash. Acad. of Sciences Journal*, xliv, Nov. 1954

Barbour, William R. "The Guns of Lewis and Clark," *Gun Digest*, 18th ed., 1964

Bayne-Jones, Stanhope. "The Evaluation of Preventive Medicine in the United States Army, 1607-1939." Office of Surgeon General, Dept. of the Army, Washington, D.C.

Beard, J. Howard, M.D. "The Medical Observations and Practice of Lewis and Clark." *Scientific Monthly*, xx, No. 5, May 1925, pp. 506-26

Beidleman, Richard G. "Lewis and Clark — Plant Collectors for a President." *Horticulture*, XLIV, No. 4, 1966

Biddle, Nicholas, ed. *History of the Expedition under the Command of Captains Lewis and Clark . . . Performed during the years 1804-5-6*. Prepared for the press by Paul Allen. 2 vols. Bradford and Inskeep, Phila: 1814

Binger, Carl. *Revolutionary Doctor, Benjamin Rush*. N. W. Norton & Co., N.Y: 1966

Blanton, Wyndham B. *Medicine in Virginia in the Eighteenth Century*. Garrett & Massie, Inc., Richmond: 1931

Bliss, E.F. "Dr. Saugrain's Note-Books, 1788." *Proceed. of Amer. Antiquarian Soc.*, n.s., Vol. XIX, 1909; — "Dr. Saugrain's Relation of His Voyage Down the Ohio River . . . in 1788," *ibid.*, n.s., XI, 1898

Brackenridge, Henry Marie. *Recollections of Persons and Places in the West*. James Kay, Phila: 1834

———. *Views of Louisiana*. Cramer, Spear and Eichbaum, Pittsburgh: 1814

Brown, D. Alexander. *The Great Adventure*. Nat. Hist. Soc., Gettysburg: 1970

Burroughs, Raymond Darwin. *The Natural History of the Lewis and Clark Expedition*. Mich. St. Univ. Press, East Lansing: 1961

———. "The Lewis and Clark Expedition's Botanical Discoveries." *Natural History*, LXXV, No. 1, Jan. 1966

———. *Exploration Unlimited*. Wayne Univ. Press, Detroit: 1953

Butterfield, L.H., ed. *Letters of Benjamin Rush*. 2 vols. Amer. Philo. Soc., Phila: 1951

Catlin, George. *The North American Indians*. 2 vols. London: 1841

Chambaugh, Benjamin F. "The Story of Sergeant Charles Floyd." Proceed. of Miss. Valley Hist. Assn., Vol. 2, 1910

Chittenden, Hiram M. *The American Fur Trade of the Far West*. 3 vols., Francis P. Harper, N.Y: 1902

Chuinard, E.G., M.D. "The Medical Aspects of the Lewis and Clark Expedition," Friends of the Library, Oreg. St. Univ., Corvallis: 1965

————. "The Actual Role of the Birdwoman." *Montana, Mag. of the West. Hist.*, xxvi, No. 3, pp. 78-79

————. "A Medical Mystery at Fort Clatsop." *We Proceeded On*, iii, No. 2, pp. 8-9

————. "Thomas Jefferson and The Corps of Discovery: Could he have done more." *American West*, xii, No. 6, Nov. 1975, pp. 4-13

Clarke, Charles G. *The Men of the Lewis and Clark Expedition*. The Arthur H. Clark Co., Glendale, Ca: 1970

————. "The Roster of the Lewis and Clark Expedition." *Oreg. Hist. Quar.*, xlv, Dec. 1944, pp. 289-305

Cockran, John. "Medical Department of the Revolutionary Army." *Mag. of Amer. Hist.*, xii, 1884, pp. 241-259

Coues, Elliott, ed. *The Expeditions of Zebulon Montgomery Pike*. 3 vols., Francis P. Harper, N.Y: 1895

————, ed. *History of the Expedition under the Command of Lewis and Clark*. 4 vols., Francis P. Harper, N.Y: 1893

————. *Forty Years a Fur Trader, the Personal Narrative of Charles Larpenteur*. 2 vols., Francis P. Harper, N.Y: 1898

Courtney, R. Hall. "Jefferson on the Medical Theory and Practice of His Day." *Bull. of the Hist. of Medicine*, xxxi, No. 3, 1957

Cox, Ross. *The Columbia River*. 2 vols., London: 1831

Crawford, Helen. "Sakakawea." *No. Dak. Hist. Quar.*, i, April 1927

Criswell, Elijah Harry. "Lewis and Clark: Linguistic Pioneers." *Univ. of Mo. Studies*, xv, No. 2. Columbia: 1940

Cutbush, Edward. *Observations on the Means of Preserving the Health of Soldiers and Sailors*. Fry and Kannerer, Phila: 1808

Cutright, Paul. "I Gave Him Barks and Saltpeter." *Amer. Heritage*, xv, No. 1, Dec. 1963

————. "Jefferson's Instructions to Lewis and Clark," *Bull. of the Mo. Hist. Soc.*, xxii, No. 3, April 1966

————. "The Journal of Private Joseph Whitehouse, A Soldier with Lewis and Clark." *Bull of the Mo. Hist. Soc.*, xxviii, No. 3, April 1972

————. "Lewis and Clark Begin a Journey." *Bull. of Mo. Hist. Soc.*, xxiv, No. 1, Oct. 1967.

————. "Lewis and Clark and Du Pratz," *Bull of the Mo. Hist. Soc.*, xxi, No. 1, Oct. 1964

———. *Lewis and Clark: Pioneering Naturalists.* Univ. of Ill. Press, Urbana: 1969

———. "Meriwether Lewis and the Marias River." *Mont., the Mag. of Western Hist.,* xviii, No. 3, July 1968

———. "Meriwether Lewis: Botanist," *Oreg. Hist. Quar.,* lxix, No. 2, June 2, 1968

———. "Meriwether Lewis Prepares for a Trip West." *Bull. of the Mo. Hist. Soc.,* xxiii, No. 1, Oct. 1966

———. "Meriwether Lewis: Zoologist," *Oreg. Hist. Quar.,* lxix, No. 1, March 1, 1968

———. *Theodore Roosevelt, the Naturalist.* Harper & Bros., N.Y: 1956

DeVoto, Bernard. *The Course of Empire.* Houghton Mifflin Co., Boston: 1952

———. *The Journals of Lewis and Clark.* Houghton Mifflin Co., Boston: 1953

Dillon, Richard. *Meriwether Lewis.* Coward-McCann, N.Y: 1965

Duncan, Andrew, m.d. *Edinburgh New Dispensatory.* Isaiah Thomas, Jr., Pub., 1805

Dunlop, Richard. "The Doctors who Helped Tame the West." *Today's Health,* xli

Du Pratz, Antoine LePage. *History of Louisiana, or the Western Parts of Virginia and Carolina; containing a description of the Countries that lie on both sides of the River Mississippi. . .* London: 1763

Dye, Eva Emory. *The Conquest; The True Story of Lewis and Clark.* McClurg & Co., Chicago: 1902

Ewers, John C. "The Indian Trade of the Upper Missouri before Lewis and Clark: An Interpretation." *Bull. of the Mo. Hist. Soc.,* v, No. 4, July 1954

Fenner, Louise. "It Can Be Deadly." *Montana Outdoors,* iii, No. 1, Jan.-Feb. 1972, p. 32.

Fisher, Sherry R. "In the Footsteps of Lewis and Clark." *Vista-USA,* Exxon Travel Club, Fall, 1977

Fisher, Vardis. *Suicide or Murder.* Alan Swallow, Denver: 1962

Ford, Paul L., ed. *Writings of Thomas Jefferson.* Vol. 9. Putnam, N.Y: 1898

Forrest, Earle E. "Patrick Gass, Carpenter of the Lewis and Clark Expedition." *Bull. of the Mo. Hist. Soc.,* iv, July 1948, pp. 217-222

Franchere, Gabriel. *Narrative of a Voyage to the Northwest Coast of America.* Redfield, N.Y: 1854

Friis, Herman R. "Cartographic and Geographic Activities of the Lewis and Clark Expedition," *Jour. of the Wash. Academy of Sci.*, XLIV, Nov. 1954

Garrison, Fielding H. *An Introduction to the History of Medicine.* 4th ed. W. B. Saunders Co., 1966

Garver, Frank H. "The Story of Sergeant Charles Floyd." *Miss. Valley Hist. Assn. Proceed.*, II, 1908-09, pp. 76-84

Gass, Patrick. *A Journal of the Voyages and Travels of a Corps of Discovery, under the Command of Capt. Lewis and Capt. Clarke of the Army of the United States, from the mouth of the River Missouri through the Interior Parts of North America to the Pacific Ocean, during the years 1804, 1805 & 1806. Containing an authentic relation of the most interesting trans-actions during the expedition, — A description of the country, — An account of its inhabitants, soil,, climate, curiosities and vegetable and animal productions.* Pittsburgh: 1807

————. *A Journal of the Voyages and Travels of a Corps of Discovery, under the Command of Capt. Lewis and Capt. Clarke of the Army of the United States.* Ed. David McKeehan. Ross and Haines, Minneapolis: 1958

Gill, Larry. "The Great Portage." *Great Falls Tribune*, Great Falls, Mt: Aug. 15, 1965

Goldstein, Max. "One Hundred Years of Medicine and Surgery in Missouri." *St. Louis Star.* St. Louis: 1900

Goodman, Nathan G. *Benjamin Rush, Physician and Citizen.* Univ. of Pa. Press, Phila: 1934

Gordon, Maurice Bear, M.D. *Aesculapius Comes to the Colonies.* Ventor Publishers, Inc., Ventor, N.J: 1949

Govan, Thomas Payne. *Nicholas Biddle, Nationalist and Public Banker, 1786-1844.* Chicago: 1959

Gray, Ralph. "Following the Trail of Lewis and Clark," *Nat'l Geog. Mag.*, Vol. 103, No. 6, June 1953

Halsey, Robert H. *How the President, Thomas Jefferson, and Dr. Benjamin Waterhouse established Vaccination as a Public Health Procedure.* Published privately by the author, N.Y: 1936

Harrell, Laura. "Preventitive Medicine in the Mississippi Territory." *Bull. of the Hist. of Med.*, XL, No. 4, 1966

Harris, Burton. *John Colter: His Years in the Rockies.* Scribner's Sons, N.Y: 1952

Hebard, Grace Raymond. *Sacajawea. A guide and interpreter of the Lewis and Clark Expedition, with an account of the travels of Toussaint Charbonneau, and of Jean Baptiste, the Expedition Papoose.* The Arthur H. Clark Co., Glendale, Ca: 1933

Holm, Don. "The Lewis and Hooke Expedition." *Portland Oregonian,* Dec. 12, 1965

Holman, Frederick V. "Lewis and Clark Expedition at Fort Clatsop." *Oreg. Hist. Quar.,* xxvii, Sept. 1926

Holmes, Chris. "Benjamin Rush and the Yellow Fever." *Bull. of the Hist. of Medicine,* xl, No. 3, pp. 253-260

Horine, Emmet Field, M.D. *Daniel Drake, Pioneer Physician of the Midwest.* Univ. of Pa. Press, Phila: 1961

Jackson, Donald. "A Footnote to the Lewis and Clark Expedition." *Manuscripts,* xxiv, No. 1, 1972

———. "Some Books Carried by Lewis and Clark," *Bull. of the Mo. Hist. Soc.,* xvi, No. 1, Oct. 1959

———. "The Race to Publish Lewis and Clark." *Penn. Mag. of Hist. & Biog.,* lxxxv, No. 2, April 1961

———. "The Public Image of Lewis and Clark," *Pac. Northwest Quar.,* lvii, No. 1, Jan. 1966

———, ed. *Letters of the Lewis and Clark Expedition with Related Documents, 1783-1854.* Univ. of Ill. Press, Urbana: 1962

Jacobs, John G. *The Life and Times of Patrick Gass, Now Sole Survivor of the Overland Expedition to the Pacific, under Lewis and Clark, in 1804-5-6.* Jacob & Smith, Wellsburg, Va: 1859

James, Edwin. *An Account of an Expedition from Pittsburgh to the Rocky Mountains, performed in the years 1819 and 1820 . . .* 2 vols., N. C. Carey & I. Lea, Phila: 1823

Jefferson, Thomas. *Message from the President of the United States Communicating Discoveries made in Exploring the Missouri, Red River and Washita, by Captains Lewis and Clark, Doctor Sibley, and Mr. Dunbar; with a statistical account of the countries adjacent . . .* Washington: 1806

———. *Notes on the State of Virginia.* Lilly & Wait, Boston: 1832

Jones, Gene. "The Mandan Indians, Descendants of the Vikings." *Real West,* ix, No. 47, 1966

Jones, John, M.D. *Plain, Concise, Practical Remarks on the Treatment of Wounds and Fractures, to which is added a short appendix on*

Camp and Military Hospitals: Principally designed for the use of young military surgeons in North America. 1775

Kennerly, William Clark. *Persimmon Hill.* Univ. of Okla. Press, Norman: 1948

Kingston, C.S. "Sacajawea as a guide — the evaluation of a legend." *Pac. Northwest Quar.*, xxxv, Jan. 1944, pp. 2-18

Koch, Elers. "Lewis and Clark Across the Bitterroot Range." Forest Service, U.S. Dept. of Agriculture, Missoula, Mt: 1962

Larpenteur, Charles. *Forty Years a Fur Trader.* Lakeside Press, R. R. Donnelley & Sons Co., Chicago: 1933

Larsell, Olaf. "Medical Aspects of the Lewis and Clark Expedition," *Surgery, Gynecology, and Obstetrics,* lxxxv, Nov. 1947, pp. 663-69

Lewis, Grace. "Financial records: Expedition to the Pacific," *Bull. of the Mo. Hist. Soc.,* x, July 1954, pp. 465-489

Loos, John Louis. "William Clark's Part in the Preparation of the Lewis and Clark Expedition," *Bull. of the Mo. Hist. Soc.,* viii, July 1954, pp. 492-93; 508-09

McKelvey, Susan Delano. *Botanical Exploration of the Trans-Mississippi West.* Arnold Arboretum of Harvard Univ., Boston: 1955

Mackenzie, Alexander. *Voyages from Montreal, on the River St. Lawrence, through the Continent of North America, to the Frozen and Pacific Ocean; in the years 1789 and 1793* . . . 2 vols., London: 1801

Maquire, Edward F. "Frequent Diseases and Intended Remedies on the Frontier, 1780-1850." *Unpublished thesis for Master's Degree,* St. Louis Univ., St. Louis: 1953

Major, Ralph H., m.d. *A History of Medicine.* Charles C. Thomas, Springfield: 1954

Marks, Constant R. "The Life of Sargeant Chas. Floyd." *Pioneers.* Deitch & Lamar Co., Sioux City: 1924

Mattes, Merrill J. "On the Trail of Lewis and Clark with Thomas Hart Benton." *Montana, the Mag. of West. Hist.,* xvi, No. 3, July 1966

Michaux, F.A., m.d. *Travels to the Westward of the Allegeny Mountains.* Barnard and Sultzer, London: 1805

Mirsky, Jeannette. *The Westward Crossings.* Alfred A. Knopf, N.Y: 1946

Nasatir, A.P., ed. *Before Lewis and Clark.* 2 vols., St. Louis Hist. Docs. Found., St. Louis: 1952

Osgood, Ernest Staples, ed. *The Field Notes of Captain William Clark, 1803-1805.* Yale Univ. Press, New Haven: 1964

Packard, Francis R. *History of Medicine in the United States.* Paul B. Hoeber, Inc., N.Y: 1931

Peebles, John J. "Rugged Waters: Trails and Campsites of Lewis and Clark in the Salmon River Country." *Idaho Yesterdays,* VIII, No. 2, Summer 1964

————. "Lewis and Clark in Idaho," *Idaho Hist. Series,* No. 16, Dec. 1966

Pepper, O.N. Perry, M.D. "Benjamin Rush: Theories on Blood-Letting after One Hundred and Fifty Years," *Trans. & Studies of College of Physicians,* XIV, Phila: 1946-47

Phelps, Dawson A. "The Tragic Death of Meriwether Lewis." *William & Mary Quar.,* 3rd series, XIII, No. 3, 1956

Poole, Edwin A. "Charbono's Squar." *The Pacific Northwesterner,* VIII, No. 1, 1964

Pryor, Nathaniel. "Documents: Captain Nathaniel Pryor." *Amer. Hist. Rev.,* XXIV, Jan. 1919, pp. 253-265

Quaife, Milo M. "Some New Found Records of the Lewis and Clark Expedition." *Miss. Valley Hist. Rev.,* June 2, 1915

————, ed. "The Journals of Captain Meriwether Lewis and Sergeant John Ordway." *Publ. of St. Hist. Soc. of Wisc.,* XXII, Madison: 1916

Rees, John. "The Shoshoni Contribution to Lewis and Clark." *Idaho Yesterdays,* II, Summer 1958, pp. 2-13

Reid, Russell. "Sakakawea, the Bird Woman," St. Hist. Soc. of No. Dak., Bismarck: 1950

Robinson, Doane. "Lewis and Clark in South Dakota," *So. Dak. Hist. Coll.,* IX, 1918, pp. 514-96

————. "Medical Adventures of Lewis and Clark." *So. Dak. Hist. Coll.,* XII, 1924

Runes, Dagobert. *The Selected Writings of Benjamin Rush.* Philosophical Library, Inc., N.Y: 1947

Rush, Benjamin. "Defense of Blood-Letting," published in *Medical Inquiries and Observations,* IV, 3rd ed., Phila: 1809

Russell, Carl P. "The Guns of the Lewis and Clark Expedition." *No. Dak. Hist.,* XXVII, Winter 1960, pp. 25-33

Salisbury, Albert and Jane. *Two Captains West.* Superior Pub. Co., Seattle: 1950

Schmidt, J.E., M.D. *Medical Discoveries.* Charles C. Thomas, Springfield: 1959

Scully, Virginia. *A Treasury of American Indian Herbs.* Crown Publishers, Inc., N.Y: 1970

Sibley, William G. *The French Five Hundred.* Gallia Co. Hist. Soc., Gallipolis: 1933

Skarsten, M.O. *George Drouillard.* Arthur H. Clark Co., Glendale, Calif: 1964

Smith, James S., and Kathryn Smith. "Sedulous Sergeant, Patrick Gass," *Montana, the Mag. of West. Hist.,* v, Summer 1955, pp. 20-27

Smith, Peter. *The Indian Doctor's Dispensatory.* Cincinnati: 1812. Republished as Reproduction Series No. 2 in Bulletin of the Lloyd Library of Botany, Pharmacy and Materia Medica, p. 86

Snoddy, Donald D. "Medical Aspects of the Lewis and Clark Expedition." *Nebraska History,* LI, No. 2, pp. 115-51

Snyder, Gerald S. "In the Footsteps of Lewis and Clark." Nat'l Geog. Soc., Wash., D.C: 1970

Sowerby, E. Millicent, comp. *Catalogue of the Library of Thomas Jefferson.* 5 vols., Wash., D.C: 1952-59

Space, Ralph S. *Lewis and Clark Through Idaho.* Tribune Pub. Co. Lewiston, Ida: 1964

————. *The Lolo Trail.* Lewiston, Id: 1970

Stanley, L.L. "Medicine and Surgery of the Lewis and Clark Expedition," *Medical Journal and Record,* Vol. 127, 1928

Stone, Eric. "Medicine Among the American Indians," *Clio Medica,* Paul B. Hoeber, Inc., 1932

Teggart, Frederick J. "Notes Supplementary to any Edition of Lewis and Clark." *Annual Rept. Amer. Hist. Assn.,* I, 1908, pp. 185-95

Thacher, James. *A Military Journal of the Revolutionary War,* Cotton & Barnard, Boston: 1827

Thwaites, Reuben Gold, ed. *Early Western Travels.* 32 vols., Arthur H. Clark Co., Cleveland: 1905

————. *Original Journals of the Lewis and Clark Expedition.* 8 vols., Dodd, Mead & Co., N.Y: 1904-5

————. "William Clark: Soldier, Explorer, Statesman." *Mo. Hist. Soc. Pubs.,* XI, No. 7, Oct. 1906

Tilton, James. *Economical Observations of Military Hospitals.* J. Wilson Pubs., Wilmington, Del: 1813

Tomkins, Calvin. "Annals of Law: The Lewis and Clark Case." *The New Yorker*, Oct. 29, 1966

———. *The Lewis and Clark Trail*, Harper & Row, N.Y: 1965

Townsend, John K. *Narrative of a Journey across the Rocky Mts. and a Visit to the Sandwich Islands, Chili &c.* Henry Perkins, Phila: 1839

Vestal, Stanley. *The Missouri.* Farrar and Rinehart, N.Y: 1945

Vinton, Stallo. *John Colter, Discoverer of Yellowstone.* Edward Eberstadt, N.Y: 1926

Vogel, Virgil J. *American Indian Medicine.* Univ. of Okla. Press, Norman: 1970

Welsh, Benjamin, M.D. *A Practical Treatise on the Efficacy of Blood Letting.* Longman, Hurst, Reese, Orme, and Brown, Edinburgh: 1819

West, Helen B. "Meriwether Lewis in Blackfeet Country," U.S. Dept. of Interior, Bureau of Ind. Affairs, Blackfeet Agency, Mus. of the Plains Indian, Browning, Mt: 1964

———. "The Lewis and Clark Expedition: Our National Epic." *Mont., the Mag. of West. Hist.*, xvi, No. 3, July 1966

Wheeler, Olin D. *The Trail of Lewis and Clark, 1804-1806.* 2 vols., G. P. Putnam's Sons, N.Y: 1904

Will, Drake W., M.D. "Lewis and Clark, Westering Physicians," *Montana. the Mag. of West. Hist.*, xxi, No. 4, Autumn 1971

———. "The Medical and Surgical Practice of the Lewis and Clark Expedition," *Journal of the Hist. of Medicine and Allied Sciences*, xiv, No. 3, 1959

Wilson, Charles Morrow. *Meriwether Lewis of Lewis and Clark.* Thomas Y. Crowell Co., N.Y: 1934

Wood, George B., M.D., and Boche, Franklin, M.D. *U.S. Dispensatory I,* Grigg & Elliott, 2nd ed., Phila: 1834

Wood, Ruth Kedzie. *The Lewis and Clark Expedition. The Mentor.*

Yates, Ted. "Since Lewis and Clark." *The Amer. West,* ii, No. 4, Fall 1965

Young, F.G. "The Higher Significance in the Lewis and Clark Expedition." *Quar. of the Oreg. Hist. Soc.*, vi, No. 1, March 1905

ADDENDA

Allen, John L. "The Summer of Decision: Lewis and Clark in Montana, 1805." *We Proceeded On*, Vol. II, No. 3, pp. 8-11

Allen, John L. *Through the Garden.* Univ. of Ill. Press, Urbana: 1975

Ambler, Charles Henry. *The Life and Diary of John Floyd.* Richmond Press, Richmond, Va: 1918

Betts, Edwin M. *Thomas Jefferson's Farm Book.* Princeton Univ. Press, Princeton: 1953

Burroughs, Raymond D. "Lewis and Clark in Buffalo Country." *We Proceeded On,* Vol. II, No. 1, pp. 6-10

Chatters, Roy M. "The Not-So-Enigmatic Lewis and Clark Airgun." *We Proceeded On,* Vol. III, No. 2, pp. 4-6

Hawke, David Freeman. *Benjamin Rush: Revolutionary Gadfly.* Bobbs-Merrill Co., Indianapolis: 1971

McDermott, John Francis. *Private Libraries in Creole Saint Louis.* The Johns Hopkins Press, Baltimore: 1938

————. "Gallipolis as the Travelers Saw It, 1793-1811." *Ohio Arch. & Hist. Quar.,* Vol. XLVIII, 1939

————. "William Clark's Struggle with Place Names in Upper Louisiana." *Bull. of Miss. Hist. Soc.,* Vol. XXXIV, No. 3, pp. 140-50

Maury, Ann. *Memoirs of a Hugenot Family.* Putnam & Co., N.Y: 1853

Muench, David, and Dan Murphy. *Lewis and Clark.* K.C. Pubns., Las Vegas: 1977

————, and Archie Satterfield. *Lewis and Clark Country.* Beautiful Amer. Pub. Co., Portland, Or: 1978

Osgood, Ernest. "Our Dog Scannon — Pardner in Discovery." *Montana, Mag. of West. Hist.,* Vol. XXVI, No. 3, pp. 8-17

Powell, J.H. *Bring Out Your Dead.* Univ. of Penna. Press, Phila: 1949

Saindon, Robert. "The Abduction of Sacagawea." *We Proceeded On,* Vol. II, No. 2, pp. 6-8

————. "The Lost Vocabularies of Lewis and Clark Expedition." *We Proceeded On,* Vol. III, No. 3, pp. 4-6

Schroer, Blanche. "Sacagawea: The Legend and the Truth." *In Wyoming,* Dec.-Jan. 1978

Selter, H. Fouré. *L'Odyssée Américaine d'Une Famille Francaise.* The Johns Hopkins Press, Baltimore: 1936

Spencer, Omar. *Story of Sauvies Island.* Binfords, Portland, Or: 1950

Steffen, Jerome O. "William Clark: A Reappraisal." *Montana, Mag. of West. Hist.,* Vol. XXV, No. 2

————. *William Clark: Jeffersonian Man on the Frontier.* Univ. of Okla. Press, Norman: 1977

Index